P9-CEG-678

WEST GEORGIA REGIONAL LIBRARY SYSTEM
Neva Lomason Memorial Library

☆
JEB STUART
The Last Cavalier

JEB STUART
THE LAST CAVALIER

BURKE DAVIS

WITH MAPS BY RAFAEL D. PALACIOS

THE FAIRFAX PRESS
NEW YORK

☆

To Robert D. Loomis

Copyright © MCMLVII by Burke Davis
All rights reserved.

This 1988 edition is published by The Fairfax Press, distributed by
Crown Publishers, Inc., 225 Park Avenue South, New York, New York 10003,
by arrangement with Holt, Rinehart & Winston, Inc.

Printed and Bound in the United States of America

Library of Congress Cataloging-in-Publication Data

Davis, Burke, 1913–
    Jeb Stuart, the last cavalier / Burke Davis ; with maps by Rafael
D. Palacios.
        p.   cm.
    Reprint. Originally published: New York : Rinehart, 1957.
    Bibliography: p.
    Includes index.
    ISBN 0-517-18597-0
    1. Stuart, Jeb, 1833–1864.   2. Generals—United States—Biography.
3. United States.   Army—Biography.   4. Confederate States of
America. Army—Biography.   I. Title.
E467.1.S9D3 1988
973.7'3'0924—dc19
[B]   87-32017
                                                                                 CIP

m l k j i h g f

☆

Acknowledgments

Grateful acknowledgment is made to the following individuals, organizations and publishers for permission to reprint material controlled by them in this biography:

A. LEOPOLD ALEXANDER, Savannah, Georgia, for permission to reprint an excerpt from THE ALEXANDER LETTERS, 1787–1900, compiled and published by G. J. Baldwin.

STUART B. CAMPBELL, Wytheville, Virginia, for permission to reprint an excerpt from a letter written by J. E. B. Stuart to his mother in January, 1860.

REV. DAVID H. COBLENTZ, Clover, South Carolina, for permission to reprint two military dispatches of General Stuart.

CONFEDERATE MEMORIAL LITERARY SOCIETY, Richmond, Virginia, for permission to reprint excerpts from letters written by J. E. B. Stuart on September 4, 1849, June 3, 1850, August 10, 1855, May 19, 1861 and July 19, 1862.

MRS. ANDREW J. DAVIS, Alexandria, Virginia, for permission to reprint the first letter J. E. B. Stuart wrote to Flora Cooke (July 25, 1855).

DUKE UNIVERSITY LIBRARY, Durham, North Carolina, for permission to reprint excerpts from letters of May 10, 1861, June 13, 1861, December 5, 1862, December 18, 1862, April 6, 1863 and May 4, 1863 which are included in the *J. E. B. Stuart Papers;* from entries in the *John Esten Cooke War Journals* of 1862 and 1863; and from a letter in the *Robert W. Hooke Papers.*

EMORY UNIVERSITY LIBRARY, Emory University, Georgia, for permission to reprint excerpts from letters which appear in LETTERS OF GENERAL J. E. B. STUART TO HIS WIFE, 1861, edited by Bingham Duncan, copyright 1943 by Emory University Library (Sources and Reprints, Series 1, No. 1).

HOUGHTON MIFFLIN COMPANY, Boston, Massachusetts, for permission to reprint excerpts from THE LIFE AND CAMPAIGNS OF J. E. B. STUART, by H. B. McClellan.

VAN DYK MACBRIDE, Newark, New Jersey, for permission to reprint a brief note written by J. E. B. Stuart to Miss Belle Hart.

RALPH G. NEWMAN, Chicago, Illinois, for permission to reprint an excerpt from a paper sent by J. E. B. Stuart to General G. B. McClellan.

LOUISE FITZHUGH PRICE, Richmond, Virginia, for permission to reprint brief excerpts from letters of Channing Price.

CHARLES SCRIBNER'S SONS, New York, N.Y., for permission to reprint brief excerpts from LETTERS FROM LEE'S ARMY, edited by Charles Minor Blackford, III, copyright 1947 by Charles Scribner's Sons; WAR YEARS WITH JEB STUART, by W. W. Blackford, copyright 1945 by Charles Scribner's Sons; RECOLLECTIONS GRAVE AND GAY, by Constance C. Harrison, copyright 1911 by Charles Scribner's Sons, 1939 by Fairfax Harrison; and JEB STUART, by John W. Thomason, copyright 1930 by Charles Scribner's Sons.

UNIVERSITY OF ALABAMA PRESS, University, Alabama, for permission to reprint excerpts from THE CIVIL WAR DIARY OF GENERAL JOSIAH GORGAS, edited by F. E. Vandiver, copyright, 1947.

UNIVERSITY OF NORTH CAROLINA LIBRARY, Chapel Hill, North Carolina, and MRS. JAMES E. COVINGTON, Richmond, Virgina, for permission to reprint excerpts from letters of J. E. B. Stuart to his cousins Betty and Jack Hairston, which are included in the *Hairston-Wilson Papers* of *The Southern Historical Collection* of the University of North Carolina Library.

VIRGINIA HISTORICAL SOCIETY, Richmond, Virginia, for permission to reprint excerpts from Volume 8 of the SOUTHERN HISTORICAL SOCIETY PAPERS; and for permission to reprint brief excerpts from the *Philip St. George Cooke Papers*.

VIRGINIA STATE LIBRARY, Richmond, Virginia, for permission to reprint a letter written by Elizabeth L. Stuart to General Robert E. Lee on April 23, 1861, the original of which is in the Virginia State Library.

McDONALD WELLFORD, Richmond, Virginia, for permission to reprint a letter written by J. E. B. Stuart to his cousin, the mother of Channing Price, and a letter of Evalina Wellford written on May 16, 1863.

☆

Contents

☆

List of Maps

JEB STUART
The Last Cavalier

☆

CHAPTER 1

Old John Brown

(OCTOBER 18, 1859)

THE soldiers were drunk, and after dark the streets were full of them, popping their guns and shouting. Mist from the rivers writhed through the town in a slow gray current, and the troops plunged about in it like comic specters. There was a drizzle of cold rain.

The saloon was open late, roaring, and men crowded the barrooms of the hotels, The Wager House and The Galt House, adding to their excitement with tales of the day's fighting.

The troops were militiamen who had swarmed into the town in the fork of the Shenandoah and the Potomac to keep the peace. They had fired raggedly all day in an indecisive battle, and the little band of raiders which had defied them was still unsubdued, hiding in the fire-engine house. Harpers Ferry waited. No one seemed to know what was to be done.

A crowd of two thousand stared at the brick fire house and its enormous doors. Behind the doors lay the raiders and their prisoners. The enginehouse was almost surrounded by the militia, but their picketing was loose and unsoldierly.

One militiaman growled that his troop had been given no orders since dark, except a few unintelligible commands "from a set of drunken fellows whooping and bellowing like a pack of maddened bulls, evidently too drunk to hold their guns."[1]

The enginehouse loomed in the darkness like a symbol of the unspoken fear of the South—a mutiny of the Negroes. The white leader in the place called himself Isaac Smith, and he had come over the Potomac from his mysterious rented farm in Maryland with

3

a tiny band of whites and Negroes to seize the Armory and call the slaves of Virginia to rebellion. It had been a long day.

At least a dozen men were dead. Among them was the gentle old Mayor of Harpers Ferry, Fontaine Beckham, who had for twenty-five years been the Baltimore and Ohio Railroad agent. One of the raiders had shot the unarmed Beckham as he peered around a water tank. Another of the dead was George Turner, a rich farmer, shot as he rode in a street, gun in hand.

Beckham's death sent a lynch mob storming into The Wager House, where it seized William Thompson, twenty-six, one of the raiders who had been snatched as he emerged from the enginehouse under a flag of truce.

The victim was defiant. "You may take my life," Thompson yelled, "but eighty million will rise up to avenge me, and bring liberty to the slaves."

He was dragged to the Potomac bridge, where two pistols were fired against his head. The body dropped into shallow water below, and all day men and boys shot the corpse and laughed at the expression of agony on its white face.

There was more of it. One of Smith's followers was William Leeman, eighteen, caught in an outpost of the raiders, also killed with a pistol. His body was left in plain sight on heights above the town. Men fired at it hour after hour, filling it with shot.[2]

Daingerfield Newby, a Negro who was shot in the enginehouse yard, fell into the hands of the Virginians and his ears were sliced off and other atrocities committed on his body. A townsman reported that a drove of hogs tore the corpse.

Two men sent out from Smith's lair under a white flag were shot down in the street. One lay in the sun for a while, bleeding; the other, mortally wounded, crawled back to the raiders. Two more raiders were shot late that afternoon as they attempted to escape over the river.

The first militia company had come at noon, from Charlestown. Others came from Martinsburg, Shepherdstown, Winchester County, and from Frederick, Maryland. Five companies from Baltimore arrived after dark.

Smith and his men had attacked yesterday, Sunday morning.

They had made no secret of their plan. One of the first captives was a guard of the Federal Armory, from whom Smith took the key, saying, "I came here from Kansas. I want to free all the Negroes in this state. If the citizens interfere with me, I must only burn the town and have blood."

He had about thirty captives, most of them snatched on their way home from a Methodist revival, but when he moved his band from the Armory into the fire-engine house, he took only nine of the most prominent as hostages. The militia freed those he had abandoned.

One of Smith's first prisoners was the dignified Colonel Lewis Washington, a great-grandnephew of George Washington. He had been taken in a midnight call; his nonplussed slaves were taken with him, given pikes and told to guard their master.

Smith now had weapons which he seemed to feel had magical significance: A pistol given George Washington by Lafayette, and a handsome sword presented to the first President by Frederick the Great. The sword did not leave Smith's hand.

Among the prisoners was a farmer, John H. Allstadt, brought in with his eighteen-year-old son in a wagon with Washington and his slaves.

"As we drove inside the Armory yard," young Allstadt wrote, "there stood an old man."

"This is John Brown," a voice said.

The old man stepped toward Colonel Washington. "Osawatomie Brown of Kansas," he said, as if he wanted no mistake about his identity, despite his assumed name.

Colonel Robert Baylor of the militia found courage, after a council, to send a man into the enginehouse yard, demanding surrender. He chose Samuel Strider. The young man approached the building under a flag of truce, a white handkerchief tied atop an umbrella.

A voice called from the enginehouse.

"I heard nothing about terms, sir." Strider said. "What terms do you want?"

"I want to be allowed to take my men and prisoners across the bridge into Maryland." There was more of this, in an old man's voice.

"Captain, you will have to put that in writing," Strider said.

"It's too dark to write."

"Nonsense. You needn't tell me an old soldier like you hasn't got all the modern conveniences. If you don't write down your terms in black and white, I won't take them back."

A light appeared in the enginehouse and a piece of paper was soon thrust out. Strider returned to Colonel Baylor with a note:

> Capt. John Brown answers:
> In consideration of all my men, whether living or dead, or wounded, being soon safely in and delivered up to me at this point with all their arms and ammunition, we will then take our prisoners and cross the Potomac bridge, a little beyond which we will set them at liberty; after which we can negotiate about the Government property as may be best. Also we require the delivery of our horses and harness at the hotel.
>
> John Brown

Several men read the note with Baylor. It was passed to Lawson Botts, a leading lawyer of the region and a kinsman of the Washington family. Botts threw down the note and ground it under his foot.

"Gentlemen," he said, "this is adding insult to injury. I think we should storm those fellows without delay."[3]

Colonel Baylor shook his head. He would sit until daylight to avoid wounding the prisoners. He rejected the plea for terms, but did not tell the mob the identity of "Smith."

Baylor sent another man to talk with Brown, a Captain Sinn of the Frederick militia. Brown complained that his men had been shot under a flag of truce.

"Men who take up arms as you have, in insurrection, must expect that," Sinn said.

"I have weighed the responsibility and shall not shrink from it," Brown said. "I had full possession of the town, and could have murdered everyone in it. We have killed no unarmed men. I think we are entitled to some terms."

"Mayor Beckham was unarmed, and you shot him."

Brown expressed "deep regret." Sinn left the enginehouse. A doctor followed him there, examined the wounded son of old Brown, Watson, saw that he was near death, and departed. The light was snuffed out, and the enginehouse was quiet.

First news of the raid had gone out at seven five A.M., a message from a railroad telegrapher reporting a plot to free the slaves. The master of transportation in the Baltimore office of the railroad replied at nine A.M.:

> Your dispatch is evidently exaggerated and written under excitement. Why should our trains be stopped by Abolitionists, and how do you know they are such and that they numbered one hundred or more? What is their object?

Before the frantic Harpers Ferry operator could reply to his critic, the railroad's president, John W. Garrett, read the message of alarm and sent telegrams to President Buchanan in Washington, to Virginia's Governor Wise, and the commander of Maryland's volunteer troops. Thus the news reached the country at large before the first of the militia entered Harpers Ferry.

The enginehouse was a solid brick structure, about thirty-five feet by thirty, with doors stoutly battened. Two "heavy, old-fashioned fire engines" were inside, with a hose cart and reel standing between them on the brick floor. The prisoners huddled at the rear with the dead and wounded raiders. It was cold in the place as night wore on.

Young Allstadt wrote: "In the quiet of the night young Oliver Brown died. He begged again and again to be shot, in the agony of his wound, but his father replied to him, 'Oh, you will get over it,' and, 'If you must die, die like a man.' "

Oliver Brown lay quiet in his corner.

"I guess he's dead," Brown said.

There were now only five raiders left alive and unwounded. Old Brown spoke occasionally, and managed a normal voice, though he had been forty hours without sleep.

"Men, are you awake?" he called at intervals.

Jeremiah Anderson and Dauphin Thompson were two of the younger raiders. They listened as Brown talked with the captive Federal paymaster, John Daingerfield. The paymaster insisted that Brown's raid was treason against the United States as well as Virginia.

One of the young men called to Brown, "Are we committing treason against the country by being here?"

"Certainly," Brown said.

"Then we don't want to fight any more, if that's true. We thought we came to liberate the slaves. We didn't know it was treason."

There were now few sounds to be heard from outside the enginehouse. The raiders had been warned that civilians no longer surrounded the place. United States Marines had come.

It had been quite a day for Lieutenant James Ewell Brown Stuart, 1st U.S. Cavalry, a fiercely bearded officer of twenty-six on furlough from his Kansas frontier regiment. He was caught up in the opening scene of a national struggle by sheer accident.

He had visited his family in the Virginia hills of Patrick County and gone to Richmond for a convention of Episcopal laymen, and had then been called to Washington to negotiate with the War Department. For Lieutenant Stuart was something of an inventor as well as an Indian fighter. He had devised a new means of attaching a saber to a belt and was trying to sell his patent to the Government.

Thus, on the morning of October 17, 1859, he was cooling his heels in an anteroom of the War Department when a flurry of excitement struck the inner offices. There seemed to be trouble in Harpers Ferry, Virginia. Something about raiders. An officer came from the Secretary's suite. Would Lieutenant Stuart deliver a message to Colonel Robert E. Lee? The colonel was fortunately at his home at Arlington, also on leave from a Western post. Stuart could almost see the familiar white-columned mansion across the river. He lost no time.

Before noon Stuart had crossed the long bridge with a message

calling Lee to the War Department with all possible speed. Lee and
Stuart left Arlington at once. The lieutenant told his old West Point
commandant all he knew or could guess of the Harpers Ferry troubles, and asked permission to go with him as an aide.

The War Department was in haste. No army troops were on
hand, but the Navy Department had sent off Lieutenant Israel Green
with 90 Marines. They left on the three-thirty train while Lee and
Stuart were at the White House in conference with President Buchanan and Secretary of War John B. Floyd. The President signed
a proclamation of martial law. Lee was given command of all forces
in Harpers Ferry. Stuart would act as his aide.[4]

There was no train, but the railroad sent a locomotive for them,
and Stuart and Lee roared through the Maryland countryside in the
jolting engine toward Harpers Ferry, where Lee had telegraphed
Green to wait for them.

Lieutenant Green met Lee and Stuart as they dismounted from
the engine. He remembered few details of their apparance. Of Lee:
"He was in civilian dress. . . . He wore no beard, except a dark mustache, and his hair was slightly gray."

Of Stuart he noticed only the rakish rolled brim of a big brown
hat. The young cavalryman was broad in the shoulders, standing
about five feet ten inches. The two might have been a pair of merchants on a holiday, for all the concern Lieutenant Green could
read in their manner.[5]

Lee marched the Marines over a bridge into Harpers Ferry, led
them into the yard of the enginehouse and relieved the militia at
eleven P.M.

One of the first to speak to him in the half-darkness was the
district Congressman, A. R. Boteler, an acquaintance. Lee assured
him there would be an attack at dawn.

Lee explained his plan to Stuart: The Lieutenant would carry
to the enginehouse a written demand for surrender. If the raiders
refused, a party of picked men would rush the doors. To avoid killing captives they would use bayonets only.

Apparently out of courtesy Lee asked a militia colonel from
Frederick, one Shriver, if his men wanted to make the attack.

"These men of mine have wives and children at home," Shriver said. "I will not expose them to such risks. You are paid for doing this kind of work."

Lee made the same offer to Colonel Baylor, who also declined.

Lee turned to Green: "Lieutenant, do you want the honor of taking these men out?"

Green solemnly shook Lee's hand and expressed profuse thanks. He chose a dozen Marines to attack and as many more to be held in reserve.[6]

It was almost six thirty A.M. when the storming party took position near the enginehouse. Stuart and Green agreed on a signal for attack; Jeb would simply wave his hat.

When the troops were lined up against the building, Stuart went to a door and called. Someone inside shouted. Stuart read Lee's message in the gray light:

> Colonel Lee, United States Army, commanding the troops sent by the President of the United States to suppress the insurrection at this place, demands the surrender of the persons in the Armory buildings.
>
> If they will peaceably surrender themselves and restore the pillaged property, they shall be kept in safety to await the orders of the President. Colonel Lee represents to them, in all frankness, that it is impossible for them to escape; that the Armory is surrounded on all sides by troops, and that if he is compelled to take them by force he cannot answer for their safety.

There was a glimpse of the man called "Smith." Stuart wrote: "He opened the door about four inches and placed his body against the crack, with a cocked carbine in his hands: hence his remark after his capture that he could have wiped me out like a mosquito. . . . When *Smith* first came to the door I recognized old *Osawatomie Brown*, who had given us so much trouble in Kansas."

Old Brown was talkative. He wanted to leave the enginehouse undisturbed, and be allowed to cross the bridge into Maryland.

The hostages inside began to clamor, and someone asked Colonel Lee to amend his terms.

A voice rose above the rest: "Never mind us! Fire!"

Lee recognized it as that of Colonel Washington, even at his distance: "The old revolutionary blood does tell," he said.

As Brown and Stuart ended their long talk the old raider shouted, "Well, Lieutenant, I see we can't agree. You have the numbers on me, but you know we soldiers aren't afraid of death. I would as leave die by a bullet as on the gallows."

"Is that your final answer, Captain?"

"Yes," Brown said.

Stuart stepped aside and waved his hat. Green and some of the Marines looked back to a slight elevation some forty feet away, where Colonel Lee stood behind a masonry pillar. Lee raised his hand. Green wrote: "He had no arms upon his person, and treated the affair as one of no great consequence, which could be speedily settled by the Marines."[7]

Three Marines pounded on the thick doors with sledge hammers; the planks shivered but did not give. Green ordered a halt and looked about for a battering ram:

"My eye caught sight of a ladder, lying a few feet from the engine house." He put his twelve storming Marines on the ladder, and had the reserve lined up beside them, ready for action. The troops walked backward for a few feet and then ran, smashing the ladder against the door; the wood caved in at the second blow. Green glanced at the opening: "This entrance was a ragged hole low down in the right hand door, the door being splintered and cracked some distance upward. I instantly stepped from my position in front of the stone abutment, and entered."

Green ran to the rear of the building and came between the two fire engines. He saw Colonel Washington.

"Hello, Green," Washington said. The men shook hands.

A gray-haired man kneeling by Washington cocked a carbine. The Marine raised his light dress sword.

Washington pointed to the man at his feet. "This is Osawatomie," he said.

Green struck with the sword. Brown turned and took a deep cut in his neck. He rolled onto his back, unconscious. Green was not through: "Instinctively as Brown fell I gave him a saber thrust in the left breast." The sword bent double.

Firing swept the enginehouse. A Marine fell at the entrance, clutching his abdomen.

Three or four Marines came, "rushing in like tigers," as Green recalled it. They bayonetted a man under a fire engine and pinned another against a wall—the young rebels, Anderson and Thompson, who had so lately been aghast to find themselves traitors to their country. Thompson died instantly; Anderson was dragged out, groaning. Green called to his men to spill no more blood, and the others were made prisoners.

The fight had lasted no more than three minutes. Green saw: "The engine house was thick with smoke, and it was with difficulty that a person could be seen across the room." Green noticed Washington, "as cool as he would have been on his own veranda entertaining guests." But the colonel would not leave the building until he had pulled on a pair of green kid gloves. The famous man then stepped into the daylight, the gesture of the gloves in strange contrast to his disheveled appearance. Congressman Boteler came to congratulate Washington.

"Lewis, old fellow, how do you feel?"

"Hungry as a hound and dry as a powder horn," Washington said. "Come to think of it, I've had nothing to eat for forty-odd hours, and nothing better to drink than water out of a horse bucket."

He went toward The Wager House for a drink with his friends: "It seems months since I've had one."

Men bore old Brown from the enginehouse and laid him on the ground outside, where he regained consciousness. Marines formed a line to keep back the curious crowds, and Colonel Lee ordered Brown carried into a nearby office.

Stuart somehow got into the enginehouse before firing had ceased. He was among the first, for he snatched old Brown's bowie knife to keep as a souvenir.

Brown was besieged in his haven. Congressman Boteler found the old man smeared with blood, "like some aboriginal savage with his war paint on."

"Captain Brown, what brought you here?"

"To free your slaves."

"How did you expect to do it, with the small force you brought?"

"I expected help."

"From whites as well as blacks?"

"I did."

"Then you have been disappointed in not getting it."

"Yes."

"Will there be more attempts to cause the slaves to rise up?"

"Time will show," Brown said.

A Catholic priest came into the room. He had just administered last rites to a Marine. Brown shouted excitedly. "Get out of here!" he called to the priest. "Go out! I don't want you about me. Go out!"[8]

A remarkable group entered Brown's room, as if summoned by some caprice of destiny:

Colonel Robert E. Lee, Lieutenant Stuart, Senator J. M. Mason, Governor Henry Wise, Congressman C. L. Vallandigham of Ohio, Colonel Washington, Congressman Charles J. Faulkner of Virginia— all soon to be drawn into the whirlwind of violence sweeping the country.

"If you are uncomfortable, I will bar all visitors," Lee began.

"I am glad to make myself and my motives understood," Brown said.

For hours the leading men of Virginia quizzed old Brown, and though he refused to incriminate others, he astonished his captors with his forthrightness. He wrung from Governor Wise the tribute: "The gamest man I ever saw."

The questions were almost endless:

Mason: "Who furnished the money for your expedition?"

"I furnished most of it myself. It is by my own folly that I have been taken. I could easily have saved myself from it had I exercised my own better judgment, rather than yielded to my feelings. . . . I wanted to allay the fears of those who believed we came here to burn and kill."

"But you killed some people passing along the streets quietly."

"Well, sir, if anything of that kind was done, it was without my knowledge."

Vallandigham: "Mr. Brown, who sent you here?"

"No man sent me here; it was my own prompting, and that of my Maker, or that of the devil, whichever you please to ascribe it to. I acknowledge no man in human form."

A young man in a volunteer's uniform: "How many men in all did you have?"

"I came to Virginia with eighteen men only, besides myself."

"What in the world did you suppose that you could do with that number?"

"Young man, I don't wish to discuss that question here."

Mason: "How do you justify your acts?"

"I think, my friend, you are guilty of a great wrong against God and humanity—I say it without wishing to be offensive—and it would be perfectly right in any one to interfere with you so far as to free those you wilfully and wickedly hold in bondage. I do not say this insultingly."

"I understand that," Mason said.

"I think I did right, and that others will do right to interefere with you at any time and all times. I hold that the Golden Rule, 'Do unto others as you would have them do unto you', applies to all who would help others to gain their liberty."

Lieutenant Stuart shouted, "But you don't believe in the Bible."

"Certainly I do," Brown said.

Mason held up a pamphlet, the "Provisional Constitution and Ordinances for the People of the United States," taken from the raider's pocket. "Did you consider this as a military organization in this paper? I have not yet read it."

"I did in some sense. I wish you would give that paper close attention."

"You considered yourself the commander-in-chief of these military forces?"

"I was chosen . . . commander-in-chief of that force."

"What wages did you offer?" Mason asked.

"None."

Stuart interrupted once more: " 'The wages of sin is death.' "

Brown turned to Stuart: "I would not have made such a remark to you, if you had been a prisoner and wounded in my hands."

There was a brief silence, broken by a bystander: "Did you not promise a Negro in Gettysburg twenty dollars a month?"

"I did not."[9]

There was much more, all recorded by a New York *Herald* reporter, and most of it, perhaps, heard by the intent Lieutenant Stuart. But in the afternoon Lee sent Stuart with a few Marines and a wagon into Maryland to search the farm old Brown had made his headquarters. Stuart brought back a wagonload of handmade pikes.

Harpers Ferry was recovering from excitement. Five survivors of the raid had lain outside the enginehouse for an hour or more. Several were led to prison at nearby Charlestown, a few had escaped, and others had died.

Young Anderson writhed in the yard too long, a visiting farmer thought. The countryman looked at the boy in bitter silence, then walked away. He returned to find Anderson still breathing.

"Well, it takes a hell of a long time for you to die," the farmer said.

But Anderson's time was near. Some bystanders spit tobacco juice into his eyes, and his face grimaced in pain as he breathed his last.

Bodies were collected from the river and the streets and buried in a pit beside the Shenandoah. One body was missing, however, for doctors from Winchester took Anderson's corpse from the yard and stuffed it into a barrel, for use in their dissections. One witness, John Barry, wrote: "Head foremost, they rammed him in, but they could not bend his legs so as to get them into the barrel with the rest of the body . . . they strained so hard that the man's bones or sinews fairly cracked."

Old Brown's son, Watson, was now in his last hours, and he, too, was put through a catechism, by C. W. Tayleure, a Baltimore reporter:

"What brought you here?"

"Duty, sir."

"Is it then your idea of duty to shoot down men upon their own hearth-stones for defending their rights?"

"I am dying, I cannot discuss the question. I did my duty as I saw it."

One of the raiders listened calmly, another "with uncontrollable terror," as the questioning went on.[10]

The roles of Stuart and Lee in the incident were near an end. They remained in the buzzing town for another day as the militia companies drifted away and the citizens went back to their daily routine. Panic subsided. There was brief excitement the night following Brown's capture—a report of a slave rebellion in Pleasant Valley, six miles out. But when Stuart and Lee rode there with Green and thirty Marines they found it a false alarm. They were greeted by yawning planters in torchlight, and Negroes who gaped at the troops, obviously more frightened by the name of Brown than by the soldiers themselves.

Governor Wise had brought other troops into Harpers Ferry, including the neatly uniformed Richmond Howitzers, in whose ranks marched the eminent young novelist, John Esten Cooke. The writer was a cousin of Stuart's wife, Flora; Jeb would soon meet him again.

Lee and Stuart took a train to Washington the next morning as casually as if Harpers Ferry had dropped from their lives, and as if there could be no aftermath to the raid by the pale-eyed old man and his band of fumbling revolutionaries.

☆

CHAPTER 2

The Young Warrior

JAMES E. B. STUART was born February 6, 1833, in a comfortable, unpretentious farmhouse in Southwestern Virginia, Laurel Hill, the seventh of eleven children, and the youngest son.

His father was Archibald Stuart, a soldier in the War of 1812, who returned to a country law practice and a career in politics. He long represented Patrick County in the Virginia Assembly, and held a seat in Congress during the Nullification crisis; he sided with John C. Calhoun.

Archibald has come down in family memoirs as "a powerful orator and advocate," a great singer and social companion, a charmer and wit, a *bon vivant* whose nature was to be reflected in his most famous son.

He reared his family in a home provided by his wife, an inheritance from the well-to-do Letcher family.

The clan was five generations old in Virginia with the arrival of the brood of eleven at Laurel Hill. The first of the American line was Archibald Stuart the elder, an Irish refugee of 1726, who was obliged to hide out in Western Pennsylvania for seven years and then drifted into the Shenandoah Valley and took up lands which made him rich.

One of his sons was Major Alexander Stuart, commander of a Virginia regiment at the battle of Guilford Courthouse in the Revolution. The major had two horses shot beneath him, and was badly wounded, captured by the British and exchanged. In his later years— he lived to the age of ninety—he became a man of wealth and influence in Virginia, a patron of education and the arts, and a founder of the college to become Washington and Lee University.

17

The major's younger son, Alexander, won distinction as a member of the Virginia Executive Council, a Federal judge in Missouri, and Speaker of the Missouri House of Representatives. Alexander was the grandfather of J. E. B. Stuart.

James's mother was Elizabeth Letcher Pannill, of a family which furnished governors for Kentucky and Virginia. John Letcher, the Civil War Governor of Virginia, was a close kinsman. She was related by marriage to Governor Sam Houston of Texas, and to the distinguished Hairston family of Virginia and North Carolina.

Laurel Hill was a big rambling house in an oak grove, with a view of the Blue Ridge. Slaves carried the burden of the plantation's work, but they seem not to have been numerous. James came to know the place well and to love its hills, trees and flowers; he formed a habit of collecting flower specimens. This training came from his mother, and remained with him. He also had tutors of ability in early years. He went to nearby Emory and Henry College at fifteen, and in need of a testimonial as to his accomplishments, wrote his old teacher of the Latin learning, "which you instilled into me partly by the mouth and partly by the rod."[1]

He also wrote this man: "It is not my intention not to read Virgil at all, but as I expect to teach school some when I leave here, then will be my time to read it."

Stuart's father was Presbyterian, his mother, Episcopalian; the home life was not fanatically religious. Young James faced a moral issue in the innocence of twelve: He took an oath that he would never touch liquor.

The few stories from his childhood emphasize young James's strength of will. One, told by his older brother, William Alexander, described the conquest of a hornet's nest by nine-year-old James, who climbed a tree despite stings of the insects and destroyed their nest, while his companion fled.

Nearing manhood James was a gangling boy with long arms and legs, short in the body, striking only when on horseback. He spent much time in the saddle.

In 1848 he worked briefly in the office of the county clerk in nearby Wytheville, when he was perhaps being urged to study law. That fall, however, he entered Emory and Henry. One item of record this year: James was swept up in a local revival, and joined the Methodist church.

About a year later his father lost his seat in Congress. Young James almost simultaneously tried to enter West Point. The first official act of the newly elected Congressman, H. T. Averett, was to appoint the son of his rival to the military academy. James seems to have had no early dreams of military glory; his decision was abrupt. He left for the Academy in late June, 1850. A letter to a relative en route revealed him as an intent tourist, as he paused in Washington:

> I am green as a gourd vine yet. Unfortunately I did not come on reception day and was thereby deprived of the pleasure of an introduction to Zack [President Zachary Taylor]. I have seen him twice on the streets. He is a plain looking old fellow with a slight squat as he walks. . . . A day in the U.S. Senate is worth no little to anyone. I think Mr. Webster decidedly the finest looking man in the Senate. He speaks slowly but forcibly, but of all the pleasant speakers give me Jeff Davis of Mississippi. I heard Mr. Clay make some remarks. He is very nervous. . . . Mr. Fillmore is a better looking man than I expected to find him. Mr. Houston is very fine looking. . . . I was in the House, but this is a rowdy place compared with the Senate.

James reported to West Point July first. He found his country schooling adequate, and worked as hard as his gay nature permitted. At the end of the term he stood high in a class of 71 which included men destined for fame: eighth in mathematics, fifteenth in French, twelfth in English. In general merit he was eighth in his class. His conduct was almost exemplary, for he was No. 82 among the 229 cadets of the corps, with 43 demerits.

In his second year he held his ground: seventh in a class of 60 in mathematics, twenty-first in drawing, eighth in French. He was seventh in general merit, and 57 among the 229 in conduct, with 29 demerits. Thereafter he seemed to abandon himself to the good life at The Point.[2]

Fitzhugh Lee, the nephew of Major Robert E. Lee, the superintendent, recalled Stuart: "It was in 1852 that I first knew him. . . .

'Beauty' Stuart he was then universally called, for however manly and soldierly in appearance he afterwards grew, in those days his comrades bestowed that appellation upon him to express their idea of his personal comeliness in inverse ratio to the term employed."

When Fitz Lee met him, Stuart was orderly sergeant of his company. Lee wrote: "His distinguishing characteristics were a strict attention to his military duties, an erect, soldierly bearing, an immediate and almost thankful acceptance of a challenge from any cadet to fight, who might in any way feel himself aggrieved, and a clear, metallic, ringing voice."

Lee remembered Stuart on the parade ground: "There was so much music in his voice . . . sounding like the trumpet of the Archangel."[3]

Stuart's belligerence was real enough. His father wrote him near the end of his third class year:

> I am proud to say that your conduct has given me entire satisfaction. I heard, it is true (but no thanks to you for the information) of the little scrape in which you involved yourself; but I confess, from what I understand of the transaction, I did not consider you much to blame. An insult should be resented under all circumstances. If a man in your circumstances gain credit by submitting to an insult as a strict observer of discipline, he loses more in proportion in his standing as a gentleman and man of courage.

Six months later, however, the father's tone became firmer:

> I have received your letter, and much regret that you have been involved in another fighting scrape. My dear son, I can excuse more readily a fault of the sort you have committed, in which you maintained your character as a man of honor and courage, than almost any other. But I hope you will hereafter, as far as possible, avoid getting into difficulties in which such maintenance may be demanded at your hands.

Academy records began to lengthen under Stuart's name. "Delinquencies for the Year of 1853" included:

July 14. Allowing a loud noise to be made in his company 4:30 and 5 A.M. 8 demerits.

July 14. Answering another cadet in a boisterous tone of voice, in the immediate vicinity of the Commandant's office, 7:30 and 8:30 A.M. 5 demerits.

Also in July:

Bedding out of order at evening inspection; wearing cap not uniform; not placing his handspike in proper position at Artillery drill; late at formation of artillery section; tent walls not raised at breakfast.

There was an odd assortment throughout the year. Stuart was charged with "occupying and causing citizens [probably girls] to occupy seats on a sentinel's post"; with "raising hand at parade"; with "swinging arms marching"; with keeping a dirty floor, unclean shoes, and, "loitering, 11 A.M."[4]

In his letters of this time Stuart revealed a sensitive spirit evidently at war with that of the heedless soldier he had become. He had been in Virginia on furlough in the summer of 1852, and wrote a girl cousin of his boat trip up the Hudson:

The lovely prospect spreads before you on either side, with here and there a magnificent country seat. . . . Among these are the princely dwelling of Forrest the tragedian, and the more plain, but no less elegant mansion of Washington Irving . . . myriads of flowers lean forth, laughing with joy, and then imagine the incessant warble of the winged songsters. . . .

You find your view suddenly confined by the Palisades which consist of an immense barrier of solid rock extending for several miles along the river on your left, rising in unique grandeur to the clouds. . . . You find yourself suddenly in the midst of the romantic scenery of the highlands. Your eyes now rest upon West Point. Its broad plain about 150 feet above the river, surrounded by high mountains, its beautiful buildings, magnificent barracks, the proud banner floating gracefully.

Stuart also wrote of the "August Ball," which attracted

... such an assemblage of beauty, fashion and gaiety as I never saw before. Notwithstanding the violent storm which raged without, all night, the Hall was crowded with ladies, and continued so until 12. Although the music and the busy whirl of the dance succeeded in drowning out the rain, yet the thunder ... roared far above every noise. With many a long face we marched into Barracks next day to resume the arduous duties of another year.[5]

He had brought from Virginia a gourd, which hung on his barracks wall, carved with "Bettie" in honor of his cousin. Fellow cadets teased him about it, but he often drank Bettie's health from the gourd. He wrote frequently and ardently of home:

> In Dear Old Virginia October and November I consider by far the most delightful months of the year.

And:

> I am very well pleased with West Point for the limited stay which I expect to make ... but so long as there is such a bright spot as Virginia I can never be content to take up my abode here permanently. If it could be grafted on Virginia soil I would consider it a paradise.

He added:

> I am as glad to see any Virginian as if he were an old acquaintance.

He became the supreme Virginia partisan when it came to women:

> The more I see of these Yankee girls the more thoroughly I am convinced of their inferiority in every respect to our Virginia ladies, in beauty especially.

His letters reveal a growing fondness for the company of young women. He met a "Miss B" walking on the Hudson and got an ornament from her hat as a souvenir; he went walking to the Crow's

Nest with several young ladies, chaperoned by Mrs. R. E. Lee, who was prevented from repeating the outing by the death of her mother, at Arlington. Stuart admired Mrs. Lee's daughter Mary "both as regards beauty and sprightliness."

But of love Stuart wrote mournfully:

> I must say that with all the array of love-seekers and heart-breakers I have escaped unscathed. Whether my escape has been effected by my own generalship or whether Cupid regarded me as too unworthy a victim I leave to your fancy to determine. . . . They say that to be in love is a glorious predicament, but if it costs as much sleep as my classmates lose in midnight communion with the stars and renders vacant seats in the mess hall as it seems to have done, save me from such a monster.

And again:

> I suppose you received the usual number of Valentines this year. For my part I did not receive any, thus showing that after all my devotion to the ladies during last summer they have forgotten me in so short a time.

Stuart formed strong attachments for two older women, Mrs. R. E. Lee and Mrs. Winfield Scott, wife of the elderly commander-in-chief of the army. He left glimpses of the relationships:

> Mrs. Lee, of whom you have so often heard me speak highly, has left us for a visit of some months to Arlington. She was like a mother to me and I miss her in proportion, but in compliance with her invitation I will stop at Arlington on my way home.

Again:

> Last Saturday I had the pleasure of dining at Colonel Lee's and found the Colonel in a fine humor. Mrs. Lee is still in Virginia. . . . I have formed a high regard for the family.

Of Mrs. Scott:

> Our honored "Alma Mater", Mrs. General Scott, too has
> been on The Point for about a month, loading us as usual with
> her kind attentions. I received from her the other day a very
> kind note with a basket of grapes. . . . She claims all the corps as
> her children, and is often asked by strangers if she has any sons,
> to which she gives the invariable reply, "250".
> I often tell Ma what an indulgent mother I have, and tell
> her there is great danger of my being spoilt, in which I fear
> there is more truth than jest.

Most telling of all his letters was one written in his final year,
when he was Cadet Captain, and an orator on the occasion of his rising to First Classman. He described his part in the ceremony:

> The reader of the Declaration was—your cousin; elected
> by the Dialectic Society. The audience was very large, for
> besides the Corps there congregated together samples of beauty
> and fashion from almost every part of the country *except Vir-
> ginia.*
> I always thought I had enough brass, but when I rose be-
> fore such an audience to perform the part assigned me I felt
> quite embarrassed and would willingly have "crawfished" if it
> had been possible. But I had to "stand up to the rack, fodder or
> no fodder", so I put on a bold face and drove ahead.

He wrote often of his favorite horse, Tony, which carried him
on cavalry exercises at The Point until a day in March, 1853, when
Stuart wrote:

> Tony was condemned by a board of officers as being unfit,
> and suffered "the penalty". But there is consolation in the
> thought that such is the fortune of war, and we are all victims
> ready for sacrifice when it shall please U.S. I propose therefore
> that we wear mourning on the *little finger* for one week. His
> loss I deeply deplore.

But there was plenty of horseflesh at home, and he asked of
Bettie:

I suppose I will have to content myself with Duroc, Bembo, Rhoderick, Don Quixote, Forager, or Jerry. Which do you prefer?

Rarely did Stuart reveal an awareness of growing tension between North and South, but at the approach of a national election he wrote Bettie in favor of the Democratic Party:

I join with you in your best wishes for the success of Democracy. Experience has fully demonstrated that its principles are the only ones which will secure the permanency of our government and preserve the Constitution and the rights of the states inviolate.

While Bettie was in school at Salem Academy, North Carolina, Stuart wrote:

I never admired Salem as an institution, but it is perhaps as good as any except those contaminated by abolitionism. I ask your pardon for introducing the subject, but I do know that I have seen more misery in a limited sphere within the period of my sojourn North than I ever dreamed of seeing South during my lifetime. This shows how perfectly absurd are all the outcries and attacks of Yankees against Southern Institutions. They seem to forget that *charity* begins (where slander never does) at home.

Near the end of his West Point career Stuart wrote two letters on his choice of profession. To his father:

I have not as yet any fixed course determined upon after graduation; still I can't help but regard it as the crisis of my life. Two courses will be left for my adoption, the profession of arms and that of the law; the one securing an ample support, with a life of hardship and uncertainty—laurels, if any, dearly bought, and leaving an empty title as a bequeathment; the other an overcrowded thoroughfare, which may or may not yield a support—may possibly secure honors, but of doubtful worth. Each has its labors and rewards. In making the selection I will rely upon the guidance of Him whose judgment cannot err, for "it is not with man that walketh to direct his steps".

He was much more outspoken to Cousin Bettie:

Were I to consult my own inclination at present I would continue in the army. It has attractions which are . . . overpowering. There is something in "the pride and pomp and circumstance of glorious war" which makes "Othello's occupation" the most desirable of all.

Now tell me candidly, had you not rather see your cousin a bold Dragoon than a petty-fogger lawyer? I have no doubt that you have a sort of partiality for the life of a farmer but the young man for whom capital has not already been accumulated is forced to adopt one of the *hireling* professions, Law, Medicine, Engineering and Arms.

The officer has his toils, but he has his *reward*. The lawyer has his cases but *seldom* receives his fee. The physician has his patients; his sleepless nights, but his patients are very patient in *waiting to pay him*. The Engineer must first have a reputation before he can get desirable employment.

But young James was only entertaining. He was already lost, for the moment mounted squadrons charged in cavalry drill, he knew he was forever a soldier.

He had expressed to Bettie Hairston what he could not to his father, his chagrin at being the seventh child of a none-too-prosperous country lawyer, denied a landed estate to provide him a start in life and comfortable leisure, and driven to be a "hireling" because clients seldom paid Lawyer Stuart their fees.

Nothing seemed to mar James's increasing gaiety. He graduated from West Point in July, 1854, and waited impatiently for a vacancy in his assigned regiment.

He finished thirteenth in a class of forty-six survivors. His accomplishments were respectable:

Engineering, twenty-ninth; Ethics, ninth; Mineralogy and Geology, thirteenth; Infantry Tactics, fourteenth; Artillery, thirteenth; Cavalry Tactics, tenth.

His conduct was deplorable by comparison: He stood 103rd among 206 cadets, with a total of 129 demerits. But his class standing was high, and above him were young soldiers of promise. G. W.

Custis Lee, son of the commandant, was first, and O. O. Howard of Maine was fourth—men Stuart would meet in the years ahead.

Just below him were others to become known in war: Stephen D. Lee, William D. Pender, Archibald Gracie.

There is a family tradition that Stuart's grades were higher in the last year, but that he feared fine marks would place him in the elite corps of engineers, a relatively dull place, and that he deliberately slowed his pace to make poorer grades.[6]

Jeb went home to Patrick County and wandered restlessly for several weeks. He fell ill in Richmond, and returned home to be cared for by a family physician. The illness was brief, but Stuart complained:

> I have not yet recovered my lost appetite, a loss which I have so seldom been made to feel that it almost grieves me, especially when I find myself unable to do justice to a meal for which I have to pay full price, for it has always been my consolation that I always got the worth of my money in the eating line, and precious little did a hotel keeper ever make off me.

When he reached home, he discovered the "long-looked-for document from headquarters"—his commission as second lieutenant in the Mounted Rifles. He was assigned to duty in Texas, October fifteenth.

He found the Rifles "a corps which my taste, fondness for riding, and desire to serve my country in some acceptable manner led me to select above all the rest."

There was a delay, however, and he made a leisurely trip west through Washington and New York, buying equipment on his way. It was this week, in Washington, that he had made the first known daguerreotype of his early manhood, a solemn portrait in a fashionable black coat, light waistcoat, white shirt with a gates-ajar collar, its points upturned about his broad mouth. The chin, derided as weak by his friends, is tucked over an enormous black tie. If the chin is weak, the fault is concealed by the camera's angle, for the face is strong, almost belligerent. The hair is swept back from a high brow, curling long over the ears. There is mysterious banter in his letters of this period about the picture, which he sent to several friends. He wrote to one from Washington's Willard Hotel:

> I send you by this mail a likeness of "Beauty". You perceive I was looking my *prettiest* when it was taken. . . . I staid in New York City just three minutes by the watch . . . Arlington yesterday, *delighted*.
>
> You are at liberty to show this daguerreotype to our mutual friends, but beware of ————.[7]

On the eve of departure he had more to say on his career:

> As regards my entering the army, I have but one aim, to do some service to my country in return for what she has done for me.
>
> I might *nominally* cancel my sense of duty to my country, by entering that portion of the service entirely unexposed to actual fighting, and thus spend my life in inglorious ease at some delightful station on the Atlantic. But when there are hard knocks to be felt, and hard blows to be dealt, a man *really desirous* to serve his country will not hesitate a moment to declare for the latter.

Impatient to join his regiment before the Comanches left the warpath, he was off for the West.

☆

CHAPTER 3

On the Frontier

LIEUTENANT STUART was seasick. He did not leave his cabin as the little steamer crept through the gulf to the West, and when it docked at Galveston, he lay in his berth for twelve hours, still suffering as if he were being tossed on the rough waters.

A noisy passenger roused him and on unsteady legs Jeb dressed and "crawled" through the streets of the town.

He had been ill almost since leaving New Orleans, for "a violent northeaster" struck as they entered the Gulf of Mexico and howled over them for hours. Stuart had never before been out of sight of land, and was an easy victim to the pitching of the vessel.

Otherwise it had been a pleasant journey. He had gone west to Louisville, and here got orders to delay his trip because of a yellow fever epidemic in New Orleans. He used the respite to visit relatives in St. Louis, and it was November twenty-ninth before he took a boat to the south:

> I felt that I had sundered the last ties that bound me to home and friends. . . . I glided down the Mississippi, which presented such beauty, novelty and variety of vegetation that the trip really seemed a short one.

Stuart was not impressed by Galveston:

> I was struck with the rusticity of the inhabitants and the extreme economy and simplicity displayed in their edifices, of which by far the most imposing and finest was the billiard saloon and bar room attached to the Tremont House.

He went back to the boat and soon landed, "with a voracious appetite" at Indianola, Texas, where he awaited a smaller boat. The final voyage was "tedious" but not perilous. Stuart and his companions slept on deck and cooked their own meals. At night they anchored off the lonely coast and most of the men slept gratefully. But Stuart wrote:

> For my own part I met with something to interest me every day and at night enjoyed an incessant serenade from sea fowls and wolves.

In Corpus Christi, Stuart found that the Mounted Rifles were some 450 miles west of Laredo in trackless Indian country, and he pushed on. He wrote home of his departure from town under escort, aware that it was the start of his career as a soldier:

> You ought to have seen what an array of wagons were mustered up on the lovely morning of the 29th of December, 1853. May the setting of my military sun be as bright as its rising sun was on that day!

Jeb saw the country with the eye of a neophyte traveler as he rode west:

> The region is almost entirely uninhabited prairie with little or no vegetation ... and remarkably scarce water. A mud hole is sought with as much avidity as we would repair to the spring under the beech tree on the hottest day in August.
>
> We found game in the greatest abundance. Deer bounded over the plain in herds with an air of defiance, taking care however to keep at a respectful distance from our rifles, though Major Hall killed two and I wounded another. Rabbits and partridges ran along before us as if inviting us to kill.

After two days he reached Laredo and headed for Eagle Pass. In this country Stuart had his first glimpse of Indians in the wild.

He rode with a companion to hunt partridge and was soon out of sight of camp. It was late evening when the wagons had halted for water. From nowhere a band of horsemen appeared, twenty or

thirty of them. As Stuart and his friend stared "in utter astonishment" the riders advanced, looking like "Indians in disguise" in their
rags, and on scrub ponies.

Stuart thought his last moment had come:

> Of course we then had to "face the music". In this dilemma
> we were left for a moment only, for the leader galloping up to
> us accosted us in plain English and relieved us from our painful
> suspense.

The Indians were "mustangers" catching horses for the market,
and wanted to buy bread from the soldiers. A relieved Stuart rode
with them to the caravan. He wrote home of his courage:

> So you see we were as brave as if they had been *Indians sure
> enough*.

Jeb did not miss occasional beauties of the country, including
"a beautiful flower on the roadside" which led him to confess a
weakness:

> Fond as I am of flowers (would you believe it?) I didn't
> pull it, but left it as an ornament to the solitude.

The caravan reached Laredo, "a little Mexican village of miserable hovels," but the Mounted Rifles seemed to be moving away like
a mirage. There was word that they had gone to the west of Fort
Clark, to a place called Limpia, more than four hundred miles west
of Eagle Pass. The campaign might last six months or longer.

On one stop Jeb found time to instruct Cousin Bettie on Shake-
speare, and revealed the extent of his own reading:

> My favorite piece is the *Merchant of Venice*. The first
> time I read Shakespeare to appreciate it was while a Plebe at
> West Point. I studied my lesson until bedtime and took Shake-
> speare to bed with me with a lamp by my side and read for
> hours. I believe *Hamlet* is his masterpiece. *Tempest* is first-rate.
> *Love's Labor Lost* nothing extra. *Midsummer Night's Dream*
> I never could bear. *Richard III* good. *Othello* is magnificent.

I was particularly struck with the author's power of true depic-
tion where Othello is modestly recounting his daring exploits to
Desdemona. I hated very much, however, the end. I hope you
will read at your leisure *Childe Harold* and *Ivanhoe*, and tell me
what you think of them. I believe Irving's are the best American
works.

This letter brought a new tone to his correspondence with
Cousin Bettie, which had earlier seemed almost like love letters, as if
he were trying his hand at the game. From Texas he wrote more like
father than lover, and the final letter of the series ended:

> Whatever may be my fate, may you be happy . . .
>
> > Your Affectionate Cousin.

It was as if he deliberately snapped whatever tenuous romantic
ties bound him to his young kinswoman.[1]

The caravan at last joined the Mounted Rifles, but there was
little action, though the command scoured West Texas for months.
Stuart wrote his cousin Jack Hairston in March, 1855, of his "bitter
disappointment":

> Notwithstanding we have threaded every trail, clambered
> every precipice and penetrated every ravine for hundreds of
> miles around, we have not been able to find Mr. Comanche.
> We are now quietly awaiting General Smith's orders, resting
> our animals, which are very jaded.

The men were as worn, he said:

> We had a great deal of walking to do over ground where
> we could scarcely *lead* our horses. I wore out a pair of very
> thick shoes such as cornfield Negroes wear in Virginia and
> would have been barefooted but for a pair of embroidered
> slippers which chance threw in my way to bring out. They had
> been given me while at West Point by Miss Helen Alexander,
> who was married last summer. I presume she little thought when
> she gave them that they were destined to tread Comanches
> trails.

He was critical of famed local scouts attached to the Rifles:

> The Texan Rangers would fire all day at deer without killing one. They have left us now, and never was a departure more rejoiced at. They were a rowdy crowd with a few praiseworthy exceptions.

He wrote Cousin Jack of fine hunting: Blue quail, Rio Grande quail, "the prettiest bird I ever saw," and Chapparal Cocks, antelope and deer. He spent hours observing prairie dogs, which he thought the most remarkable of Texas animals.

Prairie wolves howled every night, Stuart wrote, but the "most mournful cry" came from a panther. He went out with a companion after "His Panthership," but without success.[2]

Stuart was not content with private letters from Texas. He wrote at least two long ones to *The Jeffersonian*, published in Staunton, Virginia, describing in detail his adventures and the countryside.

The party pressed over rugged mountains to the camp of the Comanches, now abandoned, where Jeb admired the system of pickets and sentinels developed by the Indians, and concealment of their lodges. Here he met a soldier he would come to know well—Major James Longstreet, who was out from El Paso with a party of the 8th Infantry.

Stuart's Virginia readers were treated to a sketch of a near tragedy, a swift prairie fire that singed beards, uniforms and horses, and consumed most of the expedition's supplies. The disaster forced the party to give up the chase of Indians and join a nearby camp.

It was on this expedition that Stuart grew the huge cinnamon-red beard and mustache he wore the rest of his life. He wrote a girl back East:

> My beard (which by the way is in a flourishing condition) has so much altered my physique that you could not recognize me. Davant says that I am the only man he ever saw that Beard improved.

Stuart triumphed over rough terrain with one piece of artillery on this trip as his horses wound down a snaking cliffside trail. Jeb went to the bottom of the cliff, hoping, he said, to find an order to abandon the gun. There were no such orders from his commander, Major John Simonson:

> I determined to show the Major what a little determination could do.

Stuart led twenty-five men as they edged the big gun down the sheer bluff with ropes and lariats, lifting it over stones and snaking it along the narrow trail.

> Before night we were sipping our coffee at the Major's bivouac. The Major told me that I deserved great credit for my success, and said that he never expected to see me bring the artillery down that mountain.[3]

Stuart was becoming known outside the Rifles. In the spring of 1855, Secretary of War Jefferson Davis organized the 1st and 2nd Cavalry, and ordered Stuart to Jefferson Barracks, St. Louis, as second lieutenant of the 1st Cavalry. The commander was Colonel Edwin Sumner, with Joseph E. Johnston as his lieutenant colonel. John Sedgwick was a major, and among the captains and lesser grades were a dozen or more destined to become generals, including George McClellan.

The cavalry regiments, superbly equipped and led by picked officers from all branches, were the War Department's answer to the Indian menace on the frontier. The Mounted Rifles were outmoded. The need was for a big, swift-striking force able to find the enemy in his own country and endure long campaigns. It was the birth of a modern fighting unit for the army.

The 2nd Cavalry was led by distinguished men, too: Albert Sidney Johnston was its colonel, R. E. Lee the lieutenant colonel, George Thomas a major. Among the lieutenants was R. E. Lee's nephew, Fitz Lee.

As he left the Mounted Rifles, Stuart got the highest praise from Major Simonson:

> During your service with Company G, your duties have, at times, been necessarily arduous, and it has afforded me pleasure to notice that under these circumstances you have not

omitted to display that cheerfulness and zeal in their performance which, if perservered in, will not fail to be appreciated by
those with whom you may serve, and to secure you a favorable
reputation as an officer.

Simonson later wrote:

Lieutenant Stuart was brave and gallant, always prompt in
the execution of orders, and reckless of danger or exposure. I
considered him one of the most promising young officers in the
United States Army.

About this time Stuart had a noteworthy letter from his father
in Virginia:

Just embarking in military life (a life which tests, perhaps
more than any other, a young man's prudence and steadiness),
at an immense distance from your friends, great responsibility
rests upon your shoulders.
It is true that you have, to start with, good morals fortified
by religion, a good temper and a good constitution, which if
preserved will carry you through the trial safely. But the temp-
tations of a camp to a young man of sanguine temperament, like
yourself, are not to be trifled with or despised. I conjure you
to be constantly on your guard, repelling and avoiding the
slightest approach towards vice or immorality.

Stuart left Texas in May and was soon busy with the organization of the new force in St. Louis, though probably disappointed
when Colonel Sumner made him regimental quartermaster and commissary. He learned vital lessons as chaperon to the mounts, however, and was one of the first men with experience in mounting, feeding and supplying a modern cavalry troop.
He found companionship in St. Louis among the lieutenants and
captains, including W. N. R. Beall, George Steuart, Robert Ransom,
George Bayard, Lunsford Lomax, William S. Walker, R. H. Anderson and R. S. Garnett—all of them to become generals. He had at
least one close friend outside the regiment, Andrew Reid Venable,
Jr., a twenty-three-year-old Virginia businessman drawn to the

booming frontier town. Stuart, Venable and other Southerners felt themselves at home, for the "tone of society" was set by families from the plantation South. Stuart's relatives were part of "the Southern element," as he was, without the trouble of searching his conscience.[4]

He may have read danger in St. Louis, where the plain people were almost unanimously antislavery, and joined the Free Soilers in noisy demonstrations. The fight to keep slavery from the West seemed to center in the turbulent city. Stuart was snatched away in the summer of 1855, assigned to Fort Leavenworth, Kansas Territory.

One of his first sights of this frontier must have been the daughter of Colonel Philip St. George Cooke of the 2nd Dragoons. Her name was Flora; born in Missouri of an old Virginia family, graduate of a private school in Detroit, an accomplished horsewoman, and though not pretty, an effective charmer. Stuart succumbed with hardly a struggle. His first note to her on July 25, 1855:

> Lieut. Stuart presents his compliments to Miss Flora with the view of ascertaining whether her plans for the ride this afternoon have fully matured. . . .
> Lieut. Stuart begs leave to add that he hopes nothing will occur to prevent the ride, and with best wishes for her hasty recovery from the remotest resemblance of sickness.[5]

Little more than two weeks later he wrote a male cousin in Virginia:

> I have something of *importance*, to myself at least, to tell you and which will perhaps surprise you. . . . Our garrison is notwithstanding the presence of cholera among the troops quite lively. Some seven or eight young ladies can always hoist sail for amusement. I have been riding with one nearly every suitable evening. I hardly expected so much refinement on the frontier . . . I'm bound to be married before I am 23.[6]

A few weeks of riding with Flora brought an engagement. They planned a church wedding, and Stuart wrote his father and got parental blessings. The Cookes were well known in Virginia: The father was a distinguished Army veteran; one of his sons, John R. Cooke, was a promising young Harvard graduate, and a nephew John Esten Cooke, was one of the most celebrated American novelists, "The Sir Walter Scott of The Southern Border," author of successful books, a poet, and contributor to *The Southern Literary Messenger*.

The romance was interrupted in September when the 1st Cavalry went on an Indian raid. Stuart returned after a hard expedition, on November fourth, to find word of the death of his father. He could not return to Virginia, but the death forced cancellation of plans for an elaborate wedding.

Stuart wrote Flora that their quarters in Leavenworth's "West End" would be simple by comparison with the spacious accommodations for her father's family, and she was teased at Fort Riley about moving into "one room and a kitchen" from the commander's quarters.

They were married on November fourteenth at Fort Riley, Flora small and radiant in her white school graduation dress, dazzling her bridegroom with the glow of her blue eyes and the fine complexion which were her only claims to beauty. It was a simple ceremony with only four attendants, two men and two women. Jeb took her to Leavenworth the next day. There were no servants in the party. They began housekeeping in Leavenworth's barracks.

Stuart wrote one of his girl friends, sending a bit of the wedding cake and announcing his conquest by "Miss Flora, eldest daughter of Colonel P. St. George Cooke, U.S. 2nd Dragoons, to whom I was married on the 14th." He addressed the girl correspondent as "My dear, *dear* friend," adding:

> Our correspondence shall never stop with my consent. What say you? . . . Tell Miss Emily I fear she will take no interest in "Beauty" now that he is an old married man.

Jeb and Flora began life together on the raw post while the regiment was being trained for new duties. There was soon good news—promotion for Stuart. Flora's father, a bit dazed, wrote his novelist nephew:

Flora was married, rather suddenly—to Mr. Stuart of Virginia. . . . He is a remarkably fine, promising, pure young man, and has had so far an extraordinary promotion. He is a First Lieutenant, 1st Cavalry.[7]

The Kansas in which the Stuarts began marriage was in chaos. Open war raged as bands of Border Ruffians fought Free Soilers. Murder became commonplace, and old Osawatomie Brown was charged with massacres; there were lynchings and retaliations. In the spring of 1856 a proslavery band from Missouri invaded Kansas to avenge murders at Pottawatomie. Their leader was a soldier Stuart would meet again.

This was Henry Clay Pate, a captain of Missouri militia, deputy U.S. Marshal, and correspondent of the *Missouri Republican* of St. Louis. Pate was a fiery young Virginian of twenty-four, who had studied at the University in Charlottesville.

The Missourians had captured some of Brown's gang, including John Brown, Jr., and on June second, at Black Jack on the Santa Fe Trail, John Brown's band of nine men forced the surrender of Pate's men after a gun battle.

Colonel Edwin Sumner and a party of the 1st Cavalry arrived to free Pate and his Missourians, and in the rescue column of fifty troopers rode Lieutenant Stuart.

The soldiers halted near the camp and old Brown came out to treat with Colonel Sumner as if he were the ruler of a sovereign state. Sumner ordered the band dispersed and announced that he was there by command of President Pierce to enforce law and order in an impartial manner. Brown began moving his camp and freed the prisoners.

Stuart thus had his first glimpse of Brown and his ragged soldiers who had taken the law into their own hands in an attack on slavery. He also began an acquaintance with Pate, who was so soon to be riding at his side in the bloody sequel to the trials of Kansas.

Stuart might have learned from the wisdom of his colonel in this matter, for Sumner reported:

Things are getting worse every day, and it is hard to foresee the result. One of these things must happen: Either it will terminate in civil war or the vicious will band themselves together to plunder and murder all whom they meet.

Affairs in Kansas did not improve. Stuart's father-in-law, General Cooke, reported in mid-June:

> The disorders in the Territory have, in fact, changed their character, and consist now of robberies and assassinations, by a set of bandits whom the excitement of the times has attracted hither.

The climax came on July 4, 1856, when Colonel Sumner, under what he construed to be his orders, entered the antislavery Free State Legislature at Topeka and ordered it to disperse. Governor Woodson had declared the assembly to be in defiance of his authority, which had been clearly stated by President Pierce. Sumner felt that he could take no other course than to close the legislature as directed by the governor, but he made a bold and manly speech:

> This is the most disagreeable duty of my whole life. My orders are to disperse the Legislature, and I am here to tell you it must not meet, and to see it dispersed. God knows I have no partisan feelings in the matter, and I will have none so long as I hold my present position in Kansas. I have just returned from the border, where I have been driving out bands of Missourians, and now I am ordered here to disperse you. You must disperse. Let me again assure you that this is the most disagreeable duty of my life.

When a storm of protest broke in the North, Secretary of War Jefferson Davis, in an apparent search for a scapegoat, said sternly that Colonel Sumner had exceeded his authority, and Sumner was given leave. But barracks gossip in Kansas was that the courageous old soldier had been relieved only because he expressed his distaste for the disbanding of the legislature and had exposed the plans of the proslavery faction.

Young James Stuart, entranced with Flora and very much in love, watched the growing agonies of the frontier in crisis.[8]

Flora became pregnant in December, 1856. In the summer, when Indian troubles grew worse on the frontier the regiment was gone for weeks, and Flora must have despaired of seeing Jeb again. Before he returned he had a serious wound to report.

Far out on the border the regiment (again under Colonel Sumner) came upon three hundred Cheyenne warriors in line of battle. Stuart wrote:

> We fronted into line as soon as possible. . . . It was my intention to give a carbine volley and then charge with drawn pistols, and use the saber as a last resort; but much to my surprise the Colonel ordered, "Draw sabers! Charge!" when the Indians were within gunshot.
>
> We set up a terrific yell, which scattered the Cheyennes in disorderly flight, and we kept up the charge in pursuit.

It was the first cavalry charge of Stuart's life with flesh-and-blood enemy facing him. He dashed joyously among the fleeing Indians and lost his company in the melee. He found himself riding with other young officers at his side, including his friends Stanley and Lomax. When he rode among the enemy, Stuart wounded an Indian who was on the point of shooting Lunsford Lomax. The Indian shot at Stuart, but missed.

Lieutenant Stanley yelled, "Wait! I'll fetch him!" and knelt to fire at the Indian. His gun went off accidentally, using the last of his ammunition. The Indian advanced on Stanley with a pointed pistol.

"I could not stand that," Stuart wrote, "but drawing my saber rushed upon the monster and inflicted a severe wound on his head."

The Indian was no more than a foot or two from Stuart when he fired his pistol, striking Jeb in the breast. The bullet glanced off bone, "lodging near my left nipple, but so far inside that it cannot be felt."

He reassured Flora:

> I rejoice to inform you that the wound is not regarded as dangerous, thought I may be confined to my bed for weeks. I am now enjoying excellent health in every other respect.

Stuart began his recovery near the forks of the Solomon River under the treatment of Dr. Charles Brewer, the regimental surgeon. He was carried eight miles to the rear, where he was left with other wounded in a tiny field fort for about ten days while the command chased the Cheyenne. His wound improved so rapidly that two days after being shot he was not in pain when lying still. He wrote Flora:

> We have a pretty view up the creek for about two miles. ... I can sit up a little with props, and seize a moment now and then to jot a daily token to my wife. The day drags heavily.
> My Prayer Book—which I must say has not been neglected —and my Army Regulations are my only books. A few sheets of *Harpers Weekly* are treasures indeed.

About thirty Cheyennes attacked the fort on August fourth, but the wounded and their guards drove them off. Stuart walked a bit the next day, and at the end of that week began the long trip to Fort Kearny on horseback. The party went slowly, for some of the wounded rode on travois, Indian fashion. The command had no compass and traveled by the stars and the skill of Pawnee guides.

Stuart woke up on the second morning in a thick fog to find the Pawnees had deserted. The party was lost. With a glimpse of the starry sky at night as fog cleared briefly, Jeb set a course and took a small band to find the fort, but it was a struggle with a new guide, a Mexican, who insisted Kearny lay south of the line of march Stuart had chosen. For a day or two, alternately lashed by storms and blinded by fog, Jeb held his men to the work. To keep the proper line one man would halt in rear as others rode ahead, to be signaled into proper position. The rearmost man then rode to the front in turn. Jeb wrote Flora of a night in a violent storm:

> There we sat, every man squatted on his saddle, revealed in gloomy outlines only by the lightning's flash.
> We were all sleepy, and were dozing through the night in this way when a flash of lightning revealed, instead of the pretty grass plat, a large mass of water before us halfway up the bodies of our horses, and had barely time to make good our retreat.

After a hard day's march the party ate the last of its food, but Jeb did not despair.

"From the first I prayed to God to be my guide," he wrote, but he was willing to aid Providence. He forced the party across a swollen stream in its path, though other officers advised against it, and the Mexican guide made the plea, "Me no swim." Stuart swam first, alone, and the others followed on horseback.

They met the mail coming from Fort Kearny, carried by a government rider who had a little food in his knapsack. Stuart got a piece of hard bread, "the most delicious morsel I ever tasted." They soon reached the fort, where they found Colonel Sumner anxious for their safety. A relief expedition was sent for the sick and wounded, and the adventure was over.[9]

Jeb returned to Flora on August seventeenth. She bore a child the first week in September, a girl. Stuart insisted that she be named Flora. He was a doting father at twenty-four, and life in the skin-hung cavalry quarters of the frontier was gay and pleasant for the little family. His wound healed quickly. It was to be the last of his career until death.

In these days a nostalgia for Virginia and Laurel Hill touched Stuart. He wrote his mother:

> I wish to devote one hundred dollars to the purchase of a comfortable log church near your place, because in all my ob-servation I believe that one is more needed in that neighbor-hood than any other that I know of; and besides, "charity be-gins at home". Seventy-five of this one hundred dollars I have in trust for that purpose, and the remainder is my own contri-bution. If you will join me with a like amount from two or three others interested will build a very respectable *free* church. . . . What will you take for the South half of your plantation? I want to buy it.

Indian troubles in Kansas became less. Flora's father, Colonel Cooke, went into the Northwest with his dragoons. Stuart remained with his family at Fort Riley, where six companies of the 1st Cavalry were commanded by Major John Sedgwick. A year and a half passed quickly for the Stuarts with their infant daughter.

Jeb was not idle. For one thing, he turned to the problem of his saber, awkwardly fixed to his belt, hard to remove and replace. In spare moments he devised a simple attachment, quick and easy to use. That led him to another invention, "Stuart's Lightning Horse Hitcher," a halter with a snap enabling him to hitch and free a horse almost instantly.[10]

Stuart renewed his interest in religion, and early in 1859 was confirmed in the church of his wife and mother by the Episcopal Bishop Hawkes in St. Louis. Soon afterward the Stuarts went on a long leave to Virginia, where they visited relatives. Jeb went to Richmond for a church convention, and to Washington, hoping to sell his inventions to the War Department. He was there when chance led him to Harpers Ferry, to meet John Brown once more. The quelling of this uprising stirred his Southern passions anew and he wrote Virginia's Governor Wise, urging an enlarged militia:

> I have during my summer's stay . . . done all in my power to encourage and help organize military companies; I have found an insuperable obstacle in the cost of the uniform. Some of the best soldiers are unable to afford $25 for such a purpose. I therefore respectfully and earnestly urge you in view of the exposed situation of Virginia to attack from the North . . . to take into serious consideration the issue by the State to every organized military company in the State the same number of uniform suits as arms.[11]

Before old Brown was tried and hanged Jeb and Flora were back in Kansas. There was soon a second child, Philip St. George Cooke Stuart, named in honor of his grandfather—who was now stationed in Oregon Territory.

Fort Riley was far removed from the rising antagonisms of the East, but the post was divided, North and South, and the loyalties of officers were so well known that an accurate roster of potential Southern soldiers could be—and was—drawn up in faraway Virginia. Newspapers coming into the fort shrieked increasingly ominous news.

Stuart and Flora left no record of their talks about Secession; she seemed to seek the background instinctively, and to leave such decisions to her voluble husband. The Stuarts were certainly among the most avid readers of the New York *Herald* in April of 1860. They perhaps read aloud its stories which seemed to prophesy war.

The Reverend Henry Ward Beecher, the *Herald* reported, drew a great audience, half of it women, to the seventh of his lecture series at the Brooklyn Tabernacle—where he spoke on "How To Save the Union." He was often interrupted by applause.

There was a report of a singular debate in the Senate in Washington one April day: . . . "The Slavery Question" and "Suppression of Polygamy in Utah" were quaintly wedded. And in the *Herald's* column Mr. Etheridge of Tennessee raised a defiant Southern protest: "If the Government has the right to interfere in the private affairs of a white man, it can do the same with niggers—unless a nigger is better than a white man."

Flora Stuart must have read danger in the headlines of the *Herald* in May:

> Great doings at the Cooper Institute. Anti-Slavery froth
> and bubble. Abolition Lions and Lambs lying down together.
> Mob law recommended to People.

And this paper's hostility to abolitionism surely drew appreciative laughter from Stuart with its advice to the Republican Party, ready to convene:

"Our Friends the Black Republicans in Chicago are urged to come clean before the people." In short, to forget Seward and "give us a candidate of merit."

The ferment was also in the pages of Jeb's "treasure," *Harpers Weekly*, among the advertisements for a new Thackeray novel, *The Virginians*, Winslow Homer's drawings for a new serial, and patent remedies for common ills. Army couples in the frontier barracks saw perhaps more clearly than Easterners the implication in the triumphant advertisements of a controversial book that was splitting the country.

> Helper's *Impending Crisis*
> A Live Book
> 55,000 Copies Have Been Sold

> Now Is The Time
> This is the work that is creating
> So Much Excitement
> in Congress
> Price $1
> Paper Covers 50¢
> Active Agents Wanted

There was a story of violent passions from Washington: Senator Clark of Missouri was denouncing the Helper book when Senator Haskin "let fall a pistol from his pocket. This caused some confusion and alarm. At the close of the affray Mr. Clark apologized and all ended quietly."

Perhaps most prophetic of all was the *Weekly's* report of a brief speech in Congress when William Pennington, of New Jersey, was elected Speaker of The House. John Sherman of Ohio was the orator:

> A Republican Speaker is elected and no calamity comes;
> A Republican Speaker is elected and the people rejoice;
> A Republican Speaker is elected and stocks advance;
> A Republican Speaker is elected and cotton is worth 11 cents a pound and upwards—and may it advance higher (cheers);
> A Republican Speaker is elected and slave property remains the same in value;
> A Republican Speaker is elected and the Union is safe;
> So will it be when a Republican President is elected (prolonged cheers and cries of 'Good!').

And in the New York *Tribune* was an item of special interest to Lieutenant Stuart, who was an inveterate reader and clipper:

> The *Tribune* is requested to state that Mrs. Brown, the widow of the martyr of Harpers Ferry, is much embarrassed and annoyed by the multitude of letters addressed to her by entire strangers.

She asked them to desist.

If Lieutenant Stuart growled his rage at these gusts of news, his young wife probably heard him out in silence, going about the chores of tending her children and the small household in her rather humorless calm, determined to leave the family's politics in the hands of Jeb.

The cavalry left for the west in early summer, and Jeb rode far from Fort Riley to the headwaters of the Arkansas River where the command was ordered to build a fort. The 1st Cavalry wintered there at new Fort Wise and, in January, Stuart applied for leave to bring his family to the station.

But things in the East were happening swiftly. While Stuart was directing logging crews in the wilderness, South Carolina seceded, and Alabama, Florida and Mississippi fell out behind her. Jefferson Davis was sworn in as provisional President of the Confederate States in Montgomery, Alabama in January, 1861.

Stuart knew nothing of this when he wrote Davis in his Senate office at Washington:

> Sir: In view of the impending condition of affairs in our country, no sane man can fail to calculate on a rupture of our national bonds as a thing strongly probable. In view, therefore, of the probable dismemberment of the Army, and of your prominence as one likely to exercise a large control in the organization of the Army of the South, I beg leave respectfully to ask you to secure for me a position in that army. I have the honor to refer you to Gen. J. E. Johnston, Cols. Cooke, Lee and Emory and the Captains of my regiment, for whatever of merit I may possess. Please file this application.

On January eighteenth Stuart wrote his brother, William Alexander Stuart:

> Events are transpiring rapidly that furnish so little hope of perpetuating the Union, that I feel it incumbent upon me to tell you my course of conduct in such an emergency. Of course I go with Virginia, whether she be alone or otherwise, but I am sure that a large military force will be required for a time by the State, and I am anxious to secure from Wythe [County]

a legion of cavalry—200 men—myself as commander, or a battery of light artillery, 100 men or less. With Gov. Letcher as Governor, and you on the spot, I ought to be able to get such a command.

In later letters of the next two months to William were telling sentences:

He would go to Fort Riley and with his family "quietly and calmly await the march of events," and:

> The moment she [Va.] passes the ordinance of secession, I will set out immediately for Richmond, and report in person to Governor Letcher, unless I am certain that my service would be more needed at some other point in the State....
>
> If no war ensues upon Virginia's secession, I will quit the army, and if I can obtain no desirable position in her [Virginia's] regular army, I will resign and practice law in Memphis, Tenn.... I had rather be a private in Va.'s army than a general in any army to coerce her.... Col. Cooke will, I think, become a Missourian in the event of disruption, as he is perhaps more identified with that State than any other.

Stuart had thus already reached a decision when he had an urgent letter from Flora's cousin, John Esten Cooke, the novelist, warning him that he and General Cooke would soon be enemies of the South if they did not act.

Esten Cooke insisted that Stuart would draw none of the "prizes" of the Southern army if he lagged behind, and that the choice commissions were being gobbled up. Revolution would wait for no man, he wrote.

Jeb reached Fort Riley from the frontier in early April and was there when the Southerners fired on Fort Sumter, in Charleston Harbor. It was April fourteenth; Virginia's convention was meeting, but there was no news of her secession. On April seventeenth, President Lincoln called for 75,000 volunteers to maintain the Union and gave Virginia a quota of 8,000 men. The convention seethed, and late that night passed the Ordinance of Secession; approval by the people in May was thought to be a mere formality.

It was enough for Lieutenant Stuart, who could now lose no

time in returning East. As he and Flora began packing, he read his appointment as Captain, 1st U.S. Cavalry, which had been awaiting him at Fort Riley. He was not impressed. In the first days of May he passed through St. Louis with his family, and on May third wrote the Adjutant General, U.S. Army:

> Colonel: From a sense of duty to my native state (Va.), I hereby resign my position as an officer in the Army of The United States.

On the same day he wrote General Samuel Cooper, Adjutant General of the Confederate Army:

> General: Having resigned my position (Capt. 1st Cavalry) in the U.S. Army, and being now on my way to unite my destinies to Virginia, my native State, I write to apprize you of the fact in order that you may assign me such a position in the Army of The South as will accord with that lately held by me in the Federal Army.
>
> My preference is Cavalry—light artillery—Light Infantry in the order named, but I would prefer a position as Assist. Adjt. Gen. or Topographical Engineer if such a position would give me greater rank. My address will be: Care Gov. Letcher, Richmond.

His resignation from the U.S. Army was dated May fourteenth. He took his family by steamer to Memphis and then east by train. Somewhere on the way they met Flora's brother, John, who also cast his lot with the South. From the distant Northwest, Colonel Cooke wrote his distress: "Those mad boys! If only I had been there." His presence could hardly have deterred Stuart.

While they were en route, Jeb's mother wrote in a fury of Southern patriotism to Colonel R. E. Lee, who was in Richmond mustering Virginia's army:

> The mother of Lieutenant Stuart (of the 1st Cavalry) begs leave to introduce herself to you in behalf of her son. *He* is most anxious to offer his services to his native state, and has been

waiting at his post in the Far West of Kansas, to hear of the Secession of Virginia. I have written to him repeatedly and telegraphed to him also....

As soon as he hears of the Secession he will fly to place himself by your side. Can you save a place for him? He has been educated under your eye and was with you at Harpers Ferry. He is greatly attached to you and to all of your family. I am expecting him *every hour* with the *greatest* impatience. He has been long anxious to resign, but we advised him to await for the Secession of the State. Excuse me for troubling you if you please.

Respectfully,
Elizabeth L. Stuart.

I have been waiting for *you* two months.[12]

Stuart reached Richmond on May sixth and found an infantry commission awaiting him. The city was full of troops, spoiling for fight.

☆

CHAPTER 4

First Blood

STUART was not a stranger in swarming Richmond. He called at the home of his frontier friend and surgeon, Dr. Charles Brewer, who was now the husband of Flora's sister, Maria. The doctor was himself awaiting orders from the Confederate Army.

Jeb visited family friends and stopped at the office of Robert E. Lee, already a general, with offices in the teeming building of the Mechanics Institute.

He wrote Flora at one A.M. of May ninth: He must leave at once for the front, for he had been named Lieutenant Colonel of Virginia infantry, assigned to Harpers Ferry, where he would be second in command to Colonel Thomas J. Jackson, a strange, dedicated soldier who had come from Virginia Military Institute with his cadets.

There was good news in the letter. He had gone empty-handed to Richmond, but now his comfort in the field was assured: "Ma lets me have Jo as a Body servant for the war."

It was a stroke of luck for him to have one of the Laurel Hill Negroes to serve him, since he had no slaves of his own. He had also made a trade of sorts. His cousin Peter Hairston would act as his aide and in return furnish Jeb a fine horse from his North Carolina stock.

There was also a family matter of concern, the loyalties of Colonel Philip St. George Cooke:

> The greatest anxiety is manifested for your Pa to arrive. He is regarded as the *ne plus ultra* of a Cavalry officer—Why don't he come?

Stuart left a brief glimpse of Lee on this day:

> Gen. Lee is very much harassed by the trifling duties he has to perform.

He then gave the only explanation for his having landed in the infantry:

> As there is no post of Lt. Col. of Cavalry vacant I have been engaged as Col. of a Regiment from the extreme South West and from the counties in and about Danville.

He wrote, almost petulantly, that he would "make no effort" to get his commission in the cavalry, but, "if offered by the solicitation of others I shall accept."[1]

Harpers Ferry brought memories to Stuart. The armory buildings where John Brown had been cornered were swarmed by workmen who dismantled machinery. The place was alive with drilling troops, green, unsoldierly and sullen, for Colonel Jackson had ousted their militia officers to whom soldiering was a business of fancy uniforms and street parades. It had now become an outpost, with gun batteries frowning from the heights. The daring Jackson had actually invaded Yankee territory by seizing Maryland Heights across the Potomac. Jackson and Stuart understood each other. Jackson admired Jeb's credo: "If we oppose force to force we cannot win, for their resources are greater than ours. We must substitute *esprit* for numbers. Therefore I strive to inculcate in my men the spirit of the chase."

Before May was out Stuart wrote Flora again, with Colonel Cooke still much on his mind:

> How I hope your Pa will *resign*. If he could only see things in their true and right light—which is difficult to do so far off— he would resign instanter. He is wanted here very much. He is highly complimented everywhere and would soon take a foremost stand in the State defence. Why don't he come?

Despite Stuart's infantry commission, Jackson gave him cavalry, and provoked a quarrel by placing all horsemen of the outpost under Jeb's command. There was a protest from Turner Ashby, a mountain cavalryman who hurried to Jackson's headquarters and furiously demanded command of his own company. Ashby was older than Stuart and had come to the frontier before him. He thought he was entitled to first promotion. Jackson won Ashby's loyalty by countermanding his order and dividing the cavalry in two. Ashby thus escaped from Stuart's command.[2]

Jackson himself was soon relieved from command, for Joseph E. Johnston arrived without notice in Harpers Ferry, under Confederate orders. Stuart welcomed Johnston as an old and valued friend, and soon after his arrival got the commission he sought, Lieutenant Colonel of Cavalry.

Stuart was not long in Harpers Ferry, for the cautious Johnston evacuated the town. And on June tenth Stuart wrote a friend of the first action along the Potomac above the abandoned outpost:

> The ball is open up here at Honeywood. I sent about 100 men to repel invasion by an irregular force—of canal hands from Maryland—My pickets had already killed several—nobody hurt on our side.[3]

Stuart camped at Bunker Hill, nine miles north of Winchester, manning picket lines in the very face of the enemy.

He wrote Flora on June thirteenth:

> If you could see the strawberries, bouquets and other nice things the ladies send me you would think me pretty well off. The young men of the regiment wonder why it is that I am the recipient of so much favor. They forget that rank will tell. . . . Kiss our dear ones a thousand times and keep them in mind of their Pa.

Bunker Hill was like a nest of foxhunters. June opened with only twenty-one officers and 313 men in Stuart's command, which he called the 1st Virginia. There was little rest for anyone. Every path and road south of the Potomac in that region was under guard.

One of the young riders who joined him, a lawyer by the name of George Cary Eggleston, left a complaint. Eggleston came in with a company after a four-day march, having ridden twenty miles that day. The colonel assigned the new company a position and ordered its tents pitched. But the captain of the newcomers, "even worse disciplined than we were," scorned the muddy spot pointed out by Stuart, and moved his men to a place of his choosing. Stuart scolded the captain severely, returning him to his men with the conviction that "all West Point graduates were martinets."

Stuart had more in store for this company. The weary men had visions of a long rest and a night's sleep, but Stuart pushed them into trails along the Potomac, under the very noses of the enemy. "This West Point colonel was rapidly forfeiting our good opinion." But Stuart kept them at it; several times Federal cavalry fled before the new company, and it returned to camp with confidence.

The next morning "our unreasonable colonel again ordered us to mount," and this time took out the company himself on what seemed a madcap ride. He led them into a spot surrounded by enemy infantry, laughed at them, and told them their chances of escape were slim indeed. "I think we began about this time to suspect that we were learning something," Eggleston said. Jeb led them "jauntily out of the trap."

One morning Stuart halted Eggleston at headquarters:

"Is that your horse out there?"

"Yes, but I don't want to sell him."

"Let's slip off on a scout," Stuart said. "I'll ride your horse and you take mine. I want to try his paces."

They galloped within the Union lines and were soon being chased by Federal cavalrymen.

Stuart seemed unconcerned by pursuit in rear. "Colonel, there's a Federal post ahead," Eggleston said. "Hadn't we better oblique into the woods?"

"Oh, no," Stuart said. "They won't expect us from this direction. We can ride over them before they make up their minds who we are."

The two pounded through the group of startled bluecoats and

sent men sprawling into ditches. A hail of bullets followed them
harmlessly. Stuart rode as if he were in his own camp. He turned
eagerly to Eggleston: "Did you ever time this horse for a half
mile?"[4]

Another observant young man who came to Stuart's camp that
month was William W. Blackford, an engineer from Abingdon, Virginia, with a well-equipped company he had raised himself.

One June evening at sunset Blackford and his company came
to Stuart's camp, the first actual fighting post it had seen.

Before the tents Colonel Stuart was inspecting forty or fifty
horsemen. Blackford sketched him:

> A young officer in a United States undress uniform. . . .a
> little above medium height, broad-shouldered and powerfully
> built, ruddy complexion and blue-gray eyes which could flash
> fire . . . then about 29 years old.[5]

The commander of Blackford's company was a veteran West
Pointer much older than Stuart, one W. E. Jones, universally called
"Grumble"; he took an instant dislike to Stuart, and growled to his
men that he would take no orders from that young whippersnapper.

Blackford began that day a warm friendship with Stuart which
would last to the end of the colonel's life.

Stuart wrote Flora about this time:

> My Dearest One:
>   Things are hastening to a crisis. Every day, sometimes
> twice a day, I hear of the enemy's drawing a little closer. He
> has not yet reached the Potomac. General Johnston himself
> writes to me every day, and I have little doubt that the moment
> the enemy is near he will march out near me and meet him. . . .
>   Every one is delighted with our camp here. I got the
> drawers but they are canton flannel, rather warm. My health
> was never better, and when I do get to sleep which is not often,
> I sleep like a log.

The life of the camp was exhilarating for the young Virginia
riders, most of whom had been almost literally born to the saddle,

and were superbly mounted. George Eggleston recalled that the horsemanship of his regiment remained a model for all Confederate cavalry. He also wrote of this camp:

> We had some tents, in which to sleep after we got tired of playing poker for grains of corn; but we were so rarely in camp that after a little while we forgot that we owned canvas dwellings. . . . We slept on the ground out somewhere within musket shot of the enemy's lines, and our waking hours were passed in playing tag with the enemy's scouting parties. . . .
>
> It must have been a healthy life that we led. During that summer my company never had a man on the sick list. When the commissary managed to get rations of flour to us, we wetted it with water from any stream or brook that might be at hand, added a little salt, if we happened to have any, to the putty-like mass, fried the paste in bacon fat, and ate it as bread and went on our scouting ways utterly unconscious of the fact that we were possessed of stomachs until the tempting succulence of half-ripened corn in somebody's field set appetite a-going again and we feasted upon the grain without the bother of cooking it at all.

When shirts became indecently dirty they washed them in streams and if marching orders interrupted "we put them on wet and rode away in full confidence that they would dry on our persons as easily as on a clothesline." One advantage of such light travel was that Eggleston could carry a book under his shirt. He heard pious tales of how Bibles had stopped bullets and saved lives, but Eggleston was saved when a bullet struck him in the abdomen, to be turned aside by his copy of the racy novel, *Tristram Shandy*.[6]

Jeb had an adventure during the spring which became a legend in two armies. He rode beyond the lines one morning with an orderly and sighted a familiar figure dressed as he was, in an old U.S. Army greatcoat of blue. The approaching officer was one Duane Perkins whom Stuart had known at West Point.

Stuart assumed he had come into the Confederacy, and without a pause shouted, "Howdy, Perk! Glad to see you've come over. What's your command?"

A battery of Union artillery came into sight behind Perkins with its flag in full view. Perkins laughed and yelled, pointing rearward, "Hello, Beauty! How are you? That's my command, right there!"

Stuart turned his horse abruptly. "Oh, the devil! I didn't know you'd stayed with the Yankees!" He spurred away, and with his orderly soon outdistanced pursuit.

An innovation of this time was "Camp Cripple," a separate site where Stuart sent injured men and horses, and those not eager for war. About a quarter of his force was soon there. One day Private Peter Paul, of Company I, gave this camp a new name. In a confusion of yells—"Where's Company A?" "You Company D?" "Company K to the front!"—Paul shouted, "Where's Company Q?" The troopers took it up, and Stuart thereafter referred to the camp of cripples as "Company Q" even in official reports.

Invasion now threatened northern Virginia. From Richmond, General Lee began concentrating troops at Manassas Junction, a rail center not far south of Alexandria, where he predicted the next Federal blow would fall.

General P. G. T. Beauregard, the hero of Fort Sumter, commanded the growing army at Manassas, and in June he had over 30,000 men. General Johnston, with a force of some 10,000, was to the west around Winchester. Johnston would be able to reinforce Beauregard in an emergency with a march of two days—if he could rid himself of the Federal force in his own sector.

Two Union armies were poised to strike, a large one under General Irwin McDowell near Washington, expected to fall upon Manassas; and a smaller one under the aging Mexican War hero, General Robert Patterson, north of the Potomac above Winchester.

It was Patterson's patrols that clashed with Stuart's riders day after day, as General Johnston and his lieutenant, Colonel Jackson, watched with the infantry a few miles in Stuart's rear.

July first, at four A.M., Union infantry passed the river village of Williamsport, Maryland, wading the ford toward Virginia. By seven thirty Colonel Jackson had Stuart's report of the move and prepared for his first battle, though he was under orders to do no more than feel the strength of the enemy, and fall back in face of superior numbers. Jackson met Stuart near a settlement called Falling Waters.

Jackson carried an infantry brigade of 380 men and one battery of guns. He saw that the bluecoats had brigades beyond counting. Jackson sent three of his cannon to the rear and placed Stuart and the cavalry on the flank.

The Federals soon left their woodland cover and charged. Jackson's skirmishers fired, falling back, and gave fatal inspiration to the green Federal troops. There was a pell-mell charge down a crowded roadway toward Jackson, whose artilleryman, the Rev. W. N. Pendleton, boasted four guns named Matthew, Mark, Luke and John. Pendleton raised his hand and closed his eyes as one gun was made ready: "Aim low, men, and may the Lord have mercy on their souls!" The gun cleared the road with terrible slaughter.

Jackson's men retreated slowly before the Federal force. The enemy found the camp and tore up more than 150 tents, enough to support claims of victory.[7]

But the little skirmish was not over. Stuart could not contain himself on the flank. His riders clashed with bluecoat cavalry, and fighting spread through the wooded country. Stuart found himself alone within sight of an enemy company in a field behind a rail fence. Jeb rode near them.

"Take down those bars!" he ordered. The Federal soldiers jumped to do his bidding, misled by his blue coat and the old U. S. trousers. When the fence was down Stuart shouted, "Throw down your arms, or you are all dead men!"

The astounded bluecoats imagined the woods filled with their enemy. "They dropped their arms, fell upon their faces, and were all captured," Stuart said.

He marched gaily back into his lines with them, forty-nine in all, the entire Company I of the 15th Pennsylvania Volunteers.

This put Stuart's staid commanders into something like ecstasy. Jackson: "Colonel Stuart and his command merit high praise, and I may here remark that he has exhibited those qualities which are calculated to make him eminent in his arm of the service." Johnston praised Jackson and Stuart and asked Richmond: ". . . that Colonel Jackson be promoted without delay to the grade of Brigadier-General, and Lieutenant-Colonel Stuart to that of Colonel."

Stuart could not accept the retreat at Falling Waters. He left his prisoners and escorted his apprentice troopers to the front to further their education. Private Eggleston thought "the most natural thing to do" was to fall back with the infantry to Winchester, and when Stuart led the riders toward the river, men in the ranks muttered that the colonel was insane.

Eggleston could not forget the experience: "He marched his handful of men right up to the advancing lines and ordered us to dismount. The Federal skirmish line was coming toward us at a double-quick.

"He waited until the infantry was within about two hundred yards of us, we being in the edge of a little grove, and they on the other side of an open field. Then Stuart cried out, 'Backwards—march! Steady, men—keep your faces to the enemy!' And we marched in that way through the timber, delivering our shotgun fire slowly as we fell back toward our horses."

They mounted with the Federals almost upon them and went away at a slow trot, which Stuart would not let them speed up. The colonel led them into a road not far away and lectured:

"Attention. Now I want to talk to you, men. You are brave fellows and patriotic too, but you're ignorant of this kind of work, and I'm teaching you. I want you to observe that a good man on a good horse can never be caught. Another thing: Cavalry can *trot* away from anything, and a gallop is a gait unbecoming to a soldier, unless he is going toward the enemy. Remember that. We gallop toward the enemy, and trot away, always. Steady now! Don't break ranks!"

While Stuart spoke a shell whistled over their heads.

"There," he said. "I've been waiting for that, and watching those fellows. I knew they'd shoot too high, and I wanted you to learn how shells sound."

Stuart kept these men in the Federal lines for two or three days, "shelled, skirmished with, charged and surrounded scores of times, until we learned to hold in high regard our colonel's masterly skill in getting into and out of perilous positions." Within a week or so the troopers began to feel something "closely akin to worship" for this laughing madman on horseback.

Eggleston noted: "He could never be still. He was rarely ever in camp at all, and he never showed a sign of fatigue. He led almost everything."[8]

William Blackford won Stuart's heart one July day. His company was on a scout with Stuart near the enemy, quietly watching for a chance to attack. They waited in an apple orchard half a mile from the Federals. Horses grazed in the sunshine and all was peaceful until a "Union man" from a nearby farm betrayed them to the blue-coats. The enemy sent out a column. Stuart ordered his men to the rear.

Before the troopers cleared the orchard, shells burst about them. Blackford's company, he said, was the only one that went off in perfect order; he rode in the rear and herded the men to safety. When they reached cover, Blackford discovered that he had lost his pistol in the orchard. He knew that he must have dropped it as his fine horse, "Comet," soared over a fence.

Blackford explained to Stuart, and asked permission to ride into the open, under fire, for his pistol. Stuart looked at him "with a surprised and pleased expression" and nodded. The pistol was easily found, and the enemy shells flew high; the battery was not enough to frighten Blackford. Stuart marked this man for promotion.[9]

The Federal high command now moved to strike Johnston's army near Winchester, so that it could not go to the rescue of Beauregard at Manassas, where McDowell planned to attack in late July. But troubles developed. Old Winfield Scott, the ailing Federal commander-in-chief, was impatient with the timorous General Patterson.

While Patterson marched, Stuart's riders probed his lines on every side. Patterson seemed confused, for on July seventeenth Scott telegraphed him:

Do not let the enemy amuse you and delay you with a small force in front whilst he re-enforces the Junction [Manassas] with his main body.

McDowell had already begun his move from Washington, and expected to crush Beauregard within a day or two.

Near midnight of July eighteenth a telegram from Richmond called Johnston to action: Beauregard was under attack at Manassas. The Army of the Shenandoah must move immediately to his aid.

Johnston ordered Stuart to deceive Patterson, while the infantry marched eastward. Stuart would follow after he had blinded the enemy. The exchange of Federal telegrams of the day pointed out Jeb's success:

Patterson to Scott, one thirty A.M.:

To attack . . . against the greatly superior force at Winchester is most hazardous. Shall I attack?

Scott to Patterson:

I have certainly been expecting you to beat the enemy. If not, to hear that you had felt him strongly, or, at least, had occupied him by threats and demonstrations. You have at least his equal and, I suppose, superior, numbers. Has he not stolen a march and sent reenforcements toward Manassas Junction?

Patterson to Scott:

The enemy has stolen no march upon me. I have kept him actively employed, and by threats and reconnaisances in force caused him to be reenforced.[10]

At the moment General Patterson wrote, while Stuart's riders were cowing his pickets, Johnston's army was moving rapidly eastward. Officers shouted to the hurrying Rebels at the rare rest periods: "The commanding General hopes that his troops will step out like men and make a forced march to save the country!" Jackson's brigade was beginning to earn its title, "Foot Cavalry." By nightfall the army was on the Blue Ridge and forded the Shenandoah not long after. Colonel Jackson alone stood picket at two A.M. when they rested. By early morning they had reached the railroad, and by midafternoon were joining Beauregard at Manassas.

Stuart hung in the rear, shaking a phantom screen before Patterson, disguising his force as an entire army. He kept a line of horsemen in his rear, cutting all communication with the Valley, and the bulk of his force followed on the heels of the infantry. Captain Blackford had a night of it.

Infantry and artillery filled the road and forced the cavalry into the fields. All night they jumped ditches and fences and dodged infantrymen who fell out to sleep, sprawling everywhere. The troopers rode over some of them in the dark.

The cavalry's supply wagons did not catch up for a day or so, and the hungry troopers ate what they could find. Blackford dined on a bullfrog, legs and all, and found it delicious.

When the horsemen came onto the plain of Manassas more than 60,000 men faced each other, in armies of almost equal size.

Troops were spilling out of trains along miles of track, and marching into lines along Bull Run, six miles away. Big wagon trains of food and ammunition moved among them, and through the crowds drivers whipped their teams and cursed delays; couriers, orderlies and officers lashed horses through the melee. A yellow dust cloud boiled above everything.

As Stuart's cavalry passed General Johnston's headquarters, the commander came out and the staffs shook hands. The 1st Virginia Cavalry was settled for the night in a field of tall broom sedge, where horses and men fell asleep after their thirty-six-hour ride. It was a soft starry night, and the rumble of Yankee preparations for battle kept no one awake.

Sunday, July twenty-first, was opened by distant cannon fire. Stuart scrambled to his feet, shouting, "Hello! What's that?" The staff roused itself. Musket fire broke out far to their left, near Sudley Mills. There were no orders for the cavalry. Stuart had the horses fed and got the regiment over Bull Run on a scout. The pickets fanned out, found a party of Federal skirmishers and fell back.

Stuart retreated across Bull Run without revealing the size of his force and spent the morning in waiting.

Stuart sat impatiently as the battle roared along the stream in the direction of Sudley Ford; the Confederates were slowly giving way. Now and then a shell burst above the woodland which screened his position opposite Stone Bridge, and the shifting wind occasionally swelled the sound of musketry. As battle neared them the horsemen saw Confederate infantry regiments moving into position; it became clear that fighting would soon center near the Stone Bridge.

Stuart rode restlessly. At each infantry movement he sent a courier to the commander, advising him that the 1st Cavalry was ready to act on flanks, or wherever needed. He got no encouragement until late afternoon. He at last sent Blackford, who found Virginia infantry under Colonel Jackson, fresh from a fierce engagement on a hillside where Jackson had won from General Bee a new name: Stonewall.

Jackson had a finger wound, and was holding a bloody hand in the air as he led his men into position. Blackford gave him Stuart's message. "Good! Good!" Jackson replied absently. "Tell Stuart I will." Blackford returned to the waiting cavalry, as infantrymen were caught up in a spreading battle down the creek. Torrents of men broke out of the woods and fled to the rear: South Carolina troops, in panic. More reserves were thrown in, and firing grew. Blackford sketched the call of the cavalry to battle:

> It was about two o'clock. Stuart was striding backwards and forwards in great impatience. Presently we saw a staff officer dash out of the woods and come spurring towards us. The men all sprang to their feet and began tightening their saddle girths. . . . The supreme moment had come at last. Colonel Stuart stepped forward to meet the officer. He reined up his horse and asked if that was Colonel Stuart and then, with a military salute, said, "Colonel Stuart, General Beauregard directs that you bring your command into action at once and that you attack where the firing is hottest."

The bugles crowed and Stuart led them through a valley filled with Rebel wounded, where arms and legs lay in great piles and screaming men were held on tables as the saws whined and blood-spattered doctors worked. The troopers leaned from their saddles and retched. When they came into sight of the action Stuart halted. A blue vapor hung over the struggling infantry, lifted and lowered by the wind. Guns roared and flamed in the hot landscape. It looked as if the Confederates were having the worst of it; the gray lines were sagging.

Stuart and Blackford rode at the head of the tiny column of horsemen, almost into the midst of a regiment of scarlet-uniformed infantry in Zouave dress.

Stuart shouted to them, "Don't run, boys. We're here."

He and Blackford looked more sharply; there was something strange about the red-clad soldiers. Stuart stopped. "Blackford, are those our men or the enemy?"

"I don't know. I heard Beauregard brought up some Zouaves from New Orleans."

At that moment a breeze fanned out the flag of the strange regiment—the Stars and Stripes. Stuart ordered a charge. The galloping column reminded Blackford of an arrow loosed from a bow.

The New York Zouaves fired a volley. There were a few casualties; riderless horses galloped off. Then the weight of Stuart's column struck and with clubbed carbines and sabers cut the red line to bits. There was a second charge as the Zouaves moved rearward, and the scarlet uniforms scattered rapidly over the field. Other Federal units began to run with them toward the rear. The Zouaves yelled as they ran, "The Black Horse!" The cry echoed over the field.

Only five hundred riders had begun a panic; Stuart had lost nine men and eighteen horses. The troopers had broken to the rear after their charges, but Blackford reformed them in a woods and led them back. "Bully for you, Blackford!" Stuart shouted, and began working with a pair of guns he had borrowed from the infantry. Lieutenant James F. Beckham commanded these guns. He masked them in pine thickets and opened fire. Federal soldiers fell in windrows; the enemy retreat became faster and more widespread.

General Jubal Early, with infantry reinforcements, was just going into line through Confederate stragglers and skulkers nearby.

From his viewpoint the battle seemed lost; everywhere he saw Federals coming on:

"Affairs now wore a gloomy aspect . . . the day appeared to be going against us. As I approached, a messenger came galloping to me from Colonel J. E. B. Stuart, stating that the colonel said the enemy was about giving away, and if we would hurry up they would soon be in retreat."

Stuart sent another message, however: The enemy had only retired behind a ridge and was forming for attack. He warned Early to be careful.

Early said, "Stuart, who had been in position beyond our extreme left, had, by the judicious use of guns on his right flank, kept the enemy in check. It was mainly by the fire poured from Beckham's guns into the enemy that that column had been forced to retire."

Early watched as Stuart turned his guns on a new enemy regiment. The Federal line fell back. Early wrote:

"I immediately ordered my command forward. . . . On reaching the crest we came in view of the Warrenton turnpike and the plains beyond, and discovered the enemy in full retreat across and beyond the turnpike."

A pursuit followed and the bluecoats ran toward the rear, over-running wagon trains and carriages of Congressmen and Washington society leaders who had come to see the slaughter of the Rebels.

Early thought that Stuart had perhaps won the battle:

"But for his presence there . . . the enemy would probably have ended the battle before my brigade reached that point. Stuart did as much towards saving the battle of First Manassas as any subordinate who participated in it."[11]

Stuart's troopers rode twelve miles after the enemy before darkness fell. They turned back, lacking the strength to press even this demoralized army in the night. There was a holiday of looting among the abandoned wagons, but there were grisly scenes. Captain Blackford, suffering from thirst, sought along Bull Run a clean place to drink, but found everywhere Federal wounded who had crawled there, many of them dead with heads in the water; the creek literally flowed blood, but he forced himself to drink, and after protest his horse drank, too. Blackford captured prisoners from the broken Zouave regiment, and the enemy troops told him, "We had no cavalry that was worth a damn."

The Federal rout was evidently complete; scouts said McDowell's army had streamed back into Washington like a rabble. The Confederate army hoped to be moving forward to attack Washington soon.

The fame of Beauregard and Johnston grew by the day. Politicians, contractors and pretty women emerged from trains into the swarm at Manassas. Yet there was delay, and the army only waited. Feuds in the high command became army gossip.

Stuart received no major credit for the victory at First Manassas except from Early. Jeb's own report, one of his staff members thought, was "brief and indefinite" to the point that he could make no claims. Thus it was not easy to state precisely his contributions to victory.

Colonel Jackson had mentioned him:

> Apprehensive lest my flanks be turned, I sent orders to Colonels Stuart and Radford to secure them. Colonel Stuart, with that part of his command with him, deserve great praise for the promptness with which they moved to my left and secured the flank by timely charging the enemy and driving him back.

General Johnston wrote:

> Colonel Stuart contributed to one of these repulses [of the enemy] by a well timed and vigorous charge on the enemy's right flank with two companies of his cavalry.

It was glory, of course, but by no means glory enough.

Stuart took his staff to Fairfax Court House for a few days; they ate in a village boardinghouse, where officers under Stuart met General Longstreet. Blackford was unimpressed: "A man of limited capacity who acquired a reputation for wisdom by never saying anything." He could not remember hearing Longstreet say half a dozen words, beyond "yes" and "no."

After a few days, Stuart moved headquarters into the open country at Munson's Hill, from which he could see Washington itself; he slept there for weeks, expecting an order to advance. It never came.

On July sixteenth, orders had been drawn in Richmond: Stuart was a full colonel, Confederate States Army. They celebrated on Munson's Hill.

☆

CHAPTER 5

Gathering the Clan

VILLAGERS stared in disbelief. A handsome Confederate officer rode at breakneck speed in the dusty street, banging away with both hands at a captured Yankee drum. He careened to a halt at cavalry headquarters. It was Jeb Stuart.

It was unmistakably Stuart's headquarters. Outside the farmhouse was a gleaming Blakeley cannon. A chained raccoon scrambled along its barrel, snarling, an enormous animal with glistening fur.

Flora's cousin, John Esten Cooke, had found his way here. He would stay, for this life promised more than that of a captain of artillery. He recorded his first visit, when he found Stuart stretched on a blanket at the roadside, talking with country people:

> His low athletic figure was clad in an old blue undress coat of the United States Army, brown velveteen pantaloons worn white by rubbing against the saddle, high cavalry boots with small brass spurs, a gray waistcoat, and carelessly tied cravat. At his side lay a Zouave cap, covered with a white havelock, and beside this two huge yellow leathern gauntlets. . . . The figure was that of a man "every inch a soldier."
>
> The broad forehead was bronzed by sun and wind; the eyes were clear, piercing, and of an intense and dazzling blue; the nose prominent, with large and mobile nostrils; and the mouth was completely covered by a heavy brown mustache, which swept down and mingled with a huge beard of the same tint, reaching to his breast.

67

Cooke soon saw Stuart at work:

> In this man who wrote away busily at his desk, or, throw-
> ing one leg carelessly over the arm of his chair, you could
> discern enormous physical strength. . . . In five minutes he had
> started up, put on his hat, and was showing me his Blakeley gun.
> His satisfaction at the ferocious snarling of his coon was im-
> mense. . . . He made the place echo with laughter.

They went into the house to supper, and Cooke was astonished
to see two women captives; one was about seventeen, and pretty,
the other was elderly. They had been captured trying to evade Jeb's
pickets. The two had at first refused to eat with the Rebels, but were
persuaded by Stuart's courtly Maryland aide, Captain Tiernan
Brien. Stuart beckoned for entertainers. Cooke was fascinated:

> All were black. The first an accomplished performer on
> the guitar, the second gifted with the faculty of producing
> exact imitations of every bird of the forest; and the third was
> a master of the back-step, the old Virginia "breakdown."

Stuart wrote, couriers grinned from the door and the women
stared. Bob, a young mulatto servant, played "Listen to the Mock-
ingbird"; the bird mimic began to sing. Other songs followed. The
young woman was under a spell.

> Stuart turns round with a laugh and calls for a breakdown.
> The dilapidated African advances, dropping his hat first at the
> door. Bob strikes up a jig upon his guitar, the ventriloquist claps,
> and the great performer of the breakdown commences, first
> upon the heeltap, then upon the toe. His antics are grand and
> indescribable. He leaps, he whirls, he twists and untwists his legs
> until the crowd at the door grows wild with admiration. The
> guitar continues to soar and Stuart's laughter mingles with it.
> The dancer's eyes roll gorgeously, his steps grow more rapid,
> he executes unheard-of figures. Finally a frenzy seems to seize
> him; the mirth grows fast and furious; the young lady laughs
> outright and seems about to clap her hands. Even the elder re-
> laxes into an unmistakable smile; and as the dancer disappears

with a bound through the door, the guitar stops playing, and
Stuart's laughter rings out gay and jovial, the grim lips open
and she says, "You rebels *do* seem to enjoy yourselves!"

Stuart rose. "You have heard my musicians, ladies. Would you
like to see something that might interest you?"

"Very much."

Stuart pointed to a coat and vest hanging on a nail over their
heads. The clothes were bullet-torn and bloody.

"What is that?" the old woman said.

"They belonged to a poor boy of my command, madam. Shot
and killed on picket the other day—young Chichester, from below
Fairfax Courthouse. A brave fellow, and I am keeping these to send
to his mother."

The smiles faded. Stuart told the women of the fight in which
the boy was killed, and bowed them to their room. The next morning, when he sent them on toward Richmond as captives, he put the
women into a carriage. The girl held out her hand. Stuart kissed it
and stood laughing after them.

Cooke asked him, "Why did you put yourself out for them so
much last night, and get up that frolic?"

"Don't you understand? When they arrived they were mad
enough to bite my head off, and I determined to put them in good
humor before they left. Well, I did it, and they're my good friends
at this moment."

"I saw you kiss the girl's hand. Why didn't you kiss the old
lady's, too?"

Stuart leaned against Cooke's horse, and said in a low voice,
"Would you like me to tell you?"

"Yes."

"The old lady's hand had a glove on it." Stuart's whisper erupted
into laughter.[1]

But Stuart must have more music. He coveted a banjo player in
the Appomattox County regiment of Colonel T. T. Munford, one
Sam Sweeney, a dark, handsome man in his early thirties who made
such music as Stuart had never heard. Sam Sweeney was the younger

brother of Joe Sweeney, said to be the "inventor" of the banjo, celebrated as one of the first blackface minstrels, who had once played for Queen Victoria. Joe had died the year before, and now Sam carried on his minstrelsy. Stuart abducted him.

Colonel Munford left a plaint:

"Stuart's feet would shuffle at Sweeney's presence, or naming. He issued an order for him to report at his quarters and 'detained' him. It was a right he enjoyed, but not very pleasing to me or my regiment."

Esten Cooke liked to tease Munford: "Why don't you come over and enjoy our music, Colonel?" Munford raged helplessly.[2]

So there was always music. Sweeney on the banjo, Mulatto Bob on the bones, a couple of fiddlers, Negro singers and dancers, the ventriloquist, and others who caught Stuart's eye. Sweeney rode behind Stuart on the outpost day and night. Stuart often sang and Sweeney plucked the strings behind him: "Her Bright Smile Haunts Me Still," "The Corn Top's Ripe," "Lorena" and "Jine the Cavalry."

Esten Cooke was one of the most striking of the cast of characters Stuart was gathering. The young novelist spent much time writing in his tent; he rose before day to read the Bible by firelight, or Bourienne's *Memoirs of Napoleon*. He was soon placed in charge of Stuart's ordnance, but wrote in his diary that he favored "supervising rather than attending to details, which are left to my two sergeants and clerk. My philosophy is to give myself as little trouble as possible. I suppose I will be rated after the war as 'only an ordnance officer,' but I have really been aide-de-camp. That's not important, though."

He had an eye for odd incidents in camp. Once, for example, Stuart captured a Union officer's trunk and found touching letters from a wife, and obscene ones from a mistress, reveling in the wife's ignorance of the affair. Stuart sent all to the officer's wife. Cooke surmised, "There'll be a fuss in that family."[3]

Stuart picked up others who drew his attention. One was a grotesque giant from a cavalry regiment, a Corporal Henry Hagan, evidently a simple soul, but a burly man so hairy that only his eyes were visible through the mat. His voice was like the roar of a large animal. Stuart detailed him for headquarters duty as a bodyguard and pet. He had charge of the stables, and later became chief of couriers. Stuart was much amused by Hagan's inordinate pride, which puffed him so that he became unbearable when praised. A trooper noted:

"In a mad freak of fun one day, the chief recommended his corporal for promotion to see, he said, if the giant was capable of further swelling, and so the corporal became a lieutenant upon the staff."

A pretty woman of the region, Antonia Ford, got a gaudy be-ribboned "commission" from Stuart and his playful staff:

Know Ye, That reposing special confidence in the patriotism, fidelity, and ability of Antonia J. Ford, I, James E. B. Stuart, do hereby appoint and commission her my honorary Aide-de-Camp, to rank as such from this date. She will be obeyed, respected, and admired by all true lovers of a noble nature....

But the strange Stuart, Cooke noted, kept headquarters "looking like work," and the gaiety was deceptive. The trooper Eggleston remembered:

"For ten days ... we were not allowed once to take our saddles off. Night and day we were in the immediate presence of the enemy, catching naps when there happened for the moment to be nothing else to do, standing by our horses while they ate from our hands, so that we might slip their bridles on again in an instant in the event of a surprise, and eating such things as chance threw in our way, there being no rations anywhere within reach."

Eggleston's company, after more than a week of such service, scouted toward Federal lines: "We returned to camp at sunset and were immediately ordered on picket. We should have been relieved next morning, but no relief came, and we were wholly without food. No others came to take our place on the picket line."

Stuart at last rode by the distressed men.

"Colonel, do you know we've been on duty ten days, and here twenty-six hours without food?" one of them asked.

"Nonsense," Stuart said. "You don't look starved. There's a cornfield over there. Jump the fence and get a good breakfast. You don't want to go back to camp, I know. It's stupid there, and all the fun is out here. Besides, I've kept your company on duty all this time as a compliment. You boys have acquitted yourselves too well to be neglected now, and I mean to give you a chance."

The grumbling pickets thought Stuart was joking; they soon realized that his idea of a compliment to troopers was to push them into the faces of the enemy.

In these days the army got news of a shift in Federal command: General McDowell was out, and McClellan was in. The Confederates in ranks expected an attack on their position at Centreville in Northern Virginia.

Stuart overheard this talk as he was wrestling with some young members of his staff, and halted, puffing.

"We can do this for amusement when we go into winter quarters—if George McClellan ever lets us go into winter quarters at all."

"Why?" an officer asked. "Do you think he will advance before spring?"

"Not against Centreville. He has too much sense for that, and I think he knows the shortest road to Richmond, too. If I am not greatly mistaken, we shall hear of him presently on his way up the James River."

He then talked in a more sober tone, surprising to his staff: "I think it's a foregone conclusion that we will ultimately whip the Yankees. We are bound to believe that, anyhow. But the war is going to be a long and terrible one, first. We've only just begun it, and very few of us will see the end."

He added slowly: "All I ask of fate is that I may be killed leading a cavalry charge."[4]

Stuart enjoyed his growing reputation. The Army talked of what Joe Johnston had said of his work against Patterson:

"Stuart is like a yellow jacket. You brush him off and he flies right back on." And Johnston was soon to write Stuart, when he was transferred to the West: "How can I eat or sleep, without you on the outpost?"

Even more flattering to Stuart was Johnston's report to Richmond:

He is a rare man, wonderfully endowed by nature with the qualities necessary for an officer of light cavalry. Calm, firm, acute, active and enterprising, I know no one more competent than he to estimate the occurrences before him at their true value. If you add a real brigade of cavalry to this army, you can find no better brigadier general to command it.

This accolade perhaps prompted President Davis to act, for new cavalry troops began to gather near Centreville under Stuart's command. Fitz Lee became a lieutenant colonel in Grumble Jones's regiment. Captain Will Martin arrived with his Natchez Troop from Mississippi, with shining trunks in luggage wagons.

Stuart ran into big game on September eleventh and fought a skirmish with such skill that army gossip claimed it won him promotion.

A Federal column occupied the village of Lewinsville between the armies. It was only a reconnaissance but late in the morning someone thought to reinforce the party with most of a brigade. Lewinsville swarmed with bluecoats.

Stuart galloped out to punish the enemy with 305 Virginia infantrymen, an artillery section, and two cavalry companies. He saw that he was outnumbered, but flung his attack on the Federal flank as if the whole Confederate army were at hand.

The Federals had been on the point of withdrawal, and now fell back; Stuart's men literally tore away the enemy flank and pushed it from Lewinsville. The affair ended with sixteen Union casualties. Stuart lost not even a horse.

Jeb had an amusing correspondence with a Federal officer at Lewinsville, an old West Point comrade:

> My Dear Beauty: I am sorry that circumstances are such that I can't have the pleasure of seeing you, although so near you. Griffin says he would like to have you dine with him at Willard's at 5 o'clock on Saturday next. Keep your Black Horse off me, if you please.
>
> Yours,
> Orlando M. Poe.

Stuart laughed, but pride in the work of his troopers moved him to scribble on the back of the note, as if with one eye on posterity:

> I have the honor to report that 'circumstances' were such that they could have seen me if they had stopped to look behind, and I answered both at the cannon's mouth. Judging from his speed, Griffin surely left for Washington to hurry up that dinner.

Stuart became a brigadier general on September twenty-fourth. Just five days before he won his stars one of his troopers wrote of him: "Stuart sleeps every evening on Munson's Hill without even a blanket under or over him. He is very young . . . but he seems a most capable soldier, never resting, always vigilant."

Another of Jeb's men was less complimentary. Robert W. Hooke, who was soon to die of camp fever, wrote: "Colonel Stuart has been promoted and I don't know who we will get now for a Colonel. I don't think we can be worsted as it regards being kind to his men, for Stuart has treated us very badly. He is a real tyrant to his men!"

Stuart's happiness seemed complete. Flora had come to nearby Fairfax Court House and rode to see him daily. She was never heard to complain, but Captain Charles M. Blackford of the 2nd Virginia Cavalry saw her concern: "She is always in tears when she hears firing, knowing that, if possible, her husband is in the midst of it. . . . Her distressed look shows the constant anxiety she must suffer."[5]

She did not remain long at the front, for Stuart's duties increased rapidly. In October he was given command of the "Advanced Forces" when Longstreet moved up to major general and left the sector. Stuart called his present camp "Qui Vive." He wrote Flora from there on October eighteenth:

> I have very little time to write nowadays. I have to do what recently was done by Longstreet, Ewell, Bonham & myself. I have a very nice place here for you to visit me. . . . I can't promise that you will see much of your husband when you

come & you mustn't say it is cruel in me to leave you at short
notice for the imperative calls of duty.

I am very well. . . . Capt. Brien sends best regards to you
and La Pet [young Flora]. . . . 3 Cols. are waiting for me.

> In haste
> Yours
> Stuart

Four days later he wrote her that bad roads made her visit in-
advisable, adding, "I am almost out of heart about it." He warned
her to take the children to Orange Court House or elsewhere to
avoid the epidemics of scarlet fever, mumps and whooping cough,
and said, "Be patient, and trust in Him who can alleviate all our
cares. I want to see you all very much but must let you decide upon
coming, having reference to the health of the children."

Stuart was having family financial troubles at this time; he
hinted at them in letters to Flora, once writing of having met some
relatives:

> I don't think much of the party. Be sure My Darling to
> make no retorts to any of their remarks, dignified silence is the
> best rebuke. I have paid Sister Mary, Cousin Jane and Brother
> A—— or rather Cousin P—— in full of all demands, and Dr.
> Brewer, but I have not yet paid for my uniform suit, but it is not
> made yet.

The Stuarts felt the pinch of inflation and rising prices, for the
salary of a brigadier was niggardly, and there was little other source
of income. His brother, William Alexander, owner of White Sulphur
and a salt works among other enterprises, voluntarily insured Stuart's
life, making Flora the beneficiary.[6]

There was apparently friction between Jeb and his cousin Peter
Hairston, who left the staff in October. But Stuart recorded a general air of harmony, despite handicaps: "I find Beverly Robertson by
far the most troublesome man I have to deal with and Jones and
Field and Radford give me no trouble at all."

Robertson, in command of Stuart's 4th Virginia, was a West
Pointer destined to clash with other generals of the Confederacy.

The colonels of the cavalry were now: W. E. Jones, 1st Virginia;
R. C. W. Radford, 2nd Virginia; Robertson of the 4th; C. W. Field
of the 6th Virginia; Robert Ransom, Jr., of the 1st North Carolina;
with Major W. T. Martin, of the Jeff Davis Legion from Mississippi.

Winter began with severe cold, and Stuart's men built scores of
log huts in their camp about a mile from the Manassas battlefield.
There were frequent brushes with the enemy, who threatened to
push the Confederate line southward, but there was a growing suspicion that General McClellan, as Stuart had predicted, might drop
down the Potomac and take the water route against Richmond, by
way of The Peninsula, the tongue of land between the York and
James rivers.

In one skirmish Stuart's troopers captured a Federal captain
and took him to headquarters, where Jeb questioned him:

"Why don't your cavalry boys show themselves more?"

"I know they're not much for quality. They got bad training.
But they'll be better now."

"How's that?"

"New commander. General Philip St. George Cooke. He'll
make you smart."

"Yes," Stuart said. "I know he has command, and I propose to
take him prisoner. I married his daughter, and I want to present her
with her father. So let him come on."[7]

The affair of his father-in-law in Federal uniform seemed to
gall Stuart. He wrote Flora on November twentieth: "The *Washington Star* announces your Pa's appointment as Brig. Genl."

Four days later he wrote her once more, warning her to keep
her name out of the newspapers, where controversies over divided
families were raging:

> The best thing we can do is to let it go and be forgotten.
> By calling attention to the matter no one will regard what you
> say—and it will only revive the recollection of your Pa's course.
> His own action classes him with [General Winfield] Scott.
> How can we, however much we may desire to do so, class him
> otherwise? No, My Dear Wife, for our own and our children's

sake let us determine to act well *our* parts and bear with the mistakes and errors of others however grievous. Read well and con well those words my darling, and be consoled in what you rightly regard as very distressing, by the reflection that your husband and brothers will atone for the father's conduct.

He urged Flora to write her brother John, now an artilleryman, "and cheer him up—and tell him you expect him and us to wipe out every stain on the name by our own brilliant service."

Stuart made another wry comment on his father-in-law. Their son Philip, named for his grandfather at birth, now had his name changed. Stuart wrote Flora:

As for my boy's name, do not my Dear *Dear* wife ask me to do what I would consider an irreparable injury to our only son and *embitter* the last days of his father who up to this moment has labored to leave nought for him to be ashamed of. . . . I am willing that he should be called John, Alexander or Chapman Johnson after him who was such a Dear friend to my boyhood—but never that he should keep any part of his previous Christian name. . . . Do not think of recalling it and be assured that you will never hereafter regret it.

Flora was forgetful, and in a letter a day or so later, Stuart scolded:

My Darling, don't call our boy by his old name if you please. We settled that . . . it is not right to revive it in our letters.

He dwelt on the matter:

I wrote you about our boy's future name and would like to have a reply. I can never consent to any portion of his former name being retained except Stuart. How would you like the name of *Stuart* Stuart? It would be novel and I think pretty, but J. E. B. would be most suitable.

Later still:

You will find that very few will ever know that his name was ever other than *Jimmie*.

Flora surrendered; the boy became James Ewell Brown Stuart, Jr. and the name of her father, such an anathema to Stuart, disappeared.

Jeb unbent so far as to write Flora:

> I heard by underground railroad yesterday that your Ma is boarding at Brown's Hotel, Washington, and she remarked at the breakfast table the other morning, how much she would "like to hear from her daughter Flora." Now my Darling if you will write a small letter, put it in a small envelope, telling her how well and comfortable we all are and send it to me I can have it put under your Ma's breakfast plate, before the end of next week, and she will never know who brought it.

There was even a word of General Cooke:

> Your Pa is dissatisfied with the way he has been served by putting others over him. It is what he might have expected. He would have been Major General this moment had he come over to us.

The letters of these weeks to Flora revealed a Stuart preoccupied with private affairs.

John Esten Cooke had taken her the tale of Jeb's hand-kissing episode with the women prisoners, evidently highly spiced—and jokingly told her Stuart had shaved off his beard. Flora's anxious letter drew admonitions from Jeb not to let "that scamp of a cousin of yours humbug and teaze you so. My beard flourishes like the gourd of Jonah." He then burst into rhyme:

> And long may it wave—
> For I ne'er will shave—
> While My Flora approves
> Still to grow it behooves—
> And 'nary a hair'
> From it will I spare.

And, as to the other gossip:

If you had seen what passed in the hand kissing affair you would not I know have taken the slightest objection to it, and it was only by Jno. E.'s distortions that it could have been made exceptionable.

He added one of the several urgent declarations of his love he found necessary during the war:

My darling if you could know (and I think you ought) how true I am to you and how centered in you is my every hope and dream of earthly bliss, you would never listen to the idle twaddle of those who knowing how we love each other amuse themselves telling such outlandish yarns . . . to see how you would stand it.

Stuart was "quite out of patience" with Esten Cooke, he said, and more:

Jno. Esten is a case and I'm afraid I can't like him. He is like your Pa in some peculiarities.

But the young novelist, unaware of Stuart's displeasure, wrote: "Stuart jested roughly, but you were welcome to handle him as roughly in return. If you could turn the laugh upon him, you were perfectly welcome to do so, and he never liked you the less for it." Perhaps, but not where Flora and other women were concerned.

The letters to Flora were sprinkled with details of her general's life in camp:

It is snowing hard, and the ground is white. I have very little leisure, in fact none at all. . . .
As for that broth of a boy, tell him Lady Margrave [a favorite horse] wants him to ride her again. I wish you could get a little home of your own somewhere to have birds and flowers and books, the very best Society in the world. When 'war's dread commotion is over,' I would step quietly into such a home and xxx xx xxx x xx Kisses Dearest—your own—Stuart.

Jeb found time for chess, despite the constant alarms of patrolling the northern border. A messenger "lost the chess board, and the chess-men are not the kind I wanted. The drawers and shirts are very nice."

There was a glimpse of the musical gaiety of camp, as he wrote Flora:

> It is nearly 12 at night, so hoping that at this moment you are dreaming of Hubbie I will close, Send me the words of *When the Swallows* etc., *The Dew Is on the Blossom, Passing Away* and *Napolitain*, those songs which so much remind me of you. . . . Here are Kisses for you sleeping, While at you I am peeping.

He now and then consoled his wife, but often struck a grim note:

> If we are victorious my place will be in the pursuit, so you mustn't give yourself unnecessary uneasiness about me. Bear in mind that if I fall I leave in the sacrifice thus made a legacy more to be prized by my children and you Dearest than 10 years of longer life. . . . I have no idea of sacrificing myself rashly but I hope to do my duty with a firm reliance on Divine Aid to uphold me.

Again:

> I don't care what other Generals do, all I have to say is that while this war lasts I will not *leave* the *van* of our Army unless *compelled* to. Let that answer put to rest any hope of seeing me in Richmond.

In the same letter he showed concern for his position in army affairs:

> I have some enemy in the War Dept. or Adjutant General's Office. Ask Dr. Brewer to find out who it is.

In the depths of the coldest weather he seemed to miss his wife:

> I would like to be with you Dearest this dreary winter's night. Do you think of your old stove these cold nights? I really think you get up and down too much with the children; it seems to me that you might have your nurse to relieve you much in that respect.

As if in prophecy of tragedy to come, he wrote:

> I beg of you My Darling to have Flora's portrait painted. You will never regret the expense if a good one, and if not adjudged a good likeness let the distinct understanding be to be retained by the artist. My Dear do not neglect this longer and get La Pet's happy expression—Bless her heart Pa wishes he could see it now.

There were glimpses of Stuart's relations with officers of the new army:

> Much love to Custis Lee when you see him. He was the most intimate friend I had in my class. Jo Johnston is as good a friend as I have in the C. S.

Jeb was impatient for major action, and wrote on November twenty-fourth:

> We are still expecting the enemy. *'Why don't he come?'*

And on December fourth:

> We still expect McClellan daily. That he will advance, there can be little doubt, but when and where—aye, there's the *rub.*

In mid-December he held the first of his cavalry drills for admiring generals and the army at large. He described the scene briefly:

I had a splendid Brigade Drill of Cavalry today. The day was very favorable, the ground excellent and the performance admirable. Generals Johnston, G. W. [Smith] and Beauregard and nearly all the others were present. I was congratulated on my performance—putting them through as no Cavalry was ever put through before. I had 8 full squadrons present. They drilled admirably.[8]

The fields were so muddy that drill soon became impossible, but the army was no less hungry, and on December twentieth General Johnston sent most of the army's wagons to forage for food near the village of Dranesville. Stuart's men were stirred from the comfortable log huts to protect the wagon train.

As if clairvoyant, the Federal command had sent 4,000 infantry under General E. O. C. Ord toward Dranesville to collect forage.

Stuart was given four little infantry regiments and a battery of artillery, some 1,600 men in all, a tenth of them cavalrymen.

Jeb advanced rather incautiously. The Federals reached Dranesville first, and drove out the Confederate pickets. General Ord placed artillery on high ground in the village and threw two regiments into line. This force was soon swollen by the arrival of three more regiments, and Ord awaited Stuart's coming with 6,000 men. Jeb knew nothing of the Federal position until Captain Andrew Pitzer led the cavalry advance to Dranesville; the unprotected wagon train was at the mercy of the enemy. A desperate little battle blazed up.

Federal artillery held all the hilltops and blew Jeb's battery apart. Infantrymen had to drag off one of the guns to prevent its capture, and one caisson was left behind.

Confederate troops became excited, and the 6th South Carolina and 1st Kentucky fired at each other. Somehow Stuart held his position for two hours, exchanging fire with the enemy as the wagons rolled to safety, but one regiment lost their knapsacks, forced back over a different road than that on which they had advanced and left their gear.

As the men came off the field a Kentucky officer, one Captain Desha, hobbled with his regiment, obviously wounded. Stuart passed him and started to dismount.

"Take my horse, Captain," he said. But Desha refused and walked on with his men. Stuart rode ahead, his horse draped with harness stripped from dead artillery animals on the field behind.

It was by no means a victory, though Stuart camped five miles away, and went back to the abandoned field in the morning with reinforcements. He buried his dead and recovered a few wounded. He had lost 194 men at Dranesville; the enemy, 68.

To Stuart this little fight seemed a triumph because of his inferior force. He wrote Flora:

> Our side therefore came out first best—I am perfectly satisfied that my conduct was right, and I have the satisfaction to know that it meets the approval of General Johnston, and all others who know the facts, and my reputation has no doubt been the gainer. I was never in greater personal danger and men and horses fell around me like tenpins, but thanks to God to whom I looked for protection, neither myself nor my horse was touched.

He warned his wife to beware inaccurate newspaper accounts of this action, and he added:

> There is a good deal of envy in this army among such as Ransom, Robertson et al—but I assure you I let it trouble me precious little.

There were errors at Dranesville Stuart would not make again. In particular he wanted to improve the artillery. He had in mind a new kind of artillery, something as swift as cavalry itself, able to outrace the enemy to the high ground always so vital on a battlefield. He was already searching the army for talent.

He acquired Lieutenant Beckham, who had fought guns so well at Manassas; he had also snapped up Lieutenant James Breathed, a prewar physician of twenty-three, who had been one of his companions on the train trip to Richmond as the war opened. Breathed had turned up in a cavalry regiment, and Stuart urged him to join the gunners, promising a promotion to first lieutenant. He put John Esten Cooke to work on the artillery, too, and the novelist was soon

in Richmond advertising in a newspaper: "100 Patriotic Men
Wanted" to fight Stuart's guns for him.

Most telling of all, Stuart picked up a twenty-three-year-old
son of an Alabama country doctor, who was fresh from West Point—
John Pelham, an almost girlishly handsome lieutenant. Pelham had
left the military academy before graduating to slip over the border
disguised as one of General Scott's couriers. He had drawn Stuart's
attention with his "masterly manner" of handling a battery of guns
at Manassas. A cannoneer sketched Pelham: "Of ordinary stature
and light build, but remarkably sinewy. He was considered the best
athlete at West Point, and he was noted for his fondness for fencing
and boxing. . . . A boyish appearance, erect and neat address, as
modest as a maiden in the social circle."

Cavalrymen told tales of Pelham: The Prince of Wales, visiting
West Point in 1860, had been astonished by the boy's horsemanship;
once in early youth, Pelham had fought a larger schoolmate "until
he fainted with exhaustion."

He had pushed his guns into such exposed positions at the battle
of Manassas that an officer had deserted him: "If Pelham's fool
enough to stay there, I'm not."

He was Stuart's kind of soldier.

While Esten Cooke was in Richmond trying to persuade the
Confederate command to create horse artillery, Stuart wrote impatiently:

> Whoever is to be should be appointed at once and come
> directly here. I need a commander very much to organize the
> battery forthwith . . . get a *yes* or *no* out of the Department.

A few days later Stuart wrote Flora of progress:

> The Horse Artillery is growing rapidly. . . . Pelham is in
> command of it.

And:

> The Battery . . . under the energetic management of Pel-
> ham is going *ahead* and will tell a tale in the battle. It has taken
> the name of the "Stuart Horse Artillery."

There was no other battery like this. Not a man walked when Pelham's guns went into action; all were mounted, even on the horses dragging the big guns and caissons. The pieces literally flew, and Pelham drilled the gunners until they became teams of precision, able to dash into position, unhitch, limber the guns and open fire with astonishing speed.

Pelham began with eight guns, and his force grew as rapidly as Stuart could beg guns and teams, and dragoon promising men from other parts of the army. He gathered a colorful band about him.

One of the first was Major Dabney Ball, his chaplain, his "Foraging Parson," the troopers called him, for he was so skilled as a commissary officer that not a chicken could live in a territory covered by Preacher Ball. He not only foraged; he carried private messages for Stuart, and once set up bakeries for the cavalry. Ball was one of Stuart's myriad kin; he was a thirty-nine-year-old minister who had left a Washington pastorate after eighteen years in the pulpit and offered himself to Governor Letcher as a soldier.

Ball joined a colorful chaplains' corps. Wickham's brigade boasted of the Reverend Captain Thomas Nelson Conrad, who doubled as a scout, often riding the "Doctor's line," a chain of country physicians living between Stuart and Washington which brought information from the very gates of the enemy capital.

This Parson Conrad wrote of one of his warlike exploits: "I met a Yankee plunderer on the highway. His horse was strung with chickens, hams, ducks and turkeys. I shot him, took his feet out of the stirrups and dropped him on the road."[9]

Stuart also began to gather scouts to do secret service for him, bold men whose mysterious missions were little known even among the staff. One of the first was William Downs Farley, twenty-six, from Laurens, South Carolina: This handsome boy had won the army's attention by bravery at Manassas, fighting to the end though he could scarcely stand because of a raging fever from a case of measles. He had then turned to scouting along the northern lines. He won Stuart's heart by waylaying a column of several hundred Federal cavalry under General George Bayard, storming from a pine thicket with only three men to fire on Bayard and stampede most of his men. Farley was captured in this foray, however, and spent several months in Old Capitol prison in Washington. When he was released he returned to the area of Centreville.

Farley had "the most flattering proposals" to employ his talents in the West, Esten Cooke wrote, but: "Chancing to meet General Stuart, that officer took violent possession of him, and thenceforth kept him near him as volunteer aide."

Another of Stuart's scouts was Redmond Burke, one of his intimates, a fearless middle-aged soldier who gravitated to the cavalry command in the first months of fighting; he had three sons riding with Stuart. In a letter to Flora, Stuart left a glimpse of his work in enemy lines:

> Would you believe it? Redmond Burke rode up and reported for duty yesterday. We have made a great glorification over him. He had many narrow escapes and has a wonderful set of yarns to tell. We are delighted to see him.

Another Stuart scout was Frank Stringfellow, whose air of twenty-one-year-old innocence took him safely through many an escapade; he had become as much at home in enemy lines as among Jeb's cavalry. He once was forced into a remarkable hiding place in Alexandria which made him a legend in the Army of Northern Virginia.

Stringfellow was walking in the occupied border city one day when a Federal officer recognized him. A chase ensued through busy streets, with a growing party of Union soldiers running yelling after him.

The scout ran through the open door of a house, up a flight of stairs, and burst into a room occupied by an old woman, who sat at a table. She wore old-fashioned hoop skirts. Miraculously, she was a friend of Stringfellow's.

"Here, Frank," she said calmly, lifting her skirts. The scout crouched beneath her hoops, holding his breath, as Federal soldiers searched the house.

An officer shouted at the old woman, "Where is he? He came in here."

"Who are you looking for? Someone ran in the front door a

moment ago. He must have run through and out the back door."

The Federals gave up the search, and Stringfellow emerged, resolved, he said, "to be a better and more Christian man."[10]

Christmas passed. Jeb sent Flora a gift of fifteen yards of silk goods in from Baltimore through the blockade; she sent him a golden sash and gaudy shoulder straps, made by women of War-renton. "Bless the ladies," Stuart wrote.

Flora urged him to come to her for a visit, and allow other officers to guard against the Federal invaders.

He wrote her:

> How much better to have your husband in his grave after a career true to every duty and every responsibility, to you, his country, and his God, than inglorious existence—a living shame to you and to his children.

In January he wrote his brother-in-law, John R. Cooke:

> I have felt great mortification at Col. Cooke's course. He will regret it but once, and that will be continuously. Let us so conduct ourselves as to have nothing in our course to be regretted. Certainly thus far we have nothing that we may not be proud of. It is a sad thing, but the responsibility of the present state of the separation in the family rests entirely with the Colonel. Let us bear our misfortunes in silence.[11]

He was in a mood to scold politicians, too, for the new bill reshuffling the army's commands:

> Congress has thoroughly disgraced itself by passing the most outrageous abortion of a bill ever heard of for the reorganization of our forces.

He warned his wife not to reveal his opinion, for fear his foes would "use this speech against me."

But in camp Stuart revealed no concern; instead, as Esten Cooke saw him:

> "He was the most approachable of generals, and jested with the private soldiers as jovially as if he had been one of them. The men

were perfectly unconstrained in his presence, and treated him more like the chief of a hunting party than a general. . . . Stuart was like a king of rangers. On one side of his room was his chair and desk; on the other his blankets; at his feet his two setters, 'Nip' and 'Tuck.' . . . When tired of writing, he would throw himself upon his blankets, play with his pets, laugh at the least provocation, and burst into some gay song. . . .

"His favorites were: 'The Bugle Sang Truce, For the Night Cloud Had Lowered'; 'The Dew Is On the Blossom,' 'Sweet Evelina,' and 'Evelyn.' "

But Stuart also loved the roaring songs of his band, and was apt to cast aside his dispatches, or leave his games of marbles, quoits or snowballs with his staff, and join Sweeney and the others in "Hell Broke Loose in Georgia," "Billy in the Low Grounds," "Oh Lord, Gals, One Friday," or "Gal on the Log."

Stuart was seldom thoughtful, so far as the men of headquarters could discern. But Cooke once chided him for needless exposure on the front lines, and warned he would be killed if he did not use caution.

"Oh, I reckon not," Stuart said, "but if I am, they will easily find somebody to fill my place."

So far as one could see, he had no more serious concern for his life; the burdens of war seemed to rest lightly on him. Eggleston saw him in a railroad station at lighthearted play: "In the crowded waiting room with a babe on each arm; a great, bearded warrior with his plumed hat, and with golden spurs clanking at his heels, engaged in a mad frolic with all the little people in the room, charging them right and left with the pair of babies which he had captured from their mothers."

Despite this, there was alert watchfulness—though once during the winter the enemy drove in upon him, an event promptly reported by General D. H. Hill. President Davis was stung to criticism in a dispatch to General Johnston:

The letter of General Hill painfully impresses me with that which has heretofore been indicated—a want of vigilance and intelligent observation on the part of General Stuart. The officers commanding his pickets should be notified of all roads in their neighborhood, and sleepless watchfulness should be required of them.

It is the only complaint of record on the cavalry cordon of this period.[12]

Stuart had a countercomplaint, that his troops had not been properly recognized for their work at Manassas in the summer:

> As you well know my regiment was the only cavalry that charged the enemy. . . . No cavalry has excelled it in the zeal and effectiveness of its captains and men, none of whom have been advanced, notwithstanding the promotion of every other captain on duty at Manassas. I respectfully ask that the company officers of the 1st Cavalry be not forgotten.

And of the action at Dranesville he wrote:

> I notice that Congress voted thanks to all who have been engaged with the enemy except the brave men who were with me at Dranesville. Have I no friends in Congress?

Winter dragged by; picket duty was cruel, and the bottomless fields and roads ended Stuart's round of drills and reviews. The troops burrowed in their villages of huts to wait for spring.

☆

CHAPTER 6

The Peninsula

THE rainstorm struck muted thunder from the equestrian statue of Washington in Capitol Square; waterfalls spilled down the theatrical figure and the bronze flanks of the horse. The statue rose in the center of the square between old St. Paul's Church and the Capitol, surrounded by lesser heroes on their pedestals, beneath the bare arms of giant trees. All the people of Richmond seemed to have crowded here on this miserable day.

It was February twenty-second; the Confederacy was a year old, and Jefferson Davis was to be inaugurated as permanent President. A sea of umbrellas stretched before the pale, thin Mississippian, whose voice was hushed by the drumming of the storm as he took the oath of office. He was none too popular in the Confederate capital at this moment, but one who watched saw a hopeful sign: "Something in his mien—something solemn in the surroundings . . . for the moment raised him in the eyes of the people, high above party spite and personal prejudice.

"An involuntary murmur of admiration, not loud, but heart-deep, broke from the crowds who thronged the drenched walks; and every foot of space on the roof, windows and steps of the Capitol. As it died, Mr. Davis spoke to the people."

The President said the Confederacy's future would be as bright as tomorrow's sun. Keen listeners noted that he made no promises, no apologies for recent disasters. He spoke in a cold, calm, impersonal manner. His faith in the destiny of the Confederacy was unconquerable, he said, and his distant, almost diffident, air only emphasized his strength of will.

He drew a remarkable cheer from the people. A witness, T. C.

DeLeon, described it: "Then, through the swooping blasts of the storm, came a low, wordless shout, wrenched from their inmost natures, that told, if not of renewed faith in his means, at least of dogged resolution to stand by him, heart and hand, to achieve the common end. It was a solemn sight, that inauguration."

Men and women left the Square with serious faces, DeLeon saw, though hundreds had doubtless heard only a few words spoken by the low, firm voice.[1]

The permanent government made few changes. Secretary of War Judah Benjamin, unpopular with the public, was removed from office, but reappeared immediately as Secretary of State, where, as one witness put it, "his rosy, smiling visage impressed all who approached him with the vague belief that he had just heard good news."

The Confederacy's news had been bad for months past. In mid-January General Crittenden was defeated at Mill Springs in the West, and General Zollicoffer was dead. Men in Richmond streets muttered that Zollicoffer was uselessly sacrificed.

Affairs in the West grew worse. Fort Henry fell. This news was followed by a report of a great Confederate victory at Fort Donelson, but after a day of rejoicing in Richmond the War Department came forth with the glum truth: Donelson had fallen, a twin to Fort Henry. There was widespread complaint that the government was somehow misusing the vast resources sacrificed by the people. "Nearly half the country" was in opposition to Davis this week.

On February seventh a new blow came. Roanoke Island, North Carolina, fell with its force of Virginia troops under Governor Henry Wise. Old Wise had been calling for help for weeks, with warnings that the whole North Carolina coast would fall to the enemy. Now it was too late for anything but a Congressional investigation: The War Department was to blame. Almost as soon as this document appeared, General Burnside led a Federal column into New Bern, North Carolina, and most of the coastal area immediately south of Richmond was lost to the Confederacy.

Not even this series of catastrophes dampened the gay spirits of the new Richmond. There were almost nightly receptions in the

mansion occupied by President Davis and his family. Every fort-
night there was an "undress review," thronged by thousands; a
military band played, and cabinet and bureau heads moved in the
crowd. Generals from the front were seen, including Joe Johnston,
Longstreet and the blond giant John Hood. There were "senior
wranglers" from Congress, editors and "dancing men wasting their
time in the vain effort to talk."

DeLeon, who saw some of the revelry, wrote: "But not only the
chosen ten thousand were called. Sturdy artisans, with their best
coats and hands scrubbed to the proper point of cleanliness for shaking the President's, were always there. Moneyed men came, with
speculation in their eyes, and lobby members trying to throw up
dust therein; while country visitors, having screwed their courage up
to the desperate point of being presented—always dropped Mr.
Davis' hand as if its not over-cordial grasp burned them."

Dark-eyed Varina Howell Davis, "the Mississippi Rose,"
smiled gravely at the crowd from her husband's side; it was not long
since Captain Blackford, on his way to join Stuart, had overheard
her on the streets, cursing a Negro groom for cruelty to a horse,
with all the crude profanity of a drover.

Many houses were open nightly and the young people, who
were coming to dominate Richmond society, danced the Lancers.
There were dozens of gambling hells, too, rich saloons of a sort the
city had never seen before.

The observant DeLeon wrote as if he had visited the places:
"Senators, soldiers, and the learned professions sat elbow to elbow
round the generous table. In the handsome rooms above they puffed
fragrant real Havanas, while the latest developments were discussed.
Here men who had been riding raids in the mountains of the west,
had lain shut up in water batteries of the Mississippi . . . met after
long separation. Here the wondering young cadet would look first
upon some noted raider, or some gallant brigadier, cool and invincible amid the rattle of Minié balls, as reckless but conquerable
amid the rattle of ivory chips."

Inflation became worse by the day, but, strange to the eyes of
Richmond, those who were fortunate enough to have gold lived
like emperors, and flourished the more with each passing day, as the

Confederate Treasury ground out its banknotes in desperation, and the paper sank rapidly in value. Money halted briefly in its descent before it became almost literally worthless. Confederate bills would buy a Richmond hotel room for a day for $20, $1 in gold; a suit of clothes, $300 Confederate, $30, gold; whisky, $25 per gallon, Confederate, $1.25, gold. Prices in the North, in Washington and New York, were double Richmond's gold prices; thus a small class of speculators and blockade runners became rich beyond their dreams. Gold was the only vehicle for financial gambling.

Soldiers were being paid on the original basis, on the mythical theory that Confederate bills were truly valued. The result was that the $11 per month paid a private soon amounted to no more than 55 cents in coin. A brigadier general's income, translated into gold, was nearly $8 per month.

But though generals swarmed into Richmond during the winter, no one saw Stuart; he was with his men in the cold camp at Centreville, watching for the expected move of McClellan. Signs of Federal activity multiplied in early March.

On March second Jeb wrote Flora:

> The next summer will probably be the most eventful in a century. We must nerve our hearts for the trial with a firm reliance on God. We must plant our feet firmly upon the platform of our inextinguishable hatred to the Northern Confederacy, with a determination to die rather than submit— What a mockery would such a liberty be with submission— I for *one*—though I stood alone in the Confederacy, without countenance or aid, would uphold the banner of Southern Independence as long as I had a hand left to grasp the staff—and then die before submitting. I want my wifey to feel that sort of enthusiasm. . . .
>
> Tell my boy when I am gone how I felt & wrote. Tell him never to do anything which his father would be ashamed of— never to forget the principles for which his father struggled. We are *sure* to win, what the sacrifices are to be, we cannot tell, but if the enemy held every town and hill top—Southern subjugation would be no nearer its consummation than now. . . .

Stuart was not disheartened, even by the bad news from the West and the North Carolina coast. He thought it might serve to arouse the people of the Confederacy from their "criminal apathy."

He took no satisfaction from the evident failure of General Robert E. Lee in the mountains of West Virginia, however; his old West Point commandant had tried in vain to save a doomed campaign and the Federals had pushed forward, forcing Lee to give up his hope of holding the western Virginia frontier.

Jeb wrote: "With profound personal regard for General Lee, he has disappointed me as a General."

Stuart's own front abruptly demanded his attention.

On a frosty March morning his scouts brought ominous news: The enemy was moving on them. Stuart flung his cavalrymen toward the bluecoats on the length of his front. It was not long before he suspected that McClellan was only screening his real maneuver. He was right. Federal troopships were moving down the Potomac to Fortress Monroe, where McClellan would base his new drive against Richmond up the marshy highway between the York and the James.

General Johnston had been pleading with Richmond to allow him to evacuate the line around Manassas; one who opposed him was General R. E. Lee, now brought to the city to advise President Davis. Now Johnston reacted instantly to the Federal advance. He ordered Stuart to burn the vast stores accumulated at Manassas.

The infantry evacuated the junction and left Stuart's troopers to deal with the Federals. Captain Blackford did mournful duty, burning corn cribs with his own hands and directing his regiment in scorching a path before the enemy. Within a day or so the troopers had nothing to eat but parched corn—yet Johnston's orders destroyed millions of rations without making a fight for them. Captain Blackford lamented: "This may have been West Point science, but to ordinary mortals it looked not wise." At Manassas the troopers burned piles of bacon as high as houses, and watched unhappily as flames consumed the meat, wafting the odor for twenty miles. The cavalry fell back before the enemy. Pursuit was brief.

To Stuart this sudden withdrawal with its loss of clothing and food seemed absurd. He expressed his anger to Flora:

I am enduring the saddest, sorest trials of the soldier, to
see this beautiful country abandoned to the enemy.

But it must be abandoned now, since the enemy was clearly
planning to attack The Peninsula. And Stuart hurried his command
in the rear of Johnston's swarming army. Most of the route to Richmond was snowy and unpleasant.

As they left Manassas they rode through a severe sleet storm and
camped in a pine wood. It was too dark for the weary soldiers to
notice that the trees were bent far down with snow and ice. The
cavalrymen built fires on the edge of these woods, fed horses corn
from the burned cribs, and ate chicken and eggs snatched from
farms in their path. While the hungry men waited for supper with
the delicious odors in their nostrils, heat from the fires dumped
disaster on them.

Masses of ice and snow melted free and crashed among the men,
extinguishing the fires and ruining their meal. They salvaged such
half-cooked food as they could find and slept on the snow.

Stuart arrived late at this bivouac and slept under a brush lean-to
with Blackford on a makeshift bed of leaves. Stuart and Blackford
combined their blankets for the night.[2]

The Confederate government had watched with dismay as
Johnston's troops marched toward the defenses around Yorktown.
Davis and Lee had advised partial rather than complete withdrawal
to the new position. But the people of Richmond took courage at
sight of the soldiers, even the first of the ragged infantry coming
out of the muddy roads from the north. By the time Stuart's cavalry
brought up the rear enthusiasm was at a peak.

Last year Jeb's troopers had been mounted on horses and mules
of every description, in a variety of uniforms, armed with shotguns,
muskets, rifles or old flintlocks. But on the March day when they
trotted with precision up Franklin Street to Capitol Square and
turned out Broad Street toward the front, they seemed to the
populace the very ideal of mounted soldiers. There was little polish,
and both uniforms and trappings were worn, with a sprinkling of
captured Federal equipment.

Windows, doors and sidewalks were jammed from one end of

Richmond to the other as Stuart's men passed. Women and children waved, handkerchiefs fluttered and flowers were tossed. Many men broke ranks to greet families and friends, but officers pulled them back, and the command went into camp east of the city. For a night cavalrymen swarmed through the city.

The stay was short, for the troopers were soon with the infantry at Yorktown. There was idleness from the first, with little to do but stare out over the water. A few miles to the east was the growing Federal invasion post at Fortress Monroe. Attack might come any day.

In the very face of the enemy threat, the Confederate army gave itself over to reorganization. In the throes of a new democracy, officers of all units were to stand for re-election. Hundreds of men left the service and others were turned out by upstart candidates from the ranks who promised their men everything. Blackford recalled that discipline disappeared this week. He walked down a line of tents as roll was being called, but not a man reported for duty. All were lying abed, aware that no officer would force them to stir while elections were on, grandly answering to their names from their blankets, while an orderly sergeant passed meekly down the tent rows. Blackford noted that candidates were telling men that, if elected, they would see to it that the soldiers would not be "exposed"—in short, they would not have to fight. In his own company, a Sergeant Litchfield campaigned for captain, telling the troopers he would take them from under Stuart's harsh command and into the artillery, if elected. Blackford could not bring himself to solicit votes, and lost his place to Litchfield. The erstwhile captain returned to Richmond, to find a place in the engineer corps.[3]

The enemy did not stir while Johnston's army was torn apart by this remarkable reorganization, and for more than a month the big armies lay watching each other. Johnston was anxious, and his dispatches to Richmond betrayed his urge to fall back to the capital itself. Johnston had been in this frame of mind from his first glimpse of the Yorktown trenches and the dispirited troops of General J. B. Magruder. In mid-April, Johnston had hurried back to Richmond and called President Davis into a day-long conference. Johnston wanted to abandon the entire Peninsula, falling back to Richmond, sacrificing Norfolk and all else in the area. He would then concentrate Confederate troops from all over the South around Richmond, to stand off McClellan. Generals Lee, Longstreet and G. W. Smith debated the plan before Davis and Johnston, finishing at one o'clock in the morning. When it was over, the President ordered Johnston to defend the line of the lower Peninsula.

It was the same Johnston who had so easily given up Harpers Ferry at the opening of the war, and then literally run from the line at Manassas this spring. Yet Stuart remained loyal to him, and in the cavalryman's estimate of this time, Johnston was "in capacity head and shoulders above every other" Southern general. He was also Jeb's "dearest friend."

Life was dull around Yorktown in April, and there was little duty for cavalry or infantry. There was a bit of relief in news from the Shenandoah Valley, where a little army under Stonewall Jackson was attacking Federal forces with reckless daring, but as yet no pattern of campaign had emerged there. At Yorktown, the army waited for McClellan to jump.

McClellan hardly got the chance. On May first Johnston announced to Richmond headquarters that he would abandon Yorktown, come what may. He feared that Federal boats would move up the rivers on his flanks. On May fourth, without notifying Richmond further, the infantry left the trenches and marched up the few muddy roads toward the capital.

The Federals were so astonished that they did not pursue until noon. They first had to deal with Stuart's cavalry screen.

The main artery up the Peninsula was the Telegraph Road, leading through Williamsburg to Richmond. There was a river road, along the south bank of the York. Otherwise, there were only lateral roads crossing the tongue of land. Stuart defended a line almost from river to river.

He sent the 1st Virginia under Fitz Lee westward to guard the banks of the upper York, at Eltham's Landing. On the Telegraph Road he concentrated his strength under Williams Wickham. Smoke rose over the swamp in the early hours of the morning.

Stuart had Captain Pelham's battery placed on his left, where it could command the Telegraph Road. He ordered Pelham to fire as long as he found targets. The guns soon opened.

The Federal advance was led by General George Stoneman; it soon appeared that he had strong infantry regiments behind him. The enemy pressed hard against the Telegraph Road, expecting to approach Williamsburg and reach a Confederate earthwork known as Fort Magruder before Stuart could group his cavalry there. The Union troopers rode into Pelham's fire and took terrible losses. They were hemmed in at the roadside by marshes, and were forced back for a time.[4]

Later the superior Federal artillery swept Telegraph Road and Wickham retreated; the Federals had now cleared the way to Williamsburg. Stuart was thus left far in the Confederate rear, separated from one wing of his force by miles of swamp and forest. Unknown to him the 3rd Pennsylvania Cavalry had cut off his retreat, and a trap was opening behind him.

The scout, William Farley, helped save the day, the blithe South Carolina boy who told John Esten Cooke, "I don't know how many of the enemy I've killed. I never counted. A good many."

"A dozen?"

"Oh, yes. I can remember six officers. I never counted the men."

Today Farley was riding across country in Stuart's rear when he blundered into the enemy.

Stuart had sent Colonel Thomas F. Goode and men of the 3rd Virginia to probe the rear. Goode was galloping in the swampy road when Farley broke from cover.

"Yankees ahead, ready to charge you," Farley said. "You'd better get into the woods."

Goode put his troopers into an ambush on the side of the road, and there was a brief skirmish in the swamp track, both parties sitting in the saddles, firing with carbines. The enemy soon fell back, leaving three or four bodies in the road.[5] When the party returned to Stuart, the commander had found a new route of retreat toward Williamsburg.

Unhesitatingly, as if he knew every pig track of this country, he led the troopers and their guns to the narrow beach of the river, and they dashed upstream with two mountain howitzers firing in the rear to keep the enemy at bay. Stuart led them into Williamsburg after dark. He learned that Williams Wickham had fought a heavy cavalry action in front of Fort Magruder in the afternoon. Wickham had a saber wound in his side and would be out of action for weeks.[6]

The army had narrowly averted disaster. The bold Federal infantry had reached Fort Magruder at the edge of the village before Johnston could throw South Carolina infantry into the works. Furious artillery fire had pushed back the enemy at dusk. Weary Confederates slept everywhere in Williamsburg, but many were roused in the night: General Magruder led the advance of the retreat up The Peninsula in a torrential downpour. Johnston ordered the rearguard to hold during the coming day, to give rest to the army.

Stuart was moving before daylight and at six o'clock, with rain still falling, heard the opening Federal artillery fire. It was a long day. The cavalry was not fully engaged, though in the fields and boggy swamps the green Confederate and Federal troops charged and countercharged for hours. The fighting was desperate, especially on the Confederate left, where Jubal Early and D. H. Hill led their men in reckless frontal assaults. Longstreet commanded the defense, and was proud of the repulse of the Federals. When the army straggled up the peninsula nearer Richmond, about four hundred wounded were left behind in the rain. Early's brigade had lost 600 men; the total was thought to be over 1,500.

Difficult terrain and inexperienced officers had resulted in costly charges that won no advantage. Stuart was mentioned by Longstreet in his report as "exceedingly active and zealous in conducting the different columns to their proper destinations and in assisting them to get properly into action."

In the excitement, there had been informalities, however, and Stuart's men were not entirely idle. William Farley could not bear the inaction of the second day and had left his chief to lead an infantry regiment in an impetuous charge.

The army left Williamsburg with the Federal tide seeping after it toward Richmond. Johnston had split his forces for the retreat. Magruder was on a road nearing the Chickahominy, and G. W.

Smith, on the New Kent Road to the north, protected the flank along the York River. Johnston's fears were soon realized. Union troops poured ashore at West Point under the guard of gunboats and thus controlled the York to the limit of navigation. Smith could expect an attack on his flank, and the new threat must be met before the retreating army was mauled once more.

Fitz Lee's 1st Virginia was screening Smith's regiments, and its pickets were first to detect the Federal move near West Point. On May seventh, with the enemy pushing inland from that point, Smith sent Generals Hood and Wade Hampton to halt them with two infantry brigades. The reckless young Hood forced his way into the lead.

Hood ordered his men to unload their guns for fear of killing his own troops in undergrowth near the river; he led the column to Fitz Lee's front, and there stumbled onto the enemy. Firing broke out. Hood exposed himself by walking within a few yards of bluecoat skirmishers, and was saved as he fled by a disobedient soldier: A Union corporal lifted his rifle to shoot Hood, when a Texan in the ranks, having disregarded the order to unload his gun, dropped the enemy marksman. The Confederates thrust through thickets and pushed the Federals to the landing, in close range of the protective artillery. Smith's procession was safe, and the enemy was at bay.

The further retreat toward Richmond was uneventful, and Smith gave credit to the cavalry: "The comfort and quiet with which the march of the troops has been conducted . . . is largely due to the admirable dispositions and watchfulness of the cavalry rear-guard, first under Colonel Fitz Lee and more recently under Brigadier General J. E. B. Stuart."

Two days after this little affair, with Johnston's army settling against the outer defenses of Richmond, Stuart wrote Flora of his part in the battle of Williamsburg, including incidents not easily found in official reports. He wrote from his "Headquarters in the Saddle":

My Darling Wife—
    Blessed be God that giveth *us* the victory. The battle of Wmsburg was fought and won on the 5th. A glorious affair.

... On the 4th my Brigade distinguished itself, and on the 5th by its attitude and maneuvering under constant fire prevented the enemy's leaving the woods for the open ground—thus narrowing his artillery scope of fire. *I* consider the most brilliant feat of the 5th to have been a dash of the *Stuart* Horse Artillery to the front.

For *myself* I have only to say that if you had seen your husband you would have been proud of him. I was not out of fire the whole day.

The day before (4th) the Cavalry made several charges—and Lawrence Williams told the bearer of a flag of truce that I came within an ace of capturing my father-in-law. Our Cavalry charged their Cavalry handsomely and, even they were entirely routed—their artillery captured, the Cav. flag of the enemy was captured—but the 4th Va. Cavalry lost its standard bearer and flag....

God bless you—

The army's morale was low as it lay in camps before Richmond. Norfolk must be abandoned, and the historic ironclad *Merrimac*, now the *Virginia*, must be scuttled after her fight with the Federal *Monitor*, because the James was too shallow to carry her to safety. Enemy gunboats were perilously near Richmond. Defenses at Drewry's Bluff on the James were hurriedly strengthened, but no one knew whether they could halt the enemy. With Captain Blackford's aid engineers had thrown a bridge over the river there, and Richmond headquarters could now more easily maneuver forces.

In northern Virginia, along the line of the Rappahannock, a big Union army under General Irvin McDowell threatened the smaller Confederate force in its front. In the Shenandoah, Jackson and General Dick Ewell were marching, but faced great odds.

McClellan inched forward until his line was in places five miles from Richmond. Spies said he had more than 120,000 men. In face of this General Johnston fought a small war of his own with Richmond authority. He declined to advise the hostile President Davis of his plans; his refusal to reply to urgent dispatches stung Davis and General R. E. Lee to investigate in the field.

Lee and Davis were not cheered by what they saw. The President pointed out that a main road lay open to the enemy. On May twenty-fourth this road was used by McClellan as his advance to Mechanicsville, a village five miles from Richmond. Johnston promised an early attack.

There was a brief flare of hope. Jackson and Ewell had surprised the Federals at Front Royal, in the Valley, and on May twenty-third chased them through Winchester. The campaign there continued.

There was little relief in sight; it seemed there was nothing to prevent McDowell's joining McClellan to open the gates of Richmond. But the Federal government had fears of its own, and when Jackson pushed north through the Shenandoah, McDowell was held in check. Richmond got a breathing spell.

Johnston's relations with Davis were so strained that General Lee once felt it necessary to make peace by riding to the front and appealing for more information. At last, on May thirtieth, Johnston felt himself ready to meet McClellan. The scene was Seven Pines, an insignificant settlement in the marshes east of Richmond. As he fell back from Williamsburg on the retreat, soldiers had heard Joe Johnston humming the Stephen Foster melody, "Camptown Races,"[7] but there was no such gaiety now. On May thirty-first, the very morning serious fighting opened, headquarters officers saw Johnston leap into his saddle and ride away at the approach of President Davis and General Lee, as if to avoid them. The future was not promising.

On the eve of the fight at Seven Pines, cavalry headquarters staff acquired one of its most colorful officers: Heros von Borcke.

The newcomer was a German who spoke the most rudimentary English. He was just off a train from Charleston when Richmond first glimpsed him: An attractive young man of six feet two inches, weighing about two hundred and fifty pounds, but so light and graceful in movement that he did not seem large. His polished manners were as impressive as the huge cavalry sword he carried.

Von Borcke had been a Lieutenant of the Guard in Berlin, but had quarreled with his father over money and come to America seeking adventure. He had burned his identification papers at sea when his ship was boarded by a Yankee crew—but had already persuaded

Secretary of War Randolph to give him a letter of introduction to General Stuart.

An intelligent Richmond diarist, Constance Cary, saw him: "A giant in stature, blond and virile, with great curling golden mustaches, and the expression in his wide-open blue eyes of a singularly modest boy."[8]

Near sunset on May thirtieth von Borcke came to the camp of Fitz Lee's 1st Virginia: "Lee assured me that it would be next to impossible to find General Stuart that night, and kindly offered me the hospitality of his tent."

The camp scene was striking to the eyes of a stranger: "The horses were not picketed in regular lines as in European armies, but were scattered about anywhere in the wood, some tethered to swinging limbs, some tied to small trees, other left to browse at will. . . . In the Colonel's tent, where the officers of his regiment had assembled, and where the lively strains of the banjo alternated with patriotic songs and animated discourse, . . ." supper was served.

The main dish was made of terrapin eggs found in a nearby creek and prepared by one of Fitz Lee's Negro servants; von Borcke found it a "work of art" equal to the best Parisian cuisine.

In the morning von Borcke rode with Fitz Lee's regiment toward the enemy. This, Lee told him, was the way to find Stuart. The German inspected his new companions: "It was marvellous to see how readily these unmilitary-looking troopers obeyed the orders of their colonel, and with what rapidity the breaking up of the camp was managed. . . . The men were all Virginians, whose easy and graceful seat betrayed the constant habit of horseback exercise, and they were mounted mostly on blooded animals."

Fitz Lee soon pointed out Stuart, "a man galloping rapidly on an active, handsome horse . . . a stoutly-built man, of a most frank and winning expression . . . his eye quick and piercing."

Stuart was riding into the battle, but read von Borcke's letter from Secretary Randolph and invited the German to accompany him. He introduced him to General Longstreet. Von Borcke had vivid impressions of the stolid infantry general: "He was a stout man of middle height . . . his long brown beard gave something leonine to his appearance; an engaging simplicity . . . in manners and dress . . .

a small black felt hat, a tunic-like gray coat, much faded . . . a pair of gray trousers and military boots with Mexican spurs; a small sword was his only weapon."

Von Borcke could see little of the battle. He rode with Stuart, who was in reserve at the center, since his cavalry could be of little service on the overgrown field.

It seemed to von Borcke that Stuart, though he did not lead a charge, was "in the thickest of the fray, giving assistance, counsel and encouragement to the rest, and letting nothing escape his observation."

Johnston attacked the enemy south of the Chickahominy, hoping to cut off an exposed wing before reinforcements could cross the swollen stream. Longstreet, Magruder, G. W. Smith and D. H. Hill commanded his troops, which were ordered to move in concert. Something went wrong. Longstreet misunderstood or disobeyed orders and left his assigned position, blocking commands behind him and delaying attack.

By three P.M. it became clear that plans had miscarried. The rolling of musket fire announced the premature clash of the vanguard with the enemy, and the struggle was on, much of it a bootless hand-to-hand affair pressed with gallantry by infantry on both sides, as they floundered through waist-deep water. Casualties were heavy, and no one seemed to know just how the battle was going. The Federals were driven back, but the price was fearful.

At the beginning of the heaviest artillery barrage, Stuart sent von Borcke with a dispatch to Fitz Lee. When he returned to Jeb's side, the Federal line was beginning to give way, and only in the center were the Confederates in trouble. There a North Carolina brigade was retreating. Von Borcke wrote: "Instantly General Stuart was at the spot, encouraging the troops to hold the position until our reinforcements could arrive. I followed him into the hail of bullets, of whizzing grape and bursting bombs, one of which rolled between my horse's legs."

As the North Carolinians fell back Stuart herded them into line, "here with threats, there with eloquent entreaties and brought them forward again into the battle to check the enemy. A Virginia brigade soon came up as reinforcement. With banners flying and loud war-cries, they threw themselves on the foe, driving them before them, and taking their earthworks, which bristled with cannon."

Night fell on a field strewn with the dead, and in the dusk trains of prisoners shuffled toward the Confederate rear. Von Borcke wrote: "Terrible it was to see on every side the wounded returning from the battle; here a man with his head bleeding, there another with shattered arm or leg, reddening the path with his blood; then the more severely wounded in the ambulances, groaning and wailing."

On one stretcher was General Johnston, wounded in the shoulder by an exploding shell, and at the very end of the battle lost to his army. Before the field had begun to clear, President Davis had given the command to Robert E. Lee.

Davis passed over the senior commander on the field, G. W. Smith, because he seemed timid.

In his report of the day Smith said of Stuart: "He gave me the first information received from the right after the close of the action, and rendered me very important assistance during the night."

Stuart was on the field until late, with von Borcke at his heels. The German wrote of their departure: "The ride to headquarters was a dreadful one: hundreds of conveyances, some taking the wounded to Richmond, some coming out from the city with provisions, were crossing each other in the almost impassable turnpike, and the groans and cries of the wounded were mingled with the curses and shouts of drivers, whose vehicles obstructed the way with broken wheels or exhausted horses."

Many Richmond families had sent carriages to help take off casualties, of whom there were 6,000, thrice the toll of First Manassas.

Stuart made headquarters at Montebello, a big country house overlooking the James. Von Borcke thought it was delightful, for Stuart accepted him as a volunteer aide, and the Prussian began at once to teach the young men cavalry skills. One day Captain Blackford would save von Borcke's life with one of the imported tricks.

Von Borcke could not forget his view of the battlefield at Seven Pines the next morning: "Friend and foe were lying here indiscriminately side by side, mown down in multitudes by musketry and by the guns . . . the artillery had here lost all their horses, which lay by the dozens, piled one upon another, and all around the ground was strewn with weapons, haversacks, cartridge boxes, ammunition."

A South Carolina brigade, the German noted, with an uneasy stomach, camped amid the corpses, gaily making breakfast of loot from the field.

Stuart and his staff rode near the Confederate front as a cannon ball sang overhead and ploughed into the soft earth fifty yards behind. Other shots came nearer, but Stuart continued inspecting enemy positions with field glasses. The group was showered with earth from exploding shells, obviously a target for a Federal battery. At last, when fragments flew near his head, Stuart turned to von Borcke in surprise.

"Lieutenant, they are firing at us here; let's ride a little faster."

The two riders galloped about three hundred yards in the open to a grove of trees, with shells falling about them. The enemy battery was guided by a scout in a treetop, closely observing Stuart, but he was soon shot from his perch by a Confederate marksman.

By one P.M. firing had ceased at Seven Pines and Stuart went to headquarters, where he met President Davis and many general officers. Von Borcke sketched Davis as "a tall thin man with sharply-defined features, an air of easy command, and frank, unaffected, gentlemanlike manners. . . ." Davis inspected the German's big cavalry sword, and said he was happy that so good a blade and such a strong arm had joined his army.

With the end of fighting at Seven Pines, the army settled to another period of waiting; there was now improved morale. News from the Shenandoah was better by the day, for Stonewall Jackson was driving bigger Federal armies from the region. General Lee brought better times to the army before Richmond, too. There was more decent food and clothing and a reorganization of the brigades. Many of the old political officers were on their way out, and there were changes in the high command. The army also had a new name: The Army of Northern Virginia, thus styled in the first modest order to the troops from General Lee. Whispers of an offensive against the Yankees circulated through the camps.

☆

CHAPTER 7

Fame at a Gallop

IN early June, Federal scouts peered into Richmond from a fat orange observation balloon which hung above the Chickahominy swamps. A single Rebel cannon banged at it in slow anger, but with poor aim, and the balloonists saw all they wished.

They watched the city in mourning, its streets filled with funeral processions and the walking wounded. Richmond had the look of a doomed capital.

The cavalry seemed unaware of the depressing outlook.

One morning Stuart had breakfast with John Mosby, the young lawyer-scout whom he had called to headquarters duty. Mosby had not been reluctant, though it may have cost him promotion: "The loss of my commission did not weigh a feather against the pleasure of being directly under the orders of a man of genius."

He learned of some of Jeb's talents as they sat alone at a camp table.

"I want you to have a look at McClellan for me," Stuart said.

"Yes, sir."

"Take a small party, the smaller the better, and see what he's doing along Totopotomoy Creek. General Lee wants to know if he's fortifying his right."

Within half an hour Mosby led three men on their dangerous mission, "as joyful a party as if we were going to a wedding."

Mosby got as far as Hanover Court House, more than fifteen miles north of Richmond, and turned southeastward down the Pamunkey River. He was far in the rear of Federal lines, and took a long look at McClellan's exposed position: The line of supply ran back by many roads to White House landing on the Pamunkey. The only protection for the entire line was a string of cavalry pickets.

Mosby returned to Stuart in excitement. He found headquarters in a holiday mood, for it had just got news of Stonewall Jackson's incredible victories over Generals Fremont and Shields in the Shenandoah Valley.

Stuart was anxious for Mosby's report, however. The scout was worn from his long ride, and the day was hot: "I laid down on the grass to tell him what I had learned. A martinet would have ordered me to stand in his presence."

(It was Mosby whose sly humor had so lately outraged the proper Fitz Lee, when he reported, "Colonel, the horn has blowed for dress parade!" Fitz had exploded, "Sir, if I ever hear you call a bugle a horn again, I'll put you under arrest!")

Stuart listened to Mosby's tale of McClellan's vulnerability and questioned him about the roads, the troops he had seen, and the country people he had interviewed. Stuart was at last satisfied: "Go to the adjutant's office and write down what you have said."

As Mosby left him, Jeb called for a courier.

Mosby returned. Stuart took a sheet of paper from him and read it through, nodding.

"You didn't sign it."

"No, I thought it was just a memorandum."

"Go back and sign it," Stuart said.

He waited, with the courier standing by, holding two horses, as if the fate of the army hung on the scout's report—and when Mosby returned with it, Stuart thrust it into a pocket and rode away.

Jeb went to General Lee's headquarters where he was alone with the commander for a few minutes, studying Mosby's memorandum. He returned to camp in a gay mood.

For several days there was a stir in the army, as if great things were in the offing.[1]

Jefferson Davis watched anxiously as his new commander unfolded plans of attack so daring that Davis at first resisted, but as June wore on and trenches grew before Richmond, he weakened, and soon approved Lee's bold scheme: Jackson must be brought from the Valley, and the gray regiments would be hurled from Richmond against McClellan's flank.

As Lee's councils of war developed in the Dabbs farmhouse on Nine Mile Road, the commander had no lack of advice. He encouraged his lieutenants to speak, and though he made daily rides along the lines to study the situation for himself, he seemed anxious for the opinions of other officers.

Through it all he kept his own counsel.

One of the first to urge him to attack in the desperate situation was Jeb Stuart. Lee's command of the army was but a few hours old when Jeb sent him a remarkable manuscript, with only this introduction:

> The present imperilled condition of the Nation, I presume, will be a sufficient apology for putting forth for your consideration, convictions derived from a close observation of the enemy's movements for months past, his system of war, and his conduct in Battle, as well as our own.

Stuart then gave Lee a lecture in military affairs. He suggested that McClellan would not smash at Richmond until he had completed fortifications south of the Chickahominy, and that Lee should attack in that quarter:

> We have an army far better adapted to attack than defense. Let us fight at an advantage before we are forced to fight at disadvantage. It may seem presumption in me to give these views, but I have not thus far mistaken the policy and practice of the enemy. At any rate, I would rather incur the charge of presumption than fold my arms in silence and indifference to the momentous crisis at hand. Be assured, however, General, that whatever course you pursue you will find nowhere a more zealous and determined cooperator and supporter than,
> Yours with the highest respect,
>
> J. E. B. Stuart[2]

Headquarters did not linger long over Stuart's plan, for what he proposed was attack in the swampy fringes of the Chickahominy, where Lee's inferior force would be at a dangerous disadvantage. The attack, in Lee's mind, must be made in just the opposite fashion: Hold in the south with small force, and strike in the north.

In any event, the boldness of his youthful cavalry chief was in Lee's mind on June tenth, when he called Stuart to headquarters. If Stuart was disappointed at rejection of his battle plan, he soon forgot it in his enthusiasm for the assignment Lee gave him. The instructions were characteristic of Lee as commander—breath-takingly bold, tempered with insistent warnings of caution:

Stuart would make "a scout movement" in the enemy rear, inspecting communications, taking cattle and grain, burning Federal wagon trains. This was Mosby's foray, repeated in force. He would take only men and horses able to endure a hard ride and must leave enough cavalry to protect the main army.

Most of the order was a series of admonitions against Stuart's exuberance:

> The utmost vigilance on your part will be necessary to prevent any surprise ... and the greatest caution must be practised in keeping well in your front and flanks reliable scouts to give you information. You will return as soon as the object of your expedition is accomplished; and you must bear constantly in mind, while endeavoring to execute the general purpose of your mission, not to hazard unnecessarily your command, or to attempt what your judgment may not approve; but be content to accomplish all the good you can, without feeling it necessary to obtain all that might be desired.

Even this was not all. As if he saw in the cinnamon-bearded cavalry commander the impulsive West Point cadet of eight short years ago—the year of the 129 demerits—Lee added:

> Remember that one of the chief objects of your expedition is to gain intelligence for the guidance of future movements. ... Should you find that the enemy is moving to his right, or is so strongly posted as to make your expedition inopportune, you will, after gaining all the information you can, resume your former position.[3]

But the prospect of a cautious probe vanished as Stuart replied to Lee, "And if I find the way open, it may be that I can ride all the way around him. Circle his whole army."

There was no one in the room to record Lee's reply, but at least he did not forbid the daring elaboration of his plan. He sent Stuart to work.

Stuart picked 1,200 men. His commanders were Fitz Lee, Lieutenant Colonel Will Martin and R. E. Lee's son, W. H. F. (Rooney) Lee. Lieutenant James Breathed was ordered to make ready a section of the horse artillery.

The men knew action was afoot only when they got orders to cook three days' rations. Not even the staff knew more. The troopers gathered in the darkness of June eleventh.

Von Borcke wrote: "It was two o'clock in the morning, and we were all fast asleep, when General Stuart's clear voice awoke us with the words, 'Gentlemen, in ten minutes every man must be in his saddle!' "

In half that time the officers were galloping to the main column a few miles away. John Esten Cooke pictured Stuart at the moment of departure: "As he mounted his horse on that moonlight night he was a gallant figure to look at. The gray coat buttoned to the chin; the light French saber, the pistol in its black holster; the cavalry boots above the knee, and the brown hat with its black plume floating above the bearded features, the brilliant eyes and the huge mustache, which curled with laughter at the slightest provocation— these made Stuart the perfect picture of a gay cavalier, and the spirited horse he rode seemed to feel that he carried one whose motto was to 'do or die.' "[4]

Cooke and Stuart rode together through the moonlight until the staff overtook the column at five A.M. The march began.

Mosby overheard a final conversation. An officer called to Stuart:

"When will you be back?"

"It may be for years, and it may be forever." Stuart's laugh trailed behind him.

Stuart did not allow the bugle calls he so much admired. Troopers were shaken awake and ordered into columns of fours, and the vanguard trotted northward.

There was gossip in the gray ranks, for despite the swift pace toward Louisa Court House, some troopers believed they were being sent against the flank of McClellan. The route was familiar to moving troops: Past Emmanuel Church, over a tributary of the Chickahominy at Brook Run, by the old Yellow Tavern, veering westward a bit at Turners, across the Richmond, Fredericksburg and Potomac tracks, then sharply northward in the afternoon, toward the crossing of the South Anna River.

Near the river, late in the day, suspicions of the men were confirmed. Stuart turned the leading squadrons sharply eastward across the railroad. They camped on the farm of the Winston family, near the post office of Taylorsville. Stuart ordered "a noiseless bivouac," with no camp fires allowed. Rooney Lee invited Jeb to ride to Hickory Hill, the home of his wife's family, some five miles away. Rooney's wife was Charlotte Wickham; when they arrived at Hickory Hill after midnight they found the wounded Colonel Williams Wickham, recuperating from his injuries of Williamsburg.

Rooney talked with the Wickhams until the early morning. Jeb fell asleep in a chair, but roused himself for breakfast and led the party back to camp at daylight.

The troopers were aroused "without flag or bugle sound," and signal rockets were used to alert the column down its length. The riders turned southeast toward Old Church, some twenty miles away on a country road between the Pamunkey and Chickahominy Rivers. Here, for the first time, Stuart confided his plan to Martin and the Lees "so as to secure an intelligent action and cooperation in whatever might occur."

Stuart was with the vanguard when, at nine A.M., they got the first glimpse of the enemy. Jeb halted outside the village of Hanover Court House and studied the scene.

There was the quaint brick courthouse where Patrick Henry had made his stirring speech against American preachers and the old tavern where Henry had once tended bar. A few houses bore signs of a recent skirmish. John Esten Cooke sketched the place:

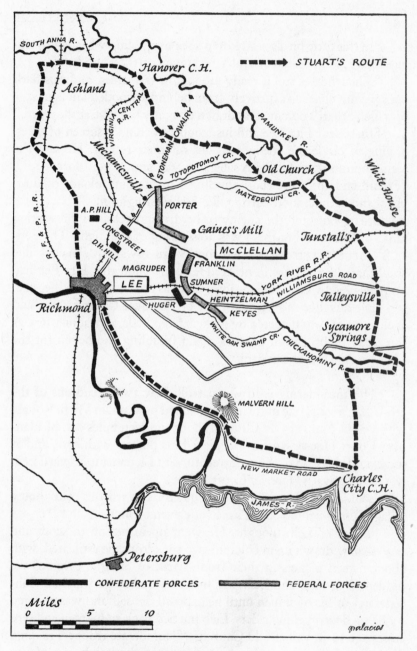

SOUTH ANNA R.

STUART'S ROUTE

•Ashland

Hanover C.H.

PAMUNKEY R.

VIRGINIA CENTRAL R.R.

STONEMAN CAVALRY

Mechanicsville

TOTOPOTOMOY CR.

Old Church

White House

R. F. & P. R. R.

MATEDEQUIN CR.

A.P. HILL

PORTER

•Gaines's Mill

LONGSTREET

McCLELLAN

Tunstall's

D.H. HILL

FRANKLIN

MAGRUDER

YORK RIVER R.R.

WILLIAMSBURG ROAD

LEE

SUMNER

Talleysville

Richmond

HUGER

HEINTZELMAN

KEYES

WHITE OAK SWAMP CR.

Sycamore
Springs

CHICKAHOMINY R.

MALVERN HILL

NEW MARKET ROAD

Charles
City C.H.

JAMES R.

Petersburg

CONFEDERATE FORCES   FEDERAL FORCES

Miles

0   5   10

palacios

FIRST FAME: STUART CIRCLES MC CLELLAN

June 12–15, 1862

"In this little bird's nest, lost in a sea of rippling wheat and waving foliage, some Yankee cavalry had taken up their abode.

"Their horses stood ready saddled in the street, and this dark mass we now gazed at furtively from behind a wooded knoll, in rear of which Stuart's column was drawn up ready to move at the word."

Stuart sent Fitz Lee and his troopers behind a screen of trees, hoping to circle the enemy and cut off their retreat. He sent the main column downhill with sabers drawn, and as von Borcke said, "Friend and foe were soon enveloped in blinding clouds of dust, pistol and carbine shots darting like flashes of lightning."

Stuart expected the enemy to be driven back into the waiting ranks of Fitz Lee, but there was no slowing of the flight. The Federals, about 150 strong, turned southward toward Mechanicsville, and Stuart let them go in peace. He soon found that Fitz Lee had been delayed by crossing a swamp, and was too late to close the road.

The advance moved south out of Hanover Court House, and at eleven A.M. was detected by pickets from Federal headquarters. A three-day nightmare of confusion and fumbling had begun for the Union command on this flank.

This meandering road was patrolled by two squadrons of the 5th U.S. Cavalry, one of them commanded by Captain W. B. Royall, who was in camp at Old Church, about eighteen miles east of Hanover Court House. Royall had placed his pickets with care, and at six A.M. of this Friday, June thirteenth, sent Lieutenant Edward Leib westward toward Hanover Court House.

Leib and F Company trotted quietly toward the court house village. They sighted Stuart's men at eleven o'clock.

"Pickets," Leib thought. He went up in person to scout and saw cavalry drawn up in column; two squadrons, he estimated, with about fifteen pickets in their front. Most of Stuart's column was hidden from him, and Leib was unsure whether he watched Confederates or his own men until he exposed himself and was charged by half a dozen yelling riders. Leib hurried back to his men and sent a message to Royall at Old Church: "Confederate troopers raiding. Two squadrons strong. Nothing to worry about." It was eleven thirty.

Leib pulled his men back, keeping out of sight of the raiders, and hurried toward safety.

There was as yet no suspicion anywhere in the Federal army that Stuart was cutting behind it in force.

The road went past remote landmarks: Taliaferro's Mill, Enon Church, and into Hawes Shop, the site of a wagon factory and forge. Here Leib halted and sent back a second report, giving his position.

Captain Royall replied with an order to fall back to Old Church, just as a sudden rush of Stuart's advance overwhelmed Leib's small picket and forced another retreat. Leib got off an appeal for help. He recalled the scene:

"I drew up in line under the brow of a hill on the side of the road, intending if my force were sufficient to charge; if not, to keep them in check with the pistol. . . . The enemy came on in large numbers. . . . I felt most seriously the superiority of the enemy, who were armed with rifles and shot-guns. . . . After I had emptied all of my pistols, I drew sabers and endeavored to charge, but finding they were coming up in greatly superior force on either flank and in front, I thought it best to fall back."[5]

Things had a different look from Stuart's column. Cooke saw the skirmish open:

"A Federal officer at the head of a detachment came on at full gallop, very nearly ran into the head of our column, and then seeing the dense mass of gray coats, fired his pistol, wheeled short about and went back at full speed."

Stuart bellowed: "Form fours! Draw sabers! Charge!" The column pounded ahead and in a chase of two or three miles took several prisoners. Fitz Lee found himself among his prewar regiment, and halted to question captured troopers: "Is Robinson still sergeant? Is Brown alive? Where's old Jones?" The Federals laughed with the twenty-five-year-old colonel.

Stuart had the 9th Virginia in front, and its riders pressed the Federals so hard that an attempted stand at a bridge of the Totopotomoy was swept aside; flanking columns splashed the creek on either side, and pursuit continued.

The chase would remain a memory with Stuart, who saw in the Ninth's adjutant, Lieutenant W. T. Robins, a man after his heart:

"On, on dashed Robins, here skirting a field, there leaping a fence or ditch, and clearing the woods beyond, when not far from Old Church, the enemy made a stand, having been reenforced."

Jeb could attack only in columns of fours along the road, and his final thought was: "I preferred to oppose the enemy with one squadron at a time, remembering that he who brings on the field the last cavalry reserve wins the day."

The next squadron went up. Its commander was Captain William Latané, a daring, handsome boy who was a great favorite with the command. Fighting spread into a woodland. Stuart poured in more troops, and the enemy broke. But Latané, riding down the nearest Federal officer, clashed with Captain Royall, who had come up with reinforcements. Latané cut a gash in the Federal's arm and chest, but Royall shot him with a pistol. Latané fell. A few gray troopers clustered about him as the column hammered on; he was dying.

The Federal horsemen wheeled twice more to receive charges, but were always driven by Stuart's yelling riders. The gray advance soon scattered, however, and Jeb called up Fitz Lee with the 1st Virginia to take the lead. Lee pleaded with his commander.

"My old regiment's camp is just over there through the woods," he said. "The old Second—the one they now call the Fifth. Let me clean it out."

Stuart sent him off with a warning that he must not be long about the task.

Lee burst into the camp of the Federal 5th, looting and burning. Von Borcke saw it as an inspiring spectacle: "The whole camp was enveloped in one blaze, hundreds of tents burning together . . . wonderfully beautiful. Many horses and mules, and two captured standards, were carried off with us."

The Prussian aide, staring through the woodlands from the roadway near Old Church, thought he saw the house occupied by General McClellan, surrounded by an ocean of white tents. He estimated the distance at two and a half miles.

Stuart now hesitated, and gathered the command. He later wrote:

"Here was the turning point of the expedition. Two routes were before me—the one to return by Hanover Court House, the other to pass around through New Kent, taking the chances of having to swim the Chickahominy, and make a bold effort to cut the enemy's lines of communication."

In brief, Stuart contemplated riding entirely around McClellan's army, completing a circle to Richmond of almost one hundred miles.

He reasoned that since he was already eighteen miles southeast of Hanover Court House, the enemy would expect him to retrace his steps and could intercept him.

He already knew what Lee had sent him to learn: The right flank of McClellan was "in the air" north of the Chickahominy. There were no trenches on the vital ridge near Totopotomoy Creek; the enemy could be struck in the flank by an infantry assault.

Esten Cooke was sitting his horse beside Stuart when the chief made up his mind:

"I looked at him. He was evidently reflecting. In a moment he turned round to me and said, 'Tell Fitz Lee to come along. I'm going to move on with my column.'"

Cooke had no doubts, from that instant, that Stuart planned to circle the enemy.

"I think the quicker we move now the better," Cooke said.

"Right," Stuart said. "Tell the column to move on at a trot."

The pace picked up. "The gayest portion of the ride," Cooke said, had begun. But he figured their chances of getting through alive at one in ten. "It was neck or nothing, now," he wrote.

The men went at half speed, picking up enemy stragglers and seizing wagons. They took wagons of champagne and cigars destined for some Federal general, and there was a quick popping of corks; officers stopped it soon, however, and the wagons burned.

There was an alarm: "Yankees in the rear!" The column whirled about, but there was nothing behind. A roar of laughter swept the column, and recurred through most of the afternoon. At almost every house women and children ran to the roadside, and riders jumped from saddles to embrace women, mothers, sisters, sweethearts. Cooke recalled: "These went quite wild at the sight of their sons and brothers. They laughed and cried and clapped their

hands and fell into ecstasies of delight." One young woman threw
her arms around a gray trooper, a brother she had not seen since the
start of the war, "bursting into alternate sobs and laughter."

The column raced on, every man aware of the enemy network
lying near them, but caught in something of the exhilaration Stuart
felt:

> The hope of striking a serious blow at a boastful and in-
> solent foe, which would make him tremble in his shoes, made
> more agreeable the alternative I chose.

He added:

> There was something of the sublime in the implicit con-
> fidence and unquestioning trust of the rank and file in a leader
> guiding them straight, apparently, into the very jaws of the
> enemy, every step appearing to them to diminish the faintest
> hope of extrication.

As Stuart's advance galloped within sight of enemy depots on
the Pamunkey River, the Federal high command in his rear reacted
strangely to news of the raid.

The Federal cavalry commander was Stuart's father-in-law,
Philip St. George Cooke, who was in camp three or four miles from
the site of the skirmish between Stuart's vanguard and the pickets of
Lieutenant Lieb.

Captain Royall got his first message from Lieb about noon, and
sent up support, but the first message sent to General Cooke was
hurried off much later. It was ten minutes before three P.M. when
a lieutenant gave Cooke a dispatch announcing the raid.

Cooke wrote: "I immediately sounded 'To horse,' and ordered
six squadrons . . . to reenforce." These bluecoats were moving by
three P.M., and "half an hour later" drove in Confederate pickets
near Hanover Courthouse; the gray riders ran. A man in a nearby
house told the pursuers the story: From 3,000 to 5,000 Rebel cavalry, with artillery, passed eastward half an hour before. The commander of the party, Major Lawrence Williams, thought this an

exaggeration—but he also picked up a report that Confederate infantry had been seen, a serious matter indeed.

Williams sent a platoon in the tracks of Stuart's column.

Back in General Cooke's headquarters, things moved more slowly. Cooke had called up some infantry support, but did not stir from his camp himself until eight P.M. when, with some cavalry and artillery, he marched for the scene of Stuart's first skirmish. He got there about ten P.M. A bluecoat infantry brigade had outmarched him there.

Already, it seemed, officers were looking askance at General Cooke, wondering if his strange lethargy stemmed from his affection for his daughter's husband.

General Fitz John Porter, commander of the sector, said: "I can only express surprise that General Cooke . . . did not join earlier his command in front and there act as circumstances required, and that when General Cooke did pursue, he should have tied his legs with the infantry command.

"I have seen no energy or spirit in the pursuit by General Cooke of the enemy or [seen] exhibited the characteristics of a skillful and active guardian of our flanks."

General Cooke was aroused "about every half hour" during the night by orders from superiors. At midnight he was ordered to make large detachments from his force.

One order said that General Sykes had been directed to take command of Cooke's force, and would arrive in the morning. Another from General Porter, arriving at eleven P.M., ordered him to bring "all the information concerning the enemy you can get hold of." Half an hour later, he was ordered to "hold your own, and maintain your position. Do not attack a superior force."

About midnight there was word that the enemy was a little over a mile away, in the Hanover road. Cooke gave orders to march, but soon found that the report was false. He called off the movement and marched instead to Old Church. It was after daylight when he began the chase. He expected, he said, to meet the enemy momentarily in the hot morning of June fourteenth. By then, the gray column had left him hopelessly behind. There was only smoking debris to mark its trail.[6]

Stuart was now among McClellan's vital lines of supply, and at almost every turn of the road the squadrons found wagons to burn and stores to destroy. The column went past Bassett, Smith's Store, over Matadequin Creek. As he passed a homestead called Garlick's, Stuart sent two squadrons to a landing on the Pamunkey, where they found two Union transports at dock, loaded with the wagon trains of two New York regiments. They put both to the torch, and smoke rose through the late afternoon.

By now even John Esten Cooke, galloping up and down the column on Stuart's errands, was wondering whether his uncle, the Federal cavalry commander, was not remiss in his duty, since there was no sign of pursuit.

Esten Cooke "laughed and joked" with the men to keep up their morale, but the strain already told on him; he was falling asleep in the saddle now and then, and would count twenty-five such lapses before the ride was over.

The column now swept down on Tunstall's Station, a depot where the road crossed the York River Railroad. Signs of Federal alarm were everywhere, wagons overturned, stores scattered.

A Negro man hailed them admiringly at the roadside, mistaking them for Union troops: "We got Richmond yet, boss? If we ain't, 't'won't be long, for McClellan and our boys is sure to fotch her!"

At Tunstall's, Stuart called artillery from the rear.

The nearest gun had fallen "into a tremendous mudhole." Its wheels sank to the axle in the pit, and neither popping whips nor swearing drivers could budge it.

One of Stuart's German-born sergeants shouted in inspiration, "Gat, Lieutenant, it can't be done! But put that keg on the gun, Lieutenant!"

A small barrel of captured whisky was placed on the gun, provoking "an exhibition of herculean muscularity." Cooke wrote:

"With eyes fixed ardently upon the keg, the powerful cannoneers waded into the mudhole up to their knees, seized the wheels of gun and caisson loaded down with ammunition, and just simply lifted the whole out, and put them on firm ground."

The gun wheeled ahead, flinging mud, its wonder-working keg drained at the gallop by the thirsty gunners. Stuart found no need for the gun, after all. His scouts took the station without firing a shot, overpowering the fifteen or twenty pickets there. They cut the telegraph wires and went to work at tearing up the rails.

From the West, in billows of smoke, came a Federal train, bound for Tunstall's and the White House landing. Stuart hurried troopers beside the tracks, and waited as the train bore down upon them. Riders galloped with it, calling on the engineer to halt the train and surrender.

Captain Farley, riding with von Borcke, took the Prussian's blunderbuss and shot the engineer as he opened his throttle. Firing broke out, and as von Borcke said, "a battle of the strangest description now arose." The bluecoats huddled on their speeding flatcars in the open, returning the shots of Stuart's riders. After a few volleys the train was out of range to all except excited troopers like von Borcke, who gave chase with a revolver, plunging down the embankment and firing almost in the faces of the enemy. The train fled out of sight and the column halted. It was near sunset.

Just four miles beyond, on the Pamunkey, was Rooney Lee's plantation home, White House, now the chief Federal base, rich in supplies, where gunboats and loaded supply transports awaited looting. Lee probably urged Stuart to strike at this tempting target, and Jeb confessed he "could scarcely resist it," but he turned to the affairs at hand.

He had his men burn the nearby Black Creek bridge and a long wagon train abandoned by the enemy. Freight cars at the station, filled with hay and forage, were soon aflame, telegraph poles were felled, and, as Stuart wrote, the flames "illuminated the country for miles."

In this glow, and the dusty light of the full moon, Stuart turned them southwest on the long route toward Richmond. There was still the flooded river ahead of them, and there would be no safety until they had crossed it.

Von Borcke rejoiced at the close of the day: "My parched tongue was cleaving to the roof of my mouth, when one of our men galloped up to me, and held out a bottle of champagne, saying, 'Captain, you did pretty hot work today. I got this bottle for you out of McClellan's wagon. It will do you good.' Never in my life have I enjoyed a bottle of wine so much."

Stuart drove them on as darkness fell, trying to keep the column closed up, pushing the vanguard in the direction of the river.

Somewhere along this section of the route the renowned New York reporter, George Alfred Townsend, riding after news of the raiders, was almost snatched up by Stuart's men. He was startled by bluecoats riding by him "as if the foul fiend was at their heels."

"The Rebels are behind!" one shouted. Townsend wrote: "I heard the crack of carbines behind ... buried myself in underbrush. ... The roadway seemed shaken by a hundred hoofs. The imperceptible horsemen yelled like a war party of Comanches, and the carbines rang ahead, as if some bloody work was being done at every rod."

Townsend found the flaming wreckage of the Federal supply train, railroad cars and buildings. He rode to the White House landing and found panic; steamers had fled downstream, tradesmen were leaving, and soldiers were in turmoil. There was no sign of pursuit of the Confederates.[7]

Far behind Stuart, behind even the incipient Federal pursuit, the lone Confederate casualty, Captain Latané, was buried. Latané's younger brother, James, a minister, dropped out of Stuart's ranks and waited with the body at the roadside "while the ruck of pursuit swept by." He then hailed a corn cart and with the aid of its Negro driver emptied it of corn and carried the captain's body to Westwood, the plantation of Mrs. Catherine Brockenbrough, a few miles away. The mistress of the plantation sent James to rejoin Stuart with a fresh horse, and with the aid of a neighbor, Mrs. Willoughby Newton, and a few slaves buried Latané in a slave-made casket, covered with a cavalry cape. They could find no minister, and held services in the graveyard of the nearby plantation Summer Hill with their Negro workmen, a scene soon to be celebrated throughout the Confederacy by poets and painters.[8]

Southeast from Tunstall's Station toward the river was the settlement of Talleysville. Stuart urged his column along the road to that place. It was none too easy, for, as Stuart recorded: "The roads at this point were far worse than ours, and the artillery had much difficulty in passing. Our march was finally continued by bright moonlight."

The vanguard soon reached the "three or four houses known as Talleysville," with several Federal hospitals nearby. Stuart said, "I deemed it proper not to molest the surgeons and attendants in charge."

The command lay there until midnight to give stragglers a chance to catch up and close the column. The troopers pounced upon a few sutlers and their wagons, and ate the delicacies intended for the enemy. Cooke ate "in succession" figs, beef tongue, pickle, candy, tomato catsup, preserves, lemons, cakes, sausages, molasses, crackers, canned meats.

John Mosby found the summer night: "A carnival of fun I can never forget. Nobody thought of danger or sleep, when champagne bottles were bursting and wine was flowing in copious streams. All had perfect confidence in their leader. . . . The discipline of the soldiers for a while gave way to the wild revelry of Comus."[9]

The riders in Stuart's front were from the New Kent County company of the 3rd Virginia, natives who knew every trail. Private Richard Frayser had led them from Old Church to Tunstall's, and when Stuart turned south toward the Chickahominy, he called on a new guide, Lieutenant Jonas Christian, who had a scheme for escape.

Christian's home, Sycamore Springs, lay along the Chickahominy below Long Bridge—a crossing sure to be under guard. A private ford at Sycamore would give the column a hidden passage. Christian assured Stuart that this ford had always been passable in the memory of the oldest inhabitants. Not even the recent rains should make it difficult. The column rode in that direction, the river now seven miles away.

As Stuart left Talleysville, Federal troops arrived at Tunstall's, only four miles behind to the north.

Esten Cooke left a vivid sketch of the column plodding toward the river whose crossing meant safety:

"The highway lay before us, white in the unclouded splendor of the moon. The critical moment was yet to come. . . . The exhaustion of the march now began to tell on the men. Whole companies went to sleep in the saddle, and Stuart himself was no exception. He had thrown one knee over the pommel of his saddle, folded his arms, dropped the bridle, and—chin on breast, his plumed hat drooping over his forehead—was sound asleep. His sure-footed horse moved steadily, but the form of the General tottered from side to side, and for miles I held him erect by the arm."

The column thus moved on during the remainder of the night, the wary advance guard encountering no enemies and giving no alarm. At the first streak of dawn the Chickahominy was in sight.

Stuart spurred out of the highway, along the farm lane leading to the river.

Rooney Lee was among the first riders Christian led to the stream. The men gazed in dismay at the dark waters surging high over the ford.

Rooney Lee wasted no time. The commanding general's son stripped off most of his clothes and rode his horse into the coffee-colored river, followed by a few of his men. They struggled against the current until they floundered among the roots on the far bank, and it was clear that the whole column could not cross in this way. Lee and his party recrossed the river. Stuart watched him reflectively. Cooke noted that the only sign of Stuart's concern was "a peculiar fashion of twisting his beard." Otherwise, he looked "cool and dangerous."

Cooke helped Lee to emerge from the stream.

"What do you think of the situation, Colonel?" Cooke asked.

The huge boy replied, "Well, Captain, I think we are caught."

The men on the bank of the stream evidently agreed with Rooney. Cooke thought that in any other but this desperate moment the troopers would be laughable:

"Some sprawled flat, half-asleep, still holding their bridles; others were asleep in the saddles, their heads hanging almost to the pommels; some gnawed on captured crackers or figs, or smoked, and looked about, yawning."

Cooke tried to cheer them up. "It's all right," he said.

The men stared at him "as sane men regard a lunatic."

But Stuart soon put them to work. The first attempt was to fell trees across the river, but as the great trunks splashed into the water they were swept downstream, and this effort was abandoned.

Stuart called for Corporal Turner Doswell and sent him to General Lee with a dispatch. He wanted the army to make a diversion for him on the Charles City Road to draw the attention of the Federals. He described his plight at the swollen river, but assured the commander he would get the column across somehow.

Stuart gave up the crossing at Christian's ford and took the column downstream to the ruins of Forge Bridge, whose abutments were still standing. Jeb put out a rear guard, set up Breathed's cannon, and put Henry Hagan and Redmond Burke to rebuilding the bridge. With a small squad the resourceful scouts worked a miracle.

While the men worked, Mosby watched Stuart, who was "lying down on the bank of the stream, in the gayest humor I ever saw, laughing at the prank he had played on McClellan."

Troopers ripped boards and timbers from an abandoned barn, and Burke soon had a rickety foot bridge to the island in midstream, stout enough to pass men who walked, holding the bridles of their horses as they swam on the downriver side of the bridge. About half the column went over in this way.

Within three hours Burke and Hagan had made the bridge sounder, using the main timbers of the old barn, which were long enough to span the crossing by a matter of inches. Now artillery and wagons bowled over, and safety lay ahead.

At the moment of completing the bridge, Stuart was helping to fit the planks in place, singing as he worked. The last man to cross was Fitz Lee, who followed the rear guard.

On the far side of the island in the river the way was barred by fords little more than mudholes, and the column splashed quickly through them. In front bluecoat prisoners rode some of the hundreds of captured mules; many rode two to a mule, and frequently fell into the shallow swamp. Guards laughed at the cursing prisoners, and Cooke recorded their protests: "How many damned Chicken Hominies are there in this infernal country?"

When Fitz Lee had herded over the last of his men, smoke

began to curl from the quickly raised bridge. Fire soon ate through the dry old timbers and dropped them into the stream.

Through the smoke the rear guard saw the first of the Federals to reach the riverside: A few cavalrymen in blue on weary horses. A shot was fired. Fitz Lee took his men out of sight. The hopelessness of pursuit would creep into the report of Colonel Richard Rush of the Sixth Pennsylvania Cavalry—the proud Philadelphia Lancers:

His major, Robert Morris, Rush said, had led a bold chase, commanding the pursuit to within four miles of the Rebels at their bridge. But when Rush took over, for some unexplained reason, it required three hours to move horsemen four miles to the river. In the words of Rush's report:

"At 2:45 I reached the Sycamore farm, and seeing smoke over the woods ahead, sent forward Major Morris, with eight carbineers. He soon returned, reporting that a mile beyond the woods he had come up to the bridge over the Chickahominy, which was broken and burning, watched by five men on the other side. He fired one shot at them, when they mounted and ran. I scouted the woods for an hour all about the Sycamore farm and mill, but getting no more trace of the rebels, and feeling satisfied that all had crossed the river, I returned with my command to Tunstall's."[10]

There was no thought of chasing the Rebels over the Chickahominy. There was only praise for Major Morris, who had followed the trail of the retreating Rebels in the morning.

A couple of hours earlier General McClellan had sent a telegram to Washington:

A rebel force of cavalry and artillery, variously estimated at from 1,000 to 5,000, came around our right flank last evening, attacked and drove in a picket guard of two squadrons of cavalry stationed at Old Church; thence they proceeded to a landing three miles above White House, where they burned two forage schooners and destroyed some wagons. They then struck the railroad at Tunstall's Station, fired into a train, killing some five or six. Here they met a force of infantry which I sent down to meet them, when they ran off. I have several cavalry detachments out after them, and hope to punish them. No damage has been done to the railroad.

Stuart gave the column no rest until it was some miles from the river, for Richmond was still thirty-five miles away, and there was danger of attack from the flank of McClellan's army.

Jeb stopped for a few minutes to drink coffee in the home of Thomas Christian, not far from the river. When the vanguard reached Charles City Court House, near the banks of the James, Stuart called a halt. He and his staff went to the hospitable mansion of Judge Isaac Christian in the village, and his men went on to Buckland, the home of Colonel J. M. Wilcox. After thirty-six hours in the saddle, the troopers needed no invitation. They fell asleep in lawns and fields and did not stir until after sunset, when Stuart prepared to leave for Richmond to report to General Lee. Fitz Lee was left in command with orders to move the column at eleven P.M.

Mosby thought their chief "gay as a lark," despite his two days and nights without sleep.

Esten Cooke thought the general would take a longer rest, but Jeb understood the army's need for information on the Federal flank, and was impatient to be off.

Cooke had an interesting conversation with Jeb.

"I believe General Cooke really tried to catch us there across the river," Stuart said.

"I can't believe it," Cooke said.

"Yes, the General is a man who'll do his duty up to the handle."

"Granted," Cooke replied, "but he was a poor cavalry officer if he couldn't find the tracks of 1,200 cavalry in a big road, and catch them ten miles off in twelve hours."

Esten Cooke thought Stuart too devoted to his father-in-law to condemn him.[11]

"I'm going to Richmond," Stuart said. "Would you like to ride with me?"

But Esten's horse was worn out, and he had to stay behind. Jeb trotted off with a small party of couriers as escort; his guide was Captain Richard Frayser. He rode the thirty miles before daylight, across country partly covered by Federal patrols. There was a halt at Rowland's Mill, six miles from Charles City Court House, where Jeb stopped for another cup of strong coffee. When they reached Richmond, Jeb turned toward Lee's headquarters. He sent Frayser to tell Governor John Letcher the news, and to advise Flora that he was safely home.

Frayser was at first rebuffed by a sleepy servant at the Executive Mansion, but insisted until he was led to Letcher's bedroom, where he found the governor and Dr. John Mayo, an old friend, in a huge bed. The youth told stories of the raid for the old men, as they laughed over Stuart's exploits. The governor promised sabers for Stuart and Frayser, and soon delivered them; Jeb's was a handsome ceremonial sword fit to commemorate the famed ride.

The Richmond *Dispatch* praised the men of the raid and published an article on its worth:

> "What, then, was the result?" asked we of a wearied, dusty trooper watering his jaded and faithful animal by a roadside spring. "The result?" answered he, proudly but much exhausted. "The result? We have been in the saddle from Thursday morning until Saturday noon, never breaking rein or breakfast. We have whipped the enemy wherever he dared to appear—never opposing more than equal forces. We have burned two hundred wagons . . . sunk or fired three large transports, captured three hundred horses and mules, brought in 170 prisoners, four officers and many Negroes, killed and wounded scores of the enemy, and had one man killed, poor Captain Latané. This is the result, and three million dollars cannot cover the Federal loss in goods alone."

Stuart's report glowed with colorful phrases, and at times the rhetoric was almost epic, as in his praise of the work of his lieutenants at the crossing of the river:

> Their brave men behaved with coolness and intrepidity in danger, unswerving resolution before difficulties, and stood unappalled before the rushing torrent of the Chickahominy, with the probability of an enemy at their heels armed with the fury of a tigress robbed of her whelps.

It had more of the sound of an imperial order to troops than a report on a reconnaissance in force—but Stuart's congratulatory order to the 1,200 troopers was in the same vein. He also gave them a new battle cry: "Avenge Latané!" He seemed to resent bitterly even this single casualty as the price of a breath-taking raid.

Stuart singled out many for praise, not forgetting his scouts, surgeon, Cooke, von Borcke, Mosby, Hagan and many others. He urged promotions for his men: Fitz Lee and Rooney Lee to be brigadiers; Lieutenant Colonel Martin to be full colonel; for von Borcke, "this deserving man who has cast his lot with us in this trying hour," he asked the highest possible rank which could be conferred. He also spoke for Burke, Farley and Robins.

General Lee's order in reply reflected the pride of the command in Stuart's feat:

> The general commanding announces with great satisfaction to the army the brilliant exploit of Brig. Gen. J. E. B. Stuart . . . in passing around the rear of the whole Federal army, taking a number of prisoners, and destroying and capturing stores to a large amount. . . . The expedition recrossed the Chickahominy almost in the presence of the enemy with the same coolness and address that marked every step of its progress. . . .
>
> The general commanding takes great pleasure in expressing his admiration of the courage and skill so conspicuously exhibited throughout by the general and the officers and men under his command.

But it was, after all, the quiet talk in the privacy of headquarters that presaged great days for the army. Robert Lee could look at the maps of the Chickahominy country and trace the dominating ridge north of that river, certain that the way was open for attack. Now he could move with hope of driving the enemy with his inferior force. Stuart reported that he was ready to lead Jackson into position.

Orders went out to Stonewall, in the Valley. He was to screen his rear and pull the victorious little Foot Cavalry into the Richmond theater. Haste and secrecy were vital.

As the army planned its first great offensive, critics already wondered what Stuart's gaudy raid had accomplished. Perhaps it served only to warn the enemy. But daily scouts showed no change

in the Federal line, and McClellan lay still, as if unaware that Lee
knew most of his dispositions. The raid gave a great boost to the
morale of Richmond and the Confederacy at large. It left Stuart in
gay spirits, at any rate.

Esten Cooke said to him, "That was a tight place at the river,
General. If the enemy had come, would you have surrendered?"

"No, there was one course left—to die game."

And he joked with Longstreet: "I left one general behind me."

"Who's that, Jeb?"

"General Consternation."

☆

CHAPTER 8

A Week of Miracles

LATE June, 1862, at cavalry headquarters was an idyll. Flora was visiting Stuart and had with her four-year-old young Flora and Jimmy, who was two. Stuart rolled on the floors at play with the children and sat in the farmhouse parlor to hear his wife sing.

Red and white roses bloomed in sheets on the walls of the house, and von Borcke was almost overcome by odors of the roses, wild honeysuckle and magnolias.

On June twentieth, "with a significant smile," Stuart sent von Borcke to the War Department in nearby Richmond. The German returned with a commission as captain of cavalry.

Captain Blackford returned to Stuart, too, this time as an engineer officer.

There were signs of a mysterious move by the army. Brigades were forever shifting position along the swamp roads.

Marching orders came to Stuart's headquarters late at night, June twenty-fifth. The regiments were in the saddle by midnight, but there was no moon, and the men could not see in the blackness; they did not move until dawn.

Stuart gave Cooke a dispatch. "This must be in the hands of our special messenger by daylight," Jeb said.

Cooke glanced at the sealed envelope. It read: "Gen. T. J. Jackson, Somewhere."

The war had abruptly changed. Cooke realized that a major attack on McClellan was under way, and that Jackson, who only yesterday was reported facing the enemy in the Shenandoah Valley, had by some miracle leaped across Virginia.

Cooke rode off on his errand.

The column moved north at dawn and by afternoon had halted around the village of Ashland, sixteen miles above Richmond. The corps had grown. Stuart had 2,000 riders: Fitz Lee and his 1st Virginia, Rooney Lee with the 9th Virginia, Wickham's 4th Virginia under a captain, Colonel Will Martin's Jeff Davis Legion, the Hampton Legion, Pelham's Artillery, and a new regiment, Colonel T. R. R. Cobb's Georgia Legion. He left behind four regiments under Colonel Tom Rosser to guard the main army.

In the late afternoon, near Ashland, the troopers discovered the startling secret of General Robert Lee's strategy. The road was suddenly filled with dusty infantrymen. Someone caught sight of the leading officer—Jackson. Men cheered.

Captain Blackford was excited by the arrival of these confident troops from the West, and by the travel-worn Jackson, whom the cavalrymen had last seen in action almost a year before, at Manassas. Jackson stopped to shake hands and talk with Stuart. Jackson's infantry cheered as it passed them. "They knew well enough what was brewing," Blackford thought, as they saw Stuart and Jackson in earnest conversation.

Blackford got a vivid impression of Stonewall: "Then thirty-eight years of age, a little over medium height, of compact muscular build . . . careless about his dress . . . and though clean . . . dressed in a threadbare, faded semi-military suit, with a disreputable old Virginia Military Institute cap drawn down over his eyes."

There was a striking contrast as Jackson sat with Stuart's young officers, elegant in Confederate gray, with polished boots and black plumes in their hats.

The troops went into camp. Jackson ordered his division to move against the enemy at two thirty A.M. in an effort to make up lost time.

Stuart was to guide Jackson to McClellan's unprotected flank which he had discovered the previous week. Stonewall was the northernmost wing of the attack; below him, and on roughly parallel routes, the divisions under A. P. Hill, D. H. Hill and Longstreet would push against the Federals. General Lee was staking everything on a sweep from his Richmond trenches against the enemy flank. Much depended on Jackson, whose troops were the army's most experienced. And Stonewall was already late, having several times lost his way in the unfamiliar swamp country.

Jackson was expected to pry loose McClellan's right somewhere near Beaver Dam Creek and force the Federals to evacuate the village of Mechanicsville. That done, the Hills and Longstreet would advance their big forces and Lee might destroy his adversary.[1]

Jackson's troops crossed the Virginia Central Railroad before daylight and pushed eastward. Von Borcke was near Stuart, and wrote: "With the exception of encounters with small patrols, we saw little of the enemy until five o'clock in the afternoon, when Jackson's vanguard attacked them, and was soon engaged in a sharp skirmish."

This action came at a bridge over Totopotomoy Creek, near their objective at Beaver Dam. Jackson seemed slow. His Maryland gunners answered Federal batteries in a thick woodland, but though the advance crossed the bridge after extinguishing flames set by the enemy, Jackson halted.

There was cannon fire and musketry from the south. There, unknown to Stonewall, A. P. Hill had grown impatient, and despite orders to await word from Jackson, had attacked at Mechanicsville; on that field casualties were mounting.

For some reason, Jackson, though behind schedule, seemed to think he had done enough for the day. He sat withdrawn and aloof, taking little interest in affairs. Stuart's amazement did not get into the official records, but he watched Jackson, stroking his beard in his familiar gesture of perplexity as he saw the smoke of roaring battle to the south.[2]

Jackson's men, in any event, were cooking supper while A. P. Hill's men were dying before the Federal rifle pits to the south—with the vulnerable end of McClellan's line almost within Stonewall's grasp.

The pickets in Jackson's front found no enemy in the night, and daylight revealed that McClellan had retreated. The line was abandoned from Beaver Dam to Mechanicsville and beyond. General Lee ordered a pursuit, and again gave Jackson a vital role: He would command D. H. Hill's force in addition to his own. Below him Long-

street and A. P. Hill drove eastward on the heels of the retreating
Federals. Stuart remained with Jackson.

Thousands of troops choked the roads and waded the shallow
brown streams. Firing was sparse, but as noon approached and Lee
moved the men of Longstreet and A. P. Hill into position, Federal
resistance became stronger. The enemy had made a stand somewhere
ahead. A battle flared around a swampy place called Gaines' Mill.
More than 50,000 bluecoats were digging in, their front especially
forbidding along a series of ravines crowned by earthworks and
sharpened logs.

Lee's headquarters became impatient as the day lengthened.
Nothing had been heard from Jackson. Lee sent an aide to find him,
and at last went out in search of Stonewall himself. Jackson found
his way through this landscape with difficulty, and was once led out
of his path by a native guide because of a misunderstanding about
place names: Cold Harbor and Old Cold Harbor, both near Gaines'
Mill.

Jackson and Lee met at one P.M., but this did not speed the attack, for the left flank still dragged as the rest of the army went into
action. D. H. Hill's men lay strung along a roadway, pinned down
by cannon fire. For several hours no one seemed to know where
Jackson was.

Stuart's command was not idle. Esten Cooke was with Jeb much
of the day, amid "shelling hotter than I ever knew it. . . . I followed
Stuart here, there, everywhere. Shells very quick and hot, evidently
directed by a signal man up a tree."

As they rode under fire, Cooke plunged forward on the neck of
his horse and tumbled to the ground. Stuart and the staff stared in
dismay, fearing that he had been killed.

"Hallo, Cooke, are you hit?" Stuart yelled.

Cooke leaped up, caught his horse and rejoined them. "I dodged
too far, General," he said sheepishly.

Jeb and the young men roared with laughter.

"You dodged too far, Cooke!" Stuart said. It was only the first
of his interminable jokes about the incident at Cooke's expense.

The troopers made quick work of the first Federal cavalry
sighted. Captain Blackford felt "a creeping of the flesh" as he saw

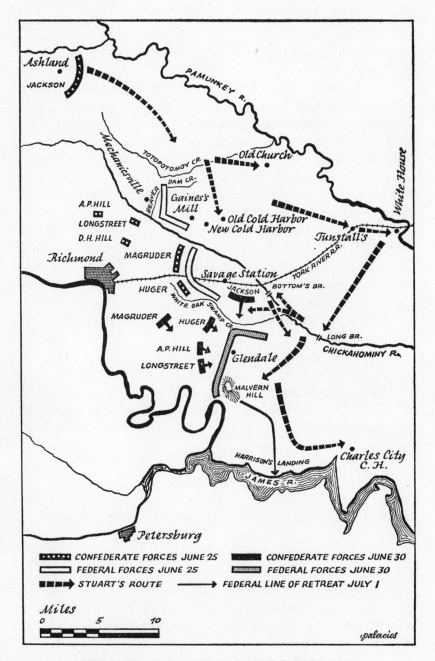

THE SEVEN DAYS: STUART IN THE ENEMY REAR

some Union Lancers drawn up in a field with steel-tipped spears glistening.

Stuart threw a regiment into line three hundred yards from the enemy and charged. Von Borcke said: "But before our Virginia horsemen got within fifty yards of their line, this magnificent regiment . . . turned tail and fled in disorder, strewing the whole line of their retreat with their picturesque but inconvenient arms. The entire skirmish was over in less time than is required to record it; and I do not believe that out of the whole body of 700 men more than twenty retained their lances."

As fighting concentrated, the cavalry was drawn up in fields in the rear of Old Cold Harbor. Cooke was sent to investigate the front and to find Jackson. He discovered Stonewall "sitting on a log near an old tumbledown log house, in his old sun-yellowed tilt-forward cap and dingy coat."

"General, I am on General Stuart's staff. He wishes to know your dispositions."

"Wait a moment," Jackson said.

"General Stuart is just across there—he could ride over."

"Ask him to gallop over," Jackson said.

Stuart soon came up and Jackson began changing the front of his fourteen brigades to bring them to the aid of Longstreet and A. P. Hill. Cavalry joined the move.

Jeb sent Pelham with two batteries to shell the enemy. The young Alabamian took guns into a field near Cold Harbor and opened fire. Federal shelling grew fiercer. Stuart, Jackson, Cooke, von Borcke and other officers rode forward. Cooke sketched it in his diary:

"Musketry terrible. Artillery duel in full roar. . . . Enemy trying it last time. . . . Stuart and Jackson in [the] thickest of it. . . .

"Not flurried one particle. Never cooler in my life. Laughing and voice steady, a sure sign with me. . . . Night coming on. Separated from Stuart. . . . Shelling awful. Whiz! Whiz-is-is-bang! whizzz! bang! whirrr!

"Went forward. . . . Our guns belching flame, and throwing shovelsful of fiery cinders from muzzles. Enemy's batteries silenced.

Found Stuart, rode forward with him to where the enemy had fired the fence and bushes on left of the road to draw our fire. . . .

"At the burning fence . . . D. H. Hill's men were heard cheering as they ran the enemy down the big hill where their twelve guns were."

The Federals had at last fallen back. Near the end of the day, when it seemed too late, Jackson's division had struck and pushed McClellan's line into the dark swamps.

Stuart and Cooke rode to the rear and halted under "a lofty, rugged and solitary oak, riven by cannon balls," where they made headquarters for the night.

During the day Cooke had halted for a moment in the yard of a Mrs. Johnson, where, he was told, General Philip St. George Cooke had made headquarters until the early morning. Stuart's father-in-law had lived in a small tent there, Mrs. Johnson said. Cooke recorded: "He is wretched, they say, and hopes the first ball will kill him."

The army had suffered horribly in the day: Some 8,000 casualties, almost half of them in Jackson's division. Many brigades were wrecked.

Stuart and Cooke had a visitor as they drowsed under their tree. At two A.M. of June twenty-eighth, as Cooke wrote, "a third personage rode up, dismounted, and lying down between us, began to converse."

"Yesterday was the most terrific fire of musketry I ever heard," the newcomer said. Cooke knew him at once in the darkness: "Anyone who had listened to the brief, low, abrupt voice would have recognized it. The speaker was Stonewall Jackson."

Jackson and Stuart talked for a few minutes, planning the continued chase of the enemy the next day. Cooke fell asleep.

Another diarist who had seen Stuart during the day and kept a vivid memory of it was Kyd Douglas of Jackson's staff. When Stonewall had called up batteries to support Pelham he said to an aide, "Ride to General Ewell and direct him, if the enemy do not retire before dusk, he must sweep them from that hill with the bayonet!"

Stuart sat nearby and cheered. "That's the order!" he said,

waving the plumed hat in the air. "Let one of my staff go with him. That order must not miscarry!"[8]

Daylight revealed a landscape of broken trees, burned thickets, and fields littered with dead. Jackson rode among the thousands of bodies, many of them John Hood's Texans, and paid tribute: "The men who carried this position were soldiers indeed."

Most of the Confederate army lay still in the morning, for General Lee had not yet puzzled out the intentions of McClellan. There were signs that the enemy was abandoning the base on the York and shifting southward to the James. Lee could not bring himself to believe that the aggressive McClellan had so soon abandoned his plan to attack Richmond. He called Stuart and Ewell to headquarters. Stuart would drive eastward to the nearest point of the York River Railroad and try to cut the enemy from their base. Ewell's infantry would move down the Chickahominy in the same direction, with Fitz Lee's cavalry as an advance guard.

Cooke had a lame horse and rode back into Richmond for a fresh one, and both he and von Borcke missed the day's action. The German watched enviously as Stuart left with the command, but found some excitement in camp, where the rumor spread that the Yankees had poisoned wells and springs in the region, and that hundreds of Confederates were dying in agony. But the sensible von Borcke concluded: "Although I do not love the Yankees, I am quite sure they were entirely innocent of this. The sufferers had been made ill by the too abundant use of bad apple brandy, which will kill anybody."

Stuart led his men toward the familiar territory through which they had galloped on the raid around the enemy. To the south, below the Chickahominy, dust clouds marked the path of McClellan's army.

The cavalry met no resistance until it was about six miles east of Old Cold Harbor, where it passed Ewell's infantry. At Dispatch Station, the first rail depot north of the Chickahominy, Jeb sent up a squadron of Cobb's Georgians and the enemy picket fled.

The cavalry turned northeast after troopers had cut telegraph wires and torn up tracks of the York River Railroad. Jeb notified

Ewell that he had struck the railroad, and sent General Lee word that the line seemed to be undefended. Jeb then gave another display of his creative interpretation of Lee's orders, taking matters into his own hands. As he explained in an official report:

"I determined to push boldly down the White House road, resolved to find what force was in that direction, and, if possible, rout it."[4]

He seized a train of wagons and its escort and galloped on. Cavalry pickets melted away before him. Prisoners told him that Generals Stoneman and Emory were near the White House with a strong force. Stuart wrote:

"The fleeing pickets had heralded the approach of what no doubt appeared to their affrighted mind to be the whole Army of The Valley, and from the valley of the Pamunkey a dense cloud of smoke revealed . . . the flight and destruction in the path of a stampeded foe."

The gray column hammered on. At Tunstall's Station, the last stop before White House, Stuart met the first serious opposition. He was called by skirmishers to inspect a Yankee position at Black Creek.

A Federal cavalry squadron sat on the opposite bank, and beyond was what seemed to be an artillery battery. The bridge over the stream had been burned, and the steep-banked creek, with miry approaches, could not be swum in the face of Federal fire. Stuart called for Pelham. A few shots from the guns dispersed the enemy cavalry and brought a surprise from the undergrowth along the stream. A neatly laid Federal ambush was flushed—scores of riflemen who had lain in hiding ready to halt a Confederate crossing. There was no reply from the guns on the hill beyond the enemy horsemen, and Stuart concluded that they were dummies.

Jeb sent over dismounted skirmishers under Captain Farley and they scoured the area for further signs of ambush; they found none.

The night was lit by the burning of White House, the estate of Rooney Lee, in whose historic home George Washington was said to have married the widow Custis. Stuart wrote: "The conflagration raged fearfully during the entire night, while explosions of shells rent the air." He was told that 5,000 Federals guarded the burning depot, a force much larger than his own.

Stuart paraded dismounted men to convince the enemy that he had infantry with him, and had Pelham fire guns at long range into the White House area, changing gun positions often to create the impression that an army was at hand. This ruse, Blackford recalled, forced the enemy to burn the vast city of sheds which had grown up about the plantation house. Somehow, in any event, the place burned, and the Federal infantry was taken away in the night by boats.

At daylight on June twenty-ninth, Stuart's column moved within sight of the White House, picking up a few Federal fugitives on the way. When they were a quarter of a mile from the smoking ruins, Stuart and Rooney Lee found a Federal gunboat at the docks.

Young Lee, as blandly as if the valuable estate were enemy property instead of his own, indicated all the strong points of the landscape. Jeb sent 75 men to duel with the vessel, the U.S.S. *Marblehead*.

Stuart's troopers went over an open meadow about forty paces apart, ready with rifles. Whistling shells from the gunboat flew overhead. Bluecoat skirmishers came ashore and from the river bank blazed away at the Confederates until one of Pelham's howitzers fired, exploding a shell just over the *Marblehead*. The boat began to gather steam, called in her skirmishers and fell downstream under Pelham's fire.

There was a strange race between the gunboat and Pelham's piece, which rumbled along the bank as far as the horses could go. Stuart and his staff trotted to the White House.

They pawed among luxuries left by the enemy: Heaps of lemons and other fruits and vegetables, canned meats and oysters and lobster, cases of beer, wine and liquor, barrels of sugar, tons of ice. There were eggs packed in salt barrels, roasted by the fire, and now plucked out as delicacies by the hungry cavalrymen.

Stuart's concern was with the historic house. He angrily protested "the deceitfulness of the enemy's pretended reverence for everything associated with the name of Washington, for the dwelling-house was burned to the ground, and not a vestige left except what told of desolation and vandalism."[5]

Perhaps this diverted him, for he reported that his soldiers ate "fruits of the tropics as well as substantials of the land." In truth, Blackford noted, the troopers dashed for the whisky, and before Rooney Lee was aware of it, scores were drunk, and had bottles hidden in their clothing. Lee spread a shrewd rumor that the enemy had poisoned the liquor and left it as a trap, and that one man had just died in extreme pain. Bottles sailed out of the column in every direction and sobriety slowly returned.

Nine barges burned at the water front, sending up millions of dollars' worth of supplies in smoke. Troopers ransacked wagons, taking their pick of valuables. Stuart put a pontoon train aboard wagons and started it southward. He debated with Blackford as to what should be done with captured locomotives. The engineer had them put out of action by blasting their boilers with Pelham's guns at a range of fifty yards.

There was a dispatch from R. E. Lee in the morning ordering Stuart to watch for any sign of enemy retreat in his direction. Stuart replied with his news that the Federals were now definitely running for the James River, since he had destroyed their base on the York. He was not the first with this information, however. Lee had got it early in the morning from two of Longstreet's engineers, who had found empty Federal entrenchments south of the Chickahominy.

Stuart remained at the White House the rest of this hot Sunday, salvaging his loot, but sent Fitz Lee and the 1st Virginia south to observe the enemy along the Chickahominy.

Far behind Stuart's party, in the swamps to the southeast, Lee's main army had spent an unprofitable day. The commander's efforts to trap McClellan had again gone awry. Jackson's wing was delayed by a burned bridge, and Magruder met the enemy alone in a costly battle at Savage's Station. Army co-ordination seemed elusive indeed. A rainstorm ended the day, with Lee making further plans to press the Federals: Jackson would cross White Oak Swamp and drive the enemy into the waiting divisions of Longstreet and A. P. Hill.

Esten Cooke galloped back from Richmond in Stuart's tracks and at last came to the White House, where he found "the General— and the flies." He found the wreckage of the depot, "wild, tragic, loathsome chaos . . . an awful stench." Cooke put his weapons in a wagon, since his new horse was already worn out, and went into the country in search of another mount. The cavalry left him behind.

Von Borcke had caught up by now, finding Stuart "in excellent spirits" and full of tales of the expedition. There was little time for a reunion, for Jeb moved them back to the Chickahominy on Monday morning, and spent the day along the river while the enemy engaged Pelham in an artillery duel. Stuart could not discover the flank of the main body of enemy infantry, and went into camp near the river. He had heard rolling sounds of battle from upstream most of the day.

Lee's army had failed once more. Jackson had been strangely delayed in crossing White Oak Swamp. No one could explain his lethargy, for though two cavalrymen, Wade Hampton and T. T. Munford, had pointed out to Stonewall means of crossing the swamp, the usually aggressive Valley conqueror had sat on a log almost all day, as if overcome by exhaustion or fever. While he waited at the northern edge of his swamp the escaping Federal army had brushed with the outnumbered forces of Longstreet and A. P. Hill and stung them badly in the battle of Glendale, or Frayser's Farm. Even yet General Lee was pressing the pursuit.

Stuart had seen none of the major action of this hectic campaign since Cold Harbor, because of his orders from General Lee to skirt the enemy flank. And not until three thirty A.M., July first, was he called to aid the main army.

At that hour a dispatch bearer roused Jeb from sleep near Forge Bridge of the Chickahominy. The note was signed by Lee's aide, Colonel Chilton, but bore no hour. The order said that the enemy had been headed off at a road intersection, and told Stuart to cross the Chickahominy and co-operate with infantry on the south side. It suggested that Grapevine Bridge was a suitable spot.

Stuart questioned the courier:

"When was this written?"

"About nine thirty last night."

"Where was the firing then?"

"It had stopped around White Oak Swamp bridge by then, over where Jackson was."

Stuart pondered the order in light of what he surmised had happened since Lee dictated it, and called for the buglers. The command was soon in the saddle. They rode eleven miles up the river to Bottom's Bridge and crossed to the south of the Chickahominy. Stuart found the road clogged with marching Confederate infantry, moving so fast and so filling the roadway that he was forced to retrace his steps.

The cavalry moved back downstream to Forge Bridge once more, recrossed the river to the south bank, and turned upstream. The troopers now came up on the left of Stonewall Jackson's troops. Stuart wrote Jackson a note to this effect, saying he would be ready to co-operate, but it was too late. The long maneuver had eaten up the hours with its marching and countermarching.

But there was a moment of rest during the hot afternoon when Stuart lay with the staff beneath cherry trees at a roadside. Men picked the ripe cherries and Stuart clambered atop a fence rail to join them. When he had eaten all the fruit within reach Jeb called to von Borcke:

"Captain, you charge the Yanks so well. Why don't you attack this cherry tree?"

Von Borcke leaped from a fence rail upon a limb, dragging it to earth and breaking down the tree. The laughing troopers had soon picked clean its branches.

They were interrupted by thunder of artillery and Stuart, as if his memory had been jogged, ordered them into the saddles once more.[6]

As the cavalry sought position, Lee's army was fighting the bloody engagement of Malvern Hill, regiments charging one by one up a slope under the murderous fire of sixty Federal cannon, standing wheel to wheel. Brigades had been decimated through a blundering of orders, and despite the gallantry of the gray columns, only Federal failure to understand the situation saved Lee from defeat. The action roared until after dark, no more than a few miles across the swamps from Stuart's approaching column. Jeb came, long after dark, to Jackson's flank near a stream called Turkey Creek.

Stuart's absence had drawn no criticism, and he probably could not have made effective use of the cavalry in the swamp fighting in any event, yet his report of the final movements of his expedition had a defensive ring:

"Passing Nance's Shop about sundown, it was dark before we reached Rock's house, near which we stampeded the enemy's picket ... soon after ... encountered picket fires, and a little way beyond saw the light of a considerable encampment. There was no other recourse left but to halt for the night, after a day's march of 42 miles."

Stuart thought he had helped to confuse the enemy despite the stumbling marches of the day, for he wrote:

"My arrival could not have been more fortunately timed, for, arriving after dark, its ponderous march, with the rolling artillery, must have impressed the enemy's cavalry, watching the approaches to their rear, with the idea of an immense army about to cut off their retreat, and contributed to cause that sudden collapse and stampede that soon after occurred, leaving us in possession of Malvern Hill."

Morning brought fog and rain. Jeb woke with his staff in an orchard near Malvern Hill, just outside a small farmhouse.

Stuart went in search of Jackson and found him riding restlessly in the fog with Captain Blackford. Stonewall was ready to charge the enemy on Malvern Hill, but Stuart halted him and sent Blackford to inspect the front. The captain rode up the menacing slope toward gun pits on the ridge and saw dim figures. Blackford knew that Stuart meant him to go close enough to draw fire if the enemy were still there, and he went to the crest. He found that the skirmishers were Confederates. The enemy had gone. Blackford took the news to Stuart.

Jeb sent him in the path of the enemy, and Blackford rode to a hill overlooking the James and two magnificent plantation houses of Colonial days, Berkeley and Westover. Around them crowded Federal troops beyond counting, with gunboats lying offshore just beyond. Blackford was near enough to hear voices of command.

Stuart took a column downriver toward the plantation, Shirley, but ran into a strong Federal rear guard and turned back. He spent the rest of the day collecting prisoners, sending captured arms to the rear, and worrying the enemy. Late in the day he galloped in reconnaissance toward Charles City Court House.

Stuart got a message from Pelham the next morning confirming Blackford's report: The enemy lay by the river near Westover with a stream—Herring Creek—to their right. A raised plateau called Evelington Heights overlooked this position. The heights were unoccupied. Young Captain Pelham urged that artillery be hurried to that hill.

Stuart sent the dispatch through Jackson to General Lee, but did not wait for army channels to bring action. He immediately aroused the men and rode to Evelington Heights. The lone Federal cavalry squadron there fell back almost docilely to Westover. Stuart looked down on the crowded regiments of McClellan's army.

Without thought of the unequal odds or concern lest he alert the enemy to the strategic importance of the commanding hill, he made ready to fight. One howitzer opened fire. Shells fell in the packed Union camp, killing men and animals. Stuart enjoyed the sight: "Judging from the great commotion and excitement caused below it must have had considerable effect."

Stuart had another surprise for the enemy, "some foreign chap" with a Congreive rocket battery, whose fat missiles flew straight enough, but once they struck leaped and turned in many directions. They threshed in McClellan's camp, scalding mules with "liquid damnation," but in the end burned only a few tents. Some of them whizzed back toward Jeb's hill, and this ancient weapon was abandoned.

Stuart advised General Lee of the situation, and was told help was on the way—infantry of Jackson and Longstreet.

The gun had opened on the Federals at nine A.M., and Stuart held the heights until two in the afternoon, when the enemy finally pushed a battery across difficult Herring Creek and began firing. Even then he clung to the position while bluecoat infantry inched up on his flank and the battery blazed at him. A courier brought a disheartening message: Longstreet had taken the wrong road, and was at least six miles away at Nance's Shop. The cavalry must soon retreat.

Pelham had just reported two more rounds left, and Stuart had ordered these fired, expecting Longstreet's vanguard at every moment. The sharpshooters trotted back from the front with all cartridges gone. Stuart wrote almost bitterly that they "had at last to retire; not, however, without teaching many a foeman the bitter lesson of death."

But Evelington Heights was lost, and soon swarmed with bluecoats, who began to fortify it.

The next day was July fourth, and Stuart spent it with Lee and Jackson, prowling about Evelington Heights, seeking some way to attack, but though Stuart urged Jackson and "showed him routes by which the plateau could be reached to the left," the high command refused to risk the army against the strong position of McClellan, now shielded by the ridge Stuart had lost.[7]

On July sixth, as if nettled by his failure to cripple the enemy, Stuart went hunting at the riverside. He rode off in the dusk with two regiments and six of Pelham's guns to lay an ambush for some of the Federal boats which passed so boldly up and down the James.

It was a soft summer night, "full of the fragrance of wild flowers and forest blossoms, and myriads of fireflies glittered," von Borcke wrote. Stuart led them to a landing, had the guns loaded, and settled to wait.

Within a few minutes a flotilla came upstream and lights glowed on the water. Five enemy transports pulled slowly past, decks loaded with troops. They were no more than a hundred yards off when Stuart ordered the gunners to fire. The effect was devastating.

Von Borcke remembered: "We could distinctly hear our balls and shells crashing through the sides of the vessels, the cries of the wounded on board, and the confused random commands of the officers."

A transport sank, and the river was dotted with struggling figures. Above the sounds of the little engagement Stuart heard the approach of gunboats under heavy steam. He called off the guns and the party trotted home through the early morning. Behind them, to von Borcke's amusement, the enemy sent hundred-pound shells crashing into the spot from which Stuart's horse artillery had been firing.[8]

Von Borcke somehow became separated from the party, and since he had been warned that Yankee cavalry was nearby, he rode in the darkness with caution. A horseman emerged from a side path.

"Halt!" von Borcke shouted. "What is your regiment?"

"Eighth Illinois," a voice replied.

Von Borcke thrust a pistol against the man's chest. The rider wore a blue Federal uniform. The German took him to camp, noting greedily that the captive rode a fine horse, which would soon be his own. The young man was talkative, full of stories about life in the Yankee army—but when they arrived in the camp of the 9th Virginia the "Federal," laughing, identified himself as one of Fitz Lee's troopers, clad in a captured uniform.

Von Borcke was enraged, and drew his pistol on the private. "Why did you tell me you were Federal?"

"I thought you were a Yankee. Your accent."

The German threatened the laughing boy with murder at any further jesting, and rode to join Stuart.

For months afterward Jeb teased von Borcke:

"Captain, how many prisoners of the 9th Virginia have you taken lately?"

The cavalry pickets hung close to the enemy for a few days, and General Lee kept the infantry in line. But on July eighth the commander concluded that McClellan intended no immediate offensive against Richmond, and most of the infantry was marched nearer the capital. The cavalry screen was pulled back. The Seven Days had ended.

The army would never be the same; Lee had suffered almost 20,000 casualties, against some 15,000 for the enemy. The country between the Chickahominy and the James was like a vast abattoir.

Esten Cooke had returned to Stuart at the end of the fighting, smarting because his search for a fresh horse had led him into a long journey. He had fretted after hearing the guns of Malvern Hill: "Was Stuart at the heavy fighting last evening? I don't know. I was not. But, *mon General*, thou canst not say I did it. 'Twas the horse I mounted in an evil hour."

Cooke was back, however, and got astonished greetings. The staff had thought him dead, shot by a Yankee infantry company and buried days earlier.

Von Borcke threw his arms around Cooke. "I cried," the German shouted. "I cried for you, and wanted to go for your remains."

Captain Farley said he, too, had wept for the loss of John Esten. Cooke was amused, and wrote in his diary: "Not this time, *mes amis!* Here I am writing on the grass under the locusts, the General sleeping yonder."

Stuart did not seem physically worn after the hard riding of the week, but his reports indicated an awareness that the role of the cavalry might have left something to be desired. At the end of them:

"I regret that the very extended field of operations of the cavalry has made this report necessarily long. During the whole period it will be observed that my command was in contact with the enemy. No opportunity occurred, however, for an overwhelming charge; a circumstance resulting from the nature of the positions . . . in woods or behind swamps and ditches."

What Jeb longed for, in short, was an "overwhelming charge." Without one, the life of the cavalry seemed incomplete.

His casualties were light, a total of 71—61 of these borne by the 1st North Carolina, on duty with the main army while Stuart was galloping his long route. But of the casualties only four men were dead, four others had deserted to the enemy. For all its losses, the cavalry corps hardly knew it had been engaged.

Stuart was free with praise of officers and men. His staff was learning:

Colonels Fitz Lee, Rooney Lee, T. R. R. Cobb, and Lieutenant Colonel Will Martin had shown "zeal and ability" in independent command, and deserved promotion.

Captain John Pelham had shown "such signal ability as an artillerist, such heroic example and devotion in danger, and indomitable energy . . . that, reluctant as I am at the chance of losing such a valuable limb from the brigade, I feel bound to ask for his promotion, with the remark that in either cavalry or artillery no field grade is too high for his merit or capacity."

Captain Blackford was "always in advance, obtaining valuable information of the enemy. . . . He is bold in reconnaissance, fearless in danger, and remarkably cool and correct in judgment. His services are invaluable to the advance guard of any army."

Von Borcke was "ever-present, fearless and untiring."

There was praise for new members of the staff, Stuart's kinsman from Mississippi, Hardeman Stuart, a signal officer, and Captain Norman Fitzhugh, just promoted from the ranks to chief of staff. There was mention of Redmond Burke, Esten Cooke, Captain Farley, Chaplain Ball and others.

Like most other commanders of the army, Stuart read with pleasure Lee's general order on July seventh, summing up The Seven Days. The commander said of his new army:

> The general commanding, profoundly grateful to the only Giver of all victory for the signal success with which He has blessed our arms, tenders his warmest thanks and congratulations to the army....
>
> Today the remains of that confident and threatening host of the enemy lie upon the banks of the James River, 30 miles from Richmond, seeking to recover . . . from the effects of a series of disastrous defeats....
>
> The service rendered to the country in this short but eventful period can scarcely be estimated, and the general commanding cannot adequately express his admiration of the courage, endurance, and soldierly conduct of the officers and men engaged....

Despite this official rejoicing, Lee sought to improve the blundering system of command which had cost him complete victory. His official report said mildly: "Under ordinary circumstances the Federal army should have been destroyed." And he wrote his wife: "Our success has not been so great or complete as we could have desired."

There were signs of reorganization within the army. For his part, Stuart wanted only an enlarged cavalry corps and promotion for his reckless young officers. When Jeb found time for a note to Flora he wrote:

> I have been marching and fighting for one solid week. Generally on my own hook, with the cavalry detached from the main body. I ran a gunboat from the White House and took possession. What do you think of that?

We have been everywhere victorious and on the 3rd I had
the infinite satisfaction of slipping around to the enemy's rear
and shelling his camp at Westover. If the army had been up
with me we could have finished his business. . . .

Stuart talked with Esten Cooke of the strategy of The Seven
Days, and of his stillborn plan which had been discarded by General
Lee at the start.

"Do you know what General Lee's object was at Richmond?"
he asked.

"No."

"He was building fortifications, in order to hold the city with
a small force, and then to attack McClellan on the right flank, as
you know. I was in favor of attacking his left flank, on the Charles
City Road."

"From what point, General?"

"Well, from about White Oak Swamp."

"Would you have had space enough?"

"Yes. But the other plan was best, after all. But McClellan
ought to have struck right for Richmond when we advanced on his
flank."

"He hadn't the nerve," Cooke said. "Napoleon would have
done it."[9] Cooke still carried in his knapsack the biography of Napoleon, and read from it daily.

For nearly a month the Confederate forces rested. The infantry camped outside Richmond and the cavalry was divided between
picket duty on the Charles City Road and a training camp at Hanover Court House, where the regiments were being drilled.

Stuart's staff was happy to move to Hanover County, for life
on the battlefields was unpleasant. Von Borcke sketched the "im-
poverishment and utter destitution of the country . . . numberless
festering carcasses of horses and mules . . . stench from human bodies
hastily buried but a few inches below the surface."

The German and Captain Hardeman Stuart dug for a whole
day in a garden near headquarters and found only "a few miserable
onions and diseased potatoes to appease our hunger."

All this was soon left behind. Stuart took von Borcke to Richmond, where he went to see President Davis, but the German, his only uniform in shreds, could not be persuaded to make the state visit. Von Borcke went to a tailor and bought a full uniform "of the newest gloss, light gray frock coat with buff facings, dark blue trousers, and a little black cocked hat with sweeping ostrich plume."

Stuart found himself a hero in Richmond, and one morning as he rode through the streets a band of young women besieged him. The girls surrounded his horse and he sat, joking with them as they put a wreath of flowers around the neck of his horse and thrust a bunch of roses beneath his arm. Jeb was reciting poetry to them when a column of infantry marched around a corner onto the scene of hero worship and began gobbling falsetto cries of derision.

Stuart was off in a clatter, shedding roses, with a hasty farewell to the young women.[10]

The new cavalry headquarters were on the Timberlake farm, on the Virginia Central Railroad near Atlee's Station, some ten miles north of Richmond. The farmhouse was pleasantly shaded by a grove of huge oaks and hickories, with well-tended fields about it. The elderly master of the place had two sons in Stuart's column, and was determined to be hospitable. Jeb arrived here on July twelfth. Flora came to a nearby plantation two days later, and was a constant visitor for meals; the Stuart children were pets of the staff, and there was endless play in the old house.

Jeb staged a review on July seventeenth. Most of the spectators were women of the region, von Borcke noticed, "among whom General Stuart had many acquaintances and admirers." The brigade went through a drill and then paraded in column. Flora watched with the other women. Captain Blackford thought she must have been proud of her husband, who little more than a year ago had been a lieutenant, and now commanded the cavalry of an army.

After the review Stuart went among the carriages to invite spectators to visit the camp. Many families accepted, and von Borcke and Fitzhugh were hurried to the Timberlake house to prepare for the crowd. The officers commandeered "a little army" of slaves and looted the house of chairs and sofas, placing them in a great circle

under a tent fly. The guests sat under the canvas in the yard, the
women drinking cold milk and eating ginger cakes, and the men
sipping juleps.

Von Borcke was impressed by the "animated talk and patriotic
songs" of the guests, who left "with the impression that camp life
was not so bad after all."

But the enemy had begun to stir. The Federal armies in Northern Virginia and the Shenandoah Valley had been consolidated, and
a blustering general from the Western theater, John Pope, was in
command. His first orders to the troops became jokes in both armies
in Virginia:

> Let us understand each other. I have come to you from the
> West, where we have always seen the backs of our enemies. . . .
> I presume I have been called here to pursue the same system.
> . . . I hear constantly of "taking strong positions and holding
> them", of "lines of retreat. . . ." Let us discard such ideas. The
> strongest position a soldier should desire to occupy is one from
> which he can most easily advance against the enemy.

Pope disturbed the repose of Stuart's command on von Borcke's
birthday. There had been a surprise celebration and a bouquet of
field flowers. News from the front ended the party: The enemy had
overcome a cavalry picket just fifteen miles away and taken several
prisoners and horses. Stuart went in pursuit with 2,000 men and two
guns, but found to his "great disappointment" that the enemy had
gone back to Fredericksburg. A night rainstorm broke, flooding
creeks and rivers, forcing Stuart to retire and end his little offensive.

Jeb left the command to rest the horses and with Blackford and
von Borcke climbed on a handcar propelled by two Negroes and
whizzed back to headquarters on the railroad tracks. He was in Hanover Court House by sunset of July twenty-fifth.

For a few more days the headquarters staff lolled about the
place. A favorite plantation house for visits was Dundee, the home
of the Price family, intimates of Stuart. One Sunday, as the staff
sat with Jeb on the porch of this house, listening to the tunes of
Sweeney's banjo, Bob's bones and the fiddlers, fire blazed from a

stable. The officers rushed to fight flames and save the livestock. They singed clothing and burned hands, but won the skirmish and for a day to two Stuart amused the women with his jokes about von Borcke's deeds of valor:

"He came running out of there with a mule under one arm and two little pigs under the other."

July thirtieth brought the biggest of the summer's celebrations. Stuart came back from Richmond with new commissions. He was a major general.

Von Borcke was a major, and adjutant general of the staff. There were other promotions, including a captaincy for Cooke, but none for Blackford. Richmond refused to advance engineer officers, but Blackford did get welcome aid: A wagon fitted for his map making, with a driver and five horses.

The cavalry command was also enlarged. There would be three brigades under Jeb commanded by Wade Hampton, Beverly Robertson and Fitz Lee as brigadiers. New regiments from North and South Carolina joined the corps. August opened with Stuart in command of some 15,000 troopers. He was ready for the new phase of maneuver against Pope on the broad fields to the west.

☆

CHAPTER 9

Easy Victories

THE trumpeting of General Pope inspired John Mosby to new visions of guerrilla fighting in the enemy's rear. He begged Stuart for a dozen men to harass Pope's communications. Jeb refused.

"I am getting ready for active campaigning," he said. "I can't spare you the men. Wait."

Mosby was determined.

"Then give me a letter to Jackson, and I will try him."

Stuart gave him a rousing recommendation:

> General—The bearer, John S. Mosby, late 1st Lieutenant of 1st Virginia Cavalry, is en route to scout beyond the enemy's lines toward Manassas and Fairfax. He is bold, daring, intelligent and discreet. The information he may obtain and transmit to you may be relied upon, and I have no doubt that he will soon give additional proofs of his value. Did you receive the volume of Napoleon and his *Maxims* that I sent you?[1]

Mosby left for Jackson's camp at Gordonsville to the west, but within a few miles was picked up with absurd ease by a crack Federal cavalry regiment, the Harris Light, of New York.

Mosby impressed his captors: "Sprightly appearance and conversation . . . displays no small amount of Southern bravado in his dress and manners. His gray plush hat is surmounted by a waving plume, which he tosses, as he speaks, in real Prussian style."

The enemy found Stuart's letter to Jackson and sent Mosby off to prison. It was a capture the Federal army would regret.

Mosby's adventure led Stuart into action on August fourth, for Jeb, stung by raids against the Virginia Central Railroad, took four regiments and a battery of guns toward Fredericksburg to punish the enemy. Chivalry intervened.

On the way north Captain Blackford caused a detour to Gay Mont, a plantation whose family he knew. Jeb followed him to the house, where they found women shaking with fright; the cavalry had been mistaken for Yankees, some of whom had just left the plantation.

Blackford was incensed: "Did they molest you in any way?"

"They were well behaved, Captain. But one of them did steal a watch from old Cye, our carriage driver."

While Stuart and the staff rested on the porch Blackford led twenty men in chase of the Federal party—though he first took one of the women aside and got further reassurance that the enemy raiders had not been discourteous.

Blackford overtook the culprits within a few miles and made a speech to the astounded Federals:

"Do you see those pine saplings there? Well, those ladies back there tell me you treated them with respect; if you hadn't, I would be hanging every one of you here by your halter straps. Now, one of you took a watch from an old Negro back there. Hand it up to me."

A sheepish prisoner produced a silver timepiece and Blackford galloped ahead of his prisoners to Gay Mont, restored the watch to the servant and joined the other officers in "a charming dinner" with the ladies before returning to the hot, dusty ride toward the enemy.[2]

Stuart took them off at dawn the next day and near Massaponax Church found a force of about 8,000 Federals moving down the plank highway. Jeb took one quick look and issued his orders. It was an impressive demonstration of his gifts for fighting cavalry as sketched by Esten Cooke:

"His instinct was unfailing, his glance that of the master . . . it looked like instinct, rather than calculation—that rapid and unerring glance which took in at once every trait of the ground . . . and anticipated every movement of his adversary."

His orders at this moment were simple, but they routed the Federal force which outnumbered him almost five to one. He led most of the column after the main enemy force and sent one regiment after its wagon train in the opposite direction. The enemy coiled in confusion, unaware of their superiority. Stuart rolled the wagons to safety and retreated with 200 prisoners toward Bowling Green. The Federals gave up their expedition and fell back to Fredericksburg.

Stuart found Flora waiting for him on his return to Hanover. Many other officers' wives were on hand, and there was gaiety at Dundee. Stuart had little time to enjoy it. Jackson was having cavalry troubles with Beverly Robertson and his command, and Jeb was called out on a tour of inspection.

From Richmond General Lee watched the unfolding of a new Federal plan of invasion. McClellan still lay on the James, but transports were moving out his troops. A large army under General Burnside was at Fortress Monroe, able to strike up the James toward Richmond, or up the Potomac to reinforce Pope.

Lee had moved Jackson into Pope's front, but held the bulk of his force near Richmond until it became clear that the capital was safe from attack in the east. In the last of July, Lee reinforced Jackson with A. P. Hill's strong force; Richmond was left with about 55,000 defenders.

While Lee debated the wisdom of shifting all his strength northward, John Mosby was freed from prison on exchange. From Fortress Monroe, Mosby had seen transports moving Burnside's army, and the captain of a ship, a Confederate sympathizer, had told him he was sailing for Washington. Mosby hurried toward Richmond, and walked the last twelve miles to reach Lee's headquarters in the August heat. He arrived "roughly dressed and unkempt," and was delayed by staff officers who tried to keep him from the commander, but finally went in to "the awful presence" of Lee.

Mosby pointed out the Federal movement on a map, but saw that Lee was not convinced. "My name is John Mosby," he said. "I was on Stuart's ride around McClellan."

Lee brightened. "Oh, I remember." He questioned Mosby with more interest and asked him where the next blow of the enemy would fall.

A courier went off with a mesage from Lee to Jackson, who was eighty miles northwest at Gordonsville. The commander seemed convinced that Mosby's analysis was accurate.[3]

On August ninth Jackson fought the vanguard of Pope's army at Slaughter Mountain, between Gordonsville and Culpeper, and in a desperate battle of three hours saw his lines broken and overrun, and 1,400 of his men shot down or captured. Only Stonewall's tactical ability had restored his lines as he led a final charge. The enemy fell back at night having lost twice as many men as Jackson.

Stonewall and the Federal General Banks staged a truce on August tenth to gather wounded and bury dead on Slaughter Mountain. Stuart reported at daybreak, a welcome sight to Jackson, who asked him to take Robertson's cavalry for a look at enemy dispositions.

Jeb first went with other officers to help arrange the truce. He saw a civilian making a sketch of the scene, his paper held on the pommel of his saddle. Stuart rode toward this man, who was the Federal reporter, George Alfred Townsend.

Townsend saw Stuart as "a lithe, indurated, severe-looking horseman" who peered at the pencil drawing.

"Are you making a sketch of our position?" Stuart asked.

"Not for any military purpose."

"For what?"

"For a newspaper engraving."

"Humph!"

Stuart rode to the group of officers nearby and Townsend completed his sketch. Jeb inquired for General George Hartsuff of the Union army, an old friend. One of the bluecoats told him Hartsuff had walked off, but would soon return.

Townsend engaged Stuart in conversation: "He described the Confederate uniform to me, and laughed over some reminiscences of his raid around McClellan's army."

"That performance gave me a major-generalcy," Stuart said. "And my saddle-cloth there was sent from Baltimore as a reward, by a lady whom I never knew."

Townsend was attracted by Stuart, but said he had a quality of "airiness" and liked to talk of his prowess. This inspection was soon interrupted. Hartsuff returned, and Stuart, "with a grim smile about his mouth," rose to meet him.

"Hartsuff, God bless you, how-de-do?"

"Stuart, how are you?"

The friends talked of old times; one of the Confederates pulled out a whisky jug, and, Townsend wrote, all the generals drank to an early peace. There was some error, for Stuart never drank.

"Here's hoping you'll fall into our hands," Stuart said. "We'll treat you well at Richmond!"

"Same to you!" Hartsuff replied. They laughed.

Some of the Federal officers were ill at ease, but Stuart sat on a log "in careless posture, working his jaw till the sandy gray beard brushed his chin and became twisted in his teeth." Stuart might have been "a plain farmer jaunting home from market," Townsend thought. Stuart gave Townsend permission to pass the Rebel lines and the reporter strolled among the dead and wounded on the mountainside.[4]

The officers held a gay reunion for an hour or more. Stuart met the enemy generals, Samuel Crawford and George Bayard, old friends who had brought lunch baskets. They ate together, laughing over recollections of the prewar army and their exploits in the field in recent months.

Someone said, "Well, the Yankee papers claim every battle a Yankee victory, however it turns out."

Stuart laughed.

"Crawford," he said, "I'll bet you a hat the northern papers claim this a victory here." He waved a hand toward the littered field where bluecoats had been driven back in defeat.

"I'll take you up," Crawford said. "Not even the New York *Herald* would have the audacity to claim this."[5]

The truce was over.

For the rest of the day Jeb rode hard. He took Robertson's troopers at an unaccustomed pace over the dusty roads beyond Jackson's pickets and had them probing the lines of the enemy until after dark. He reported to Stonewall that his army was in danger.

Large Federal reinforcements had come up. Jackson began a retreat to Gordonsville.

Stuart had seen enough of Beverly Robertson to convince him that the veteran West Pointer, center of so many cavalry quarrels, must go. Within a month Robertson was to be transferred. He would finally go, as one of Stuart's staff noted, "much to the joy of all concerned."

This observant officer was young Channing Price, son of the family of Dundee and a kinsman of Stuart, snatched from the Richmond Howitzers and added to the staff.

Stuart had only a day in headquarters at Hanover, for he got marching orders for the bulk of his corps, and had a final dinner at Dundee with the Prices, Flora and his staff. Mrs. Stuart took von Borcke aside and wrung from him a promise to "watch over" Jeb in battle and do all possible to prevent his rash exposure.

Stuart sent Fitz Lee with the troopers to meet him near the village of Verdiersville a few miles south of the Rapidan, very near the enemy's lines. Jeb would travel by train, confer with General Lee at Orange Court House, and be ready for action when he reached Verdiersville.

The strategic situation now demanded speed. To the east McClellan had completed the evacuation of his army and was moving up the Potomac to reinforce Pope. General Lee must strike Pope before he grew too strong, and since the Federal commander was settling in a vulnerable spot between the Rapidan and the Rappahannock, the Confederate command saw a golden opportunity. Stuart's cavalry was to play an important role.

Stuart and a few staff officers boarded a train at Hanover the afternoon of August sixteenth, bound for Gordonsville. Their horses were led into a stock car, but there was no place for Jeb and his young men. The train was packed with troops, and sprawling men covered the tops of the cars. Stuart would not disturb the soldiers. He led the staff to the tender behind the locomotive, where they sat on the fuel logs, and, von Borcke wrote: "filled the time with talk and song as we rolled rapidly through the beautiful country, of which, by reason of the thick clouds of smoke that enveloped us, we could catch only occasional glimpses." It was daybreak when they reached Gordonsville, looking at each other and erupting in laughter. The engine's soot had made them as black as crows. After "many ablutions" the party went to Lee's quarters at Orange Court House, where Stuart talked with the commander-in-chief and other officers for an hour.[6]

There was a gay dinner at Jackson's quarters at three P.M.—a most un-Jacksonlike meal, for farmers of the region had almost filled his small tent with delicacies and there was a banquet.

There was hilarity over Stuart, for he found a gift waiting for him, sent through the lines by the Federal General Crawford, who had lost the bet made during the Slaughter Mountain truce. Stuart laughingly accepted the tribute, a new brown hat, appropriately plumed, accompanied by a copy of the New York *Herald* which claimed Jackson's victory for John Pope's vanguard.

Stuart soon left the table and went with von Borcke and Mosby up Clark's Mountain, where a Confederate signal station commanded the country for miles about.

The two armies were in plain sight. Von Borcke wrote: "Many thousands of tents, the thin blue smoke of their camp fires rising straight up in the still air; regiments of infantry were marching and counter-marching, and long wagon trains were moving along the distant roads."

There was more than met von Borcke's eye. General Lee had already examined the landscape, and could hardly believe that the enemy would hold this position on the line of the Rapidan. Behind them, where this river flowed into the Rappahannock, was a ready-made trap. If Lee could cross the Rapidan below Pope with infantry, Stuart could cut off the enemy rear, burn the big bridge over the Rappahannock, and make Pope helpless before a major assault. From the top of the mountain Jeb could see the possibilities; like the Confederate high command, he counted the Federal army already a victim of Pope's blunder, caught between the two rivers.

Stuart had ordered Fitz Lee to bring the troopers across country, and expected to meet them near Raccoon Ford on the Rapidan, one of the crossings planned for Robert Lee's infantry. Fitz Lee had a march of only thirty-two miles from his last reported position, and should make it with ease.

Stuart rode down Clark's Mountain with his small escort about sunset of August seventeenth, toward Verdiersville, which Fitz Lee must pass on his way to the rendezvous at Raccoon Ford. Captain Norman Fitzhugh and Chiswell Dabney of Jeb's staff were sent ahead to search for the cavalry corps. Fitzhugh bore an important document—the detailed order from General R. E. Lee to Stuart outlining the plan to trap Pope.

The party rode into Verdiersville after midnight. The village was quiet. Fitzhugh reported that there was no sign of Fitz Lee and the corps; something had gone awry. Stuart sent Fitzhugh through the little town in the direction the troopers must come, and with his staff turned into the gate of the first farmhouse he saw, the home of a family named Rhodes. Most of the officers made their beds in the garden, but Stuart spread his scarlet-lined cloak on the porch of the house and fell asleep with his haversack and his new hat beside him.

Von Borcke was nervous, "being so far outside of our lines," and he and his companions did not unsaddle their horses, removing only their blankets. The Prussian lay down with his pistol and huge sword buckled at his waist. There was little time for sleep.

Not long after four A.M. there was a stir in the village. Cavalrymen were crossing the plank road about four hundred yards from the house where Stuart slept. A newcomer was first to wake up, one Gibson, a young man who had come from Federal prison with Mosby. Gibson roused Mosby.

"Cavalry on the road," he said. "And guns, too. It's probably Fitz Lee, but it might be Yanks."

Mosby shook Stuart, explained the unidentified troopers and said he would investigate with Gibson. The two young men mounted and Stuart walked to the farmyard fence, bareheaded, looking down the road after them.

The two Confederates soon halted; two troopers rode out of the village and fired pistols. Mosby and Gibson galloped back to the farmhouse. Stuart and his staff scattered. Jeb vaulted into his saddle and leaped a fence, leaving his hat, cloak and haversack.

Von Borcke saw his chief escape and ran for his own horse. A woman ran from the farmhouse, opened the gate, and von Borcke dashed through it into a ring of Federal horsemen. He disregarded a command to surrender, whirled his horse and went off under a hail of bullets, some of which cut his uniform. He outdistanced the enemy and at last got the horse under control. This, at least, was von Borcke's recollection of his escape.

Mosby saw it in another light: "A Prussian on Stuart's staff dashed through the front gate and went down the road ahead of us as fast as his horse could carry him. We never overtook him. . . . He described an encounter he had with the Yankees that morning as more wonderful than the feat of St. George and the Dragon. We ran as fast as we could, but the Prussian ran faster. That was all the distinction he won."

Behind them the bluecoats made merry. Federal troopers tossed Stuart's hat about with sabers, laughing at the flopping plume. Captain Fitzhugh, who had been captured by the enemy, laughed at sight of Stuart and the staff escaping while the blue troopers played with his hat. The Federal commander was curious.

"Captain, who was that party?"

Fitzhugh saw that Stuart on his fleet "Skylark" would soon be safely beyond enemy reach.

"Do you really want to know who that was, Colonel?"

"I do. Yes, yes."

"Well, it was General Stuart and his staff."

The Union officer exploded: "General Stuart! Quick. A squadron there! Fire on them. Pursue that party! Was that General Stuart?"

Fitzhugh yelled with laughter: "Yes! And he has escaped."

Stuart disappeared into the woods and the bluecoats did not press the pursuit. The Federal colonel recalled his men and went northward with Fitzhugh under guard.

Von Borcke described Jeb's return to the main army: "Stuart covered his head with his handkerchief as a protection against the sun, and we could not look at each other, despite our heat and indignation, without laughing heartily."

A sutler gave Stuart another hat from his wagon, but the story of the cavalryman's narrow escape and his loss spread through the army, and at every turn the infantrymen shouted, "Where's yer hat?"

When Stuart reported to headquarters the army's move ground to a halt. Without the cavalry thrust, the crossing of the river could not be undertaken—though Stonewall Jackson argued still for attack. The regiments settled to wait. Stuart was fiercely impatient, and in his report blamed Fitz Lee for failure of the maneuver against Pope. The army did not agree. The aggressive young cavalry lieutenant, it was thought, would surely have been in position if he had understood orders.[7]

There was no time for investigation. Fitz Lee was late by twenty-four hours because he had not seen the need for haste in his orders, which were apparently verbal. He had taken the troopers to Louisa Court House for food from their supply train, and then made his leisurely way toward the main army. When he arrived, it was too late.

General R. E. Lee had other troubles. The near-capture of Stuart was due to another vexing failure of command. When the cavalry did not come into position, Longstreet sent men of General Robert Toombs's brigade to guard the fords of the Rapidan. Toombs had been away when the order was carried out. With his return he angrily countermanded it and withdrew his men from the riverbank. That left open the fords for bluecoat cavalry and the party which chased Stuart had crossed the stream unchallenged. These raiders had, in fact, made an important capture. The papers Fitzhugh carried, including Lee's order to Stuart, were soon in the hands of General Pope, who was thoroughly frightened.

Pope only now saw through Lee's plan and moved to safety. He reported to Washington that Lee's order "made manifest the disposition of the enemy and their destination to overwhelm the army and my command before it could be reinforced by any portion of The Army of The Potomac." It was an accurate summary.

Confederate headquarters ended August nineteenth in frustration. Longstreet had Toombs under arrest, but the fiery Georgian made rebellious speeches to his cheering troops and refused to lay aside his sword. He was finally ordered back to Gordonsville, to remain under arrest until the army went into battle.

Amid this comedy of errors in command Robert Lee rode to the top of Clark's Mountain with Longstreet. Old Pete wrote of the scene as the enemy wagons moved in the distance toward the safety of the Rappahannock crossing, the clouds of dust marking the loss of a rare opportunity for Lee: "Watching without comment till the clouds grew thinner as they approached the river and melted into the bright blaze of the afternoon sun, General Lee finally put away his glasses, and with a deeply-drawn breath said, 'General, we little thought that the enemy would turn his back upon us thus early in the campaign.'"

The commander issued new orders for the chase of Pope. When he had come down from the mountain, Lee wrote Stuart of the enemy's retreat and ordered:

> You will therefore have to bear well to your right after crossing the Rapidan, unless you can get other information. I propose to start the troops at the rising of the moon tomorrow morning, which will give the men and horses a little rest. . . . If you can get information of the route of the enemy, you will endeavor to cut him off; otherwise, make for Kelly's Ford over the Rappahannock. . . . If you can get off earlier than the time I have appointed to advantage, do so.

Stuart spent the rest of the day in preparation, as if determined that the cavalry would not again fail the army. He was ready to move before dawn, but found time to write Flora, still in a jovial mood:

> I am greeted on all sides with congratulations and "Where is your hat?" I intend to make the Yankees pay for that hat.

He began to exact payment near daylight of August twentieth. General Lee had the infantry divided into two big corps: Longstreet would cross the Rapidan at Raccoon Ford and vicinity; Jackson would cross to the west, at Somerville Ford. The cavalry went out first.

Fitz Lee's brigade preceded Longstreet to Kelly's Ford on the Rappahannock, where it drove in a small force of Federal cavalry.

The gray infantry was not far behind and camped around the ford late in the day.

Stuart rode with the rest of the cavalry corps to the west, toward the village of Stevensburg through open, rolling country. In the afternoon they came upon the enemy, five regiments under Stuart's old friend, General Bayard.

Von Borcke was stirred by the welcome from villagers, who had seen nothing but Federal troops in recent days: "Men, women and children came running out of all the houses with loud exclamations of delight, many thanking God on their knees for their deliverance. . . . A venerable old lady asked permission to kiss our battle flag . . . and blessed it with tears." The cavalry went through with old men and boys straggling after it with a variety of household guns; they hung on despite the pleas of officers to go back to their homes, determined to help drive off the invaders.

Stuart rode through boiling dust clouds to find Grumble Jones and the 7th Virginia pecking away at the enemy. The bluecoats lay in a mile-long line at the edge of a woodland. Stuart sent Robertson with three regiments on a sweep at the Federal flank, and a courier was sent to bring up Fitz Lee.

The first unit met by the Confederates was the 2nd New York, the Harris Light, which had captured Mosby. This regiment had been mustered in by the famous horseman, Colonel Alfred Duffié, who harangued his recruits in Napoleonic vein: "Volunteers to ride into the cannon's mouth—step forward!" His entire regiment had stepped out, and come south for glory.[8]

Today Stuart's first rush broke the New Yorkers and they had milled in confusion until a stand on the hilltop united Bayard's command. For a few moments, then, the massed troopers seemed invincible, but at last Robertson galloped up with his regiments.

Stuart had not forgotten the drama of the scene when he wrote his official report, much later:

> I knew the country and considered it necessary to advance along the road. . . . The remaining regiments were hurled in rapid succession in column of fours upon the enemy's main body. It was perfectly plain that the enemy's force was superior

in number to ours; but as Pope had evidently with his main body reached the other side of the Rappahannock, it was not probable that a fierce onset of such cavalry as ours, animated by such incentives and aspirations, could be withstood.

Stuart saw that he was right: "Sure enough, before the clash of their sabers could make havoc in his ranks, he turned in flight."

The Federal regiments ran for the river in the rear and the plain soon filled with scattered little fights. Stuart sent 64 prisoners to the rear, many of them wounded. His own loss was small, three killed, thirteen wounded.

The chase halted at the river. Stuart wrote: "The remainder of the day was devoted to rest."[9]

It had been a stirring day for von Borcke, who recorded a rather heroic role for himself in bringing up Robertson's men: "I reached the regiment and with a loud voice commanded them, in the name of their General, to move forward at a gallop. As I was well known to every man in the division, the order was at once obeyed. I arrived to dash onward with the wild Virginia yell to the rescue. The enemy received us with a rattling volley, which emptied several saddles; but a few seconds more and we were in the midst of them, and their beautiful lines had broken into flight. I had the satisfaction here of saving my life by a magnificent blow upon one of my antagonists who, at the very moment of firing at me, received my full right-cut on the lower part of the neck, severing his head nearly from his body."

Von Borcke won Stuart's acclaim in orders for leading "an important flank attack." And Captain Redmond Burke, "that brave and venerable patriot animated with the fires of youth," also won mention for his courage, and for the severe leg wound which would keep him out of action for some weeks.

Stuart ended the day with kinder feeling for Robertson and wrote: "General Robertson had cause to be proud of the command which his superior discipline, organization, and drill had brought to the stability of veterans." There was even greater praise for Grumble Jones, with whom Stuart had so long been at odds: "Colonel Jones, whose regiment bore the brunt of the fight, behaved with marked courage and determination. The enemy, occupying woods and hedge rows with dismounted men, armed with long range carbines, were repeatedly dislodged by his bold onslaughts."

Even so the day ended with little gained. Stuart was still impatient for major action. He had none of the satisfaction von Borcke had at the finish: "I had a happy feeling riding out of the battle and wiping the blood from my sword on my horse's mane. I was complimented by General Stuart most warmly."

The cavalry camped for the night on the field. Sleep was interrupted by the arrival of Confederate infantry. The next day passed in brief skirmishes, with Stuart urging General Lee to permit a big cavalry raid in the Federal rear.

Before daylight of August twenty-second, he got the order he had longed for: Lee approved a strike at Pope's communications. Stuart was to move immediately, in such force as he thought necessary.

Jeb set to work with glee to carry out "my proposition." His troopers were ready within two hours.

He took a raiding party of 1,500 men and two guns.

At ten A.M. they were off upriver, their target the railroad bridge over Cedar Run at Catlett's Station, far in the Federal rear. As they left Captain Mosby had a glimpse of Stuart.

"I'm going after my hat," Jeb called, laughing.

The column poured unchallenged over the upper Rappahannock at Waterloo Bridge and Hart's Ford, and turned back to the northeast. Some five miles beyond the river crossings they reached Warrenton, where women crowded about Stuart with tears of joy.

The troopers rested an hour, allowing the rear of the column to close up. The general had a pretty visitor, a Miss Lucas, a young woman of the town who had a joke that appealed to Stuart.

She had wagered a bottle of wine with a boastful Federal captain that he would not be in Richmond "within thirty days." She was confident that Pope would soon be defeated, but the Federal captain, of Pope's quartermaster department, had only laughed at her.

"Now, General Stuart," Miss Lucas said, "if you will only capture that captain, why he will win his bet with me, for he'll surely be in Richmond as a prisoner soon. And if you'll bring him by here, I will pay him his bottle of wine. Won't that be too funny for anything?"

Stuart gave a laughing order: "Blackford, take his name and look out for him."

The column pushed on. Before dark a sudden storm burst upon it, rain fell in sheets, filling roads and bogging artillery. Night came down early. "The darkest night I ever saw," Stuart said.

A guide was almost providentially at hand. Someone approached in the dark, singing loudly. Jeb called for quiet: "Carr—eeee me back to Ole Virginny!" There was a drumming of a tin bucket in accompaniment to the song, and a trooper soon led a frightened Negro to Stuart. When the man made out the general's features he recovered from his fright. He said he remembered Stuart from a camp of last fall in Berkeley County. He could lead them to General Pope, he said, for he knew the place well. He served one of the Federal officers. Under threat of death if he betrayed them, the Negro was mounted behind a trooper, with others riding on either side.[10]

Jeb also sent Blackford around the camp, disguised in an oilcloth cloak. The captain found only a party of pickets lying carelessly at a crossroad. The big camp was almost unguarded. Stuart sent up Rosser with a few men and the pickets were quietly taken; Confederates were put in their places. From prisoners Jeb got a welcome bit of news: General Pope's own tent was nearby, full of headquarters baggage. Revenge was at hand.

Stuart ordered an attack. At the bugle sound the lead regiment would dash for the railroad station, the next would turn to Pope's camp, burning, looting and taking prisoners. The enemy tents came in sight—big, well-furnished tents with lamps hanging over the heads of officers who were drinking whisky before turning to their suppers. Odors of coffee and food crept from the camp, which was lighted "bright as day."

One clever Rebel trooper left the column, edged up to a Federal supper table, and began a quiet meal with the enemy, with no questions asked him.

In one tent Federal officers listened idly as an old army veteran who had known Stuart in frontier days warned them: "This is something like comfort. I hope Jeb Stuart won't disturb us tonight."

Not far away Stuart called to his chief bugler: "Sound the charge, Freed." The bugles gobbled and a chorus of Rebel yells burst out.

The prophetic Federal officer banged his fist on a table: "There he is, by God!" Table and glasses were abandoned as fury burst on the camp. Lights went out at the first shot.

The lead regiment plunged through one volley from a waiting line of Pennsylvania troopers and broke resistance with a saber attack. Men jumped into the depot and fell among the supplies.

Random pistol shots scattered Federals in the camp itself. Blackford saw: "supper tables kicked over and tents broken down in the rush to get out, the tents catching them sometimes in their fall like fish in a net."

Tents and wagons began to burn, and hundreds of horses, mules and prisoners were herded together. A train puffed by the depot. Blackford ordered the engineer to halt, and when he refused shot him from the throttle. Blackford's horse stumbled and the train rolled toward Washington with an empty engine. Blackford turned to the cutting of telegraph lines with a small crew of men. A seventeen-year-old trooper shinnied up a pole under fire and hacked wires with his saber.

Federal soldiers hid in the tents and behind bushes, under horses. The rain "fell in buckets," Blackford recalled. "Whole regiments of horses would rear and wheel around to get their backs to the storm." Most of the animals escaped. Union soldiers followed suit. One lightning flash would show a road filled with them, and the next would reveal it empty, the bluecoats vanished into the night.

Raiders in the main camp piled wagons full of spoils, chests and papers, food, drink, clothing.

But there was trouble at the railroad bridge. The torches would not ignite the wet timbers, and after a delay to find axes, it was found impossible to cut the double-hung beams. Federal fire broke out from across the stream and drove off some of the axemen.

Stuart abandoned the attempt. It was near midnight, streams in the rear were already rising, and the men were worn with long marching. He left with the greatest reluctance, and wrote General Lee: "The commanding General will, I am sure, appreciate how hard it was to desist from the undertaking, but to any one on the spot there could be but one opinion—its impossibility. I gave it up."

He took them back over the same route and reached Warrenton at daylight. Pope's quartermaster was among the prisoners, and he reported Pope had narrowly escaped capture by going on a brief visit just before the attack. Among the loot was Pope's personal and official baggage: Clothing, money chest, papers. There was about $350,000 in the money chest. Even more important was the dispatch book, with copies of letters which made clear Pope's plans and his fears of being attacked before help could reach him. Stuart sent these documents to General Lee.

Blackford had found among the prisoners the Federal captain Miss Lucas of Warrenton sought, and took him to Stuart. Jeb laughed.

"Go on ahead, Blackford," Stuart said, "and get the lady ready with the wine. She can have it there when we pass."

The general halted the column when he reached the Lucas house, the young woman appeared, blushing amid cheers of prisoners and the cavalry staff, and the Federal captain took his bottle of wine off toward a Richmond prison. The staff hurried back to the column.[11]

As they left the town á young gunner of the column made a note for his diary: "Raiding with General Stuart is poor fun and a hard business. Thunder, lightning, rain, storm nor darkness can stop him when he is on a warm fresh trail of Yankee game. This morning our battery, guns, horses and men look as if the whole business had passed through a shower of yellow mud last night."[12]

They camped near White Sulphur, on the fifth day that they had lived on a three-day ration. They had not seen supply wagons since the eighteenth, far back at Orange Court House.

The next day, August twenty-third, the cavalry fell back down the river, and Stuart rode off to R. E. Lee's headquarters, not far from Waterloo Bridge. As the troopers passed General Field's infantry brigade, Fitz Lee and his staff dismounted at the roadside.

Fitz hailed General Field: "Wait a minute, General. Something to show you."

Fitz slipped behind a tree with a bundle and "in a moment or two emerged dressed in the long blue cloak of a Federal General that reached nearly down to his feet, and wearing a Federal General's hat with its big plume." The infantrymen roared with laughter when they heard the story of the raid on Catlett's Station and the seizure of Pope's tent. Fitz Lee had not only snatched up this uniform, but had taken his victim's waiting supper from the table.[13]

Fitz turned over the uniform to Stuart, and Jeb spent a day or so joking about it, carrying it rolled behind his saddle, displaying it at every chance, and laughing over Pope's plight. He showed Stonewall Jackson the label: "John Pope." Jackson was shaken by his curious silent laughter, and listened in delight to Stuart's tale of the capture. Jeb scratched out a dispatch:

> Major Genl. John Pope
> Commanding, U. S. Army
>
> General: You have my hat and plume. I have your best coat. I have the honor to propose a cartel for a fair exchange of the prisoners.

Jackson laughed aloud, and made one of his rare jokes: "Stuart, I believe I'd rather you had brought General Pope instead of his coat."

Stuart sent the coat to Richmond where his kinsman, Governor Letcher, put it on display in the State Library. The city's newspapers made much of the boastful Pope's loss.

Stuart's raid on Catlett's was the talk of the army. It may have inspired the popular song published about this time: "Riding a Raid," sung to the tune of "Bonnie Dundee." Its Richmond publisher used an engraving of Stuart on the cover, resplendent in a plumed hat.[14]

But the raid had done little to alter the strategic situation. General Lee reported to President Davis that it "accomplished some minor advantages, destroyed some wagons, and captured some prisoners."

In Stuart's report the raid emerged in a different light. It was clear, Jeb wrote, "what a demoralizing effect the success of this expedition had upon the army of the enemy, shaking their confidence in a general who had scorned the enterprise and ridiculed the courage of his adversaries . . . it compelled him to make heavy detachments from his main body. It inflicted a mortifying disaster upon the general himself in the loss of his personal baggage and part of his staff."

Not only that. The troopers who had shared the rigors of the night attack seemed peerless to Jeb: "The horseman who, at his officer's bidding, without questioning leaps into unexplored darkness, knowing nothing except that there is certain danger ahead, possesses the highest attribute of the soldier. It is a great source of pride to me to command a division of such men."

No one knew Stuart better than General Lee, and the commanding general clearly appreciated his dashing horsemen. In one report of Stuart's exploits to Richmond he wrote: "I take occasion to express to the Department my sense of the boldness, judgment and prudence he displayed."

But perhaps the galloping rhetoric of the reports on Catlett's offended Lee's sense of propriety, for the commander soon wrote of Stuart: "The General deals in the flowery style, as you will perceive if you ever see his reports in detail."[15]

But Stuart wrote Flora gaily of his "rapid dash" at the enemy rear, proclaiming: "I have had my revenge out of Pope."

The army now turned to more decisive action against the enemy.

CHAPTER 10

Exit John Pope

AMONG the captives in Stuart's camp was a pretty woman who had been taken in a Federal private's uniform. She got no mercy from Jeb. She begged for release, but the horseman said, "If you're man enough to enlist, you ought to be man enough to go to prison."

Von Borcke took her to General Lee's headquarters and the staff there enjoyed teasing her. She continued her pleas that her sex should exempt her from a common prison, but headquarters sent her to Richmond. Von Borcke forgot her in the joys of the day, for his share of the loot from Catlett's was two boxes of fine Havana cigars, which he puffed endlessly.[1]

Von Borcke carried back orders for Stuart which presaged a lightning change in the battle front.

The armies still lay with the Rappahannock between them, sputtering musket and cannon fire when skirmishers met.

On Sunday, August twenty-fourth, R. E. Lee began another of his daring maneuvers. He went to Jackson's headquarters and asked him to get his men ready to march—all of them, a total of 25,000. Lee had not many more than 50,000 on the south bank of the river, and Pope lay opposite with about 80,000. There was no advantage in fighting across the river against these odds. Lee and Jackson were quick to agree on the remedy.

Jackson's corps would slip up the river, cross it, and swing northwest until in the enemy's rear. The objective was Pope's lifeline from Washington, the Orange and Alexandria Railroad. The march would be screened by cavalry.

Lee would remain behind with the balance of the army, confronting Pope until Jackson was well on his way. He would then follow in his path, and the army would concentrate. Ewell's division led Stonewall's column out in the gray light of August twenty-fifth.

Stuart remained behind for the day. He sent Captain Hardeman Stuart of his staff to a curious adventure. The captain was to seize a Federal signal post known as View Tree and supplant it with a Confederate flagman.

Hardeman Stuart found the hilltop held by a strong picket which drove off his handful of men; he was left afoot by an orderly who fled with his horse. Jeb's young cousin retreated until he met Jackson's passing column and fell in with an infantry regiment, to fight with Stonewall for a time.

Jeb was called to headquarters at midnight and ordered to take the cavalry in Jackson's path. Buglers called reveille at one A.M. and the squadrons were soon moving: Amissville, a sleeping village, then across the Rappahannock just above Waterloo Bridge and into the small town of Salem. Here the way was blocked by Jackson's wagons and artillery and Stuart took them out of the road. His report of it had a casual sound: "I got no sleep, but remained in the saddle all night. . . . Directing the artillery and ambulances to follow the road, I left with the cavalry and proceeded by farm roads and by paths parallel to General Jackson's route to reach the head of his column. . . . The country was exceedingly rough, but I succeeded, by the aid of skillful guides, in passing Bull Run Mountain without incident worthy of record."[2]

A few Federal pickets were snapped up, but no alarms were given, and when Jackson's men poured across the Bull Run range by Thoroughfare Gap, they broke into the plain in rear of the enemy. The Confederates were in great strength, ready to stand between Pope and Washington.

Until they turned back east through the pass and caught sight of the railroad, Jackson's veterans were ignorant of their objective. Allen Redwood, who marched with the 55th Virginia Infantry, sketched the men as they neared the point of decision:

"Such specters of men they were—gaunt-cheeked and hollow-eyed, hair, beard, clothing, and accouterments covered with dust—

only their faces and hands, where mingled soil and sweat streaked and crusted the skin, showing any departure from the whitey-gray uniformity. The ranks were sadly thinned. . . . Our regiment, which had begun the campaign 1015 strong and had carried into action at Richmond 620, counted off just 82 muskets!"[3]

The sweep around Pope had been no secret to the watchful Federals. The dust cloud raised by Jackson's men hung within sight of a dozen signal stations on the morning of August twenty-fifth, and signal flags waved accurate estimates of Stonewall's strength. But Pope's army lay along the Rappahannock as if unconcerned. Jackson might be headed for the Shenandoah Valley, or in any of three or four directions on a raid. By some miracle it did not occur to Federal headquarters that the maneuver placed Pope and his army in peril. The dash of Jackson, as it developed, might as well have been secret, after all.

Pope's order on the twenty-fifth instructed General Irwin McDowell to move his corps on Waterloo Bridge to see what was going on there, but there was little movement.

At the close of August twenty-sixth, when Jackson was striking the railroad far to the north, Pope's headquarters were at Warrenton Junction, and the units of his army were still scattered along the Rappahannock. Federal cavalry under General Buford was ordered westward at dawn to find Jackson's route.

In the night, scouts reported Jackson was marching for Thoroughfare Gap. The news did not seem to signal danger to Pope, who began to issue orders for a sort of castles-in-Spain battle, planning to line his forces on an east-west front between Warrenton and Gainesville. He was writing orders for this move when he was interrupted: Confederate cavalry had cut the railroad at Manassas Junction in his rear. Pope ordered a regiment "to ascertain what had occurred, repair the telegraph wires and protect the railroad there until further orders."

At midnight Pope sent a message to McDowell: The question of whether the entire Confederate army "has gone round is a question which we must settle instantly, so that we may determine our plans." It was eight thirty A.M., August twenty-seventh, before Pope ordered a concentration at Gainesville, near Manassas.

The Federal commander learned the truth—that Jackson's whole wing was behind him—only when he arrived at Bristoe Station on the railroad, where in the afternoon of the twenty-seventh General Hooker had driven back Ewell's vanguard after a sharp skirmish. Pope belatedly began his fight for life.

Stuart emerged from the cross-country ride with his troopers in the afternoon of August twenty-sixth at Gainesville, where he reported to Stonewall. Just before dusk troopers pounded into Bristoe Station and scattered the enemy picket.

Confederate infantry was flowing into the place when a wailing engine and a train of empty cars fled past to the north. It was too late to derail it, but soldiers hurried it with musket fire.

Jackson was told that troop and supply trains were due in the station, and he ordered switches opened so that they would plunge down a bank to destruction. He put a brigade of infantry along the tracks to fire on the bluecoats when they piled from the cars, and Stonewall rode to a nearby knoll, where he sat in the darkness with Stuart. When a train was heard, Jeb became anxious and turned to Stonewall: "Are you sure the switch is turned?"

"I suppose so. I sent my engineer officer to see to it."

Stuart was not satisfied, and sent Blackford to inspect the trap.

The engineer went off in the dark, found he could not ride up the railroad bank, and dismounted as the train was rushing upon him. A sharp volley came from the infantry as the train drew near. The quick-thinking Blackford jumped across the track in front of the racing engine and stumbled down the opposite bank, safe from spattering Confederate bullets. The train hurtled through the open switch at about fifty miles an hour, and half the cars tumbled down the bank.

When Blackford at last recrossed the railroad he learned that Stuart had left for Manassas. Jeb thought Blackford was dead, friends said, and had gone off with the staff, someone leading Blackford's horse. The engineer joined Jackson's staff to watch the trapping of more trains.[4]

Soldiers smashed red lanterns on the rear of the standing train
and a second engine rammed into it, plunging through three cars
and knocking them across the track. Blackford broke out the rear
lanterns of the second ruined train. A third headlight appeared, but
soon halted, and a shrieking engine backed up swiftly, sounding the
alarm. Confederates set fire to the jumbled box cars, and wrecking
crews pulled up the tracks.

In Blackford's brief absence, Jackson learned of an enormous
enemy supply depot at Manassas Junction, four miles up the rails
toward Washington. His troops were worn, but old Ike Trimble,
one of the most belligerent of his general officers, insisted that he
be sent to the Junction. He marched at about nine P.M. with two
infantry regiments, anxious for spoils and glory.

Jackson had sent Stuart on the same errand. This was the beginning of a bitter army feud, for Jeb understood only that Stonewall told him "to take charge of the whole." He did not know what
Trimble's orders had been, and the infantryman was not aware of
Stuart's assignment.

Stuart hurried his troopers through the night and reached the
place ahead of the infantry. He was halted by artillery fire and
settled down to wait for morning. His version was that General
Trimble, when he came up, asked for the delay until dawn. Trimble
later denied this with heat and engaged in a controversy that was to
crowd army records for months.

Before daylight North Carolina and Georgia infantrymen drove
off Federal artillerymen in the village and captured their guns.
Jackson's vanguard fell upon such spoils as they had never seen.

Von Borcke wrote:

"It was amusing to see here a ragged fellow regaling himself
with a box of pickled oysters or potted lobster; there another cutting
into a cheese of enormous size, or emptying a bottle of champagne;
while hundreds were opening packages of boots and shoes and other
clothing."

The cavalry and infantry fought for these spoils, and von
Borcke enjoyed carrying out an order from Stuart to divide plunder
among Stuart Horse Artillerymen who pressed around a wagon:
"The different boxes were speedily opened by my sword, and were

found to contain shirts, hats, pocket handkerchiefs, oranges, lemons, wines, cigars."⁵

Stonewall had the whisky and wine of the depot destroyed, and hundreds of kegs were smashed. Major Roy Mason of General Field's staff saw a depressing sight: "Streams of spirits ran like water through the sands of Manassas, and the soldiers on hands and knees drank it greedily from the ground as it ran."⁶

Jackson ordered depot sheds burned, and stores began to flame long before all the hungry Confederates had been fed.

The enemy was already pressing in. A New Jersey brigade had come from Alexandria to protect the depot, unaware of Jackson's strength. The little bluecoat force at first faced Fitz Lee's command, and the amused trooper met General George Taylor's demand for surrender with a joking reply. He agreed solemnly that he was surrounded, with Taylor in his front and Pope in his rear, but asked for an hour to consider the demand.

Within a few minutes Jackson came with infantry and the brave New Jersey troops, still thinking they faced only a few cavalrymen, charged into ruinous fire. Jackson himself went to the front, waving a white handkerchief and yelling a demand for surrender, but the Federals broke only when overwhelmed from front and both flanks. The New Jerseymen were routed, leaving 300 prisoners behind.

Stonewall marched to Groveton, leaving Manassas Junction a burning ruin in his rear.

To the west of him General Lee should soon be coming over the mountain at Thoroughfare Gap, and his approach had suddenly become a matter of concern. Until Longstreet's big corps came up with General Lee, Jackson might have to face the whole of Pope's army alone—and the result of the miraculous march might be Stonewall's destruction.

And on the searing morning of August twenty-eighth, as the blue columns pushed nearer Jackson over the dusty plains, the men in ranks feared the worst. Those in the rear could see signs of fighting on the slopes around Thoroughfare Gap, where the enemy was trying to halt Longstreet.

Stuart's troopers were in position, except for Fitz Lee's regiments, which were raiding toward Alexandria. Most of Robertson's men were near Sudley Church on Jackson's flank, and Colonel Tiernan Brien, with the 1st Virginia, and Colonel Tom Rosser, with all his force, were in front of Jackson, facing Manassas and Gainesville. Firing increased, but Jackson continued to wait on his wooded ridge.

Stuart went to Stonewall with a captured dispatch: Bluecoat cavalry were marching on the nearby village of Hay Market. Stuart was anxious to welcome them: "I proposed to General Jackson to allow me to go up there and do what I could with the two fragments of brigades I still had."

Jackson agreed, for the Federal infantry did not seem near enough to threaten him yet. Stuart skirmished with enemy cavalry at Hay Market until he heard Jackson's front erupt behind him in heavy fighting. Jeb then turned back, but he was too late. Darkness fell and the battle sputtered out before he arrived.

Jackson had spent the late afternoon with his men packed into the hot woods of his hillside, waiting. Federal columns marched, but none came within easy reach, and Stonewall paced nervously until, just before dark, a bold bluecoat column came straight toward him. Jackson almost joyously gave his command, "Bring up your men, gentlemen," and the battle was on. Captain Blackford, watching, thought the men went into the open like so many ravenous beasts.

In the sharp engagement that crackled until nine P.M. the Confederates pushed back the enemy slightly, but sustained many casualties. Dick Ewell was lost to the army for months with an amputated leg; losses in officers were heavy, and many ranks were riddled. One who served Stonewall well was John Pelham. Jackson remembered him in his report: "Owing to the difficulty of getting artillery through the woods, I did not have as much of that arm as I desired at the opening of the engagement; but this want was met by Major Pelham, with the Stuart Horse Artillery, who dashed forward on my right and opened upon the enemy at a moment when his services were much needed." Stuart added: "Pelham is always in the right place at the right time."[7]

In the night Jackson moved his men back to their original position, and placed one flank on the banks of an old railroad cut.

His front was about half a mile long, with no more than 18,000 infantrymen left to guard it. Stuart's troopers patrolled the flanks.
Stonewall's men heard the news that Longstreet had forced the
mountain pass in their rear last night, and they craned anxiously to
see if there were signs of his coming.

Before nine A.M. Jackson sent Stuart rearward to bring Longstreet in on the flank. Jeb soon saw to the west a thick dust cloud
and went into a gallop. Longstreet had come.

Longstreet and General Lee were in advance of the column to
avoid kicking dust in the eyes of the lead infantrymen. They rode
for a mile or more with Stuart as he described the positions of Jackson and Pope, and when they were almost within sight of Jackson's
line, turned to the roadside and dismounted. Stuart shook out a map
of the country and pointed out the situation. Longstreet's veterans
plodded by them, so covered with dust that they looked like clay
men cast in one mold. The troops cheered as they recognized Lee,
Longstreet and Stuart.

There was soon cheering from the front, where Jackson's men
could see the reinforcements. But there would be strange delays
during the day, when some mysterious conflict between Lee and
the stubborn Longstreet postponed the coming of the new corps
to action.

Blackford had only lately rejoined Stuart, to be hugged affec-
tionately by the general and hailed by the staff as if risen from the
dead, an ambulance having been ordered to bring his body from
Bristoe Station. The engineer now rode with Stuart as he carried out
Lee's orders.

Stuart soon found a good gun position, and opened fire on
Federals in a woodland. The enemy began to move.

Jeb went forward for a look: At least half an army corps was
moving against him, and if it kept its present line, would pass over
the commanding knoll he held. Jeb's guns were still firing, but that
was not enough. He sent several squadrons up and down the road,
and into a field, where they dashed back and forth, dragging behind
their horses branches hacked from pine trees. The dust they stirred
up seemed to slow the enemy and convince them a large force was

moving in the area. The bluecoats waited in the distance. In the end this Federal corps—under General Fitz John Porter—lay all afternoon in idleness, while Pope's attacks lashed against Jackson's line and were driven back in bloody remnants. This incident would grow into a court-martial and cost Porter his command; it was probably Longstreet's presence that did most to halt Porter this hot afternoon, but Stuart's ruse also had its effect.

Stonewall's regiments had been through desperate fighting, their lines broken by Federal assaults time after time. In some places men had used stones to drive off the enemy. It had been a near thing, with officers exhorting their men to die in their tracks rather than abandon the line. All the while Longstreet's big corps had been at hand, but had not joined, for Old Pete had opposed throwing his men into the battle so early and persuaded General Lee to allow Jackson to beat off Pope alone. Near the end of the day, however, Longstreet pushed his line forward and by nightfall the army was united at last, facing the enemy in a long, hinged line. Somehow, incredibly, General Pope was not yet convinced that Longstreet was on the field.

During the day's uproar Stuart had taken part in a defense of Jackson's wagon train, which was assailed by enemy cavalry. Pelham's guns had broken up the attack with heavy casualties, but Major William Patrick, a promising young commander of six of Stuart's companies, was shot down. Stuart wrote: "He lived long enough to witness the triumph of our arms, and expired thus in the arms of victory. The sacrifice was noble, but the loss to us irreparable."

Stuart moved over the field long after dark. Von Borcke wrote casually of a narrow escape: "Late in the night I was requested by General Stuart to bear him company in a little reconnaissance outside our lines, which came very near terminating disastrously, as on our return, in the thick darkness, we were received with a sharp but fortunately ill-aimed fire from our own men."

Stuart and his staff slept near an artillery battery. They did not unsaddle the horses, and most of them used empty cartridge boxes for pillows.

Morning was hazy and sultry. There was an occasional shell

burst, and dry grasses burned whitely across the fields. For some reason the Federals waited. Stuart pushed forward early in the day to a farmhouse, where he had a trooper climb a tree and inspect the Federal lines. The distant fields were covered with blue masses, slowly moving toward the Confederate left, which was held by Jackson, but there were many halts, and the hours dragged.

At two thirty P.M., when Federal attack was obviously near, Stuart was called to headquarters, and sat with Lee, Longstreet and Jackson. They talked briefly and then separated. A few minutes later the Federal guns opened; the Confederate lines lay out of sight during this storm and soon the bluecoats moved up, three lines of them, straight as if on parade, under bright flags and hedgerows of bayonets. Almost at once, it seemed to the watching Captain Blackford, gray puffs broke over the rows of toy soldiers, and figures went down in heaps. Confederate artillery had seldom been more effective. On Jackson's flank Colonel Stephen D. Lee, of Stuart's West Point class, commanded twenty-two guns which fired directly down the oncoming files. The gunners could hardly miss their targets.

From Longstreet's wing a far greater chorus of guns soon opened. When Jackson asked for reinforcements, Longstreet replied that the guns would break up the assault before support could arrive. He was right. When Jackson's infantry fired point-blank at the charging Federals, and the enemy line was staggered, Longstreet's artillery blazed in cross fire. There was chaos on the dusty field.

At some interval during the roaring of battle Stuart fell asleep, while Longstreet watched in amazement.

Stuart had ridden to report to General Lee the coming of Federal reinforcements in the front.

"Any further orders, sir?" Stuart asked.

"None. Wait awhile, if you will, General."

And then, by Longstreet's account: "Stuart turned round in his tracks, lay down on the ground, put a stone under his head and fell instantly asleep."

General Lee rode away. He was back in an hour and Stuart was still asleep. Lee asked for him, and Jeb, as if he had heard every word, scrambled to his feet.

"Here I am, General," he said.

"I want you to get a message to your troops on the left to send a few more cavalry to the right."

"I'd better go myself," Jeb said, and went off at a gallop. Longstreet noted with amusement that he sang at the top of his voice, " 'Jine the Cavalry! If you want to see the Devil . . . have a good time, Jine the Cavalry!' "[8]

But the battle was to be brief, and when the climax came Stuart was stirred by the spectacle. He wrote of it:

"About 3 P.M. our right wing advanced to the attack. I directed Robertson's brigade and Rosser's regiment to push forward on the extreme right, and at the same time all the batteries that I could get hold of were advanced at a gallop to take position to enfilade the enemy in front of our lines. This was done with splendid effect, Colonel Rosser, a splendid artillerist as well as a bold cavalier, having the immediate direction of the batteries.

"The fight was of remarkably short duration. The Lord of Hosts was plainly fighting on our side, and the solid walls of Federal infantry melted away before the straggling but determined onset of our infantry columns."

Robertson's cavalry now looked down on the retreat from a ridge above Bull Run. Stuart rode there, saw no enemy threat, and was galloping back toward his artillery position when a courier overtook him: Robertson was now fighting desperately at Bull Run against Federal cavalry, which had swept suddenly upon him. Stuart hurried back with two reserve regiments, but when he arrived on a lathered horse, the last bluecoat riders were splashing over Bull Run in retreat. It had been, in Stuart's words, "a brilliant affair." Colonel T. T. Munford and his 2nd Virginia won most of the glory. Robertson's brigade had lost but three dead and thirty-two badly wounded. Colonel Munford had a saber wound.

This brush seemed grand to Stuart: "Nothing could have equalled the splendor with which Robertson's regiments swept down upon a force greatly outnumbering them . . . indicating a claim for courage and discipline equal to any cavalry in the world."

Stuart thought there was still time for attack, for some Federal infantry had not retreated over Bull Run. He asked Colonel Lewis Armistead, the nearest infantry commander, to join him in an assault. Armistead declined. Stuart sent a courier to Lee, explaining the opportunity. Lee did not respond. Stuart wrote for the record only: "The attack was not made."

In the dusk the army was licking wounds as severe as any of those of the Seven Days. The field was blanketed with dead and wounded. Though the Federals had been driven from the field, many a Confederate brigade was wrecked.

Stuart found that one among the dead infantrymen was his young cousin, Hardeman Stuart, for whom he grieved: "No young man was more universally beloved or will be more universally mourned. He was a young man of fine attainments and bright promise." Hardeman died in the last moments of the fighting.

John Esten Cooke had met Hardeman Stuart in the Seven Days, a twenty-one-year-old with "a laughing face . . . exquisite frankness . . . large honest eyes . . . the model of an aide-de-camp . . . exposing himself to the heaviest fire, in the thickest portion of the fight . . . gay, laughing, and unharmed." Cooke caught a glimpse of him early in today's fight, recognizing one of the tattered infantry figures as Hardeman Stuart: "But what a change! He had always been the neatest person imaginable . . . his brown hair had always been carefully parted and brushed, his boots polished . . . his new uniform coat, with its gay braid, had been almost too nice and unwrinkled for a soldier."

No more. Captain Hardeman Stuart, turned infantry rifleman, was a strange contrast to the staff officer who had so lately lost his horse on an errand for Jeb: "Coatless, unwashed, his boots covered with dust, and his clothes had the dingy look of the real soldier. His hair was unbrushed, and hung disordered around his face." But the smile was the same, as he told Cooke the story of the loss of his horse.

"Well, Hardeman," Cooke said, "you've had bad luck. But get another horse and come on."

"I intend to. Tell the General I'll soon be there."

Cooke left him, and within a few minutes Hardeman Stuart died in a charge of Mississippi infantry. A short time afterward Jeb's cavalrymen swept upon Federal troopers in a tavern near Manassas and found a captive with Hardeman's coat. There was no mistaking it. Young Stuart's captain's commission was in a pocket.[9]

At ten P.M. firing died out around Manassas, and a rainstorm broke on the armies, making more miserable the fields of wounded among whom men moved with ambulances and stretchers by lantern light.

Stuart had only praise for the cavalry corps and his staff. Munford had shown "resolute bravery" in face of superior numbers. Pelham had been as valuable as ever, and Stonewall Jackson had said, "Stuart, if you have another Pelham, give him to me."[10]

Captain W. D. Farley of the staff had carried a dispatch near the climax of battle at the Chinn House "under circumstances of great personal danger." Farley's horse was killed beneath him.

The division surgeon, Dr. Talcott Eliason, "besides being an adept in his profession, exhibited on this, as on former occasions, the attributes of a cavalry commander." In the heat of battle the doctor had led charges, as some of Jeb's chaplains were prone to do.

There was also praise for Captain Blackford, "quick and indefatigable in his efforts to detect the designs of the enemy and improve the positions within our reach." There was mention for von Borcke, for Lieutenant Channing Price, Chiswell Dabney, and others of the staff.

Stuart also had complaints:

"Twenty or thirty ambulances were captured and sent back, with orders to go to work removing our dead and wounded from the battlefield . . . those ambulances were seized as fresh captures by a Texas brigade . . . a large number of prisoners I sent to the rear were fired upon by our infantry."

And General Trimble's report raised his ire:

[This report] "does the cavalry injustice. . . . There seems to be a growing tendency to abuse and underrate the services of that arm by a few officers of infantry, among whom I regret to find General Trimble. Troops should be taught to take pride in other branches of the service than their own."

The fighting around Manassas had been much more bloody than that of the previous summer. Federal losses were about 15,000, and

Confederate at least 9,000. Stuart's share of these casualties had been
trifling. Most regiments had not reported, but the three nearest at
hand had losses of six dead and 48 wounded.

Stuart's staff spent most of the night carrying water to the
wounded and bringing men to cover from the rain. Von Borcke had
but a few hours of sleep before Jeb shook him awake "at peep of
day" and sent him to Jackson with dispatches, and to Fitz Lee with
orders to march toward Fairfax Court House. Stuart would meet
Fitz's troopers in the afternoon.

Von Borcke had a rain-swept ride of five miles or more along
the Confederate line, wrapped in a black oilcloth coat with his hat
brim turned down over his face. He was dry, but his bizarre appearance brought him an adventure with alert Rebel patrols.

One of Jackson's quartermasters was made suspicious by the
German's accent and curious costume. Two horsemen soon caught
up with von Borcke, and pressing him on either side, asked him "im-
pertinently inquisitive questions." Other horsemen came up and demanded his surrender. Von Borcke threw open his raincoat to expose
his gray uniform.

"If you still doubt me, ride to Jackson's headquarters with me
and learn your mistake. But you will not see my papers. They were
entrusted to me, and I will die to defend them."

"Any Yankee can tell the same story. It's an old trick."

Von Borcke spurred his horse past these sentries into the open,
but his tormentors followed with drawn pistols a few yards to the
rear until von Borcke met an officer of his acquaintance, who identified him and set him free. The German sent his card as summons to
a duel to the suspicious quartermaster—but the culprit never appeared at Stuart's headquarters to face the giant and his avenging
Damascus blade.

Von Borcke found Jackson with Robert E. Lee as the commanders returned from a scout across Bull Run. They laughed at his
tale of mistaken identity, and the Prussian delivered his dispatch and
rode to Fitz Lee's camp.[11]

Stuart joined them in the afternoon and the cavalry force
walked through the rain parallel to the route of the enemy on a

nearby turnpike. By ten P.M. of August thirty-first Jeb had them in camp near the settlement of Chantilly. He had friends in the neighborhood whom he had not seen since the early weeks of the war, and took his staff six miles through the countryside for a visit.

A dozen or more bedraggled horsemen rode into the dooryard about midnight, von Borcke recalled. Two big and "ferocious" hounds howled. The family of the place was asleep.

"Let's try 'em with a serenade," Stuart said.

The staff gathered on horseback beneath a window. Sam Sweeney swung his banjo from under cover and opened the song. Von Borcke wrote: "The discordant voices that joined in the effort sounded so very like the voices of the wild Indians in their war whoop, that the proprietor, at once awakened, and fully persuaded that his peaceful residence was surrounded by a party of marauding Yankees, carefully opened a window."

The plantation owner begged "most anxiously" that the lives of the household be spared, and promised to do anything demanded of him.

When Stuart spoke, the man recognized his voice, roused his family and took Stuart and the staff into the house. Von Borcke wrote: "We remained talking with our kind friends until the morning sun, stealing through the curtains of the drawing room, reminded us that it was time to be off." They had breakfast and rode back to camp.

They found the army had halted. Late in the morning Jeb was sent with Jackson down Little River Turnpike and in a downpour of rain the vanguard ran into ambush. Von Borcke and Colonel Rosser were in front when firing ripped the woodlands about them, but the enemy had sprung the trap too soon, and casualties were few. Stonewall brought up several regiments, threw them into line and pushed against the enemy. They met stiff resistance, and despite the driving rain a sharp battle blazed in the late afternoon.[12]

Stuart's staff became anxious, for the fire grew into an ominous chorus at dusk, and in case Jackson met defeat the cavalry would be dangerously exposed. But Jeb's riders in front reported withdrawal of Pope's army toward Alexandria, and after dark it was obvious that the enemy was in full flight.

The action between Jackson and a wing of the Federal army was known as Chantilly or Ox Hill, and in its few moments had been spirited and bloody. One of the enemy casualties, found in Confederate lines that night, was a one-armed general.

"It must be Phil Kearny," someone said.

Stuart rode with a small escort to identify the body, since he had known the Federal for years. Stuart and Blackford found the body in a farmhouse in a plain undress uniform. It was Kearny. His death was reported to General Lee, who ordered the body sent into Federal lines.

Blackford had suffered a casualty during the day. His fine horse, Comet, had been wounded in the neck by a shellburst and Blackford had left him on a nearby farm. Stuart was saddened, for, as Blackford said, "next to having a staff composed of handsome men about him, he liked to see them mounted on fine horses."[13]

The cavalry camped in a pine grove where men dried their clothing by roaring fires all night. There was a welcome surprise in the morning: Wade Hampton had come up from his picket duty below Richmond with a brigade of troopers from South Carolina and Mississippi. The new brigade took the lead in the day's pursuit of the enemy and there was light skirmishing around Fairfax Court House.

The action ended with the enemy driven from a ridge about two miles from the center of the village, but the enemy left a trail of burning houses and barns, and Stuart, looking down from a hilltop, told von Borcke, "Major, ride as quick as you can, and bring up some of Pelham's guns so I can salute those rascally incendiaries. At the gallop!" Von Borcke snatched the headquarters battle flag from the color bearer and planted it in the square of Fairfax. The town had been occupied by Northern troops for months, and there was a warm welcome for the gray horsemen.

Stuart visited the home of the Ford family, whose daughter Antonia had charmed from him an honorary commission the year before. Von Borcke noted mournfully that the pretty girl betrayed Stuart's trust by marrying a Yankee officer and taking the oath of allegiance to the Union.

There was a brief respite in Fairfax, for the cavalry had orders to push toward Washington, probing enemy positions. Stuart had the staff busy. Sam Sweeney left on some errand, and a young woman, riding a public coach in the Shenandoah Valley, had a vivid recollection of the musician: "Never shall I forget that moonlight stage ride to Harrisonburg. There were three ladies and four gentlemen on the inside and three on top of the stage, one of whom was General Stuart's banjoist. His music was so bright and gay, that I could not keep my feet still."[14]

Stuart took the troopers toward Dranesville, where he had been so soundly punished by Federal infantry the year before, and they went into a quiet camp. For a few hours headquarters rested.

A campaign had ended. In two months General Lee had driven two invading armies from Virginia, shifting the front from within five miles of Richmond to the gates of Washington. The fumbling army of Joseph Johnston had become daring, slashing, and was learning precision. There was already talk of invading the North to teach the Yankee aggressors a lesson. The end of the war seemed near in these first days of September, 1862.

The cavalry corps had more than doubled in size since the Seven Days, and was now at a peak of strength and morale. Horses were good and fairly plentiful. Unlike the enemy cavalry, Stuart's troopers had to furnish their own mounts, and until now the farm and plantation homes had sent superior stock. The enemy had to be content with horses from Government stables, often inferior.

On September fifth General Beverly Robertson finally went out of the corps to organize cavalry in North Carolina, and Colonel Munford took temporary command of his squadrons. Stuart wrote Flora on September fourth:

> Long before this reaches you I will be in Maryland. I have not been able to keep the list of battles, much less give you any account of them. Our present position on the banks of the Potomac will tell you volumes . . . all the officers on the other side speak kindly of me. May God bless you.
>
> I send $200 in draft and $50 in notes. Can you pay my tailor bill?
>
> The Horse Artillery has won imperishable laurels!

On the same day General Lee's infantry began fording the Potomac into Maryland, and the invasion was on. Deserters and stragglers had stripped Lee's strength of almost 30,000 men, and those who remained were often barefoot and in rags. There was a fear, the commander wrote President Davis, of running out of ammunition in the North. But the Virginia countryside was picked clean and the army must move to feed itself.

Lee had painfully injured himself just after Second Manassas. Traveller had been frightened, lunged, and the commander had small bones broken in one hand. He was jostled over a Potomac ford in an ambulance.

☆

CHAPTER 11

Bloody Maryland

FOR three days Confederate columns crossed the river into Maryland. Bands blared ceaselessly at every ford, as if the lank-haired scarecrows needed stimulation. The musicians played "Dixie" and "Maryland, My Maryland," until the echoes might have carried downriver into Washington, where Pope's army hid in the trenches.

There was no one to stop them on the Northern shore; only wide-eyed civilians looked at the most ragged, dirty and profane men they could remember. Leighton Parks, a Maryland boy of twelve, saw them as "a hungry set of wolves," but he admired the horsemanship of Stuart's troopers; they rode like circus riders, he thought.

A gunner of the Horse Artillery, George Neese, was a diarist who found the passage was interminable. His battery was forever being stalled in the road behind the wagons. They had waited for three hours near Goose Creek, south of Leesburg, Virginia; when they did ford, water almost poured into the mouths of the cannon. They had halted at Leesburg on September fifth:

"Thousands of soldiers camped around Leesburg this evening, and all seem to be in joyous gayety, caused, I suppose, by bright anticipations of crossing the Potomac and entering Maryland. As I am writing I hear soldiers shouting, huzzahing all around us. Just now a brass band has struck up, which helps to swell the cheer of the merry throng."

They reached the Potomac before sunset of the next day, but Neese and his battery mates could not cross until late, and lay on the bank in dust so thick "as to make it impossible to discern a man three rods distant."

"It was midnight when we left the Southern Confederacy . . .
forded the Potomac, and landed in the United States, Montgomery
County, Maryland."[1]

The ford at this place was two and a half feet deep, the bottom
smooth, and the river some four hundred yards wide. The artillery
pressed north through the town of Frederick, and then turned back
to the village of Urbana, seven miles to the southeast.

Stuart crossed the Potomac at White's Ford, where the banks
soared sixty feet above the water, covered by huge vine-wrapped
trees. The cavalry staff rested for a moment on a sandbank in midstream, and von Borcke gazed at the column of troopers: "A magnificent sight. . . . The evening sun slanted upon clear placid waters,
and burnished them with gold, while the arms of the soldiers glittered and blazed. There were few moments . . . of the war of excitement more intense . . . than when we ascended the opposite bank
to the familiar but now strangely thrilling music of 'Maryland, My
Maryland.' "

Within two or three miles the cavalry reached the village of
Poolesville, where they flushed a small Federal party and took thirty
prisoners. A staff officer recorded: "The inhabitants of Maryland
whom we met along the road . . . did not greet us quite so cordially
as we had expected. . . . It was different, however, at Poolesville."

The cavalry was in the village for half an hour, beseiged by
eager civilians with questions about the army. A few young men on
horses insisted upon joining Stuart, and two merchants, swept up by
war fever, enlisted in the corps and sold their stock on the spot—for
Confederate money. Von Borcke wrote: "Our soldiers cleared out
both establishments to the last pin. Soldiers, on such occasions, are
like children. They buy everything." The German could not resist
buying cigars, sugar, lemons and a pocketknife.

Stuart's pickets soon spread from the Potomac to the Baltimore
& Ohio Railroad tracks, which were just south of Frederick. Fitz
Lee held the northern end, at the settlement of New Market; Wade
Hampton was posted in the center, around Hyattstown; and Munford commanded the lower section, including a signal station on
the top of Sugar Loaf Mountain. Munford's pickets were strung
southward to Poolesville and beyond. This screen was to protect the
army's eastern flank.

At noon on September sixth Stuart entered Urbana, where he planned to make headquarters. He did not stop there, but sent von Borcke to establish camp while he rode into Frederick for a conference with the infantry commanders.

Jeb found acquaintances in the town. Dwight Dudley, a young Federal medical cadet left behind to nurse the wounded, saw several Confederate officers on a porch. One of the officers, "of noble and distinguished military bearing" beckoned to Dudley, and came from the porch to meet him. This Confederate was talkative and anxious to impress: "I want you to tell your commanding general when he comes that we have treated his friends here with great kindness, and that we expect the same treatment for ours, and unless they receive it, I will doubly retaliate at each and every opportunity. . . . I am General Stuart."[2]

Jeb also had a heated exchange with Captain Elijah White, of the 35th Battalion, Virginia cavalry, a troop of wild young riders styled "The Comanches." White drew Stuart's wrath, perhaps because of the behavior of some of his troops in Frederick or simply because they were as yet irregulars. Jeb ordered White to return to Virginia with his company.

White protested, "I've fought as hard as any man for the chance to come here and fight in my native state."

Stuart flushed. "Do you say you have done as much as any man for the South?"

"No, sir. I didn't say that. But I've done my duty to the best of my ability, as fully as anybody."

"You did say you had done as much as any man."

"I said no such thing."

Stuart again ordered White back into Virginia. White refused. "I'll go see General Lee about it," the captain said.

"Come on," Stuart said. "I'll go with you."

At headquarters, Stuart disappeared into Lee's tent. Lee met White at the door and asked him to wait outside.

Stonewall Jackson emerged to find White in tears. White explained that he did not want to be sent back to Virginia.

Jackson seemed surprised. "Why, I just heard General Stuart tell General Lee that you wanted to be sent back, and recommend that you be sent."

White was so choked with emotion that he could not speak. Jackson told him he should obey orders no matter how unjust they seemed.

Stuart came out and called to White, "Did you say you were a Marylander?"

"Yes, sir."

"Ah. I didn't know it. General Lee wants to see you. Go in."

White entered, and got orders to scout with his company toward Harpers Ferry, and report to Lee in person; for the time, he was free of Stuart's orders, and though he was forced to return to Virginia, the commander had salved his feelings with his customary diplomacy.[3]

There was a holiday air about headquarters. The army had learned that General Pope had been removed from his command, replaced by McClellan. But there was as yet no Federal movement. The big army of the enemy was still around Washington.

General Lee was hopeful that Maryland would join the Confederate cause, and issued a proclamation urging her to aid the army, promising that there would be no depredations. Enoch Lowe, a former governor of the state, was expected to come to Frederick and cast his lot with the Confederates; he had not arrived.

Visitors thronged about them, for Frederick, though it offered no support, seemed strongly Confederate. Von Borcke noted that doors of Union sympathizers were barred, but otherwise: "The greater number of citizens had thrown wide open their doors and welcomed our troops with the liveliest enthusiasm. Flags were floating from the houses, and garlands of flowers were hung across the streets. Everywhere a dense multitude was moving up and down, singing and shouting in a paroxysm of joy and patriotic emotion, in many cases partly superinduced by an abundant flow of strong liquors."

All officers with plumes in their hats were mistaken for Jackson or Stuart, and von Borcke was soon followed by a mob, insisting that he was Stonewall Jackson, cheering and pressing bouquets on him. The Prussian left the town and returned to the country quiet of Urbana.

Stuart was soon in the village, busy with orders to his outposts.

The next morning a delegation of citizens invited Stuart and his staff
to dine at the home of the Cockey family. Jeb and his young men
spent the afternoon at the house, laughing, talking and singing with
several young women. The most attractive and most fervently Confederate of them was a kinswoman of the Cockeys from the North,
and a favorite of Stuart's. He called her "the New York Rebel." Von
Borcke remembered: "In the agreeable conversation of these ladies,
in mirth and song, the afternoon of our dinner party passed lightly
and rapidly away; and then came night . . . with a round moon,
whose beams penetrating the windows suggested to our debonair
commander a promenade."

Stuart proposed a walk, and several couples strolled through the
little town to a deserted academy building, walked through its empty
rooms, and watched the moonlit landscape from its galleries. Stuart
called to von Borcke:

"Major, what a capital place for us to give a ball in honor of our
arrival in Maryland! Don't you think we could manage it?"

There were yelps of delight, and the party scattered to make
ready for the dance. Stuart agreed to furnish the music; von Borcke
would decorate the hall, light it and send cards of invitation. There
must be no delay. The ball would be held the next night, before
military duties could interfere.

Cavalry headquarters devoted the next day to the frolic. Couriers took invitations to families for miles around Urbana. Von
Borcke directed troopers as they aired out the big hall of the
academy, swept its floors, and decorated it with roses and battle
flags. The place literally glowed at dusk with hundreds of borrowed
candles.

The streets of Urbana filled with carriages and buggies, as the
Maryland community joined the cavalrymen at play. Captain Blackford noted a grim detail—every horseman picketed his mount near
the academy, and the troopers were fully armed. Just before the
huge moon rose there was music, and the crack band of the 18th
Mississippi Infantry came, loudly playing "Dixie." The applauding
crowd followed into the ballroom.

Von Borcke was master of ceremonies. He announced a polka,
and reached for "the New York Rebel" to dance with him as queen

of the festival. The young woman refused, giving the German a lesson in provincial American manners: Ladies could "round dance" only with their brothers and cousins. Von Borcke quickly changed the program, and the band played for a quadrille. The officers hung their sabers on the walls and joined, and the ballroom shuddered to the music and dancing. Von Borcke and Blackford thought all the women lovely, and were captivated by the gaiety of the spectacle.

An orderly pushed roughly through the crowd. Those nearby heard him report to Stuart: "The enemy, sir. They've driven the pickets and are coming on. They're in camp, lots of them."

Pistol shots outside sounded dangerously near. Music scraped to a halt, and the ballroom soon cleared of men; horses pounded off in the moonlight. Women screamed, and some families collected their children to go home. Most of them waited. Firing outside the village grew louder. Artillery roared.

Stuart found that the 1st North Carolina had broken the enemy attack. A few of Pelham's guns barked until the Federals were out of sight. Pursuit lasted for several miles, and the column straggled back with prisoners. By midnight all was quiet once more.

By one A.M. Stuart and his officers were back at the academy, where candles still burned and most of the young women were waiting. The band struck up again and volunteers scattered to the homes of women who had left in their absence and brought them back, laughing happily.

A woman with whom Blackford was dancing screamed in his ear. She had seen loaded stretchers passing in the hallway—casualties of the night's skirmish. The women left the dance floor to work with the wounded.

"The New York Rebel" leaned over a boy with a bullet in his shoulder, but fainted at sight of so much blood. When she revived, Blackford and von Borcke begged her to go home, but she refused, and continued nursing, saying, "First I must do my duty."

One wounded soldier said, "I'd get hit any day to have such surgeons dress my wounds." It was daylight when officers took the last of the young women home and turned to their camp for a few hours of sleep.

In the late afternoon Stuart heard cannon fire from the east, and got a report from Fitz Lee of a lively skirmish at the village of Barnesville. But there was no serious threat, and Stuart remained for the evening at the home where "the New York Rebel" entertained him. There was a cavalry serenade, probably with Sweeney's banjo, Bob's bones, the fiddlers and chorus. It was September eighth, the last gay evening in Maryland for the troopers.[4]

On the picket line to the east the corps felt pressure increasing almost hourly as the Federals pushed from Washington. Munford's force got the worst of it, for his squadrons were already thin. Munford had left all but three regiments in Virginia to police the battle-field of Second Manassas, and casualties had cut those remaining. Only seventy-five men rode in the 12th Virginia, and the 2nd Virginia had fewer than two hundred.

The bluecoats had driven them through Poolesville on September seventh, and the next day two huge Federal cavalry regiments, the 8th Illinois and 3rd Indiana, took Poolesville. Munford tried, but the decimated 12th Virginia broke and ran, and the front fell back to Barnesville, some seven miles north. The next day, September ninth, was no better; the enemy defeated the 12th Virginia once more and took the regimental colors. The blue tide surged around the signal post on Sugar Loaf Mountain, but did not take it until the eleventh, when Federal infantry came in. Stuart's line in this sector fell back to Frederick. The enemy was beginning to stir.

General Lee had already launched another of his audacious moves. An estimated 90,000 Federal troops confronted him. He had less than half that number. Yet he was once more dividing his army, this time into five parts.

Lee had thought enemy garrisons at Harpers Ferry and Martinsburg would be evacuated when he crossed the Potomac, but after almost a week these Federal strongholds remained defiantly in the rear. They must be reduced before invasion could proceed, and Lee calmly detached his strength in the face of McClellan's advance. He sent Jackson southward across the Potomac with three divisions to strike the garrisons; Lafayette McLaws took a division across rough country to the river, north of Harpers Ferry, with J. G. Walker's division on a nearby course. D. H. Hill would guard the rear of

Longstreet's big command, which would march west toward Hagerstown.

A story illustrative of Lee's calm was soon being enjoyed by officers of the army. General Walker had gone to Lee's tent for orders, and stared in astonishment as he was told of the daring maneuver.

"You doubtless regard it as hazardous to leave McClellan on my line of communication and to march into the heart of the enemy's country?" Lee said.

"Yes, I do."

"Are you acquainted with General McClellan? He is an able general, but a very cautious one. His enemies among his own people think him too much so. His army is in a very demoralized and chaotic condition, and will not be ready for offensive operations—or he will not think it so—for three or four weeks. Before that time I hope to be on the Susquehanna."[5]

The infantry marched out of Frederick on September tenth toward its various objectives, and in the rear the cavalry fought delaying actions.

Urbana fell to the enemy the next day, September eleventh, in a cold drizzling rain. In the late morning Fitz Lee's riders passed through on the retreat; Wade Hampton followed, and only Munford's little squadrons remained behind, some five miles away.

Not until the last moment would Stuart leave the company of the charming "New York Rebel." He was at the Urbana house of her kinsmen as his column trotted by and gunfire drew nearer. Von Borcke left a protest: "I was kept riding to and fro directing the retreat in the name of the General who, with the other members of the staff, to my intense disgust, still lingered on the veranda with the ladies."

Jeb left with the last of them, finally, at two P.M., closely pursued by bluecoats; artillery shells were exploding around the house when he left it. Women and children cried, waving handkerchiefs, and the head of the household was so stirred that he rode off with Stuart's men, to join Confederate ranks. The enemy seized Urbana.

Stuart was still in a gay mood. He spent the night at the farmhouse of an old Irishman near Frederick, on the banks of the Monocacy River, joining in a dance of his officers and the "spirited Irish girls" of the house.

He wrote Flora:

> The ladies of Maryland make a great fuss over your husband—loading me with bouquets—begging for autographs, buttons, etc. What shall I do?[6]

The town had a gloomy look, his officers thought, though not all the people were downcast. Von Borcke saw an "impudent" Union man wave a United States flag from the roof of his house, and was so incensed that he ordered the civilian to take down his colors or be shot. The flag disappeared.

In the dusk of September twelfth Stuart's rear guard fell back from the Monocacy westward through Frederick in the track of General Lee's main body of infantry. Von Borcke escaped a final scattering of buckshot from the house of the defiant waver of the Union flag. There was one more welcome missile: A pretty girl tossed Captain Blackford a plum pudding as he passed her door. The staff ate it for supper that night, a few miles west in a farmhouse near Middletown.

One of the first Federal officers into Frederick was General Jacob D. Cox, to whom it appeared "a loyal city, and as Hampton's cavalry went out one end of the street and our infantry came in at the other, while the carbine smoke and the smell of powder still lingered, the closed window-shutters of the houses flew open, the sashes went up, the windows were filled with ladies waving their handkerchiefs and the national flag, and the men came to the column with fruits and refreshments for the marching soldiers."[7]

The Federals went into camp around Frederick. One of them, Private B. W. Mitchell of an Indiana regiment, found three cigars on an abandoned Confederate campsite. The wrapping drew his attention: General Order 191, it appeared to be, an order from General R. E. Lee outlining marching routes of the Confederate army. This document was soon in the hands of General McClellan, and made this cautious general surprisingly perceptive and bold. The slow

Federal advance became faster, and pursuit poured into the roads west of Frederick.

Going westward in Maryland the armies toiled over successive ridges of mountains. The first barrier, three or four miles from Frederick, was Catoctin Mountain, where Stuart left patrols of horsemen; he entered Middletown in the valley below.

The second barrier, higher and more rugged, was South Mountain, rearing about thirteen hundred feet in rocky, timbered ridges; the two chief passes were a mile apart: Turner's Gap and Fox's Gap. Farther south on this ridge, near the Potomac, was yet another pass, Crampton's Gap.

A couple of miles westward was a shorter third barrier, Elk Ridge, overlooking the Potomac near Harpers Ferry.

When the Federal drive from Frederick began, Jackson's divisions were already south of the Potomac. Stonewall was closing in on Harpers Ferry, with its 11,000 Federal troops. McLaws and Walker were aiding him from the Maryland side.

General Lee waited anxiously for news that would permit reconcentration of his army before the enemy fell upon him. The signs were unexpectedly ominous.

Stuart's cavalry was pushed off the first barrier, Catoctin Mountain, a little after noon of September thirteenth. Stuart felt no danger, for the army did not intend to fight in this country. He warned General D. H. Hill to occupy Turner's Gap, but he was no more alarmed than Wade Hampton's son Preston, who, left with his father's coat when the general went into action, impatiently tossed aside the garment and followed: "I've come to Maryland to fight Yankees, and not to carry Father's overcoat."[8]

By nightfall of September thirteenth the rear of the army was drawn along South Mountain's crest and Stuart held Turner's Gap with the support of an infantry brigade sent back by General Hill. It was easy to read trouble after dark, for in the valley to the east were thousands of Federal campfires; this was a full-scale advance, and not a mere cavalry thrust. General Lee reacted by turning Longstreet's men about and marching them rearward to help defend South Mountain. It would be ruinous to have the enemy cross it before the army's divisions pulled together once more.

Stuart had a mysterious caller in the night, a Southern sympathizer who had heard the story of the Federal discovery of the fateful cigar wrapper. Confederate plans were known to the last detail. Stuart sent the report to headquarters, but even now showed no concern, "still believing," he said, "that the capture of Harpers Ferry had been effected." He sent Hampton's cavalry south to bolster Crampton's Gap, since it was "now the weakest point of the line." He then left Turner's Gap, posting Fitz Lee there. He spent the night near the little town of Boonsboro.

Jeb said he left Turner's to join the "main part" of his force because "this was obviously no place for cavalry operations, a single horseman passing from place to place on the mountain with difficulty." Near midnight he had a caller, General Ripley of Hill's command, seeking information on the gaps, which Stuart gave "cheerfully," and included maps of the mountain. But when D. H. Hill reached Turner's Gap on the morning of September fourteenth he was surprised to find Jeb gone. Hill also saw from the hilltop the masses of McClellan's ninety thousand, with enemy parties already pushing toward the crest. He called up more infantry from the west.[9]

Federal sharpshooters swarmed along the base of the mountain, and Union guns opened fire. The battle for South Mountain crackled along the ridge, and Hill's men held on in desperation, saved more than once by the timely arrival of reinforcements from the rear. The enemy was soon pouring through Crampton's Gap.

Stuart found an opportunity to lead infantry in the perplexing retreat that night, and he reported it with apparent pride.

He "rode at full speed" toward Crampton's Gap when he heard of the enemy victory there, and on the way he met General Howell Cobb's Georgians, "retreating in disorder down Pleasant Valley."

"Yankees two hundred yards behind!" General Cobb said. "In great force. We can't stand."

Stuart halted the column, sent men into the brush at the roadside, commandeered an artillery battery that he "accidentally met with," and prepared to sell the position dearly.

There was a long wait, but the enemy did not come. Stuart sent out scouts, and after half an hour or more they returned: No enemy within a mile. Stuart ordered pickets put out, and rather disgustedly reported: "The command was left in partial repose for the night."

Stuart was alarmed by a report that John Pelham had been captured, but in the morning Pelham returned with tales of narrow escapes through the enemy lines. Headquarters of the cavalry corps were now near the Potomac, with some squadrons to the west in the passes of Elk Ridge. The troopers heard fighting from along South Mountain, where Hill and now General McLaws were engaged, and from the south, at Harpers Ferry, the fire of Jackson's guns was plain. Heavy lines of Federal infantry came toward Stuart's positions as if they would sweep over them to the relief of Harpers Ferry. But for some reason the enemy advance slowed and bluecoat skirmishers dallied for hours with Stuart's dismounted cavalry in picket lines.

So long as firing from Harpers Ferry continued, Blackford reasoned, there could be no retreat in that direction.

Even now, Stuart moved as if oblivious to danger. He was fighting across a beautiful valley of farmland, whose inhabitants had fled, leaving houses locked behind. Captain Blackford noticed an attractive farm with a commanding view of the bluecoat columns. Ripe peaches and grapes were plentiful around the house, and Blackford called to Stuart. Inside, the engineer suggested, they might find more food. Blackford crawled through an unlocked window and was soon passing out to Jeb and the staff meats, bread, milk, butter, cheese and pies. They gulped down delicacies and thrust others into their knapsacks. Enemy bullets snipped leaves above them as the party scampered back to the Confederate lines.

Almost as the blue and gray skirmish lines collided in earnest, Blackford noted, there was a hush from the south. Jackson's guns had fallen silent across the river, and the enemy on Stuart's front halted as if something had gone awry. Then, fluttering down the valley, from one Confederate unit to another, came a ragged chorus of cheering. A courier from the south found Stuart with a message: Harpers Ferry had fallen, and the garrison was captured.

A Federal leaped to an exposed stone wall: "What in hell are you fellows cheering for?"

"Because Harpers Ferry is gone up, God damn you."

"I thought that was it," the Federal called, and jumped back to safety.[10]

Stuart soon pulled his command from this front. Von Borcke

had a memory of the moment: "Stuart now came back to us, and was so delighted that he threw his arms around my neck and said, 'My dear Von, isn't this glorious? You must gallop over with me to congratulate old Stonewall.'"

And with von Borcke, Blackford, Captain Farley and Lieutenant Dabney, Stuart crossed the Potomac and reached Harpers Ferry for a glimpse of the surrender. The young officers were struck by the contrast between the new uniforms of the captive garrison and the dusty rags of Jackson's men. There was an immense store of booty, especially ammunition and small arms. Von Borcke hurried to congratulate Jackson, who replied, "This is all very well, Major, but we have yet much hard work ahead of us."

The infantry hurried off upstream, in reply to a desperate call for help from General Lee, who was assembling his troops on the north bank of the river at the little town of Sharpsburg, Maryland. As yet, he had only 18,000 in line, waiting for the enemy.

Stuart was gone from Harpers Ferry even before Jackson, riding up the Maryland side of the river with the brigades of Hampton and Robertson, who had fallen back in the general retreat. Stuart reached Sharpsburg during the night and slept on the porch of a doctor's house. Jeb reported the Harpers Ferry victory to General Lee in detail, and said Stonewall's men would soon join him.

Jackson reported at noon, September sixteenth, and his men filed into place on the upper end of the line Lee had drawn just east of Sharpsburg. It was still a pitifully small force that was digging in, the winding Potomac at its back. The men lay along a rocky ridge, looking across Antietam Creek to the Federals, who came in from the east.

General Lee rode anxiously along his front in the morning, and when he saw blue skirmishers slipping farther to his left, he called for Stuart.

"Find out what they are after, and if they are in force. Take all your cavalry if you need it, and attack."

Stuart turned to Blackford. "The ground is bad for mounted attack," he said. "See if you can spy them out with a few men, and save us a reconnaissance in force."

Blackford left with three men. Jeb waited with the cavalry corps drawn up in column. He would wait half an hour, unless he had word from Blackford.

The engineer captain had some of the army's most powerful field glasses, and when he came to a rise, found the crouching enemy skirmishers in the distance; he saw by the blue piping of their uniforms that they were infantry, and not cavalry. The move to the Confederate left was being made in earnest.

Blackford went back to Stuart, who then rode forward to see for himself. They fell back from the advanced position under fire, without loss, and reported to General Lee. It was the first indication of a powerful thrust against the exposed left flank, held by Jackson's men.[11]

September sixteenth passed with the gathering of the Federals in front, obviously preparing for an assault.

Jeb lost his staff officers as he rode back and forth in the evening, placing troops and preparing for battle. He had promised to meet von Borcke and Blackford behind the lines, but when he did not appear, the young officers made supper from the remains of the stolen farmhouse treasures and slept in a haystack. They awoke to a roar of gunfire such as they had not heard before: McClellan was tearing at Jackson's flank, and already there was retreat. Panic was in the air.

Stuart had slept quite near his staff, in a farmyard, and rode in a thin rain to Jackson's front. There was little for him to do; the cavalry was drawn up in a line, from the Potomac to Jackson's flank, ready for action. The horse artillery joined the fury of firing as Hooker's bluecoat infantry broke Jackson's line and the cavalry horses were led to the rear, the troopers fighting dismounted as infantry.

General Lee hurriedly crossed small regiments from the right to patch Jackson's front, but for hours in the morning it was a smoky chaos. Fighting surged into a woodland around the Dunkard Church near the center of the line, and receded. After a pause, other Federal corps were flung forward toward the right of the thin four-mile Confederate line. Not even the Seven Days had seen such fighting. Today, Lee battled for survival.

Several men glimpsed Stuart while the guns rolled in the growing heat. John Mosby rode with him past some of Jackson's batteries, over ground so strewn with dead and wounded that the horses had to pick their way with slow care. A farm road nearby was piled fifteen feet deep with bodies; it was to be remembered as Bloody Lane.

In the rear Stuart's troopers halted all the wounded who walked back, holding under guard those who were not bleeding, and finally barring the way to all who could walk and hold a musket. It was the building of a last pitiful reserve, for use if the enemy should break through.

Von Borcke rode down the line with Stuart, despairing over the ragged barefoot infantry. The German said he doubted they could endure the fight.

Stuart was optimistic: "I'm confident that, with God's assistance and good fighting, we'll whip these Yankees badly enough."

Within a few minutes Jeb was with his guns on Jackson's flank, the twenty-five pieces of the Horse Artillery which were banging away rapidly, but under severe fire. Von Borcke could not persuade Stuart to leave them while the duel went on.

Blackford reported Jeb constantly riding over the field, watching every turn of the action, and Esten Cooke said that Stuart was once fired upon by a whole bluecoat regiment, and escaped only because his horse was too fast to give enemy marksmen a fair aim.

In the afternoon there was work for Jeb. Jackson, incredibly enough, planned a counterattack, though the enemy push was so strong that Longstreet's men were driven into Sharpsburg. Stonewall asked Stuart to scout the enemy right. If there was room on the river bank, they would attack on the flank, relieve pressure on the line, and perhaps cause McClellan real trouble. Stuart went off to investigate.

Stonewall summoned General J. G. Walker, and as he sat his horse beneath an apple tree, one leg carelessly over the pommel, munching fruit, asked Walker to lend him an infantry regiment.

"I want to make up a force of four thousand to five thousand men," Jackson said, "and give them to Stuart, so he can get at the enemy right and rear. I want you to attack with your division when you hear Stuart's guns. We'll drive McClellan into the Potomac."

Hours passed, and there was no further sign of the attack. Walker at last learned what had happened: Stuart took a few riders and some infantrymen to the river, and saw that Federal guns were placed very near the stream—within eight hundred yards, he said. The position was too strong to be stormed by a small force. He took the news to Jackson, who was bitterly disappointed: "It's a great pity. We should have driven McClellan into the Potomac." But he had respect for Stuart's practiced eye, and the attack was forgotten.[12] The sun set on a final burst of fighting, as General A. P. Hill came up belatedly with his troops from Harpers Ferry, stormed through the village, and restored Lee's line. Sharpsburg was over, the most costly day of the war. Confederate losses were about ten thousand; Federal were twelve thousand.

Lee held a council of war in the night, and after his generals reported, decided to hold his ground. Stuart, as he would soon say in his official report, could tell only of light casualties today, and for the entire campaign: "My command did not suffer on any one day as much as their comrades of other arms, but theirs was the sleepless watch and the harassing daily *petite guerre*, in which the aggregate of casualties sums up heavily. There was not a single day, from the time my command crossed the Potomac . . . that it was not engaged with the enemy."

Jackson had praise for Stuart's role at Sharpsburg: "This officer rendered valuable service throughout the day. His bold use of artillery secured for us an important position, which had the enemy possessed, might have commanded our left."

The officers returned to their commands with the chilling order: Dig in. We will meet them here, if they want more fight. Day came in silence, with the Confederate 27,000 facing some 75,000 Federal survivors. There was no sign of attack, and the sun rose higher over the exhausted armies and the acres of their dead and wounded.

Stuart rode the lines; his troopers waited in the rear. One of Stuart's staff noted that the thin infantry line had "hardly one man to a rod of ground," yet the enemy did not come.

The first shots of the day were fired by Jeb's troopers in Sharpsburg, killing pigs and chickens; there was soon a maddening scent of cooked meat down the lines, some of whose men had not eaten in two days.

Sporadic shots were exchanged by skirmishers, but the day passed with the armies lying, watching. There was a truce in the late morning for gathering dead and wounded, but the bodies remained "a sickening sight" to von Borcke.

Lee called a second council in the late afternoon, and Stuart rode back for orders. He returned quickly with a task for Blackford:

"I want you to go to the Potomac crossing near Shepherdstown, somewhere above the regular ford, and find a place cavalry can cross. Ask no questions of civilians. I want you back here by sundown. Leave some men at the crossing and take enough to station them two hundred yards apart, all the way back. I want you to be able to guide a column to the river in the dark."

He told Blackford nothing of the purpose of this scout; his engineer needed no explanation. He took a party of horsemen to the river and began his work.

He rode a horse back and forth through the swift water, often going over his depth, and being forced to swim. After several attempts he found a shallow spot below a fish dam; the bottom was rocky and rough, but it was the best of the crossings. He left pickets with orders to respond only to his call in the dark, scattered a chain of riders in the road behind him, and reported to Stuart. A cold sifting rain made the road treacherous.

When night fell on the field before Sharpsburg every command built fires, until lines of them burned from one bend of the river to the other; regiments moved off in the rear. Retreat had begun, and the invasion was over.

Wagons, artillery and infantry went off first, recrossing into Virginia over many fords. Blackford led Hampton's column to his ford, and found it without incident. A few horses and men were lost in the deep water, but most of them clambered, dripping, up the bank into Virginia.

Von Borcke rode with Stuart to the river: "I can safely say that the ride to the Potomac was one of the most disagreeable of my life. A fine rain, which had been falling all the evening, had rendered the roads so deep with mud and so slippery that it was difficult to make any progress at all."

The German fell with his horse five times. Jeb's horse fell in the path of a heavy wagon, and only von Borcke's shout stopped the vehicle and saved the cavalry chief from death beneath its wheels.

The accident did not improve Stuart's temper, for he pushed forward yelling for the wagoners and soldiers to clear the way for him. He was answered in profane defiance by men who did not recognize his voice.

Munford's command narrowly averted disaster. It was skirmishing with the enemy on the extreme right of the Confederate line, and Munford discovered his isolated position only by accident, when he rode rearward and met Fitz Lee in Sharpsburg. Munford's was the last cavalry command to recross the river.

The final scenes in the river were tragic to men who had begun the invasion with high hopes.

In the Shepherdstown crossing an ambulance full of wounded soldiers was left in the river by a cowardly driver who had unhitched his horses and fled. General Maxcy Gregg begged his infantrymen to help: "Men, it's a shame to leave the poor fellows here in the water. Can't you take them over the river?"

A dozen men dragged the wagon through the ford, struggling in waist-deep water; watching troops sang: " 'Carry me back to old Virginny!' "

General Walker, who passed General Lee as the commander sat his horse in the river at a ford, assured him that the army had now crossed, except for a few wagons of wounded and a battery of guns, all nearby.

Lee sighed. "Thank God," he said, and rode to the southern shore.

The cavalry had a short respite from the punishing campaign. Troopers led their horses through pitch-blackness after fording the river near Shepherdstown, and at last, near dawn, were allowed to halt. They made beds on the wet ground in the open while rain still fell. Buglers called them up after an hour.

Stuart had orders to recross the river and worry General Mc-

Clellan in an effort to prevent pursuit of the infantry, and took two brigades and a few of Pelham's guns over the river at Williamsport, entering Maryland once more. They drove out a Federal picket and when the bluecoats returned in force, Stuart fought them off with a blustery show of strength and a great deal of noise.

There were two days of minor skirmishing near Williamsport, ending when Stuart tangled with heavy infantry columns, and got Wade Hampton and his men into a trap from which they barely escaped with their skins. There were more hair-raising adventures for von Borcke's journal, in which he appeared as the hero; there was a moment when a young woman fired one of Pelham's cannon at the enemy, to be known thereafter to gunners as "the Girl of Williamsport." And in the end, on the night of September twentieth, the cavalry escaped into Virginia, defended by artillery from the south shore as they forded the Potomac. Von Borcke wrote: "The whole landscape was lighted up with a lurid glare from the burning houses of Williamsport, which had been ignited by the enemy's shells. High over the heads of the crossing column and the dark waters of the river, the blazing bombs passed each other in parabolas of flame through the air, and the spectral trees showed their every limb and leaf against the red sky."

When the cavalry returned to the army, they found that the enemy had crossed the Potomac and lunged at the rear, taking a number of cannon. Jackson's men had driven the invaders into the river, seizing hundreds of prisoners and drowning many bluecoats in the current. The army soon settled down unmolested, in camps around Winchester.

On September twenty-eighth Stuart moved to The Bower, the plantation of Stephen Dandridge, eight miles from Martinsburg, and the cavalry rested for weeks in idleness, rarely interrupted by prowling Federal patrols. General Lee's headquarters were seven miles away, the cavalry command was left largely to itself, and the campaign was forgotten in pleasant fall days.

Lieutenant Channing Price wrote home the gossip of the command: Colonel Rooney Lee's name was up for a brigadier general's commission, and he would take over most of Robertson's old brigade;

Stuart wanted to divide the cavalry of Colonel Ashby, "so as to make it more efficient, it never having received any discipline under Ashby's hands"; Fitz Lee had been painfully hurt when kicked by a mule, and Rooney Lee had taken his command for the time.[13]

Somehow, between rounds of social activity, Stuart's work was not neglected; patrols covered the wide front, and paper work in headquarters was relentlessly attacked.

Among the papers of the first days of October was a heated one from Stuart to General McClellan, a protest over recurring reports that prisoners, when paroled, were sent to Minnesota to be used in fighting Indians.

> I am reluctant to believe that the U. States authorities would thus violate the spirit of a prisoner's parole by putting arms into his hands before he is exchanged, and hope therefore to receive a disavowal at your hands. . . .[14]

The days passed swimmingly. There were minor strains and jealousies among the staff: Blackford noted that von Borcke's vanity led him to forget that he owed everything to General Stuart. But when Stuart discovered a coolness between the German and his engineer he forced them to shake hands and watched carefully to see that they did not quarrel again. Cavalry headquarters devoted itself to gaiety once more.

Cook Collection, Valentine Museum, Richmond

The Jeb Stuart of legend, with the plumed hat, high boots, French saber, golden sash and cinnamon beard he made famous. Probably photographed in the winter of 1863-1864.

Confederate Museum, Ri...

Stuart in 1854, a West Point graduate of a few days, 21 years old. This likeness, mad⟨e⟩
in Washington, belies the report that his later beard hid a weak chin. He wrote a gir⟨l⟩
friend of this daguerreotype: "I send you a likeness of 'Beauty.' You perceive I wa⟨s⟩
looking my *prettiest* when it was taken."

Cook Collection, Valentine Museum, Richmond

Perhaps the only surviving photograph of Stuart in the field in wartime, here in the rougher clothing he probably wore more often than his celebrated finery.

The National A

General Philip St. George Cooke, U.S. Cavalry, Stuart's father-in-law who led the
hapless chase of Jeb on his first daring raid around the Union Army. Of Stuart and
his own son joining the Confederacy, General Cooke growled, "Those mad boys. If
only I had been there!" Of Cooke, when he failed to appear in the Confederacy,
Stuart wrote: "He will regret it but once, and that will be continuously."

Courtesy Mrs. A. J. Davis, Alexandria, Virginia, granddaughter of J. E. B. Stuart

Flora Cooke Stuart. Almost certainly a prewar daguerreotype, probably taken about the time of her 1855 marriage to Stuart at Fort Riley, Kansas, where her father commanded the 2nd U.S. Dragoons. Fresh from a Detroit boarding school, an excellent horsewoman, she was courted by Stuart on evening rides and, as her father said, married Jeb "rather suddenly."

Key Men of Jeb's Staff

Los Angeles County Museum, Los Angeles, Calif.

Sam Sweeney

Courtesy Mrs. A. J. Davis, Alexandria, Virginia

John Esten Cooke

Cook Collection, Valentine Museum, Richmond

"The Gallant Pelham"

John Pelham

Courtesy Miss Louise Price, Richmond

Channing Price

Courtesy Miss Louise Price, Richmond

Heros von Borcke

Virginia Historical Society

William Farley

Field Commanders Under Stuart

Cook Collection, Valentine Museum, Richmond

Fitzhugh Lee

Cook Collection, Valentine Museum, Richmond

Wade Hampton

Cook Collection, Valentine Museum, Richmond

W. H. F. Lee

Library of Congress

Williams C. Wickham

Library of Congress

John B. Gordon

Cook Collection, Valentine Museum, Richmond

Calbraith Butler

Cook Collection, Valentine Museum, Rich

Yellow Tavern. Probably about 1880, thought to be a view over the bridge charged by Custer's Michigan cavalry in the opening of the battle in which Stuart lost his life.

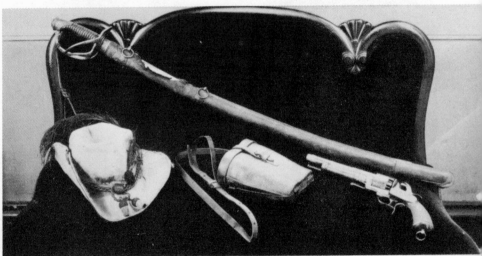

Confederate Museum, Rich

Stuart's hat, binoculars and side arms in the Confederate Museum, Richmond. The huge pistol is a LeMatt, with nine chambers and over-and-under barrels, firing .52-caliber bullets and a charge of shot.

☆

CHAPTER 12

Enemy Country

STUART'S headquarters entourage was now perhaps the army's largest, and his camp at The Bower was the envy of all commands. About the tents under giant oaks on the plantation lawn was an endless procession of officers, couriers, scouts, the general's escort, musicians and servants.

Half the staff were in love with the Dandridge girls or their visiting cousins, and the house was under constant siege. Young Pelham courted several and squired them in a captured army wagon painted an unmilitary yellow. Couples wandered in the woodland and boated on Opequon Creek. Dancing shook the big house almost nightly, and tea was an inevitable rite of the afternoons. There were charades and parlor games; public kissing was a feature of every gathering, with Stuart in the midst of it.

But the candid Blackford, perhaps Stuart's most intimate companion, scolded gossips: "Though he dearly loved to kiss a pretty girl, and the pretty girls loved to kiss him, he was as pure as they. . . . I know this to be true, for it would have been impossible for it to have been otherwise and I not to have known it."

Meals were served under a tent fly at a long table, and drew many visitors; food was plentiful, for people of the region showered Stuart with gifts.

When he had finished headquarters paper work in his tent, Stuart would emerge and call for the band. The singers accompanied Sam Sweeney and the violinists, and the mulatto, Bob, rattled the bones. They played "Alabama, Alabama," and "The Girl I Left Behind Me," and "Lorena," and always, "Jine The Cavalry." People came miles to hear the concerts.

Von Borcke left a memory: "Every evening the Negroes would ask for the lively measures of a jig or a breakdown, and then danced within the circle . . . like dervishes or lunatics, the spectators applauding to the echo."

Once after a skirmish near Shepherdstown, Stuart took his staff to visit Lily Parran Lee, the young widow of his friend of the frontier, William F. Lee, who had been killed at First Manassas. Von Borcke witnessed a romantic scene: "A mob of young and pretty girls collected . . . all very much excited . . . the General's uniform was in a few minutes entirely shorn of its buttons, taken as souvenirs; and if he had given as many locks of his hair as were asked for, our commander would soon have been totally bald. Stuart suffered all this very gracefully, with the greater resignation as every one of these patriotic young ladies gave him a kiss as tribute."

While he was in Lily Lee's house Stuart wrote an ode to his new horse, Maryland, a comic parody:

> I hear your old familiar neigh,
> Maryland, my Maryland!
> Asking for your corn and hay,
> Maryland, my Maryland.
> But you must wait till break of day,
> And Bob will then your call obey,
> And make you look so sleek and gay,
> Maryland, my Maryland.
>
> I feel secure upon your back,
> Maryland, my Maryland!
> When danger howls upon your track,
> Maryland, my Maryland.
> You bore me o'er the Potomac,
> You circumvented Little Mac,
> Oh, may I never know your lack,
> Maryland, my Maryland!

It was an outing his young men did not forget, long after the poetry was forgiven.[1]

On Monday, October sixth, Stuart was called from his merriment to army headquarters for a private talk with Lee and Jackson, and when he was recalled several times during the week, the young men prepared for action. Major Kyd Douglas of Jackson's staff dared repeat to Stonewall the gossip that Stuart was to make a bold stab into the heart of the North. Douglas asked permission to go. Stonewall refused, scolding him for prying into secret army matters —but said wistfully that he wanted to ride with the raiders himself, even as a cavalry private.

The interruptions came during a round of parties at The Bower. On Tuesday scores of guests came at the invitation to mingle with the officers at a ball. At its height there was an hilarious apparition, a "Pennsylvania farmer and his bride," two figures in outlandish costumes, the woman towering over six feet and weighing 250 pounds or more, swathed in a white gown. The company stared as the gigantic couple waltzed around the room, and roared with laughter at a glimpse of von Borcke's yellow cavalry boots beneath the skirts of his disguise.

Stuart laughed until tears streamed on his face and hugged von Borcke: "My dear old Von, if I ever could forget you as I know you on the battle field, I will never forget you as a woman." The dance lasted until dawn.[2]

On Wednesday morning the news spread: "We're raiding into Pennsylvania!" Stuart sent von Borcke to Jackson with dispatches and a gift, a new uniform coat created by a fashionable Richmond tailor. The German found Jackson in the weather-stained coat he had worn throughout the war, and drew out the gift.

Jackson blushed and stammered. "Give Stuart my best thanks, Major," he said. "The coat is much too handsome for me, but I will take the best care of it, and will prize it as a souvenir. Now let's have some dinner."

Jackson began to fold away the coat, but von Borcke and staff officers protested until he put it on. Soldiers ran to whoop over the wonder, and von Borcke reflected that not even the foppish Louis XIV had stirred such excitement with his new garments at Versailles as this strange soldier in the Virginia backwoods.

On his return to camp von Borcke was told of the planned foray into the North and was disappointed to learn that Stuart was leaving him at The Bower, "to fill his place." Blackford recorded that von Borcke was actually left behind because his careless handling of horses had left him without proper mounts for a swift raid.

By now the secret was out at headquarters. Wednesday night Stuart ordered Lieutenant Channing Price, the boy adjutant of these days, to gather all papers requiring Jeb's attention so that they could be signed later in the night without halting the revelry. Price recalled: "We had a pleasant time, music and dancing, until 11 o'clock, then returned to our tents. The General finished up all his business, and about 1 o'clock we got the music (violin, banjo and bones) and gave a farewell serenade to the Ladies of The Bower."

Half a dozen or more pretty girls smiled down from their bedroom windows on the torchlight concert, applauding an extensive program. Stuart sang four solos for the young women.

The strains of music had hardly faded from the moonlit lawn before Lieutenant Price, looking over the dispatches, learned of the raid in detail. There was an order from General Lee:

> An expedition into Maryland with a detachment of Cavalry, if it can be successfully executed, is at this time desirable. You will, therefore, form a detachment of from twelve to fifteen hundred well mounted men . . . to cross the Potomac . . . and proceed to the rear of Chambersburg, and endeavor to destroy the railroad bridge over the branch of the Conococheague.
>
> Any other damage that you can inflict upon the enemy . . . you will also execute. You are desired to gain all information of the position, force and probable intention of the enemy which you can. . . .
>
> Should you meet with citizens of Pennsylvania holding State or government offices . . . bring them with you, that they may be used as hostages, or the means of exchanges. . . . Such persons will, of course, be treated will all the respect and consideration that circumstances will permit.
>
> Should it be in your power to supply yourself with horses . . . you are authorized to do so. . . .

Stuart sent couriers in search of Price early the next morning; they dragged him from the young women at The Bower to complete the general's address to his troopers. The phrases were clearly Stuart's:

> Soldiers: You are about to engage in an enterprise which, to insure success imperatively demands at your hands coolness, decision and bravery, implicit obedience to orders without question or cavil, and the strictest order and sobriety on the march and in bivouac. . . . Suffice it to say, that with the hearty cooperation of officers and men, I have not a doubt of its success —a success which will reflect credit in the highest degree upon your arms.[3]

Stuart improved upon Lee's order and chose 1,800 men to ride with him, led by the best of his available lieutenants: Wade Hampton, Rooney Lee and W. E. Jones would each take a division of 600 men. Next in command were the daring lieutenants, Williams Wickham and Calbraith Butler. Pelham would take four guns of his horse artillery. Parties of horsemen made rendezvous in the village of Darkesville on the morning of October ninth.

Though the raid had the sound of desperation, broad strategy made it important to the Confederacy; young Price was so impressed by its promise that he resolved to keep an account of the raid for his family.

President Davis, with his usual anxiety for Richmond, was uncertain whether the capital was safe for the winter, despite Lee's presence in Northern Virginia and McClellan's position in Maryland. There was, for example, little to prevent another water-borne attack down the Potomac and against The Peninsula.

Lee felt that Stuart, given a glimpse of Union lines of communication through Maryland and Pennsylvania, would be able to interpret the enemy's plans. If, in addition, he could destroy the Cumberland Valley Railroad's bridge near Chambersburg, the expedition would justify its risks. With that bridge removed the Federals would be left with the single line of the Baltimore & Ohio for movement of men and supplies in that region.

The horsemen were to ride almost into the face of McClellan's army; they must cross rivers, canals, railroads and turnpikes, and on their return would be in danger of entrapment because of a great network of telegraph lines.

Yet the squadrons met at Darkesville as if bound for a holiday and through the afternoon moved casually toward the Potomac. Stuart met Hampton and his command on the riverbank. All was quiet, but men whispered that an outpost across the river was screened by woods, with a Federal picket nearby. Somehow the crossing must be made without spreading the alarm.

Jeb slept with his staff in a straw rick in an open field. There was not long to sleep that night.[4]

The column stirred at four A.M. in a heavy fog, and men mounted without fires or breakfast. Stuart waited with the rest as Hampton's advance moved to clear the way. For an hour or more there was no sound but the rushing of the river.

Unseen by the enemy, thirty men from the 10th Virginia and the 2nd South Carolina waded the river above the ford. A burst of firing broke the silence, and Colonel Calbraith Butler saw from the ford a winking of carbines and pistols. He sent the advance squadron into the water. Horses splashed across.

Just north of the river crossing a party of the 12th Illinois Cavalry had camped around the ruined stone walls of old Fort Frederick, a landmark of the Indian wars. Captain Thomas Logan, the commander, was at an old ironworks, Green Spring Furnace, when, at five thirty A.M., a civilian reported to him: Rebels crossing the river, thousands of Rebels.

Logan had but a handful, but he got his reserves in the saddle and sent a message downstream by a courier. In five minutes he had men in line of battle.

At five forty there was firing, but Logan simply watched as daylight grew stronger and Rebels trotted past his position. He could not put a party on their trail because of his weakness, but he had an eyeful to report:

An estimated 2,500 Confederate horsemen, eight pieces of artillery [that was Pelham's four-gun battery, looming large in the fog], a few wagons and ambulances. The Rebels took the road north to-

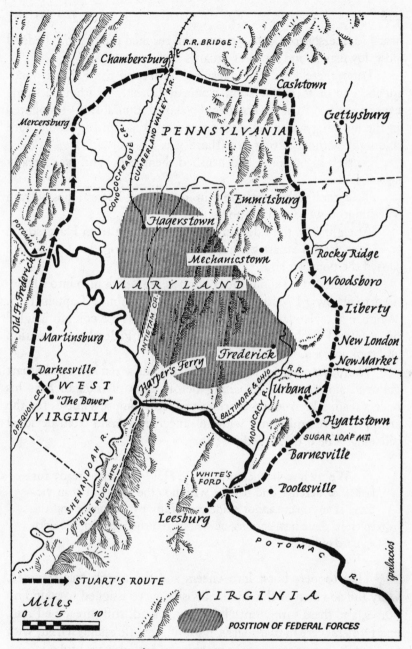

R.R. BRIDGE

Chambersburg

Cashtown

Gettysburg

Mercersburg

PENNSYLVANIA

CONOCOCHEAGUE CR.

CUMBERLAND VALLEY R.R.

POTOMAC R.

Old Ft. Frederick

Emmitsburg

Hagerstown

Mechanicstown

Rocky Ridge

Woodsboro

MARYLAND

Liberty

Martinsburg

ANTIETAM CR.

New London

Darkesville

Frederick

New Market

O.PEQUON CR.

"The Bower"

WEST

VIRGINIA

Harper's Ferry

BALTIMORE & OHIO

R.R.

Urbana

Hyattstown

MONOCACY R.

SUGAR LOAF MT.

Barnesville

SHENANDOAH R.

BLUE RIDGE MTS.

WHITE'S FORD

Poolesville

Leesburg

POTOMAC

R.

galacios

STUART'S ROUTE

VIRGINIA

Miles

0   5   10

POSITION OF FEDERAL FORCES

STUART'S 1800 RAID CHAMBERSBURG
October 10–12, 1862

ward Mercersburg. Logan's news soon reached the first big Federal post downriver, and word of Stuart's raid was out.

Later there would be querulous echoes in the Federal documents, one of them the stout claim of Logan: "Without a single exception the men of my command behaved admirably. We mounted in the morning without breakfast and remained in the saddle until midnight without eating, yet there was no murmur. . . ."

Stuart's big column had brushed them aside, and was already at full speed.

Telegraph keys chattered in dozens of Federal posts from Washington westward by now.

At eight A.M. the riders crossed the turnpike from Hagerstown to Hancock, and Stuart was told that a Union brigade of 5,000 had passed the point an hour earlier.

Fog still drifted about the column as Jeb led his men into a little-used road toward Mercersburg. His guide was now Captain B. S. White, a Marylander who knew the terrain. As the column jangled on, a few of Butler's Carolinians surprised a Federal signal station and took its men.

There was a halt on the Pennsylvania line at ten A.M., and Stuart galloped along the road, halting before each division to hear his orders read. The troopers were instructed to impress horses for the army, to leave ranks only with an officer, to refrain from personal pillaging. The order ended:

> We are now in enemy country. Hold yourselves ready for attack or defense, and behave with no other thought than victory. If any man cannot abide cheerfully by the order and the spirit of these instructions, he will be returned to Virginia with a guard of honor.

The troopers burst into cheers and the march was resumed. Only the 600 men of the middle division were assigned to round up horses, and these turned into by-roads. Clouds still threatened rain, and farmers were in their barns, most of them threshing wheat, with fat draught horses turning the machines. Confederates broke in, and excited Dutchmen sputtered helplessly as riders drove off the fine

Norman and Belgian horses, harness and all, to pull Stuart's wagons and guns. Many farmers could not believe that Rebels were among them, and thought they were Federal soldiers sent to harass those suspected of disloyalty. Many of them yelled after the Confederates, "I'm just as good a Union man as any of you!"

There were pauses while soldiers raided the houses, too. Stuart said he observed no pillaging, but Blackford saw it on every hand. Riders ate in the saddle. Some had roasted turkeys, hams and beef strapped to the saddles; haversacks bulged with rolls of butter, crocks of cream and loaves of fresh bread. They rode northward through occasional showers. Only once or twice during the day was gunfire heard by the central division of the column.

A few of Butler's soft-spoken South Carolinians led the way into Mercersburg. They crowded into a store and refitted themselves in shoes and boots, stunning the merchant with payment in Confederate scrip, assuring him that the Washington government would make good the damages.

The main column passed Mercersburg about noon. Here Blackford was told that a family had an accurate map of Franklin County, and he entered a house in search of it, beset by a bevy of scolding women. He pushed past them to a framed map on a wall, cut it out with his knife and retreated through the "rather rough specimens," who reviled him as he left.[5]

Near this town an old woman at the roadside asked excitedly for news from the Rebels. The waggish troopers told her an involved tale of the destruction of the Confederate army. "We're on our way back from whippin' 'em now," they said.

The old woman beamed. "Would any of you good Union boys like some good brandy? It's good and old. I've been saving it for Union soldiers."

There were volunteers, and many riders went off with canteens full of her brandy. One of them called to her, "We're Jeff Davis' guerrilla boys." The graycoats laughed at the consternation on her face as she dropped her spectacles and threw her hands over her head.

The command halted five miles north of the town to feed the horses. Price wrote: "We took corn right from the field, having no trouble about a quartermaster buying forage." By this time rain fell in torrents, and Stuart, like many of his riders, wore an oilcloth coverall as he rode in the downpour.

Major Henry McClellan reported continuing thefts. One lean private of the 9th Virginia entered a house defended only by women and young children and growled, upon being told there was no food, "I've never eaten human flesh. But I think I'm hungry enough to try one of them babies, if there's nothing else to eat." The household, McClellan said, quickly spread a meal for the marauder.

Soon after dark Stuart saw the lights of Chambersburg. He had come forty miles with scarcely a sign of opposition. The column halted and Pelham set up guns to command the town in case of resistance. The front ranks heard drums in Chambersburg and saw figures darting about the streets. Hampton, who led the vanguard, sent in a lieutenant and nine men under a flag of truce to demand surrender. The column waited just outside town.

The Confederates met some citizens, among them Colonel A. K. McClure, a newspaper editor and Republican politician. He sketched the leader of Hampton's squad as "a clever-looking 'butternut,' dripping wet, without any mark of rank, bearing a dirty white cloth on a little stick. . . . He refused to give his name, or the name of the general commanding, and he could not state on what terms they would accept a surrender."

Confederates had hardly reached the town square before the local provost marshal got off a telegraph message of alarm to Governor Andrew Curtin, who had been directing from Harrisburg a day-long effort to surround the Rebels. It was the final telegram of the night, for wires were soon cut.

McClure and two or three others rode through the rain on the dark turnpike to the Confederate main body. They were halted before dim mounted figures, one of which was General Hampton. McClure explained that the town was undefended. Hampton replied "in a respectful and soldier-like manner" that resistance would be futile; he wished to avoid loss of life and property. His soldiers would take only what the column needed. Wounded soldiers would be paroled, and only U.S. property would be seized or destroyed. After a brief parley the column moved into town. Colonel McClure was too late to save ten fine horses in his stables, but outraced the thirsty Rebels to his liquor stock. He drained two kegs of old rye on the ground and broke every bottle in the place.

By now telegraph operators in distant towns were aware of the progress of the raid, since Chambersburg's line was dead. About the time Stuart rode into the town square, Governor Curtin was telegraphing from Harrisburg to Secretary of War Stanton in Washington:

THE PEOPLE HAVE SURRENDERED CHAMBERSBURG

Stuart ordered Colonel Butler to empty the vault of the town's bank, but found that a fleeing official had taken the money to safety. The courtly manners of Butler's squad of plunderers so impressed the bank's cashier that he had his wife and servants bring food to the raiders. Blackford was surprised that people of the town came to their doors as Confederates rode by, speaking courteously to the troopers. Stuart took no chances. He posted the men of Jones and Hampton on one side of town and Rooney Lee's on the other. Rather grandly, he named Hampton "military governor" for the overnight stay.

A party under Jones galloped off in the dark to destroy the bridge which was a major object of the expedition, but the structure over the Conococheague was built of iron, and defied their torches and axes. They returned to report complete failure. The raiders could do no more.

Stuart settled for the night in a small tollhouse at the edge of town. He had the mulatto, Bob, make him a pot of coffee and stretched on the kitchen floor with his staff. By now the rain was hard and steady, and Stuart could not sleep. Three times during the night he rose to shake Captain Smith:

"Won't all this rain make the rivers rise before we can get back? Can we ford the Potomac in this weather?"

The patient guide assured him the column could ride back down the Pennsylvania and Maryland slopes as fast as the flood waters ran, but Stuart was not content, and tossed fitfully through the rainy night. Heavy-eyed guards squatted outside, and headquarters horses stood saddled until dawn.

Colonel McClure spent a remarkable night nearby with his Confederate guests.

"They had my best cornfield beside them, and their horses fared well. . . . One entered the yard, and after a profound bow, politely asked for a few coals to start a fire." That was the beginning. The raiders did not use McClure's woodpile, as he suggested, but tore down his fences for kindling.

Confederate courtesy amused the Colonel. Squad after squad trooped to his pump, politely asking permission for their every move. No soldier crossed his yard without this formality.

At one A.M. a few Rebel officers came on the porch to ask for coffee and bread. They saw a fire blazing on the hearth of the library, and, shivering, asked permission to enter. McClure ended with the house full of them, chattering about the war, their generals, the Yankees, battles—everything except their movements of tomorrow. Some were men of culture, McClure discovered. When he found courage to tell them he was a Republican, they thanked him for his candor. They drank his coffee with great relish, said they had had none for weeks, and that it brought ten dollars a pound in the South. They asked for more and brought friends to drink until the supply had vanished. More squads came, and soon the tea, too, was gone. In the meantime the kitchen filled with raiders. McClure thought he fed more than a hundred: "All, however, politely asked permission to enter, and behaved with entire propriety. They did not make a single rude or profane remark."

McClure's fine kinnikinnick tobacco was taken, but the Confederates did not smoke until their host assured them that it was permitted. McClure was relieved to hear Rebel buglers blow Boots and Saddles at four o'clock. His guests went into the town.

McClure followed and saw Stuart in the square, surrounded by his staff and command: "General Stuart is of medium size, has a keen eye, and wears immense sandy whiskers and mustache. His demeanor to our people was that of a humane soldier."

But McClure was put on his guard by a Confederate, one Hugh Logan, a native of Franklin County who had deserted to the South. They met in the street.

"You're not safe on your parole," Logan said.

"Why not? They gave me their promise."

"Hampton gave it to you. And if you are arrested and can reach Hampton, he will parole you, for he's a gentleman. But Jeb Stuart wants you, and I'm not sure he would let you go on parole."

Most of the town's stores were closed, and were not disturbed. McClure noted that only one was entered by force. Stuart's provost guard arrested several raiders who had taken private property. McClure himself was not molested.[6]

But as McClure observed this admirable Confederate discipline, Channing Price helped himself: "I went into town to get some plunder. I got to the Government depot just as operations commenced, and supplied myself with a nice black overcoat, a pair of blue pants, one dozen pair of woolen socks, a pair of boots and various other little items, as much as I could carry."

A Gettysburg newspaper correspondent sketched the scene as troopers selected their loot:

"The whole town was converted into one vast dressing room. On every hotel porch, at every corner, on the greater portion of the street doorsteps, might be seen Rebel cavalry donning Yankee uniforms, and throwing their own worn out and faded garments into the street. Each took as many coats, hats, and pairs of pants as he could conveniently handle."[7]

Price rode after the column, which was already on the road toward Gettysburg, in a direction surprising even to the troopers. In Chambersburg the rear guard cleared civilians from around the depots, which they set afire. They burned machine shops and stores of supplies, some 6,000 firearms, and a warehouse of ammunition. The morning resounded with explosions. Price reckoned the damage in the town at about $1,000,000.

The moving column was a strange sight, for many of the men wore blue Union overcoats against the chill, and there was a motley array of garments. Stuart rode between the vanguard and the main body, watching as the raiders collected horses and hostages—the mayors and other officials of small towns. He spoke to Blackford with an unusual earnestness:

"Blackford, I want to explain to you why I took this route for the return. And if I don't survive, I want you to vindicate my memory." He drew out a map.

"You see, the enemy will think I will try to recross the river above, out west somewhere, because it is nearer to me and farther for them. They will have strong guards at every ford and scouting parties will be looking for us, so that they can concentrate at any point. They will never expect me to move three times that distance and cross at a ford below them and so close to their main army, and so they won't be prepared for us down there to the east."

Stuart looked to Blackford with an expression of concern.

"Now, do you understand what I mean?"

"Perfectly."

"Don't you think I'm right?"

"You are. They won't think of it. And if anything should happen to you, and I get through, I'll see that the army understands."

Blackford noted that Stuart's eyes were filled with tears as he left him to speed the march of the column.

Jeb led the men to within seven miles of Gettysburg, to the village Cashtown, back into the road toward Hagerstown for a mile or so, to confuse pursuit, and then turned southward towards Emmitsburg, Maryland. There was a brief halt to feed the horses near Cashtown, and here Stuart took his only rest of the long ride home, leaning against a tree to sleep for less than half an hour. The column was in motion again before Blackford finished feeding his horse, and he thoughtfully broke up green corn cobs and gave them to his ravenous mount throughout the long day of October eleventh.

South of them, along the Potomac, a vast Federal net was spread for the raiders. Early last night Henry Halleck, the Federal general-in-chief, had ordered McClellan to exert every effort to trap the Rebels: "Not a man should be permitted to return to Virginia," the commander telegraphed.

McClellan had replied late in the night, while Stuart lay restlessly on the floor of the Chambersburg tollhouse:

> Every disposition has been made to cut off the retreat of the enemy's cavalry.

This Saturday morning, as Stuart neared the Pennsylvania-Maryland line, McClellan recovered his poise and telegraphed more fully to Washington:

> I have made such disposition of troops along the river that I think we will intercept the Rebels in their return. All of my available cavalry was ordered in pursuit last night, but as yet nothing has been heard from it.
>
> Cox's division is loaded in cars at Hancock, with cavalry well out toward the Pennsylvania line, and if the Rebels attempt to cross below Hancock, I have infantry at or near all the different fords.
>
> I have six regiments of cavalry now up the river between Hancock and Cumberland. All of these troops have been ordered to keep a sharp lookout for the return of the Rebels. . . .
>
> I have given every order necessary to insure the capture or destruction of these forces, and I hope we may be able to teach them a lesson they will not soon forget.

During all the anxious hours of the chase there was scarcely a word of the Rebel column. A new network of signal stations lay over the region, but morning fog still hid Stuart's horsemen.

George McClellan's trap was complete, and he could only wait. Men in remote telegraph offices waited at their keys, men in far signal towers stared over the foggy hill country, cavalrymen pounded on wet roads, and in two towns, Hancock to the west and Poolesville to the east, with steam up and black engine smoke trailing, two bluecoat infantry divisions waited in profane impatience in their railway cars, ready to hurtle down the tracks after Stuart.

From General George Stoneman came reassurance for the Federal high command. In the eastern sector, near the junction of the Monocacy and the Potomac, Stoneman had eight regiments and strong artillery batteries.

Surely there was no hole in the net through which Stuart and his 1,800 men could slip.

Only one Federal party got so much as a glimpse of the raiders on Saturday evening. In Jeb's path was Colonel Richard Rush, commander of one of the most spectacular of Federal units, the 6th Pennsylvania Cavalry. These were the Philadelphia Lancers who had such woeful luck against Stuart in The Seven Days—their lances now discarded.

Rush was stationed in Frederick with a force large enough to stun the raiders; in addition to the Lancers he had the 1st Maine, a battalion of Maryland troopers, two infantry regiments and a battery of New York artillery. At eight A.M. of October eleventh he sent four Lancer companies, about 140 men, north toward Emmitsburg and Gettysburg.

Like other Federal cavalry in this season, the Lancers were in poor condition, with many horses unshod and going lame; there had been no remounts since the summer fighting on The Peninsula below Richmond. But the four companies sent out by Rush galloped ahead with the confidence of a division. For eight hours they had no sign of the Confederates.

Stuart's column was five miles long as it re-entered Maryland. Troopers of the foraging division rode with two or three captured horses on each lead rein. There were frequent changes of mounts, but the column moved swiftly, and gave Rush's scouting party no hint of its presence until four P.M., when the Rebel vanguard charged into Emmitsburg, threw out pickets and closed the roads. These men chased off the last of Rush's scouts; the main body of the Federal vanguard had passed through an hour earlier.

Colonel Rush had given orders to send back couriers to him with news, but though his men made an effort, they could tell him nothing. Every courier sent toward Emmitsburg in the late afternoon and evening was caught or turned back by the watchful Confederates; the way remained blocked until after midnight. Rush was temporarily foiled.[8]

In the last hours of daylight Stuart's caravan rode in growing weariness. Blackford ranged far in front with three horsemen, using his strong binoculars to report signs of danger to Stuart. The general rode near the center and kept couriers pounding back and forth. There were strict orders against use of firearms. If an enemy party appeared, it must be sabers.

It was almost sundown when the bulk of the column reached Emmitsburg, to a warm welcome. Food was brought from the houses by townspeople who were as astonished, Blackford said, "as if we had fallen from the clouds." The grateful troopers ate in their saddles, but Stuart gave them little time; he pushed the column south in the twilight.

The advance platoon was now led by Captain F. W. Southall and John Pelham. Stuart trotted with them for a mile or so, giving orders.

"Keep this pace," he said. "Slow the gait for nothing, and ride over anything that gets in the way."

Within a few minutes there was confusion in front. Southall had caught a Federal courier, a frightened boy from the headquarters of Rush in Frederick. Stuart was soon reading his dispatches, and what he saw sent him to his map. He consulted with guides.

The Federals in Frederick were so strong that the town must be avoided. Worse still, General Alfred Pleasanton, with a big cavalry force, was heading for the village of Mechanicstown, which was just four miles west of Stuart's present position. Jeb must change his route. An all-night ride was now a pressing necessity. They were six miles south of Emmitsburg, at the village of Rocky Ridge, still some forty miles from the river. Pleasanton had the shorter route to the Potomac.

To emphasize the danger, the column drove off a Union scouting party in the darkness—probably one sent by Pleasanton. Stuart turned the horsemen eastward on a road leading through the settlement of Woodsboro, some eight miles away. Captain White advised that this was the most likely road to safety.

The vanguard stumbled upon an enemy in the dark—a lone Federal in a buggy, a gentleman wearing a fine suit of oilcloth against the rain. He drove into the column.

"Move aside, men," he said, "move aside."

When troopers barred his path he shouted, "I'm an officer of the 79th Pennsylvania on recruiting service, and I must get on."

The grinning men closed in around him.

Stuart appeared. The Federal yelled at Jeb, "Are you the officer in command?"

"I am."

"Then be good enough to order your men to make way. I'm a Pennsylvania officer on recruiting duty, and it is important for me to get ahead."

"Very well," Stuart said; he muttered an order to a nearby trooper.

The soldier dismounted and climbed into the Federal's buggy.

"What do you mean, sir?" the bluecoat spluttered.

"Nothing."

"Who are you?"

"Nobody."

"Who is that officer?"

"General Stuart."

"What General Stuart?"

"Jeb Stuart, Major General of Cavalry, Confederate States of America."

The Federal whistled. "By God, I'm procured!" he said.

"I rather think you are," the trooper said, and turned the buggy, trailing his horse behind as he rode with the new prisoner. The gray column hurried southward.[9]

Behind them, Colonel Rush made another effort to spring the trap. At seven P.M. he had a report on Rebels in Emmitsburg, and, aware that Pleasanton would cover the main roads, Rush sent two cavalry companies east of Stuart; one went to Woodsboro, the other to the tiny village of Johnsboro. They were to report frequently.

These Lancers rode into Woodsboro at ten thirty and immediately fell back, except for one man. The head of Stuart's column was passing through the village, and only Corporal John Anders of the Federals remained to watch. The brave Anders went into the town in disguise and talked with Confederates until he was suspected, seized as a spy and passed along for questioning. He escaped in the confusion and darkness.

In Stuart's column it seemed "a long, terrible" night march. The jingle and clatter of spurs, arms, stirrups and hoofs became a drowsy hum, Blackford remembered, and to escape sleep men dismounted and walked for short distances. Even so, many fell asleep in the saddles and their snores could be heard above other sounds.

They now rode on a line to the east of Frederick, generally southward toward the Potomac. Scouts brought in fragments of news: Federals were closing in. The way went southeast out of Woodsboro to Liberty, then more directly south through remote villages, New London and New Market. In the latter place a crew cut telegraph wires and placed obstructions on the Baltimore & Ohio tracks. Most of the riders hurried on; the river was more than fifteen miles away, and it was nearing midnight.

There was a dim moon.

Just after midnight Stuart left the column on an incredible mission. With the enemy almost literally snapping at his heels, Jeb proposed a diversion.

"Blackford," he said, "how would you like to see The New York Rebel tonight?" He laughed.

The captain needed no reminder. Stuart and Blackford had both become attached to the young woman in their brief stay at Urbana in the Sharpsburg campaign. Urbana was now just six miles out of the way, and a slight detour from the route of the column would take them to the friendly Cockey house.

Stuart seemed unconcerned for his safety or that of the expedition. "Come on," he said to Blackford, and they were off in the moonlight.

With them rode a handful of officers and a detail of about ten men from the 1st North Carolina, under Captain Rufus Barringer, to guard the party. The back roads were familiar to them from the recent invasion, and the riders soon arrived before the Cockey home in Urbana. A knock on the door brought a sleepy call in a woman's voice from an upper window: "Who's there?"

Stuart laughed. "General Stuart and his staff."

A head thrust from a bedroom window and riders heard squeals and rushing about within the house. Another woman's head bobbed out a window, adorned with curl papers. "Who did you say it was?" she asked, in tones of disbelief.

"General Stuart and staff!" Jeb repeated. "Come down and open the door."

The window banged, and a flurry of dressing followed. Slippers and bare feet drummed on a stairway, and soon the yard filled with young women, laughing and talking with their unexpected guests. Stuart allowed himself but half an hour, and they were on the road again. If Jeb got information from his New York Rebel, as he frequently did from women behind enemy lines, it did not creep into official reports. War seemed far away as the party rode in the dark morning to the tinkle of Sweeney's banjo and the clacking of Bob's bones.

The wayward band went hard after the column, and rejoined it at daylight of October twelfth in Hyattstown, Maryland. It was a pleasant Sunday morning, but safety was twelve miles away and Stuart kept the pace fast. The peak of Sugar Loaf Mountain was in sight; the Federals surely had a signal post there. South of Hyattstown the column clattered through the village of Barnesville, a few minutes after the troopers of the dashing Federal Colonel Alfred Duffié had cleared it. Stuart read this as a final sign of danger in their path. The enemy was steadily narrowing the segment of the river open to him.

Not only was General Pleasanton just to the west of them, where the Monocacy emptied into the Potomac—General Stoneman's force was to the east, guarding against a crossing near Leesburg, Virginia. The area must be thick with bluecoat hunters.

Stuart consulted with the guide, Captain White, who was now in the place of his boyhood and knew every trail. There was an abandoned farm road ahead, White said. It would be easy to turn into it from the well-used road leading south to Poolesville, and perhaps the column could then dash between the two large bodies of Federal troops and reach the river.

Stuart moved the riders into plain sight of the Sugar Loaf Mountain signal post to give the enemy the impression he was moving on Poolesville, but when he was hidden from the sentinels by a woodland he found the old road of Captain White's boyhood memory. The vanguard removed rail fences and the column entered a weed-grown cart track through the woods.

For more than a mile and a half White led them across country until, at about eight A.M., the advance trotted into the east-west road between Poolesville and the mouth of the Monocacy—a road roughly parallel to the winding Potomac, which was now just below them. As they came into the road they saw Federal riders, fast approaching.

Alfred Pleasanton, like every other Federal general in Maryland, had spent a hectic two days, darting this way and that in pursuit of Stuart, until his troops and horses were worn. As he wrote: "My force had marched, in twenty-four hours . . . upwards of 78 miles, and had crossed the Blue Ridge over a very rugged, rough and rocky road, which crippled up a great many of my horses."

After many false alarms he had word, just after midnight of this Sunday, that Stuart had passed near Mechanicstown and was headed for Woodsboro. Pleasanton struck for the Monocacy River to head him off. He got through Frederick by five A.M. and near eight o'clock to the Monocacy's mouth.

The general crossed the river, halted to pick up parts of his straggling command, and with a battery of artillery lumbering behind horses nearing the limit of their endurance, went toward Poolesville.

Within a mile and a half he met Stuart.

His account of the meeting was almost petulant: "My advance squadron . . . discovered a body of cavalry moving toward them, dressed in the uniform of U.S. soldiers. The officer in command of the squadron made signal in a friendly way, which was returned, and the parties approached within a short distance of each other, when the commander of the opposite party ordered his men to charge. They were received by the carbines of my men, and some skirmishing took place which forced my men to retire."

Stuart was in the very front of his column, surrounded by men who still wore the blue coats seized in Chambersburg. He saw the Federal leader hesitate as the Confederate riders began to reach for their sabers.

"Wait," Stuart said. The horses trotted nervously a few more paces toward the enemy as Jeb held back the riders, and broke into a gallop as he shouted, "Charge!"

The Federal advance fired one quick volley and ran. The only

Confederate casualty was a wounded horse. Stuart led the chase westward for almost a mile until his men climbed a ridge to look down across the Little Monocacy at the enemy. The river was a welcome sight, for its shielding ridge ran two miles southward to the Potomac, and would screen the last leg of the retreat.

Rooney Lee's men came up and tumbled from their horses. Their rifles blazed for a few moments before Pelham's guns joined the chorus. Federals began digging in on the opposite side of the stream. Stuart sent the main column over a farm road to approach White's Ford on the Potomac, with Rooney Lee in command. The advance must be cautious, for the rim of a rock quarry overlooked the ford, and if Federals were there in force crossing might be impossible. Lee rode off. Stuart and Pelham, with a small rearguard, remained behind to hold off Pleasanton.

Lee pushed within sight of the river and read danger at first glance. Federals were on the bluff of the quarry, probably riflemen who could riddle a column attempting to cross. He sent a courier to summon Stuart to the river; Jeb replied that Lee must solve the problem himself, for danger in the rear was growing.

Lee talked with his officers. The best plan, they agreed, was to attack the quarry in front and flank, while part of the column dashed for the river. If some riders got across with a piece of artillery, the gun could open upon the Federals from the Virginia side of the river. The riders formed for attack, but Lee held them up and attempted a bit of bravado. He scratched out a note to the commander of the strongly posted enemy force, demanding surrender. General Stuart, he wrote, was at hand with an overwhelming force. Resistance was useless. If he had not surrendered within fifteen minutes, Lee would charge him.

There was an anxious wait, during which men forgot to study the rising Potomac, or to look to safety on the southern bank. The Federals gave no sign of their intentions. There was no white flag, but when Lee ordered two guns to fire on the quarry, and the men went forward, the enemy began to retreat.

Confederates yelped with delight at the unexpected scene: With flags flying and drums beating the bluecoat infantry fell back in good order downriver, giving up the ford without a struggle. Lee sent a gun over the ford and into position on the Virginia shore. A second gun was soon in place on the Maryland side, and as other Federal parties approached the bridgehead over the rough terrain, the cannon blazed sporadically.

The cavalrymen and captured horses now struggled across. The horses, gaunt and heaving after their long ride without water or food, fought savagely to drink as they crossed, but there was soon an orderly procession in the ford, including the Pennsylvania hostages being borne to Confederate soil.

As Lee waited at the riverside, Pelham fell back along the ridge in the rear, his guns holding Pleasanton at bay. Stuart at last came down from his position with the rear guard, leaving Colonel Butler behind with orders to follow.

A Marylander who watched the Confederates at the crossing kept an observant eye on Stuart. Jeb, he reported, said "in a sarcastic manner" that he had fooled the whole Federal army, but regretted that he had been unable to sack Frederick, burn its depot and a nearby bridge of the Monocacy. "But," Stuart said, "all things considered, I have carried out my program with success."

The visitor thought Stuart's men and horses "looked extremely exhausted, but the former were in high glee." Jeb sent his compliments to old army friends stationed with the Federals at Frederick.[10]

Stuart kept Blackford busy with errands at the river crossing. He sent the captain into the water to help keep the captured horses moving. When Blackford returned, he found Jeb in distress. The commander's eyes were filled with tears, and there was a catch in his voice.

"Blackford, we're going to lose our rear guard."

"Why, General? How's that?"

"Why, I've sent four couriers back to Butler, and he's not here yet. And look! There's the enemy closing behind us."

Federals appeared in growing numbers on the hillsides.

"Let me try it," Blackford said.

Stuart studied him. "All right. If we don't meet again, goodbye, old fellow," he said dramatically. Blackford spurred from sight.

The captain passed the couriers who had been sent for Butler and galloped to the Poolesville road, where there was furious firing.

Captain W. H. H. Cowles, who had the 1st North Carolina in the rearmost position, had just reported to Butler that Federals had caught up with him on the roadway. Butler made a characteristic reply, boldly forming his little regiment in line of battle, and turning his single gun on the enemy.

Blackford reached the scene of this defiant stand and found Butler ignorant of danger at the river, but determined to lose nothing despite his desperate plight.

"General Stuart says withdraw at a gallop or you will be cut off," Blackford said.

"But I don't think I can pull off that gun," Butler said. "The horses can't move it."

"Leave the gun and save your men," Blackford said.

"We'll see what we can do," Butler said. His troopers whipped the weary horses, and at last the wheels lurched from the mud and took the gun to safety. Butler's little command fell back under fire through Federal forces storming the ridge on both sides, and was received with shouts at the river crossing.

Close behind was Pleasanton's struggling vanguard, its horses "so thoroughly exhausted," as the Federal commander said, "as to be unable to move the guns up the steep hills." The bluecoats pushed cannon uphill by hand as the last of Stuart's men splashed over the long, rough ford to Virginia.

Pelham waited on the Southern bank with his guns as Federal columns crowded to the entrance of the ford. But though Stuart's troopers halted to water their thirsty horses within sight and close range, the enemy did little more than threaten.

Behind, the Federal command had already begun recriminations over the failure to trap Stuart's raiders. Brigadier General Hobart Ward galloped to the ford with a few men at ten fifteen A.M. and reported to Pleasanton. He studied Stuart's riders through field glasses and tried to form a chase.

"It's too late," Pleasanton said. "There's nothing to be done now."

"Is there anything I can do?" Ward asked.

"Too late. You should have been here three hours ago."

Ward tried, through General Stoneman, to persuade Pleasanton to give him cavalry to go after Stuart in Virginia. Pleasanton refused "peremptorily," and for the rest of the afternoon the Federals watched the Confederate rear on the Virginia bank. Night came, with torrents of rain, and the chase was over.

The tale of President Lincoln's reaction to the failure soon circulated through the armies:

Lincoln was on a boat in the Potomac, surrounded by friends and officers. The President seemed in a high humor.

"Mr. President," someone asked, "what about McClellan?"

Lincoln pursed his broad lips into a solemn grimace, and with a stick drew a circle on the deck. "When I was a boy," he said, "we used to play a game—three times around, and out. Stuart has been around McClellan twice. If he goes around him once more, gentlemen, McClellan will be out."[11]

Stuart soon discovered a serious loss. Somewhere in Maryland his mulatto, Bob, had succumbed to sleep at the roadside—drunk, Major McClellan said. Bob had been leading two of Stuart's most highly prized mounts, "Sky Lark" and "Lady Margrave," and as he held their reins, snoring away, the enemy had seized him.

In all, the command had left about sixty horses behind, most of them lame or unable to keep the pace. The herd of captured mounts was immense, at least 1,200 strong, enough to see the cavalry division through the winter. There were also the thirty-odd mayors, postmasters and other town officials, who could be used as exchanges for Confederate generals and other important prisoners in the North.

The head of the column moved two or three miles into Virginia before halting. Hundreds, like Lieutenant Price, fell to the ground and were soon asleep, worn from two days and a night of ceaseless riding, but all were "soon roused up." The command went into Leesburg where there was a riotous greeting from the people of the town. Stuart and his staff stayed in the home of a Leesburg physician, where, Price wrote happily, he slept "elegantly in a nice bed."

The 1,800 spent the next morning in Leesburg, beginning to recover from their 130 miles in three days—the last 80 in twenty-four hours. There were tales to tell, but Jeb's staff was anxious to see The Bower and its lovely ladies just now.

The first riders reached the Dandridge plantation house just before daylight of October thirteenth, and did not wait for a decent hour. The banjo began and buglers joined the corn-shucking music of the Stuart band; there was another serenade before the house which "roused all hands," Price recalled. The women came down. Stephen Dandridge soon had coffee for the staff, and the young men spun tales of the raid for the girls as they ate bread and sipped hot coffee. Price and a companion went into the house and slept for several hours.

Stuart arrived at noon with good news from headquarters. General Lee was "excessively gratified" and sent his warm thanks to the cavalry.

Major Douglas of Stonewall Jackson's staff saw the return of Stuart to army headquarters. Jackson grinned, making one of his clumsy jokes in greeting:

"Howdy do, General. Get off and tell us about your trip. They tell me that from the time you crossed the Potomac until you got back you didn't sing or crack a joke, but that as soon as you got on Virginia soil, you began to whistle 'Home, Sweet Home.' "

The returning cavalrymen celebrated the success of the raid on October fifteenth with a ball, and the music was as gay as ever, though the general missed Bob and his bones. Von Borcke noted that Stuart was "the hero of the occasion, and received many a pretty compliment from fair lips." During the evening von Borcke and others staged their pantomimes and charades, and the uproar lasted most of the night.

Stuart's wife had arrived in camp, and Flora entered into the spirit of the occasion. Her husband had just received some golden spurs from Baltimore, the gift of women admirers.

In a letter to Lily Parran Lee of Shepherdstown, Stuart wrote a line with an emphasis he perhaps did not intend:

> Did you know a lady in Baltimore (anonymous) had sent me a pair of elegant gold spurs? They came while Flora was here and *she* buckled them on.[12]

There was gaiety at The Bower, at any rate, but beneath it there was thankfulness, in the reverent strain with which Stuart closed his report to General Lee.

> Believing that the hand of God was clearly manifest in the signal deliverance of my command from danger and the crowning success attending it, I ascribe to Him the praise, the honour and the glory.

He restrained himself from signing this formal document as he signed many private letters in these days: "The Knight of The Golden Spurs."

☆

CHAPTER 13

War in Winter

THE Knight of The Golden Spurs was elated by the success of the raid into Pennsylvania, and his report rang with triumphant phrases:

> The results of this expedition, in a moral and political point of view, can hardly be estimated, and the consternation among the property-holders in Pennsylvania was beyond description. . . . My Staff are entitled to the highest praise. . . .
>   I marched from Chambersburg to Leesburg, 90 miles, with only one hour's halt, in thirty-six hours, including a forced passage of the Potomac—a march without parallel in history.

Stuart was not alone in his admiration for his feat. The North was disturbed, and President Lincoln, who had been vainly urging General McClellan to invade Virginia since the battle of Sharpsburg, wrote impatiently to his field commander:

> Stuart's cavalry outmarched ours, having certainly done more marked service on the Peninsula and everywhere since. . . . Will not a movement of our army be a relief to the cavalry, compelling the enemy to concentrate, instead of foraying in squads everywhere?

A surprise for the returning raiders was Norman Fitzhugh of the staff, exchanged from a Northern prison and full of tales of his capture at Verdiersville.

There was a ball in the Dandridge House on October fifteenth, enlivened by von Borcke and Colonel Brien with more of their charades and tableaux. The cavalry officers had hardly returned to their tents when Stuart's buglers roused the camp: The enemy had crossed the river.

Jeb reached the front in the early morning, and he had not far to look. A division of bluecoat infantry had pushed south toward Winchester, and was already passing the settlement of Kearneysville: 6,000 infantry, 500 cavalry, and a number of guns.

Stuart took one of Jackson's infantry brigades from its work of tearing up railroad tracks and put it into line with his troopers. They fought all day, falling back slowly.

Jeb left a double line of pickets to watch the enemy, and returned from this skirmish with the staff through rain to The Bower, to the winged tunes of Sweeney's banjo. They trooped into the Dandridge drawing room and met two distinguished visitors, Francis Lawley, a member of Parliament and correspondent for the *London Times,* and Frank Vizetelly of the *London Illustrated News.* The English guests of the army had come in search of the famed chief of cavalry and seized him for interviews lasting late into the night. Von Borcke thought it a "delightful parley," and drank in news from abroad.

William Blackford's brother Charles noted that dancing remained popular despite Vizetelly, and remarked that things were gay as if there had been no war. He added, "The General and William led the dance until one o'clock."[1]

Vizetelly was an artist; he sketched scenes of the cavalry camp, including the dancing and banjo playing, and Stuart with a group of his officers. The artist-correspondent also became a sensation as a chef when he ousted the cooks and boastfully attempted to improve Stuart's cuisine. Von Borcke recorded that he once produced in triumph "a roast pig, with the conventional apple in its mouth, raw on one side and burned to a cinder on the other. This work of art . . . was served as *cochon a l'Italienne,* but it proved by no means so happy an accident as the original roast pig, done *a la Chinoise.*"

In the shortening days of October the cavalry kept watch from the passes of the Blue Ridge, and patrolled the southern bank of the

Potomac. Federal parties occasionally pushed hard against the pickets, as if General McClellan were impatient to know where Lee's big army lay.

Stuart came back from a foray against the enemy to Jackson's camp and spent the night with Stonewall. He arrived late, and crawled into bed with Jackson. During the cold night he wrapped himself in the single blanket, and in the morning he awoke alone in the cot, fully clothed. Jackson made a wry joke of it.

"Stuart, I'm always glad to see you. But General," he sighed, rubbing his legs, "you must not get into my bed with your boots and spurs on and ride me around like a cavalry horse all night."[2]

Religious revivals began to sweep the army, and preachers swarmed. Stuart was not noted for his participation in the services, but he once scolded an officer who sneered at the preachers:

"I regard the calling of a clergyman as the noblest in which any human being can engage," Stuart said angrily.

Esten Cooke found Stuart in thoughtful moods during this time. Jeb told Flora's cousin two things that stuck in his memory:

"My proper place would be as Major of Artillery, and not as General of Cavalry."

And,

"If I am ever wounded, don't let them give me any whisky or brandy. I promised my mother when I was twelve that I would never touch it."[3]

Couriers galloped into headquarters in the night of October twenty-sixth. The time of leisure was over. General McClellan had thrown two divisions over the Potomac below Harpers Ferry; Stuart's pickets were driven back as far as Snickers Gap in the Blue Ridge. Headquarters prepared to leave The Bower for the last time.

The cavalry moved off into the rain of October twenty-ninth "with heavy hearts indeed," as von Borcke said. The rain ceased as they left the house and a cold wind blew in their faces. By late afternoon the weather was freezing.

The ranks were thin, for disease had cut Fitz Lee's command to fewer than 1,000 riders. Stuart was concerned about what he called "greased heel" crippling the horses.

Fitz Lee was ill and unable to ride with his men. Big Rooney Lee could not command in his stead because of a lingering wound from the Sharpsburg campaign. Stuart put Wickham in command. The objective of the brigade was Snickers Gap, which the cavalry was to hold while Robert Lee moved his two infantry corps to meet the growing Federal threat. Stuart was ordered to cover Longstreet's flank, keep the enemy from the Blue Ridge passes, and post a fifty-mile cordon of pickets between the army's wings. It was an impossible assignment.

On October thirtieth, Jeb opened a season of his *petite guerre* which was to become almost endless skirmishing. He caught three companies of the 1st Rhode Island Cavalry in Mountsville, and by circling them on a back road with the 9th Virginia took the Federal camp with fifty prisoners and drove survivors as far as Aldie in the Bull Run Mountains.

But before Stuart dealt fully with the enemy he beat off another foray by Southern Womanhood. Von Borcke instigated it, riding through the street of Upperville, where he was halted by a group of girls carrying refreshments to the soldiers. "I was not strong enough to decline," he said. The girls pressed him for news of Stuart, whom they were anxious to see. The German promised to get them an audience. When Jeb galloped into the village, fifty or more women met him. The German wrote of Jeb: "surrounded by the ladies, all eager to catch the words that fell from his lips, and many with tears in their eyes kissing the skirt of his uniform coat or the glove upon his hand."

This was too much for Stuart. "Ladies," he said, "your kisses would be more acceptable on the cheek."

The young women hesitated but an elderly one threw her arms around his neck and kissed him soundly. Von Borcke watched in admiration:

"The kisses now popped in rapid succession like musketry, and at last became volleys, until our General was placed under as hot a fire as I had ever seen him sustain on the field of battle."

Stuart mounted at last, "almost exhausted," and rode off with von Borcke.

"Von," he said, "this is a pretty little trick you have played on me, but in the future I shall detail you for this sort of service."

Stuart felt the first serious pressure from the Union cavalry on November first near the hamlet of Mountsville. He clung to his position, but only John Pelham's guns held off the enemy late in the day.

General Pleasanton returned with support the next day and drove Stuart through the little town of Union, though Stuart fought his dismounted troopers behind stone fences so well that Pleasanton mistook them for infantry. It was again Pelham who made the contest almost equal.

The boy major was harassed by Federal sharpshooters who ran near his guns, picked off his horses, and went into a woodland to reload. When the bluecoat troopers had withdrawn to fill their rifles, Pelham followed unseen, took a gun to a concealed hilltop and surprised them with a load of canister. He then led a charge which took several prisoners and a regimental flag, without loss of a man.

But it was not a day of victory, even in Stuart's report: ". . . the enemy finally enveloped our position with his superior numbers . . . so as to compel our withdrawal; but every hilltop and every foot of ground was disputed, so that the enemy made progress of less than a mile during the day."

The enemy claimed complete victory, but the cavalry screen still hung before the infantry. Stuart praised Pelham: "The incomparable Pelham . . . made a gallant and obstinate resistance."

Stuart had other matters on his mind at night, for there were disturbing letters from his brother-in-law, Dr. Charles Brewer—young Flora was ill, perhaps critically. Jeb spent the night in the plantation yard of an acquaintance, and with his officers ate "a gigantic saddle of Virginia mutton." He wrote his wife:

> Dr. Brewer's first dispatch was received yesterday, and I answered it at once. The second came today, saying our darling's case was doubtful, and urges me in your name to come.
>
> I received it on the field of battle. I was at no loss to decide that it was my duty to you and to Flora to remain here. I am entrusted with the conduct of affairs, the issue of which will affect you, her, and the mothers and children of our whole country much more seriously than we can believe.
>
> If my darling's case is hopeless there are ten chances to one

that I will get to Lynchburg too late; if she is convalescent why should my presence be necessary? She was sick nine days before I knew it. Let us trust in the good God, who has blessed us so much, that he will spare our child to us, but if it should please Him to take her from us, let us bear it with Christian fortitude and resignation.[4]

The next day was Sunday, November third; the enemy came on in even greater force. A cannonade burst about Union, and there was soon a pitched battle. Many of Stuart's men fell under enemy guns, a caisson blew up, and fire was so hot that von Borcke had to force frightened ambulance drivers to pick up the wounded by holding a pistol on them. In less than half an hour one of the batteries lost fifteen men. More and more lines of dismounted bluecoats attacked, and Stuart began his withdrawal. Pelham again covered the rear.

Captain William Blackford was sent scouting along the mountain ridges and returned with a discouraging report: McClellan's whole army was coming south. Jeb pulled the command back into the slopes of the Blue Ridge.

Blackford got his first wound during the day, a painful rip in his calf from a bullet passing through his boot. The shock nauseated him; many bullets cut his clothing in the fighting. He had three horses shot under him, and lost half a dozen of his friends among the officers.

A day and night of confusion followed. Stuart took von Borcke and Dr. Talcott Eliason, the corps surgeon, and a few other officers to the headquarters of Jackson, seeking new orders to cover the changed positions of the armies. He left Rosser to hold the mountain passes and shield the cavalry's wagon train, not far away at the town of Piedmont.

The weather became bitter as Jeb led his little party over the rough trail the dozen or so miles to Stonewall. They forded the Shenandoah at midnight in cold so intense that their clothes froze stiff on their backs. They reached Jackson's camp at two A.M., but Stuart refused to wake up the commander, and they sat around a big fire, thawing, until Jackson stirred and gave them breakfast at dawn.

While the staff gratefully gulped hot coffee and cold venison, Stuart got his orders: He would not follow Longstreet's corps east, but remain near the Valley, to be on McClellan's flank.

Stuart led the group back along mountain ridges, the route often so wild that they had to hack their way through briers and grape-vines. At five P.M., with the sun almost down, they came to a peak and saw, not far below: "the dark masses of the enemy with glitter-ing arms, and beyond them the rapidly-disappearing lines of our horsemen." Stuart said quietly to von Borcke: "The Yankees have taken Ashby's Gap. Rosser is retreating. We're cut off."

They were so high on the mountain that no guides were to be had; they could return by Jackson's camp only with a circling sixty-mile ride—and Stuart must reach his command before morning.

They stumbled through the night over the ridges, often losing their way, until at last the German found a ragged mountaineer with whom Stuart bargained:

"You lead us to Barbee's Crossroads, over there, and I'll give you a reward. Betray us, and I'll shoot you down as quick as thought."

They often dismounted to lead horses around precipices and over huge rocks; thorns tore their uniforms and scratched painfully. Before morning they came to a Confederate camp near the village of Macon, a point from which Dr. Eliason knew his way. Stuart gave the delighted guide a fifty-dollar bill, and galloped for his men.

He found one squadron on picket at Barbee's Crossroads, and angrily sent von Borcke for Rosser, who had retreated seven miles beyond, to Orleans.

"Tell him to bring the men back here. I'm not going to give it up without fighting, and I'll meet them here tomorrow."

Rosser was "exceedingly annoyed," but got up his command and brought them back to Stuart.

There were brave stories of the mountain fighting that had blazed in Stuart's brief absence. One of the tales was that some of Pelham's Horse Artillery, manned by adventurers from many na-tions, had a battery overrun in a Federal attack, and that the gunners, "The French Detachment," had fought their guns until the enemy fell back, the graycoats shouting the "Marseillaise" at the tops of their voices.

Stuart fought again the next day near the crossroads, where the chief casualties were in the 1st North Carolina, under Colonel James B. Gordon, who led a daring charge. Stuart ended the day by withdrawing once more, and repeated the process through the week. He was, as ever, moved by Pelham's tenacity:

> The Stuart Horse Artillery comes in for a full share of praise, and its gallant commander, Major John Pelham, exhibited a skill and courage which I have never seen surpassed. On this occasion I was more than ever struck with that extraordinary coolness and mastery of the situation which more eminently characterized this youthful officer than any other artillerist . . . his *coup d'oeil* was accurate and comprehensive, his choice of ground made with the eye of military genius, and his dispositions always such in retiring as to render it impossible for the enemy to press us without being severely punished for his temerity.

In the midst of the rearguard fighting Stuart got bad news from home. Young Flora was dead, just after her fifth birthday. He wrote his wife on November sixth:

> The intelligence reached me this morning. I was somewhat expecting it, and yet it grieves me more the more I think of it. When I remember her sweet voice, her gentle ways, and affection for "Papa," and then think that she is *gone,* my heart is ready to burst. I want to see you so much. I know she is better off, but it is such a hard blow to us. . . .
>
> I have been harassing and checking a heavy force, believed to be McClellan's. God has shielded me thus far from bodily harm, but I feel perfect resignation to go at his bidding to join my little Flora.

A few days later he wrote to Lily Parran Lee of his sorrow:

> I can think over her sweet little face, sweet temper and nature and extraordinary sensibilities and weep like a child to

think that their embodiment who loved her Pa like idolatry is
now lifeless clay. May you never feel such a blow. . . .

In the same letter he threw off his grief to add:

I want a pair of *very* high top Russian leather boots No. 9.
Can you go into as extensive a business as this?[5]

But there was no question of Stuart's grief—and no question of
his being able to leave the front to attend Flora's funeral. The enemy
pressed him relentlessly.

On November seventh Stuart had retreated as far as Waterloo
Bridge, and that day was forced to watch his troopers fall back before the enemy "in disgraceful stampede," which was checked
only by Pelham's guns. He burned the bridge at dark and spent the
night at Jefferson in a blinding snowstorm, in a windowless abandoned house whose old chimneys filled the place with smoke. Jeb
and the staff were driven outside to escape these discomforts.

The disheveled force met the enemy again the next day and
Stuart was forced back over the Hazel River, suffering the mortifi-
cation of burying two of his cannon to keep them from the enemy.
The shrunken ranks crossed the river with von Borcke riding behind the noncombatants of "Company Q," now grown to 500 men,
shouting at them, "The Yankees are close on you!" Still the hungry
men straggled, halting to gather persimmons at the roadside.

The command crossed the Rappahannock in a fresh snowstorm
—but the following day was sent on reconnaissance and met the
enemy once more. Von Borcke noted a significant bravery among
the blue regiments which had begun to beset Stuart with such fury
in recent weeks:

"I could not help admiring . . . the excellent behavior of a
squadron of the 5th New York Cavalry, who received with the
greatest coolness the heavy fire of our battery, maintaining perfect
order while shell after shell exploded in their ranks, and saddle after
saddle was emptied—quietly filling the gaps in their lines."

The days of the early war were gone, when Stuart's fearless
riders, on superior horses, stampeded the poorly trained bluecoats almost at will. The enemy had found his courage.

Stuart had a narrow escape on this day. "Greatly provoked" at the withdrawal of his troopers, he concealed thirty riflemen in a woodland and waited until Federal horsemen were within two hundred yards.

"General, we're in danger here," von Borcke said.

Stuart was "in a very bad humor," and snapped: "If it's likely to be too hot for you, retire. I'll stay."

"My duty is with you," the German said—but when the fire broke, he discreetly went behind a tree. Bullets whizzed about them, several tearing bark on von Borcke's tree.

The German looked at Stuart, who passed his hand swiftly in front of his face with an expression of consternation. Von Borcke almost collapsed in laughter. An enemy bullet had cut off half of Stuart's "beloved mustache" as neatly as it could have been done by a barber's razor.

The Federal attack was soon halted, and Stuart had thirty prisoners to show for his ambush. That night he sent von Borcke to General Lee's headquarters, but did not go himself. The German told the story of Jeb's lost mustache to the great amusement of Lee, Longstreet and their staffs.[6]

Flora arrived in "Camp No Rest" the next day. As Jeb wrote a friend, "she is not herself since the loss of her little companion." Von Borcke was impressed by the courage of the Stuarts in their grief, but wrote: "Her manner was composed, but her eyes betrayed their frequent overflow of tears; and the warm pressure of the hand she silently gave me upon our meeting, indicated that words could not describe the agony she had endured."

Flora had brought young Jimmy with her, and this three-year-old did much to enliven the grieving family. Von Borcke thought the infant much like his father; at every opportunity the child wandered among the cavalry horses, and the German aide took him on many gallops around the camp.

General Lee came as soon as he heard of Flora's visit. Von Borcke wrote: "I was touched by the gentle sympathizing way in which he talked with Mrs. Stuart."

Lawley and Vizetelly again appeared in camp, and the days became gay once more. The enemy was quieter. Stirring news came into camp: General McClellan had been removed from Federal command, and Ambrose Burnside had succeeded him.

Longstreet said he was happy to see the change, because McClellan was developing into an aggressive officer. General Lee said thoughtfully, "McClellan and I always understood each other so well. I am afraid they may continue to make these changes until they find someone I don't understand."

Stuart told John Esten Cooke that "Little Mac" had not only botched The Seven Days before Richmond, but had thrown away victory in the Sharpsburg campaign as well:

"McClellan wasn't the man for the occasion. The Maryland campaign was full of faults. He ought to have pressed on McLaws after Boonsboro. That was a great oversight. If Harpers Ferry hadn't surrendered, we would have been in a bad way, up there."

Headquarters moved in late November, for on the nineteenth Burnside shifted the big Federal army eastward, halting on the northern bank of the Rappahannock overlooking Fredericksburg, as if he intended to leap the river and drive on Richmond. To his surprise the watchful Robert Lee had Longstreet's men fortifying heights south of the river on the same day; within two weeks Jackson's corps joined them. Lee's line was dug along a curving ridge overlooking the flat river bottom, an impregnable position from which he waited to be attacked.

Stuart's headquarters were five miles from Fredericksburg, in a tent made comfortable by two big fireplaces. Von Borcke found Jeb "as proud as an Indian nabob of his sumptuous palace." Mulatto Bob had returned from captivity, to Stuart's delight, and the bones rattled with the band as they had in the days before the raid on Chambersburg.

A newcomer was Channing Price's brother Thomas, another of Stuart's cousins. Tom became a staff lieutenant, a young man whose air of sophistication had been gained in a German university.

Lawley and Vizetelly were still in camp, and several other Englishmen with them, drawn by the prospect of coming battle. December came in, bitter cold.

Death touched the staff once more. The daring Redmond

Burke, who had been raiding in the border counties along the Potomac, had been killed in Shepherdstown in a night attack of Indiana infantry. Two of his sons were captured. Stuart was saddened. He wrote Flora:

> He died as he lived, true as steel. . . . His child-like devotion to me is one of those curious romances of this war which I will cherish next to my heart while I live.

He also issued a general order to the cavalry:

> The Major General of Cavalry announces with the deepest regret the death of Capt. Redmond Burke whose valuable services and heroic conduct on our border are historic.
> He was killed by a lurking foe in a night attack on his little band. . . .
> He possessed a heart intrepid, a spirit invincible, a patriotism too lofty to admit of a selfish thought, and a conscience that scorned to do a mean thing.
> A devoted champion of the South, his grey hairs have descended to the grave leaving a shining example of patriotism and devotion to those who survive.

And to his intimate friend, Lily Lee, from whom Stuart first learned of Burke's death, Jeb wrote:

> . . . His death was a severe blow to us and to our cause. . . . I deeply regret that he was not spared to enjoy the peace his prowess deserved.
> I intend to put a monument over Capt. B. if I live. Have the place marked.

But from the same letter Stuart's irrepressible spirit shone, betraying once more his unflagging interest which was second not even to war: Women.

> If a truce . . . should take place I shall be sure to visit you to get that kiss I have strived in vain for heretofore.
> Do kiss the girls for me if you please, and tell them all the

sweet things you know I would write if time allowed. Tell Miss
Folly that someone stole her picture and another one I had and
circumstances make Mrs. Stuart an object of strong suspicion.
I have demanded immediate restitution. . . .

Much love and kisses to the girls.

But he did not forget the war:

We are all all right here and trust very soon to have a
glorious victory. Tell our friends everywhere to pray for us:
Our army is in better fighting trim than it has been for six
months.

One morning Stuart's plan to go fox hunting was spoiled by
Federal gunboats ascending the river; he went to watch Pelham's
guns turn them back after a brisk duel. He rode back to camp
through a snowstorm. The next morning brought one of the war's
fiercest engagements, a snowball battle between the infantry divisions of Generals Hood and McLaws. The men fought over a field
half a mile square, and did not spare Jeb and his staff.

This fight had been brewing for weeks, with skirmishes at every
light snowfall, but today there was ammunition for a decisive meeting. Hundreds of McLaw's men raided Hood's camp. The Texans
boiled out with officers barking orders, regimental flags flying, and
lines of battle forming. Hood's division charged. Von Borcke recorded: "The air was darkened with snowballs." The fight came
nearer Stuart.

He pleaded neutrality and von Borcke hoisted a white flag, but
volleys burst around the cavalrymen and hundreds of men charged
around the tents. Stuart watched with von Borcke from atop an ammunition box, cheering and calling suggestions to the infantry.
McLaws' division at last chased the Texans into their camp. The
day's casualties were one broken leg, an eye lost, myriad bruises.
Von Borcke commented that the sham battle "gave ample proof of
the excellent spirit of our troops, who, in the wet, wintry weather,
many of them without blankets, some without shoes . . . still maintained their good humor, and were ever ready for any sort of sport
or fun."[7]

Two lieutenants of the staff, "Honeybun" Hullihen and Thomas Turner, left this week on a dangerous mission; they crossed the Rappahannock into the enemy rear in an effort to bring Robert Lee's daughter, Mary, south to safety from the plantation house where she was marooned by war.

Stuart knew that a major clash of the armies impended, and he was busy; he was not too busy to charm the women who still besieged him. A note of December tenth, "delivered by hand" to a girl at the plantation "Heartsease," was an example:

> Major General Stuart presents his affectionate regards to Miss Belle Hart and regrets exceedingly that an unavoidable circumstance will prevent the consummation of his wishes to-day. Should there be a concert tonight however he hopes she will hold herself unengaged in order to accompany him to it.[8]

Jeb was thus forced to forego a party at the home of a courier near Chancellorsville on this night. He allowed his officers to go, however, on their promise to return by sunrise, and they went off in Pelham's yellow wagon. Von Borcke drove four mules borrowed from the medical department, his companions Sweeney, two fiddlers, Major Pelham, Captain Blackford, Lieutenant Dabney and an English visitor—and a couple of other musicians and dancers. They jounced over the frozen road, making the woods ring with music.

The wagon overturned, giving Blackford a bad cut on the head, but the determined celebrants pushed on, and enjoyed a rollicking party, a big supper and night-long music.

They were back in camp at daybreak, at about the time the army awoke to the roar of massed Federal artillery which filled the valley of the Rappahannock with thunder. The town of Fredericksburg was being destroyed.

Most of the townspeople had been evacuated, and Blackford saw them, pitiable bands of women and children, wandering the roads and camping in the cold woods. But on December eleventh, when Burnside turned his guns on Fredericksburg, Blackford found a few civilians still hiding there, accompanied only by some Mississippi infantrymen.

Blackford studied the wintry landscape where the hills dominated the river as if he anticipated that history would be made here:

The Confederate army lay in a five-mile line just south of the Rappahannock, its upper end on the river half a mile above Fredericksburg, running farther south as it followed the crest of hills downstream. At the eastern end infantry was a mile and a half from the river; the gap was filled with cavalry.

Cannon dotted the hills, dominating the river flats where the enemy must come—if he came.

Over the river, where Stafford Heights soared, the enemy's columns wound out of sight and tents crowded the hills. Work parties threatened crossings at the riverside.

Fog covered the lower valley and lay in the streets of Fredericksburg. At a hill on the Telegraph Road the army's commanders peered through the fog at the enemy. Their own men had dug in so industriously that hardly a Confederate remained exposed. Men and guns were so thick on the wooded slopes of Jackson's front that thousands of troops were at the rear, in reserve.

Stuart sent Blackford to scout in Fredericksburg, and the captain and two men crept to the river through the ruined streets and saw an incomplete Federal pontoon bridge, its near end just a hundred yards away. Dead and wounded bluecoats lay on the bridgeway, dropped there by the Mississippi riflemen. Blackford judged that the enemy would soon launch boats and try to storm the river crossing. He returned to Stuart.

The fog rose, and the barrage began anew. The opposite hills were one great cloud of cannon smoke, and shells rained among the Colonial houses of the town. Fredericksburg began to burn.

Federal bridges spanned the river after fierce fighting in the bottoms, and the Confederates spent the rest of the day watching the enemy; endless blue columns crossed to the south of the river and camped in the flats below.

Stuart saw enemy parties digging along the river road from Fredericksburg, and about two P.M. rode with von Borcke to investigate. Jeb led the German to a barn, where they tied their horses and crept down a ditch near the enemy. Field glasses revealed growing earthworks; blue infantry and artillery were massed before

Jackson's lines. Von Borcke counted thirty-two guns in one battery. Stuart sent him to General Lee with a report.

Half an hour later von Borcke led Lee and Jackson to the spot. The commanders stared for a few minutes and went back to their hillside, apparently pleased at what they had seen.

Stuart was not idle during the night. He called up extra couriers and ordered Fitz Lee and Rooney Lee to unite at the right of the line.

Cavalry headquarters breakfasted before dawn, and the officers rode to the front. Infantry bands greeted the day in a cold wind which searched the hillside. As if summoned, the commanders rode out. Jackson was dazzling in his new uniform, and officers teased him. "It's the doing of my friend Stuart, I believe," Stonewall said.

Troops shouted, "Great God! Old Jack's drawed his bounty money and bought clothes! I'm afraid he won't get down to work."

Jackson went to a hill overlooking his own front, with A. P. Hill, Stuart and their staffs, "looking out through the white mists of the morning into the plain below, from which rose an indistinct murmur, like the distant hum of myriads of bees."

Jackson and Stuart were in agreement: They should attack the enemy where he lay and drive him into the river. The commander would entertain no such notion; he would wait. After half an hour, Stuart and his officers left Jackson for the cavalry front.

Captain Phillips, a visiting Englishman, passed John Pelham a red-and-blue tie, the colors of the Grenadier Guards, which he asked him to wear in battle and return as a souvenir. Pelham blushed as he wound the tie around his cap.

Stuart rode to the extreme right, where Pelham had posted his guns. There was a cold wait in the dense fog.

The cavalry was ready, but it seemed unlikely to see action, unless the enemy attempted a flank attack to pry Stuart from the river. Jeb probably gave no thought to one unattended detail on the infantry front which had been pointed out to him by von Borcke. On Jackson's line, in the sector commanded by A. P. Hill, some six hundred yards of marshy, wooded front was unmanned. Von Borcke had suggested that a triangle of woodland be cut down so that the enemy could not hide there. Stuart thought the position safe enough, and A. P. Hill agreed.

On the upper end of the line, where Longstreet commanded, things were in such a state of readiness that when Old Pete proposed the addition of spare cannon on Marye's Hill, Colonel E. P. Alexander said, "General, we cover that ground now so well that we comb it as with a fine-tooth comb. A chicken could not live in that field when we open on it."

Lee made a last-minute inspection of Stuart's position, with the thought that the Federals might attack there, the weakest point of the line. He warned Jeb to have the Horse Artillery ready.

Stuart and von Borcke were waiting on the flank when the Federal guns opened with such a crash that they seemed to have fired in unison. Hundreds of shells dropped into the woods on Jackson's front, stripping and felling trees.

Von Borcke saw the morning as if it were a drama:

"And now the thick veil of mist that had concealed the plain from our eyes rolled away, like the drawing up of a drop-scene at the opera, and revealed to us the countless corps, divisions, brigades and regiments of the Federal army forming their lines for attack."

About this time Jeb sent Robert Lee a characteristic message: "Jackson has not advanced, but I have, and I am going to crowd them with artillery."[9]

Stuart sent von Borcke to warn Jackson of an attack forming on his front. The German found Stonewall standing amid the fire, using his field glasses. From this hillside von Borcke saw two thirds of the field, with bluecoats marching as far as he could see. He had never beheld such grandeur: "On they came, in beautiful order, as if on parade, a moving forest of steel, their bayonets glistening in the bright sunlight as they came, waving their hundreds of regimental flags . . . while their artillery beyond the river continued the cannonade with unabated fury over their heads."

Von Borcke was anxious, and told Jackson so. Stonewall gave a firm reply: "Major, my men have sometimes failed to take a position, but to defend one, never! I am glad the Yankees are coming."

He sent the German back to Stuart with an order: Open fire with the Horse Artillery.

Stuart passed the order to Pelham, who begged Jeb to allow him to hurry to a fork of a road with only two guns, which he could have firing long before he could advance all his artillery. Stuart waved him on and the crews galloped into the open, cheering as they followed Pelham. One piece, an old Blakeley, was soon disabled by enemy fire.

Pelham and his lone gun opened a duel with the Federal army.

The brass Napoleon was an old one captured from the enemy at Seven Pines and fought in Pelham's first bid for fame at Gaines' Mill. This morning, on the largest arena of his career, the twenty-four-year-old Pelham fired from the flank down the thick Federal lines as if playing tenpins. The enemy stumbled in confusion, unsure where the shells came from; men fell rapidly. The Confederate army looked downstream from its heights to see the toy figures of Pelham's gunners working with the cannon, whose deadly fire had snarled the enemy flank. Union guns were turned on the exposed crew—four batteries of them. Pelham lost men, but he doubled his rate of fire. One Federal commander thought there was a whole battery in the road junction.

The firing went on and on, with the one gun somehow surviving the hail of shot from thirty-two enemy guns. So many men were dead or wounded that Pelham himself helped load and fire. From far up the line General Lee peered with his glasses, saw Pelham and muttered, "It is glorious to see such courage in one so young."

Stuart sent von Borcke to Pelham. He was to pull back the cannon if the Alabaman thought the time had come. Pelham shook his head: "Tell General Stuart I can hold my ground."

Stuart repeated the message three times, but Pelham hung on, still blazing away. At last, when ammunition was gone, Pelham hitched horses to the gun and pulled it away. He turned then to the full battery, which joined the chorus of the army's artillery. The battle passed to the infantry.[10]

The enemy threw waves of men into Jackson's front until two P.M., piling bodies in the open. The attacks were broken everywhere except in the wooded gap on A. P. Hill's front, where the bluecoats penetrated and were driven out only by fierce counterattack. Against orders a few butternuts followed the retreating Federals onto the plain; each time the blue wave receded, officers were hard put to prevent their elated men from leaving the hillside to follow.

On the upper end of the line, all but hidden from the cavalry by battle smoke, Longstreet's corps faced enemy attack. The blue columns rolled forward and the morning's slaughter was repeated. At the base of Marye's Hill gray infantry behind a stone wall, standing in a sunken road, poured deadly fire on the blue ranks; from overhead the big guns dropped shells precisely in their planned zones of fire. The gallantry of the Union army was marked only by long rows of casualties left at high tide of futile attacks.

A gunner in the Washington Artillery wrote: "Great gaps appeared; we gave them canister again and again; a few left the ranks—more followed . . . running in great disorder toward the town . . . the field before us was dotted with patches of blue."

A fresh division stormed toward the hill, and within a quarter of an hour had been broken like the rest, with 2,000 of its 5,000 men dead or writhing on the field. General Lee watched in the grip of powerful emotion: "It is well that war is so terrible," he said to nearby officers, "we should grow too fond of it."

In late afternoon the last enemy attack was ebbing on Jackson's front when Stuart, evidently impatient from long inaction, gave a rash command.

Fitz Lee's men were at rest behind a protective hill, most of them lying on the ground, awaiting orders. Stuart ordered the whole brigade to charge the enemy.

Beyond the hill the way was swept by hundreds of enemy cannon, and within range of most of the Federal small arms. But Fitz Lee did not hesitate. He climbed into his saddle and got the column in motion.

Charles Blackford was with him at this moment, and as the troopers went into a trot he said, "This will be a second Balaklava."

"Yes, I know it," Fitz said, "but we must obey orders."

The foremost riders were spilling onto the plain when a messenger came at breakneck speed from Jackson, waving madly with his saber and shouting. The cavalry halted as Jackson's officer approached.

"General Jackson wants to know where you're going."

"I'm about to charge the enemy under orders from General Stuart."

"There's some mistake," the messenger said. "General Jackson says to go back to your position or you will not have a man left alive."

The cavalry returned to its post as daylight ended, and this attack was forgotten.[11]

Night was very cold, with a dwindling of gunfire. A minor chorus of sobs and cries from the wounded rose from the frozen field.

Not even yet could Stuart relinquish the thought of attack, and this time found Jackson willing. They privately agreed on a night assault, and Stonewall sent a courier to Lee, asking permission. Jackson went so far as to gather white rags to tie about the sleeves of his men to identify them in the dark—but General Lee refused to permit the attack.

Stuart had ridden forward in darkness on the assumption that the assault was coming off as scheduled. The troopers rode behind sharpshooters, who began clearing the way; for almost half an hour he pushed against the enemy front. Stuart got a bullet through his haversack and another cut the collar of his coat. A messenger from Jackson came with a curt order: General Lee had canceled the attack, and Stuart would return to the lines at once. The horsemen rode back in the garish light of an aurora borealis.

Kyd Douglas of Jackson's staff reported a brief council at army headquarters this night:

Most officers thought Burnside would renew his attacks on the heights next morning. Stuart disagreed; he thought the enemy had enough of slaughter. Jackson was silent until Jeb saw that he was sound asleep, and shook him.

Stonewall opened his eyes and said wearily, "Drive 'em in the river."[12]

The cavalry had scarcely suffered, but the army had paid for its victory. Two generals were dead, Maxcy Gregg and T. R. R. Cobb. Flora Stuart's brother, John R. Cooke, was seriously wounded. The enemy had lost about 13,000 men; the Army of Northern Virginia, some 5,000, most of them on Jackson's front. One artillery command on Jackson's hillside lost ninety horses under the heavy fire.

Stuart's staff showered Pelham with congratulations and watched the smiling gunner return the soiled regimental ribbon to

Captain Phillips, the grenadier. They also welcomed Lieutenant "Honeybun" Hullihen and his companion from their expedition to rescue Mary Lee: They had found Mary far behind Federal lines, and offered to take her to safety, but her friends dissuaded her. On the way home an enemy cavalry patrol picked them up, and they escaped by overpowering the guard, shooting their captors, and dashing over the river.

The armies passed the next day watching each other. Troopers noted the woodland in Jackson's front, where trees a foot in diameter had been snapped, the ground was furrowed by cannon shot, and metal and the bodies of men and horses littered the hill. In front of Marye's Hill, William Blackford said, the ground looked as if it were covered with a blue cloth.

Jeb went out with a flag of truce the next day and met an old friend, Joe Taylor, General Sumner's chief of staff. Taylor, in a strange burst of indignation, told Stuart of General Magruder's attempted treason to the Confederacy. Magruder had first asked President Lincoln to make him a brigadier, Taylor said, and when he was refused, had come south. Jeb wrote in outrage to his friend Custis Lee, the commander's son, in Richmond headquarters:

> Joe thinks he ought to be kicked out of the Confederacy. I think his appointment should be revoked. Do not fail to lay this matter before the President and give its authority.

He boasted of Fredericksburg:

> The victory won by us here is one of the neatest and cheapest of the war. Englishmen here who surveyed Solferino and all the battlefields of Italy say that the pile of dead on the plains of Fredericksburg exceeds anything of the sort ever seen by them.
> Fredericksburg is in ruins. It is the saddest sight I ever saw. . . . Come up to see us right off. I will share my blanket with you.[13]

Rain fell before the brief quiet ended, and the cavalry staff went shivering to headquarters. Stuart growled: "These Yankees always have some underhand trick when they send a flag of truce. They'll be off by daylight."

The night roared with storm, and before dawn Stuart had word of a Federal retreat. Burnside had crossed the river and gone back into camp without having aroused one Confederate picket.

Pelham and von Borcke prowled the battlefield in the wet morning. They found numbers of torpedoes, or small mines, left as traps by the enemy, now worthless because of the wetting of their powder. And they came upon the entire band of a Federal regiment, sound asleep in a wooded corner, unaware that their army had retreated. The musicians were aroused, but quickly accepting their plight, seized instruments and broke into "Dixie" as if it were their favorite tune.

Jefferson Davis and Virginia's Governor Letcher visited the army in the afternoon and took a tour of the grim hill, looking across at the defeated enemy. From the opposite heights, a few days earlier, Abraham Lincoln had peered hopefully at Fredericksburg.

☆

CHAPTER 14

Pelham's Last Fight

STUART'S big tent was a mecca for touring British officers and politicians as the army settled for the winter in cities of log huts. Among the visitors were Colonel Garnet Wolseley, who was to become commander of the British Army, and a Colonel Leslie, chairman of the military committee of the House of Commons.

Stuart and his officers took these men to the far grander headquarters of Jackson, in the plantation office of Richard Corbin's home, Moss Neck, a dozen miles away. It was a strange setting for Jackson, lined with medical, scientific and sporting books, and the walls decorated with fishing tackle, guns, skins, deer antlers, stuffed birds and expensive prints.

Captain James P. Smith of Jackson's staff looked in amusement as Jeb paid Stonewall his first visit in the place: "With clanking saber and spurs and waving black plume he came, and was warmly greeted at the door. Papers and work were all hastily laid aside. No sooner had Stuart entered than his attention turned to the pictures on the walls. He read aloud what was said about each noted race horse and each splendid bull. At the hearth he paused to scan with affected astonishment the horrid picture of a certain terrier that could kill so many rats a minute. He pretended to believe that they were General Jackson's selections; with great solemnity he looked at the pictures and then at the general.

"He paused and stepped back, and in solemn tones said he wished to express his astonishment and grief at the display of General Jackson's low tastes. It would be a sad disappointment to the old ladies of the country, who thought that Jackson was a good man.

General Jackson was delighted beyond measure. He blushed like a girl, and said nothing but to turn aside and direct that a good dinner be prepared for General Stuart."[1]

Stuart teased Jackson about a bottle of old wine at the dinner table, and roared with laughter at finding the print of a gamecock on the butter. "I swear, Jackson," he said, "it's your coat of arms."

Stuart wrote Flora of a small tragedy of camp life, the burning of a Confederate flag she had made for him, which had fallen from its staff into a fire:

> I send you fragments. It had proudly waved over many battlefields and if I ever needed a motive for braving danger and trials, I found it by looking upon that symbol placed in my hands by my cherished wife, and which my dear little Flora so much admired.

Within a few days Flora came to visit and stayed in a farmhouse half a mile from headquarters, expecting to spend a gay Christmas with him. The cavalry's wagons scoured the country for delicacies, and returned with chickens, turkeys, hams, sweet potatoes, butter and thirty dozen eggs. There was also some apple brandy, hidden from Stuart by the staff—and from the neighboring tent of some medical officers, whisky. Von Borcke planned a party and a feast.

Most of the cavalry's officers thronged Stuart's tent on Christmas Eve, enjoying the music of the band and the company of Flora and other wives. Stuart was as cheerful as if he might celebrate forever, but he already had marching orders. General Lee had called for a raid in force. There was not a word during the party, but before dawn on Christmas Day buglers called out the men, who were shocked to learn they had only an hour to saddle, collect rations and be off. Von Borcke was once more caught without a decent horse, and left behind. This time he seemed pleased, for Jeb was hardly out of sight before the Prussian took over his tent with musicians and servants, commandeered the thirty dozen eggs, and had guests crowding around a gigantic bowl of eggnog.

Stuart led 1,800 raiders almost twenty miles to Kelly's Ford; they crossed without incident, trotted ten miles north of the Rappahannock before dark and camped at the village of Morrisville.

Their objectives lay far north and east, along the highway from Fredericksburg to Washington, by which the enemy drew many supplies. This road lay almost parallel to the northward course of the Potomac, and was heavily patrolled.

Stuart divided his force for a three-pronged attack on the highway: Fitz Lee would cut the road on the south, near Quantico; Rooney Lee would hit Dumfries, five miles to the north; and Wade Hampton ten miles farther north, at Occoquan. The forces would unite on the road. They drove hard through December twenty-sixth, for the nearest goal was twenty miles away. The column met no resistance.

Fitz Lee fell upon enemy wagon trains the morning of the twenty-seventh and herded them north to meet Rooney Lee. There had been heavier skirmishing at Dumfries, where Rooney's troopers took about 70 prisoners and drove out the garrison. When Fitz Lee came to Dumfries there was a clash, but little progress, and when dark approached Stuart concluded that he could not budge the enemy, and pulled away.

The command spent a miserable night near the hamlet of Cole's Store, where Hampton joined with a few wagons and prisoners. Stuart sent a party homeward during the night, the wagons, prisoners and broken-down guns under an escort.

Fighting continued through the next day. The command took about 100 more prisoners and rode so far north that they were almost within sight of Alexandria.

Stuart had his men close in quietly on the railroad telegrapher at Burke's Station and take him from his key while he was sending messages about the chase of Jeb's raiders. Stuart then put his own telegrapher at the wire and sent a message to become historic.

> Quartermaster-General Meigs,
> United States Army:
> Quality of the mules lately furnished me very poor. Interferes seriously with movement of captured wagons.
> > J. E. B. Stuart.

Troopers then cut the wires, burned a bridge in the neighborhood and followed Stuart to Fairfax Court House, where he hoped to surprise the garrison. But heavy fire from ambush halted the head of his column and Jeb led them even farther north, beyond Falls Church, to Vienna. Then, aware that pursuit would be concentrated in the south, he moved west through hill passes by Middleburg and Warrenton and back into Confederate lines at Culpeper.

The expedition cost him one dead, thirteen wounded, fourteen missing. He estimated the enemy loss at 200. Beyond the increased anxieties of Federal commanders in the rear, however, military results were insignificant. Stuart returned to camp.[2]

The enemy attempted an offensive in the worst of January weather known as "The Mud March," a day or so of futile struggling by men and animals in bottomless roads beside the Rappahannock, with wagons and guns sinking almost out of sight, and cumbersome pontoons lost. Captain Willard Glazier, a Federal trooper, wrote: "The Rebs seem to know all about our move. To tantalize us, they have erected an enormous sign board on their side of the river, but in full view of our pickets: Stuck In The Mud!"

Esten Cooke, busy now with a biography of Stonewall Jackson, did not neglect his diary, and recorded Jeb's outlook on the war:

> Dropped in at the General's to see Cousin Flora, but she had gone. Chatted, the General asking my opinion about the Northern news [of confused Washington leadership]. I think, I said, there'll be a great big thundering Spring campaign, and then it will end.
>
> The General replied, "If there is a Spring campaign, it will last through the year, and if so, it will go on to the end of Lincoln's time."
>
> It strikes me that the high officers of the Army perhaps are agreed among themselves to discourage peace reasoning—and they are right. War requires nerves always strung: there must be no looking forward to peace and ease; that unstrings.
>
> We talked about Lincoln and I said he had a great deal of muscles, and was pig-headed. The General agreed and said, "He has what they call iron nerve—but is not a man of ability."

On other days Cooke's diary gave small glimpses of life in Stuart's camp:

> Spent an hour with the General in his tent, recalling old battles. His resemblance to Longstreet is very striking, and his gaiety amazing.

Again:

> Banjo going as usual in the General's tent, but I believe I won't go. 'Something too much of that.'

One day Stuart had a poem from Paul Hamilton Hayne, the famous South Carolina poet, entitled "Stuart," and Jeb, rather than expressing gratitude, replied with a joking letter, teasing Hayne about his status as a civilian in wartime. "That's Stuart's way," Cooke noted.

On another day Cooke wrote:

> Came back from Richmond and have been a little blue. The General came and chatted with me. He is charming when he throws off business. He said of little Flora's death, "I shall never get over it. It is irreparable." Never spoke of it but once to me.

The army was undergoing reorganization, with many changes in command. There were feuds, too, and frequent court-martials. Jackson and A. P. Hill carried on their endless squabble, exchanging angry notes. Stuart wrote some of his reports scolding Ike Trimble. Unknown to the command, General Lafayette McLaws was writing home bitter criticism of other officers, including the chief of cavalry:

> Stuart carries around with him a banjo player and a special correspondent. This claptrap is noticed and lauded as a peculiarity of genius, when, in fact, it is nothing else but the act of a buffoon to get attention.[3]

Stuart was sublimely unaware of such criticism. He held a review of Fitz Lee's brigade on January tenth, despite a rain that poured on the field near Fredericksburg and kept ladies of the region from attending. Lee, Longstreet, Stuart and their staffs were the only spectators. Charles Blackford, now transferred from the cavalry to Longstreet's headquarters, recorded: "It rained so hard we could see only fifty yards ahead of us down the line. The men and horses had been roused before daylight, marched fifteen miles through the mud, and then thoroughly wet and worn had to march back. Could anything be more foolish, and all for the sake of a 'grand review' by which a parade might be made before a few women? I have little patience with such vanity, and I think Fitz Lee and his command agree with me."

Stuart tried to remain above the army's petty squabbles. He wrote his brother-in-law, John Cooke, when he learned of a general's wife making pleas to Lee's headquarters staff:

> I accidentally heard the other day that Mrs. Ransom wrote to Chilton informing him that A. P. Hill was trying to get Pender promoted instead of Ransom and complaining of such treatment to her husband. What do you think of that?
>
> Now if Mrs. Jeb ever takes it upon herself to write any official a letter of that kind in my behalf, she will have an account to settle with the aforesaid Jeb. It is *far better* to be neglected than to be promoted by such a means.

He gave Cooke some practical advice on Army personalities:

> I don't see how you can avoid either Ransom or D. H. Hill, who is worse—but Pettigrew I thought well of on slight acquaintance. Be sure Dear John to keep out of snarls of every kind, they are perfectly abominable. Submit to almost anything but degradation to avoid them—"a soft answer turneth away wrath".
>
> "Promotion cometh neither from the east nor the west", etc. Take good care of yourself. . . .
>
> Do you like Beauregard? No better man to excite enthusiasm and keep up the morale of an army. I liked him very much, though I rank Lee and Joe Johnston above him.

He added a bit of political prophecy on the future of the Confederacy:

The Emperor of the French will help us yet. *Mark you.*[4]

Stuart was concerned about the cavalry's mounts. Hundreds of horses were dying of disease and lack of forage. Men were little better off, and General Lee wrote Richmond that scurvy was raging, and that he had squads of men in the woods to gather roots, herbs and buds of trees. The ration was reduced even more.

The army learned that General Burnside had been replaced by General Joseph Hooker, who had a reputation as a fighter. Captain Glazier took note of a vital change in the bluecoat cavalry which became obvious to Stuart's men:

The ill-fated young General Bayard had tried in vain to consolidate Union cavalry, "but it was reserved for General Hooker to bring about the desired result."

George Stoneman was now commander of the cavalry corps, Army of the Potomac. Glazier wrote hopefully that the long-scattered regiments, now consolidated, should fight better, and with stronger morale. There were already wonders—new schools for riders, camps of instruction for grooms, hostlers and troopers. Old and incompetent officers went out, and aggressive young men rose to command the Federal brigades.

Glazier wrote: "The Rebel cavalry under Stuart has long been organized into an efficient body which, at times, has sneered at our attempts to match them . . . the general successes of the Rebel army have made them all very insolent, in the hope that final victory is already in their grasp."

Stuart was not contemptuous of the Federal cavalry this winter, however. He wrote a friend, Colonel William H. Payne, authorizing him to open a cavalry camp near Richmond, where men on parole could be trained for the field. There was still the handicap of the law requiring each man to furnish his own horse, a system before which Stuart was helpless. They must look to the enemy for a horse supply.

The Confederate cavalry system seemed an outrage to Major McClellan of Stuart's staff. The government provided feed, shoes and blacksmithing, in theory, and paid owners forty cents a day for use of their mounts. If the animal was killed in action, the government paid for it—but if it were captured, worn out, or lost in any other way, the trooper must find a new mount or transfer to the infantry.

McClellan thought this policy "a calamity against which no amount of zeal or patriotism could successfully contend. . . . The cavalrymen were kept mounted, but at an enormous loss of efficiency, and by a system of absenteeism which sometimes deprived the cavalry of more than half its numbers. . . . Whenever a cavalryman was dismounted it was necessary to send him home to procure a remount. This required from thirty to sixty days."

Almost as bad, horseshoes, nails and forges were always scarce, and more than once McClellan saw troopers leading limping horses, "while from the saddle dangled the hoofs of a dead horse, which he had cut off for the sake of the sound shoes nailed to them."

Jeb went to Culpeper in a snowstorm to inspect Hampton's troopers, and staged a dance and minstrel show. Von Borcke and Pelham were in the crowd, the latter squiring a pretty girl, Bessie Shackelford. Stuart left them in the town for a few days while he made a brief visit to Richmond. He made it obvious to observant men of the staff that parting from Pelham was painful to him.

John Pelham and William Blackford had become close friends in the winter. Their tents adjoined and they stabled their horses together. On quiet days they read to each other from military volumes, especially an army favorite, Napier's *Peninsula War*. Pelham's modesty made him a favorite in many commands; there was a report that his commission as lieutenant colonel was on its way. President Davis was said to have agreed instantly to his promotion, and when he was offered documents on the young major's record, said, "I do not need to see any papers about Major Pelham." Now only Senate approval was lacking on the commission, a mere formality.

As long ago as November Stuart had written insistently to Richmond:

> I have the honor to renew my application for the promotion of Major John Pelham to the rank of Lieutenant Colonel of Artillery in my division. He will now have five batteries;

and always on the battlefield, batteries of other divisions and
the reserve are thrown under his command, which make the
position he holds one of great responsibility, and it should have
corresponding rank.

I will add that Pelham's coolness, courage, ability and
judgment, evinced on many battlefields, vindicate his claims
to promotion. So far as service goes he has long since won a
colonelcy at the hands of his country.

Blackford thought Pelham "so innocent looking, so 'child-like
and bland' in the expression of his sparkling blue eyes, but as grand a
flirt as ever lived . . . tall, slender, beautifully proportioned and very
graceful, a superb rider, and as brave as Julius Caesar."

Blackford saw that Jeb was more fond of the artillery major
than the rest of them: "Stuart loved him like a younger brother, and
could not bear for him to be away from him."

On a hazy springlike day, about the middle of March, Pelham
went shrewdly about the business of obtaining leave from Stuart. At
night he persuaded Jeb to give him an order to inspect artillery at
Orange Court House—where he would have a chance to see some
pretty girls. Jeb agreed good-naturedly, and Pelham had Norman
Fitzhugh of the staff write the order and left immediately.

Pelham feared that Stuart would countermand the order and so
rode away before daylight without breakfast, telling Blackford that
he would eat at an artillery camp on the road.

Stuart was bound for Culpeper that day to testify at the court-
martial of his old friend of frontier days, Colonel Henry Clay Pate,
who had become involved in the army's administrative troubles. But
he missed his gunner at breakfast.

"Where's Pelham?"

"He's already gone to Orange, General. He's been gone."

"Didn't wait for breakfast?"

"He said he would eat at some battery camp."

Stuart sent a courier after Pelham. "Tell him to come back. I
want to see him."

But it was too late. Pelham had foreseen Stuart's move, and
paused in the camp for no more than a cup of coffee. The courier

caught him only when he was safely in Orange. Stuart was in Culpeper by then, on his army business.

Circumstance, aided by Pelham, soon united the cavalry chief and his artilleryman. For while Pelham was visiting in Orange, a train hurried in from Culpeper with interesting news: A big enemy cavalry force had struck upriver, about 3,000 troopers under General W. W. Averell. There was no Confederate infantry nearer than Fredericksburg to stop them.

Pelham climbed aboard the train to Culpeper, certain that Stuart would approve his violation of orders to get nearer the raiding enemy.

Jeb seemed glad to see Pelham. The court-martial was over—and there were reports from Fitz Lee that the enemy column was coming near. Fitz had a nominal strength of 1,900 in his brigade, but from losses of horses and men could assemble no more than 800 men. Company G of the 3rd Virginia, which was typical, had just thirty of its eighty riders in the saddle on March sixteenth.

Stuart and Pelham spent the night in Culpeper. Jeb probably showed the Major a note he had just received from Nannie Price, his pretty cousin of Dundee:

> Dear General: We had a little candy stew last night, and knowing your fondness for "sweets" of all kinds, I send you some of it this morning. Miss Brill sends some of it for the "Gallant Pelham," which you must be sure to give him. If you could see the burns on our fingers I am sure it would seem much sweeter....

Pelham perhaps saw his pretty Culpeper girl friend, Bessie Shackelford, on this night, but he was also seen in a hotel room in the company of some hard-riding cavalry veterans: Colonels Welby Carter, Tom Rosser, Harry Gilmor, Henry Clay Pate and Major J. W. Puller.

At seven thirty A.M. of St. Patrick's Day, March seventeenth, the enemy brushed aside Fitz Lee's picket at Kelly's Ford, swept up prisoners, and began to overrun the country south of the Rappahannock.

Fitz Lee led his five thin regiments north of Culpeper, toward Brandy Station.

Stuart was astir early. Harry Gilmor saw him on the Culpeper streets "all ready, with Pelham by his side, looking as fresh, and joyous and rosy as a boy ten years old." Gilmor rode with Stuart as a substitute aide.

Jeb and Pelham borrowed horses, the latter mounting a rawboned black mare. They trotted out of town behind Fitz Lee's column; Gilmor waved to Bessie Shackelford, who stood on the upper balcony of her father's house, fluttering a handkerchief as long as the party was in sight.

When they passed the 5th Virginia, Major Puller shouted to Gilmor, "Harry, leave me your haversack if you get killed!" Gilmor nodded.

The party rode until the advance was in sight of Kelly's Ford, half a mile from the river, where the first Federals were flushed. They did not look dangerous—a few riders strung across the road, with both flanks hidden in woods.

Stuart studied the enemy. Fitz Lee formed the men in a field and rode to Jeb:

"General, I think there are only a few platoons in the woods yonder. Hadn't we better take the bulge on them at once?"

Stuart agreed, and the 3rd Virginia trotted out with dismounted sharpshooters in front. Gilmor went with them, at the side of Captain James Bailey. When Bailey's horse went down, Gilmor took over for a moment, leading a charge on a stone fence which shielded Federal riflemen. The squadron pounded to within two hundred yards of the wall. A fire from carbines broke the ranks; "at least a regiment" fired, Gilmor thought. And from the flank hidden guns knocked men to the ground. The regiment turned and ran. Gilmor begged them to halt, but they continued to the rear.

Stuart was suddenly among them: "Don't leave me, men. If you leave, I'll be here by myself!" He waved the big hat in the air. "Confound it, men! Come back!"

Gilmor was lost in admiration: "Never did I see one bear himself more nobly. I stopped to gaze on him, though I expected every moment to hear the dull *thud* of a bullet and see him fall."

Captain Bailey returned, and Stuart sent him with the 3rd Virginia behind a sod fence some fifty yards nearer the enemy, where they were sheltered from the carbines.

The men were hardly in position when a shell burst atop the fence, spilling troopers about; there were three dead and seven wounded. Gilmor wrote of the next few moments:

"The General sent me to order the Third to charge the woods directly in front. The poor fellows went in gallantly, but it was a fatal mistake, and I thought so at the time, for that stone fence extended from the road on our right to the river on our left, and was utterly impassable for cavalry throughout its whole length. But the gallant Third dashed on in splendid style, with their long bright sabers raised in tierce point, and with a wild ringing yell. But when within 150 yards of the barricade a deadly fire poured into their ranks, which emptied many a saddle, and threw the column into some confusion. They pushed on, however, right up to the fence, killing men behind it with the pistol, and tried to make a gap; but that it was impossible for mounted men to do, and the poor fellows were forced to fall back out of range and reform the regiment, now looking no larger than a good squadron."

Pelham had gone to the rear to find a good gun position for Major James Breathed, and in his absence the regiments fought desperately without artillery support. The action was a nightmare, for wherever they turned the troopers were mauled by superior force—and the affair had only begun.

When the 3rd Virginia fell back a big blue column of fours drove on the Confederate position; the 2nd Virginia met it head-on, and formations broke like pinwheels in a savage battle of sabers. A flank attack of two gray squadrons at last drove off these Federals. Fitz Lee was heartened by this, and sent Tom Rosser to sweep around the left and cut into the enemy rear.

Gilmor rode with Rosser, anticipating easy progress, but they approached the river under a fury of carbine fire. When they could see behind the woods, as Gilmor described it: "There, to our astonishment, we beheld about two brigades of cavalry. We should, therefore, have been obliged to retreat even had there been no dismounted men at the fence; and their fire was very heavy, killing a good many men and horses. Rosser strove hard to keep the regiment in order, but, owing to the nature of the ground and the severe fire from the fence, they went back in some confusion."

As they scrambled back toward safety Rosser shouted, "Major Puller, why in the name of God don't you help me rally the men?"

Puller, white-faced, lifted his head from the horse's mane with an effort. "Colonel, I'm killed," he said.

"My God, old fellow, I hope not," Rosser said. "Bear up, bear up."

The Colonel left to herd the rest of the regiment to the rear. Gilmor tried to help Puller, but when the injured man reached for his reins he pitched to the ground. Gilmor had men catch riderless horses and carry him to an ambulance. Puller died almost immediately.

Fighting became general, with Jeb and Fitz Lee in the thickest of it. Charges littered the field and sabers rang endlessly. Fitz had two horses shot under him. The Federal Colonel Alfred Duffié led a charge which pushed Fitz Lee into a field on an adjoining farm. Lee formed his line within reach of Breathed's guns. The Federals halted in a woodland, and Fitz launched a charge. Artillery crashed from both sides.

Pelham watched Breathed and his gun crews as they blasted the enemy, nodding his satisfaction, but when Federal fire dwindled and Breathed's men worked more slowly, Pelham was impatient: "Major, do not let your fire cease. Drive them from their position."

Gilmor stood with Pelham near the 2nd Virginia Cavalry; shells burst overhead.

Fitz Lee rode the line. "Keep cool, boys. These little things make a deal of fuss, but don't hurt anyone."

The regiment cheered him, but looked anxiously toward the smoke of the guns as Lee rode away. The troopers filed off to take part in the attack. As the last of the regiment wheeled into line, Captain Bailey shouted, "My God, they've killed poor Pelham!"

Gilmor had heard no bullet strike. He whirled to see Pelham's riderless horse moving off. Pelham lay on the ground "on his back, his eyes open, and looking very natural."

He seemed fatally wounded.

Federal cavalrymen rode near, and Bailey and a lieutenant from Fitz Lee's staff lifted Pelham onto Gilmor's horse. Gilmor saw that the wound was in the back of the head, bleeding profusely. He rode a short distance, put the body over Pelham's borrowed horse, and summoned two dismounted men.

"Take this officer to the nearest ambulance and call a surgeon. Hurry!"

Gilmor galloped to find Stuart. Jeb saw blood on his hands. "You're hurt," he said.

"No, General. It's not my blood. It's Pelham. He's dead. They killed him a few minutes ago. I sent his body off."

Gilmor stared at the general: "I shall never forget his look of distress and horror."

Stuart stopped. "Tell me about it," he said. "Tell me everything that happened." When Gilmor had finished Jeb dropped his head and sobbed. Gilmor heard only a few mumbled words from him: "Our loss is irreparable!"

There was little more fighting. Partial attacks threatened Breathed's guns near the end, but General Averell had not met Lee with all his strength, evidently fearful of an ambush by infantry, and at five thirty P.M. the bluecoats retreated. In the final moments the 4th Virginia, charging in the open, had stopped to tear down a rail fence and galloped on, though about forty men fell at the spot. Gilmor observed: "This must have convinced the enemy of our determination to lose every man before they should enter Culpeper."

Stuart reported to General Lee by telegraph, a small party hung on the Federal rear, and survivors of the command went back toward Culpeper.

Gilmor overtook the two men he had ordered to care for Pelham. They were walking in the dusk just as they had on the battlefield, leading the horse with the body of the gunner draped over it, arms and legs dangling. Pelham's face, hair and hands were caked with mud and blood. Gilmor angrily halted them and stretched the body in a fence corner. He was astonished to find Pelham still breathing.

"Imagine my indignation and vented wrath when I learned that, instead of looking for an ambulance, they had moved on toward Culpeper, a distance of eight miles. . . . I firmly believe that, had surgical aid been called to remove the compression on the brain, his life might have been saved."

Gilmor soon had Pelham in an ambulance, and within a few minutes the young gunner was in bed at the Shackelford home, where three surgeons worked over him. Bessie Shackelford and other women aided with hot water, wrapped his hands and feet in flannel, and brought brandy.

Gilmor recorded the details: "The piece of shell that struck him was not larger than the end of my little finger. It entered just at the curl of the hair on the back of the head, raked through the skull without even piercing the brain, coming out two inches below the point where it entered. The skull was badly shattered between the entrance and exit of the shell. As the surgeons removed the pieces I selected one as a memento of one of the most gallant and highly esteemed officers of the Southern army."

The surgeons announced that the case was hopeless. Gilmor and Bessie remained in the room with him by candlelight.

At one o'clock Pelham opened his eyes. He gave Gilmor "an unconscious look," closed his eyes, and breathed deeply. He was dead.

They put a fresh uniform on the body. Stuart entered, Gilmor wrote, and "great tears rolled down his cheeks as he silently gazed."

H. H. Matthewe, a gunner with Breathed's battery, described the final scene in the Culpeper house:

"General Stuart also came. With measured step, his black plumed hat in hand, he approached the body, looked long and silently upon the smiling face, his eyes full of tears, then stooping down he pressed his bearded lips to the marble brow. As he did so . . . a sob issued from his lips, and a tear fell on the pale cheek of Pelham. Severing from his forehead a lock of the light hair, he turned away, and as he did so there was heard in low deep tones, which seemed to force their way through tears, the single word, 'Farewell.' "

When everyone else had gone, Gilmor slept in the room beside the body of the boy Major.[5]

Stuart telegraphed the Alabama Congressman, Lamar Curry:

The noble, the chivalrous Pelham is no more; he was killed in action; his remains will be sent to you today. How much he was loved, appreciated and admired let the tears of agony we have shed and the gloom of mourning throughout my command bear witness. His loss is irreparable.

He also telegraphed von Borcke to meet the train bearing Pelham's body at Hanover Junction and accompany it to Richmond.

Von Borcke had to quell a mutiny of Pelham's two tearful slaves, Willis and Newton, who begged to be taken. He boarded the train at Hanover and found Pelham's body in a wooden coffin identical to scores of others on the car. He got into Richmond late in the night, found that no hearse met the train, as he had ordered, and carried the coffin into the city in a common dray.

Von Borcke went to Governor Letcher, who offered a room in one of the halls of Congress; the coffin was put there under a guard of honor and covered by a Virginia flag. The Prussian helped undertakers transfer the body to a handsome metal coffin the next day. Von Borcke wrote: "I was overcome with grief as I touched the lifeless hand that had so often pressed mine in the grasp of friendship. . . . By special request I had a small glass window let into the coffin-lid just over the face, that his friends and admirers might take a last look at the young hero."

The people came "in troops," most of them girls and young women who covered the casket with flowers. A day later, with the Richmond infantry battalion marching around it, the body went to the railroad station, where a home-bound Alabama soldier became its escort. Reports were that women stopped the train at every station in Alabama, piling the casket with flowers. In Virginia, three young women went into mourning for Pelham.

Stuart paid a final tribute in orders to the cavalry corps:

He fell mortally wounded with the battle cry on his lips and the light of victory beaming in his eyes. His eye had glanced over every battlefield of this army, from the First Manassas to the moment of his death, and he was, with a single exception, a brilliant actor in them all. The memory of the gallant Pelham, his many victories, his noble nature and purity of his character is enshrined as a sacred legacy in the hearts of all who knew him. His record has been bright and spotless, his career brilliant and successful. He fell the noblest of sacrifices on the altar of his country.

To outward appearances, at least, Stuart never mourned another like this.

From the Deep South one of the dead hero's kinsmen, Major Peter Pelham, wrote of the scene in Alabama, when the casket arrived at the family home. People thronged the place from the whole county: "It was a beautiful moonlight night the last of March and as the casket, covered with white flowers ... [was] borne by white-haired old men, followed by girls with uncovered heads, to us who stood in the porch at his home, waiting ... it seemed a company 'all in white.' ... And I heard a voice near me say, 'Made white in the blood of the Lamb' and I knew it to be the voice of his Mother. The Father and Sister were crushed in sorrow and kept their rooms, but that Spartan Mother met her beloved dead on the threshold as she would have done had he been living, and led the way into the parlor and directed that he ... be laid where the light would fall on his face when Sunday came."[6]

Pelham's commission as Lieutenant Colonel, delayed in slow Richmond channels, was hastened by Robert Lee's letter to President Davis:

I mourn the loss of Major Pelham. I had hoped that a long career of usefulness and honor was still before him. He has been stricken down in the midst of both, and before he could receive the promotion he had richly won. I hope there will be no impropriety in presenting his name to the Senate, that his comrades may see that his services have been appreciated, and may be incited to emulate them.

The army quickly forgot the insignificant affair of cavalry at Kelly's Ford, and turned to the looming threat of a spring offensive. Stuart would never forget Pelham.

He wrote Flora:

You know how his death distresses me. He was noble in every sense of the word. I want Jimmie to be just like him.

And this moment moved him as if Pelham's death had somehow made the Southern cause more sacred to him than ever. He admonished his wife:

I wish an assurance on your part in the event of your surviving me—that *you will make the land for which I have given my life your home and keep my offspring on Southern soil.*

Esten Cooke learned of Pelham's death while he was in cavalry headquarters at "Camp No Camp," and was saddened by the contrast of the bleak news with the blaring of an army band nearby. He was moved to poetry:

Oh, band in the pine woods cease,
Cease with your splendid call.
Oh, the living are noble and just,
But the dead are the bravest of all.[7]

☆

Chancellorsville

ESTEN COOKE'S diary revealed the dull life at the cavalry camp as spring approached:

Wake about 8, find my fire burning and boots, cleaned with real Day & Martin, setting by it. Dress leisurely, gazing into fire with one boot on, or cravat in hand. An old weakness, this. Finish, and read my Bible. Then say my prayers. Then if breakfast isn't ready, read a novel or paper or anything.

Lige then rushes in violently with a coffee pot, breakfast follows, of steak and biscuits nearly invariably. A strong cup of coffee. No molasses now. And I commence the real business of the day, and charm of life, smoking and reading something.

This over I go to writing and write away till three or four—or I don't write. I ride out, to Col. Baldwin's, or elsewhere, and come back, and smoke and lounge in the tents till toward dark when dinner is ready—pretty much the same—a little stewed fruit being the sole addition.

After dinner, smoke, smoke—chat, chat—or read, read! *Voila ma vie!* The storm rages and I must smoke.

Cooke also reported his conversations with Jeb:

General Lee says he wishes he had a dozen Jacksons for his lieutenants. General Stuart again repeats that Jackson is a man of military genius. And I reply, "That hits it exactly. He certainly has the knack of whipping the Yankees." I believe I am regarded as the Jackson Man of headquarters.

Stuart returned to the gaiety of camp life as if he had forgotten his losses. Cooke recorded one late March day:

> The General has got his banjo and is gone out frolicking. He is a jolly cove.

There was a lightness in some of Jeb's correspondence. In a letter to one of his cousins of the Price family he fired a barrage of puns:

> I wonder how you all can keep your heads above water when the whole country is crying, "Down with the *Prices*." It must be consoling to the financiers to observe that the *Price sterling* is not as much above the *Prices* current, as before Channing's promotion.
>
> I will spare you any further affliction now, but you see I must have my joke—
>
> "No rose without its thorn, *nary Jeb, without his joke*."[1]

Channing Price, the adjutant so recently promoted, had won a reputation as the finest military secretary in the army. His father, a blind Richmond merchant, had for years dictated his correspondence to Channing.

Now, when they rode in the field, Stuart would signal Price and without halting dictate to him three or four orders, each different, often bristling with figures of strength, mileage, routes, and time of departure. Price would listen attentively, and without taking a note or asking a question, rein to the roadside and write orders for Stuart's signature. Jeb rarely made changes in Channing's dispatches.

But Channing's brother Tom, who had been so short a time with the staff, came to grief in a way that afforded gossip for months. Tom was already a distinguished young scholar, a law graduate of the University of Virginia who had studied Latin, Greek and Sanskrit with renowned German scholars in Berlin universities, had studied archeology and languages in Greece, and French literary criticism in Paris. He had run the blockade to join the Confederate army, but life with Stuart soon palled on him. He missed European gaiety and the world of letters.

Tom kept an intimate diary, and unfortunately filled it with secret thoughts on his superiors. He heaped scorn upon Stuart, his officers and their way of life in camp, and showed no appreciation for Jeb's having saved him from service as a private.

Tom lost the diary in a skirmish and bemoaned it at length. Staff officers thought it strange that he attached such value to the book—until Stuart got by mail a Northern newspaper reprinting the diary in full.

The staff saw the cause of Tom's misery, for he had written, "Oh, for Berlin!" and such phrases. And of his generous kinsman: "General Stuart in his usual garrulous style exclaimed," and so on. Jeb was hurt. Tom was soon assigned to the engineers and left the staff. In after years he would become a famed philologist.[2]

Jeb lost neither his good humor nor his interest in women. In early April an anonymous woman sent him some homemade gauntlets through one of his officers, to whom Stuart wrote:

> The best gloves of the kind I ever saw, they speak well for the fertility of resource and readiness of adaptation to the labor of love or necessity, which shine so conspicuously in our Southern heroines. I am proud to see that Virginia is behind none, and that her fair women vie with her brave men in devotion, and cheerful endurance.

He then came to the point:

> I must beg of you the further privilege to inform me of the lady's name and residence, for I am anxious to know more of one to whose favor I am so much indebted.[3]

On April eighth Stuart wrote Flora:

> I go forth into the uncertain future. My saber will not leave my hand for months. I am sustained in the hour of peril by the consciousness of right, and upheld by the same Almighty hand, which has thus far covered my head in the day of battle, and in whom I put my trust.

He was hurried off the next day to Culpeper, where Fitz Lee's little force of 2,000 held the river front. A new campaign was on.

North of the Rappahannock the enemy stirred. General Hooker was fond of proclaiming his force of 130,000 "the finest army on the planet," and he laid a shrewd plan to pry the Army of Northern Virginia from the ridge at Fredericksburg, strike it in the flank and take Richmond.

His cavalry had now grown to 12,000 troopers, by current Southern standards superbly mounted; 13,000 well-fed horses waited in Hooker's camps. Stuart's regiments were pitiful by comparison. Hundreds of men in every regiment had no horses. Wade Hampton's brigade had to be left behind near Fredericksburg for lack of mounts, and many of Hampton's riders were on furloughs to South Carolina and Mississippi, in search of fresh horses at home. Meanwhile, only 2,700 riders picketed the army's front, "from the Chesapeake to the Blue Ridge."

Only the flooding Rappahannock and muddy roads postponed war as April, 1863 advanced.

Headquarters acquired another character in these days, Captain Justus Scheibert, a German whose jollities in broken English made him the leading social attraction in Culpeper. He entertained women at the pianoforte almost nightly. William Blackford and a friend once took him to visit some girls and while they waited in the parlor, Scheibert began playing the piano. In his ardor the fat German bounced hard on the stool, crushed it, and tumbled to the floor. As he scrambled up he heard the girls on the stairway and hurriedly shoved the smashed furniture under the piano. He snatched up a broken stool leg and hid it behind his back as the girls entered. Blackford and his companion laughed so loudly that they could not introduce the stranger, and Scheibert faced the young women staring, red-faced and perspiring. He became a favorite staff amusement.

Scheibert was also a painter, and helped Rooney Lee's wife to complete portraits she had made. He once went to her house near headquarters dressed in his usual short jacket and white trousers, looking, Blackford said, as if he had been melted and poured into the uniform. When he had finished a painting he placed the wet canvas on a chair and talked with Charlotte Lee, bouncing about the room in rapid conversation, gesturing nervously, jumping in and out of chairs. He sat on the freshly painted picture, but was unaware of it, and Mrs. Lee saw it only when he knelt to look under the piano in search of it.

Charlotte Lee laughed and pulled the canvas from his clothes— leaving the print of a woman's face on the seat of his trousers. Scheibert tore out of the house and across the fields to camp, where he arrived roaring, waving his arms, and, overcome by mirth, tumbled on the grass where Stuart and the staff lay in the sunshine. Each time he turned over the officers saw the portrait on its white background, and howled with laughter.

Scheibert was a sort of fat Don Quixote on horseback, for he was a beginning rider, and when he traveled, tied packages to his saddle; he rode with a flapping and jouncing of boxes, bags and objects of every sort, many of them dropping behind him. Scheibert once took the wrong road and galloped directly toward enemy lines with his pendant belongings, and when Stuart sent a rider to warn him, only spurred his horse in fear. When caught, he had scattered his goods over a wide area and exposed himself and an orderly to gunfire in collecting them.

Such headquarters revelry was interrupted on April thirteenth.

Stoneman's big cavalry corps gathered on the upper Rappahannock, threatening Kelly's Ford and a railroad bridge a few miles above. Stoneman had simple orders:

Cross the river, drive off the Confederate cavalry at Culpeper, and ride eastward to get between Lee's army and Richmond. Burn supply depots and destroy Lee's lifeline, the Richmond and Fredericksburg Railroad.

General Hooker would be at hand to supply the cavalry when rations ran out.

The orders to Stoneman closed with an imperial flourish:

It devolves upon you, General, to take the initiative in the forward movement of this grand army, and on you and your noble command must depend in a great measure the extent and brilliancy of our success. Bear in mind that celerity, audacity, and resolution are everything in war, and especially is it the case with the command you have and the enterprise upon which you are about to embark.

But celerity, audacity and resolution deserted Stoneman's advance when the blue columns struck Stuart's tiny guard at the river crossings. So certain of success was Hooker that his big infantry corps in the rear cooked eight days' rations and prepared to move behind the cavalry. There was a fumbling start.

Rooney Lee guarded Kelly's Ford with only two regiments, plus some 250 men of the 2nd North Carolina, more than half of these without horses and on foot.

Stuart was called from "Camp Pelham" on April thirteenth and dashed to Kelly's Ford; it was all over when he arrived. The Federals had made a show of crossing at daylight, but retreated under sharp fire.

There was more trouble upstream at the railroad bridge, where a small party manned rifle pits and a blockhouse. General Gregg's division approached and its advance crossed the river. The 9th Virginia charged the enemy, who astonishingly recrossed the stream.

A few Federal parties crossed the next day and fought briefly with Stuart's outposts, but all retreated. The Rappahannock was now rising swiftly, and it appeared that the Union cavalry chief had lost an opportunity.

President Lincoln telegraphed General Hooker on April fifteenth:

General Stoneman is not moving rapidly enough to make the expedition come to anything. He has now been out three days, two of which were unusually fair weather, and all three without hindrance from the enemy, and yet he is not twenty-five miles from where he started. To reach his point he still has sixty miles to go, another river to cross, and will be hindered by the enemy. By arithmetic, how many days will it take him to do it? I do not know that any better can be done, but I greatly fear it is another failure already. Write me often, I am very anxious.

Lincoln's fears were justified. He had developed at last a cavalry corps superior to Stuart's in numbers, equipment, horses, supply and arms. He had not yet found its match in bold leadership.

Stoneman's failure gave the Confederates a respite of almost two weeks, for the Rappahannock surged high over its banks and made crossings perilous. Stuart's tents were often flooded and the staff miserable.

It was April twenty-eighth when the blow fell at last. The big Federal army had covered Kelly's Ford and the railroad bridge nearby with infantry for several days, and now they moved. Von Borcke was shaken awake at three A.M. by Stuart, and the staff rode off, yawning. They found Fitz Lee's brigade in line at dawn, near Brandy Station. The enemy were entirely hidden by fog. There were sounds of regiments marching on pontoon bridges; scouts said bluecoats were pouring over.

Stuart pulled his men into line in an effort to contain the big force—prisoners said 20,000 blue infantry had crossed and marched upriver, cutting off Kelly's Ford. One prisoner caught in the net was a blustering Belgian in Federal uniform who spoke French with von Borcke, and would say only, "Gentlemen, I can give you one piece of advice—that is, to try and make your escape as quickly as possible. If not, your capture by the large army in front of you is a certainty."

Stuart soon found what the Belgian meant. Couriers brought the same news from all directions: Yankees were pouring over the river at every crossing. Stuart cut an infantry column near Madden's, and though he scattered it but briefly, found in his catch of prisoners men wearing the badges of three corps, the Fifth, Eleventh and Twelfth. The new Richmond offensive was on. Stuart telegraphed the word to Robert Lee.

There was an immediate order in reply: Stuart would try to protect the railroads as best he could, but the main body of cavalry must retreat eastward and join the left flank of Confederate infantry.

Lee was now moving into the gloomy thickets of The Wilderness, a tangle almost fifty miles square which lay in the path of the

Federal columns. To complicate matters, Hooker was also crossing in force at Fredericksburg, and coming into line on the site of the battle of December. Lee was forced to leave a strong rear guard there. The infantry force he carried into The Wilderness was depressingly small, for Longstreet's corps was far away, at its post around Suffolk, in Tidewater Virginia.

Stuart sent Fitz Lee's men, "in a jaded and hungry condition," to Raccoon Ford, which they would hold until infantry came to their aid. Rooney Lee's brigade went to the upper Rapidan to guard the railroad.

Stuart went to the rear. Von Borcke wrote of it: "By the time we reached Raccoon Ford it was already dark. The night was wet and chilly, a fine sleet drizzling down incessantly; and we felt cold, hungry, and uncomfortable." They wound along the Orange Plank Road, which led from Germanna Ford to Chancellorsville, little more than a clearing in The Wilderness. They were on the road all night.

The first graycoats to face the enemy were the 3rd Virginia, who met the 6th New York Cavalry in a brisk fight at Wilderness Run and fell back, fighting, toward Chancellorsville.

Stuart was not far behind, in camp at Todd's Tavern. The bulk of the Federal cavalry had already left The Wilderness—on a raid in the rear, it was reported. Stuart had time to do no more than help save Lee's infantry; there was no hope of chasing Stoneman.

Jeb was not long at Todd's Tavern. He called von Borcke and two or three others, including Captain Scheibert, and rode in the light of a new moon toward Robert Lee's headquarters at Spotsylvania Court House. Von Borcke urged him to take a cavalry escort, but Jeb refused:

"It's only twelve miles. The roads are clear."

They rode near enemy lines in the overgrown country, until a pistol popped ahead of them and a courier came back with the story that Yankees had fired on him. Stuart was incredulous. "You mistook some of our own men for them," he said. He sent von Borcke and another officer to investigate.

A group of men in light blue overcoats sat horses in the road.

"What regiment are you?" von Borcke yelled.

Horses galloped. "You'll see soon enough, you damned Rebels!"
Riders filled the road, and Stuart took his party into the underbrush.
Von Borcke enjoyed seeing Stuart fly: "I had the pleasure of seeing
our General, who had now lost all doubts as to the real character of
these cavalrymen, for once run from the enemy."

Jeb sent for help; Fitz Lee came in and cleared the roadway, but
touch-and-go fighting lasted most of the night. Von Borcke sketched
a skirmish:

"General Stuart and his staff were trotting along at the head of
the column, when, at the moment of emerging out of the dark forest,
we suddenly discovered in the open field before us, and at a distance
of not more than 160 yards, the long lines of several regiments of
hostile cavalry."

These lines fired, dropping men around the staff, but Jeb drew
his saber and trotted toward the enemy, shouting to the troopers.
"For once," the German recorded, "our horsemen refused to follow
their gallant commander; they wavered under the thick storm of
bullets; soon all discipline ceased, and the greater part of this splendid regiment . . . broke to the rear in utter confusion.'"

Stuart, von Borcke and others tried vainly to stop it, but rallied
only thirty men around them. The enemy drove them through The
Wilderness, "a wild exciting chase, in which friend and foe, unable
to recognize each other, mingled helter-skelter in one furious ride."

Before they reached Lee's headquarters there were two or three
more brushes, in one of which von Borcke got a bullet through his
hat and lost a horse. He found a new mount, a tiny Federal pony
with short legs almost covered by von Borcke's big English saddle,
"leaving only his ears sticking out."

Stuart was angry at the panic of his men, but laughed at sight of
von Borcke on his new charger. At headquarters they learned that
the enemy they had met in the darkness was the advance of the main
Federal body, which now lay near Chancellorsville.[4]

Evalina Wellford, who lived in this forest, had a premonition of
terrors to come:

The Yankees were down at the Furnace not a mile from us,
shouting and shooting, and we four unprotected females every

moment expecting their appearance at the house. As soon as they came so near, Uncle C. and Charlie made their escape to the woods, as certainly they would have been captured had they remained. We sat up all night looking for the Yankees, but they did not come till Friday morning, when about 20 visited us, searching the house for arms and Confederates, shooting the fowls and stealing provisions, of which we had a scant supply.

Several who came behaved very well, and did us no harm whatever. They seemed confident of success, and thought Richmond was almost within their grasp. Of course we were amused at their boasting, and gave them to understand as much.

On this Friday morning, May first, Robert Lee astonished Joseph Hooker; rather than falling back to Richmond, he had pushed his infantry toward Chancellorsville, and by eleven A.M. there was musketry in the dense woods. Lee sent Stuart's riders to the flanks of his line, and they probed through the brush, seeking a route for attack.

Stuart ranged in the front during the morning and when the gray infantry stalled short of Chancellorsville and General McLaws called for a flank attack from the left, Stonewall Jackson got a message from Jeb:

> General: I am on a road running from Spotsylvania C. H. to Silvers, which is on Plank Road three miles below Chancellorsville. I will close in on the flank and help all I can when the ball opens.... May God grant us victory.

Jackson's reply:

> I trust God will grant us a great victory. Keep closed on Chancellorsville.

Jeb rode during the afternoon: Evalina Wellford saw the riders:

> We were looking forward to another anxious night, when to our great joy the glorious Confederates under Stuart came tramping by, on their way to meet the enemy.

By four P.M. Stuart reached the iron works called Catherine Furnace, where he found Jackson, who with his dingy old Virginia

Military Institute cap crushed down on his forehead stared through field glasses at the enemy. Cannon fire was dropping men of Major Beckham's battery of the Horse Artillery.

Shells fell nearer the group in the clearing, and one burst over a gun crew, wounding all but one of its men.

Captain Joe Morrison, Jackson's aide and brother-in-law, watched Jeb:

"The Federals got the range. Stuart laughed and said it might be prudent of Jackson to retire from the guns."

At that moment a fragment struck in the group behind Stuart. Channing Price fell to his horse's neck. His leg was shattered. "I saw the death pallor on his face as they took him from his horse," Morrison said.[5]

But Price would not leave. Doctors found that no bones were broken, and the lieutenant insisted upon staying with Stuart. He kept up for a few minutes, then fainted in his saddle. Men carried him back to the home of Evelina Wellford; he was bleeding severely, but Stuart thought him in no danger.

Jeb visited Price at night in the plantation house. He was shocked to find the boy so white. Price smiled at the staff officers, but was so weak that he could give only a weak squeeze of his hand in farewell. He died at midnight.

Von Borcke said he was too grief-stricken to rest, but Evelina Wellford wrote:

> General Stuart and his staff remained until after breakfast next morning. They slept under the trees in the yard and seemed to have a good time.[6]

But Stuart left the Wellford yard in the night. Fitz Lee's men had found the end of the Federal line, in a clearing. It had the look of a vulnerable spot, a flank "in the air." Stuart did not trust the news to a courier, but rode to Lee's headquarters near Chancellorsville, where he found a conference in progress.

Lee and Jackson sat on cracker boxes in firelight, surrounded by their staffs, poring over a map.

"Hooker's maneuvering in some way," Jackson said. "They won't be on this side the river tomorrow."

Lee disagreed. "I hope you may be right, but I believe he will deliver his main attack here. He would not have gone to such lengths and then give up without effort."

They had just sent two keen engineer officers into the brush to probe the front lines. Stuart made his report. Lee and Jackson turned to the map once more, and their fingers traced the route toward Wilderness Church, on the far left of their line.

"Are there good roads? Can we pass guns?"

Stuart did not know. He went off to investigate. In his absence Lee and Jackson made one of the war's most momentous decisions. Lee felt certain that Stuart, or someone, would find a way to the exposed enemy flank and make possible an audacious attack which might make the armies equal.

"Jackson," Lee said, "how can we get at those people?"

"You know best. Show me what to do and we will try to do it."

Lee indicated a route sweeping to their left over country unmarked by roads. "General Stuart will cover your movement with his cavalry."

Jackson stood and gave an awkward salute. "My troops will move at four o'clock."

Somewhere in the night Stuart found Jackson's chief chaplain, the Reverend B. T. Lacy, who had lived in the area and knew it intimately. He sent Lacy to headquarters, where the preacher roused Jackson. When Stonewall learned that Charles Wellford and his family could act as guides, he sent Lacy and his map maker, Jed Hotchkiss, to find them.

Lacy and Hotchkiss were back at dawn, and Hotchkiss sketched new lines on his battle map. The Wellfords had indicated an old wagon road by the iron furnace, which ran around the Federal position to Wilderness Corner. It was passable to guns—in short, a perfect solution. General Lee heard the last of the explanation and drew up a cracker box beside Jackson.

"General Jackson, what do you propose to do?"

"Go around here," Stonewall said, moving his finger on Hotchkiss's map.

"And what do you propose to make this movement with?"

"With my whole corps."

Onlookers saw no hesitation in Lee. "And what will you leave me?"

"The divisions of Anderson and McLaws."

"Well, go on."

The flank sweep would leave Lee with some 14,000 troops to face Hooker's host, which might be as large as 100,000. But Lee's calm was unstudied as he watched Jackson leave to get his men under way. Not long after the sun rose, Jackson and Lee parted for the last time, at the roadside where Stonewall's troops marched.[7]

Lee sent a message to President Davis in Richmond:

I am now swinging around to my left to come up in his rear.

Lee made a show of strength on his front during the day and waited. An enemy attack struck Jackson's rear, but the sounds soon died away. The Federals had evidently concluded that the column was retreating. The day grew hot.

Jackson's men shrugged out of their coats and thronged the few springs they passed on their twelve-mile march. They did not go fast enough for Jackson, whose physician, Dr. Hunter McGuire, saw him with concern: "Never can I forget the eagerness and intensity of Jackson on that march. . . . His face was pale, his eyes flashing. Out from his thin compressed lips came the terse command: 'Press forward! Press forward!' " Many men fell out, in spasms and fainting spells.

The cavalry led the column. Von Borcke and his friends knew nothing of the object of the march, but did not think of questioning Jackson's lead: "We marched silently along through the forest, taking a small by-road, which brought us several times so near the enemy's lines that the strokes of axes, mingled with the hum of voices from their camps, was distinctly audible."

Some enemy cavalry was sighted about two P.M. but disappeared. Within a few minutes, when the column struck the Plank Road five miles west of Chancellorsville, Fitz Lee made a discovery—Union infantry in camp:

"What a sight! The soldiers were in groups, laughing, chatting, smoking . . . feeling safe and comfortable. In the rear of them were other parties driving up and slaughtering beeves."

Fitz went quickly back to Jackson: "Ride with me, General."

Fitz took Stonewall to his hill of observation and watched with enjoyment:

"His eyes burned with a brilliant glow, lighting up a sad face; his expression was one of intense interest; his face was colored slightly . . . and radiant at the success of his flank movement."

Fitz pointed out the vulnerability of the enemy line but Jackson did not reply. He moved his lips in silence, took one last look and galloped back to his men, his elbows flapping in his curious graceless way. He issued quick orders for putting the infantry into line across the road, and sent a note to Lee, now far behind him across the quiet Wilderness:

> General,
> The enemy has made a stand at Chancellor's which is about 2 miles from Chancellorsville. I hope as soon as practicable to attack.
> I trust that an ever-kind Providence will bless us with great success.
> The leading division is up and the next two appear to be well closed.

It seemed a long time before the attack was ready. Von Borcke had a close look at the unsuspecting enemy, and was surprised by a patrol of bluecoats, who gaped at him in astonishment and fired as he rode away.

The German returned to find Stuart and Jackson and their staffs stretched under an oak, resting while the infantry went into position. When the officers were called to the front about five P.M., Stuart took troopers to the left flank. Bugles sounded, guns roared and Rebel yells startled the enemy. Panic broke on the Union flank, and men who tried to stand in the path of the attack were driven back in the dusk. The Stuart Horse Artillery kept up with the advance.

The road was wide enough for two guns, and Stuart had cleared it for Major Beckham and his crews. The gunners worked in a fury, firing, hitching their teams, advancing, firing again. The cavalry's

little guns worked with precision. When two had fired for a few
minutes, they pulled aside and the two rear guns went into action.
They had driven a mile or so when Jackson passed the artillerymen
and leaned down to Beckham with his hand out: "Young man, I
congratulate you."

Others saw Jackson in strange poses: "He would stop, raise his
hand, and turn his eyes toward Heaven, as if praying for a blessing
on our arms . . . as he passed the bodies of some of our veterans, he
halted, raised his hand as if to ask a blessing upon them, and to pray
to God to save their souls."[8]

Stonewall disappeared from the cavalry, pressing ahead in The
Wilderness with his main body as he sought to cut Hooker's army
in two.

Stuart had found no way to use his troopers in the brush, and
asked Jackson to give him some infantrymen to seize the important
river road to Ely's Ford. Jackson had sent him off with the 16th
North Carolina. On their way these men stumbled through a Federal
camp. Von Borcke wrote: "Entire regiments had thrown down their
arms, which were lying in regular lines on the ground, as if for inspection; suppers just prepared had been abandoned. Tents, baggage, wagons, cannon, half-slaughtered oxen, in chaotic confusion,
while in the background many thousand Yankees were scampering
for their lives." Confederates took them by hundreds.

Soon after dark, however, a great cannonade swept the woods,
and the infantry tide halted; the graycoats milled about. Stuart
worked to barricade the Ely's Ford road. Jackson planned more attacks in the dark.

Van Borcke was riding with Stuart when they saw firelight in
the woods ahead. They crept near enough to see Federals in camp.
Stuart could not resist. He ordered about 1,000 of the infantry to
make ready for attack.

Jeb was busy at this when two couriers came from A. P. Hill.

"You'll have to come, General. Quick! General Jackson's shot."

Jeb did not hesitate. He called the commander of the 16th
North Carolina: "Have your men fire three rounds into that camp
and fall back to their regiment."

He galloped off in the bright moonlight.

Von Borcke was soon riding after his chief, making his way by moonlight and the glare of brush fires. He rode for almost an hour before he found Stuart seated at a roadside, writing dispatches by lantern light. Jeb must now become an infantry commander, with a scattered corps to prepare for battle before morning.

Jackson had been shot by his own men, they said, somewhere on the front where he was scouting. He had been carried to the rear painfully hurt, leaving command to A. P. Hill, until he, too, had been wounded.

Captain W. F. Randolph of Jackson's staff brought the depressing news to the cavalry. Jackson had been riding with a few officers, seeking a road to the river, when they passed a Confederate regiment, its men firing nervously at shadows. Jackson sent Randolph to find their officers and stop the fire:

"I rode up and down the line and gave the order, telling them also that they were endangering the lives of General Jackson and his escort, but it was in vain. Those immediately in my front would cease as I gave the order, but the firing would break out above or below me. . . . I rode back to Jackson and said: 'General, it is impossible to stop these men. I think we had best pass through their line and get into the woods behind them.' 'Very well said,' was the reply. So, making a half whirl to the left . . . our little company commenced to pass through the line. . . . A few more seconds would have placed us in safety, for we were not over three seconds from the line, but as we turned, looking up and down as far as my eye could reach, I saw that long line of shining bayonets rise and concentrate upon us. I felt what was coming, and driving my spurs into my horse . . . he rose high in the air and as we passed over the line the thunder crash from hundreds of rifles burst in full in our very faces. . . .

"Then sick at heart I dashed back to the road, and there the saddest tragedy of the war was revealed in its fullest horror. I saw the General's horse standing close to the edge of the road, with a stream of blood running from a wound in his neck . . . and the General himself lying in the edge of the woods. He seemed to be dead. . . . I threw myself on the ground by his side and raised his head and shoulders on my arm. He groaned.

" 'Are you much hurt, General?' I asked.

" 'Wild fire, that, sir. Wild fire,' he replied, in his usual rapid way. That was all he said. I found that his left arm was shattered by a bullet just below the elbow, and his right hand was lacerated by a Minié ball that passed through the palm. . . . In a few moments A. P. Hill rode up . . . ordered me to mount my horse and bring an ambulance. 'But don't tell the men that it is General Jackson who is wounded. . . .'

"I met Sandy Pendleton, Jackson's adjutant general, and he ordered me to go and find General Jeb Stuart and tell him to come at once."

Stonewall had gone to the rear in an ambulance.

It was midnight when Stuart arrived at a fireside on the front near the spot where Jackson had fallen. The last echoes of a wild attack by Federals had just died away. His command, more than 25,000 men, lay in disorder in the darkness, no one knew where. Jeb knew only vaguely Jackson's plan of attack, and when he called up Stonewall's commanders, found that they knew no more—it was one of Jackson's secrets.

Since there could be no further orders from Robert Lee tonight, Jeb tried to determine the position of the troops; he learned little: A. P. Hill's division, a part of it thrown forward against the enemy front, was at right angles to the Plank Road. Stuart could not make out the exact positions of Generals Rodes and Colston, since their men had become tangled in the chase, and order had disappeared.

Stuart sent a courier to ask the wounded Jackson for instructions. He returned with a message: Tell General Stuart to act on his own judgment and do what he thinks best. I have implicit confidence in him.

Jeb waited for daylight.[9] Few of his staff were at hand, and of Jackson's staff only Sandy Pendleton could be found. Von Borcke was willing to help, but spent a sleepless night nursing Lieutenant "Honeybun" Hullihen, who had a shoulder wound.

A night reconnaissance by young E. P. Alexander, Jackson's artilleryman, got the guns into position, and at the first faint gray light Stuart's men moved.

At this hour Jeb got his first order from the distressed General Lee:

> It is necessary that the glorious victory thus far achieved be prosecuted with the utmost vigor, and the enemy given no time to rally. As soon, therefore, as it is possible, they must be pressed, so that we may unite the two wings of the army.
>
> Endeavor, therefore, to dispossess them of Chancellorsville, which will permit the union of the whole army.

In brief, Lee's army was so divided in The Wilderness as to be in peril; he would attack. Stuart had thought of nothing else.

Fire broke out at dawn and raged without ceasing until afternoon. Stuart's men drove through woodlands to a bristling Federal line, where infantry regiments faced each other at close range for hours; ranks were decimated. Stuart could move his artillery in but two ways: Down the Plank Road, which was swept by Union cannon; and by a lane in pinewoods half a mile south. The chief target of Jeb's attack was Hazel Grove, a cleared ridge which was the key to Hooker's position. Stuart seemed to feel that he must take the hill personally, for he was in the front of charges and countercharges in the open, waving his hat or sword, urging on the troops. There would be criticism of his bloody frontal assaults, but in the end he led them to storm the ridge. An officer who lay with his men in sight of the Chancellor House watched Stuart in "the bravest act I ever saw. He led in person several batteries down Plank Road, which was swept with the Federal artillery, and planted his guns on an eminence in advance of our infantry line."[10]

From the new position Alexander's guns dominated the clearing around the Chancellor House, where Hooker had headquarters. They fired as infantry launched three charges near the white-columned dwelling. The last attack carried over a carpet of bodies, and the enemy were swept out of sight.

General James Lane reported Stuart's leading the 28th North Carolina in two charges, and said, "Its colonel, Thomas L. Lowe, was perfectly carried away with Stuart. He heard him singing, 'Old Joe Hooker, come out of the Wilderness!' And he wound up by saying,

'Who would have thought it? Jeb Stuart in command of the 2nd Army Corps!' "

On the Plank Road wagons, guns and ambulances were blown up. "How General Stuart and those few staff officers with him who had to gallop so frequently through this escaped unhurt seems to me quite miraculuous," von Borcke said. Many couriers were wounded; Stuart's horse was shot in the fight.

As Stuart tried to deliver his own orders, he passed the 1st Virginia Artillery and was surprised to see his old friend of St. Louis days, Reid Venable, now captain of a battery. There was a brief reunion.

"Venable," Stuart yelled, "I've sent off my last man. You must take this order to the left. There is no one else. I will take all the responsibility."

"Certainly, sir," Venable said. He rode out of sight.

Venable carried orders for Jeb the rest of the day, and when there was a moment of quiet, told him how he chafed at being in the "bomb-proof" artillery positions, and longed for real action.

Stuart clapped him on the back: "I'll ask for your services to-day, to be assigned to my staff."

Venable thus began his career as Jeb's assistant adjutant and inspector general, with the rank of major; he would ride with him until the end.[11]

Robert Lee sent an encouraging message at ten thirty A.M.: The wings of the army had joined. This was the signal for the drive which broke the enemy line.

From near Chancellorsville von Borcke saw: "A magnificent spectacle . . . the long lines of our swiftly advancing troops, their red flags fluttering in the breeze, and their arms glittering in the morning sun, and farther on, dense and huddled masses of the Federals flying in utter rout toward United States Ford, whilst high over our heads flew the shells which our artillery were dropping amidst the retreating foe."

The enemy was not through, for in the afternoon General Lee learned that an attack—or a misunderstanding of orders—had led General Early to abandon the Fredericksburg position in the rear, and the army was again exposed. Lee calmly sent men to turn back this threat. Stuart slept near the ruins of the burned Chancellor House, where Lee joined him. Enemy shells ploughed earth around them all night; one burst atop a cherry tree, covering von Borcke with litter. Within a stone's throw a barn full of wounded Federals moaned ceaselessly.

Officers were already marveling over Stuart's performance of the day before. E. P. Alexander said: "I do not think there was a more brilliant thing done in the war than Stuart's extricating that command from the extremely critical position . . . as promptly and boldly as he did. We knew that Hooker had at least 80,000 infantry at hand, and that his axemen were entrenching his position all night, and in that thick undergrowth a rabbit could hardly get through. The hard marching and the night fighting had thinned our ranks to less than 20,000. . . . But Stuart never seemed to hesitate or to doubt for one moment that he could just crash his way wherever he chose to strike . . . unlike many planned attacks that I have seen, this one came off promptly on time, and it never stopped to draw its breath until it had crashed through everything. . . .

"I always thought it an injustice to Stuart and a loss to the army that he was not from that moment continued in command of Jackson's corps. He had won a right to it. I believe he had all of Jackson's genius and dash and originality, without that eccentricity of character which sometimes led to disappointment. . . . Stuart possessed the rare quality of being always equal to himself at his very best."

Monday morning was hot, sultry, with an early misting of rain. There was "an almost insupportable" stench of the dead in the thickets, many of them roasted by fires which had swept The Wilderness. The army marched confusingly through the woods, as Lee tried to trap Hooker with another stroke in his rear. But the offensive was delayed until six P.M. The enemy escaped, and Lee was reduced to shelling the retreat. A severe rainstorm broke early on May sixth. When Lee discovered the failure to crush the enemy he blazed at Dorsey Pender, who brought the news: "Why, General Pender! That is the way you young men always do. You allow those people to get away. I tell you what to do, but you don't do it."

Stuart, however, remained jubilant. He had written one of his officers:

A glorious victory yesterday—I commanded Jackson's Corps. I have directed Gen. Fitz Lee to relieve you. Can you hear which way Stoneman has gone?

He was reported coming down the Plank Road yesterday or last night. Let me hear from you.[12]

The next day he sent Flora a message:

God has spared me through another bloody battle and given us the victory yesterday and the day before. I commanded Jackson's corps.

On May seventh, with A. P. Hill recovered, Jeb was back in command of the cavalry and was off westward, trying to catch Stoneman, who was returning from his raid near Richmond. The little column was too late; the bluecoats had already passed Raccoon Ford.

Stoneman's thrust had done only minor damage, but General Lee read a danger, and wrote Jefferson Davis of the enemy cavalry:

It is very large and no doubt organized for the very purpose to which it has recently been applied. Every expedition will augment their boldness and increase their means of doing us harm, as they will become better acquainted with the country and more familiar with its roads. . . . You can see, then, how difficult it will be for us to keep up our railroad communications and prevent the inroads of the enemy's cavalry. If I could get two good divisions of cavalry, I should feel as if we ought to resist three of the enemy.

Lee's orders to the army praised Stuart, and to the regiments which left 13,000 casualties around Chancellorsville, he said:

Under trying vicissitudes of heat and storm, you attacked the enemy strongly entrenched in the depth of a tangled wilderness, and again on the hills of Fredericksburg 15 miles distant,

and by the valor that has triumphed on so many fields, forced
him once more to seek safety beyond the Rappahannock.

The Federals had lost 17,000 men in this fighting.

Lee appointed May tenth a day of Thanksgiving, and on that
day Jackson died, murmuring: "It's all right, I always wanted to die
on Sunday. . . . Let us cross over the river, and rest under the shade
of the trees." Lee spoke for the Confederacy, saying, "I have lost my
right arm."

Stuart learned of Stonewall's death in a dispatch from Lee:

> I regret to inform you that the great and good Jackson is
> no more. . . . May his spirit pervade our whole army; our
> country will then be secure.

Colonel Rosser told the grieving Stuart: "On his death bed
Jackson said that you should succeed him, and command his corps."

"I would rather know that Jackson said that," Stuart said, "than
to have the appointment."

But though command of a corps of Lee's infantry seemed much
in Jeb's thoughts, he did not seriously consider it, and wrote Flora
that "there has been a great deal of talk of my succeeding General
Jackson, but I think without foundation in fact." There may have
been wistfulness in the remark, but he never declared an ambition
to leave his horsemen.

Esten Cooke said that Jeb's troops at Chancellorsville, "although
quite enthusiastic about him, complained that he led them too recklessly against artillery; and it is hard to believe that, as an army commander, he would have consented to a strictly defensive campaign.
Fighting was a necessity of his blood, and the slow movements of
infantry did not suit his genius."

Cooke said more with which Stuart probably agreed: "Some
men are born to write great works, others to paint great pictures,
others to rule over nations. Stuart was born to fight cavalry."

On May tenth Stuart wrote his cousin, the mother of Channing
Price:

Let me share with you the deep grief. . . . The dear boy fell at my side, displaying the same devotion to duty, and abnegation of self which signalized his whole career.

As an Adjutant General he had no superior. . . . He was known most favorably to General Lee, who knew and appreciated his worth. His career though brief was so spotless and successful that it is well to consider whether, amid the mutations of human events, it is not better to have a career ended nobly, as his was, than to risk the fluctuations of fortune in an uncertain future. . . .

He was a universal favorite. . . . I miss him hourly now. His ready pen and fine perception saved me much labor, and contributed amazingly to the success of operations under my control. . . .

The staff wore mourning for thirty days for Channing, soon after it had removed black sleeve bands in memory of Pelham. The entire army mourned Jackson.

The camp where Stuart learned of Jackson's death was in a green valley overlooking the village of Orange Court House, a rich country of growing crops and plentiful farm animals—and pretty girls. The staff recovered overnight from Chancellorsville. Stuart, like Robert Lee, was unable to go to Richmond for Jackson's funeral. As Lee said, "Those people over the river are showing signs of movement."

Von Borcke became a ghost this week. He stopped in Verdiersville to call on the woman who had helped him escape Federal riders the summer before, when Stuart lost his hat on her porch.

The woman came to her door, glimpsed von Borcke, screamed, and fled into the house. The German entered, curious, and she handed him a newspaper. He read:

Among those who fell at the battle of Chancellorsville we regret to report the death of Major von Borcke. . . .

He found that the rumor had spread over the state, and he was hailed on the roads and in camp as one returned from the dead. Stuart got many letters of condolence, among them a request from Governor Letcher: Von Borcke's body should be forwarded to Richmond, where it would be given a burial of honor by Virginia. Letcher got a reply which the cavalry found hilarious:

> Can't spare body of von Borcke. It is in pursuit of Stoneman.[13]

☆

CHAPTER 16

Prelude to Invasion

FIGHTING Joe Hooker was uneasy. His big orange observation balloons were in the sky over the Rappahannock from dawn to dusk in early June, and his officers questioned the aerialists almost desperately.

Hooker reported to President Lincoln on June fifth that new divisions had joined Lee: "This could be for no other purpose but to enable the enemy to move up the river . . . a movement similar to that of Lee's last year."

Another Rebel invasion of the North, perhaps.

But though Hooker bridged the river the next day, he did not discover Lee's intention; he concluded that the enemy was still in front of him "in full force."

In fact, Robert Lee left the old Rappahannock battleground that day, going upriver behind his infantry near Culpeper, where Stuart's cavalry was resting.

Hooker had planned to strike Lee if he made any such move, and telegraphed Lincoln:

I am of the opinion that it is my duty to pitch into his rear.

Lincoln did not agree:

I would not take any risk of being tangled up on the river like an ox half jumped over a fence, and liable to be torn by dogs front and rear without a fair chance to gore one way, or kick the other.

302

Thus, in the first week of June, while Lee shifted his strength westward and held the Fredericksburg front with only A. P. Hill's men, Hooker waited.

Lee had grown stronger. Longstreet had returned and there were now three army corps, under Longstreet, A. P. Hill and Dick Ewell, the new lieutenant general replacing Jackson. Ewell had just rejoined the army, after recovering from his leg wound at Second Manassas. He returned with a wooden leg and a pretty bride.

Culpeper County in June was like paradise for the cavalry corps. Stuart had moved his headquarters to Fleetwood Hill, four miles south of the Rappahannock above Brandy Station. Recruits flocked in, most of them on fresh horses from home. Grumble Jones brought his troopers from the Shenandoah, and Robertson came up from North Carolina. The month opened with 9,536 riders in Jeb's command. The Horse Artillery had grown, and had new horses. Forage was plentiful, grass was thick on the rolling plains. The army's infantry was comfortingly near at Culpeper.

Stuart ordered a celebration. The staff sent invitations to hundreds in adjoining counties. Hotels and homes for miles about were made ready. Von Borcke went on a flag-bedecked train to meet George Randolph, Stuart's friend, who was the former Secretary of War. Visitors came from as far as Charlottesville and Richmond, and cavalry escorts took them from the station to lodgings. General Lee, who had been urgently invited, seemed to be the only missing guest.

There was a ball in the county courthouse on June fourth, dimly lit by "a few tallow candles." The gay music of Sweeney's band continued for hours. It was late when Culpeper quieted for the night.

At eight A.M., his staff in new uniforms, Stuart led the way through the streets to the review field near Brandy Station. Trains halted on the adjoining tracks with crowded cars; the rest of the field was surrounded by wagons and carriages of guests. The 10,000 cavalrymen sat horses in lines almost two miles long, and at about ten o'clock Stuart galloped onto the field. His gunner George Neese gazed raptly from the ranks of the Horse Artillery:

"He was superbly mounted and his side arms gleamed in the morning sun like burnished silver. A long black ostrich plume waved gracefully from a black slouch hat cocked up on one side, held with a golden clasp. . . . He is the prettiest and most graceful rider I ever saw. I could not help but notice with what natural ease and comely elegance he sat his steed as it bounded over the field . . . he and his horse appeared to be one and the same machine."

When Stuart and the staff had inspected the ranks they went to a natural reviewing stand, a small, steep knoll near the railroad where, Neese said, Jeb "wheeled his horse and sat there like a gallant knight errant, under his waving plume . . . a chivalric cavalier of the first order."

Three bands played as the cavalry passed in review which Neese thought: "One grand magnificent pageant, inspiring enough to make even an old woman feel fightish."

The regiments charged with sabers and the artillery banged in mock battle. Women fainted. The show went on until four P.M.

There was a dance in the evening, but the crowd spurned the courthouse, von Borcke said: "As the night was fine we danced in the open air on a piece of turf near our headquarters, and by the light of enormous woodfires, the ruddy glare of which . . . gave the whole scene a wild and romantic effect."

On the eighth, they did it all over again, for General Lee came up. The ladies were gone, but infantrymen were on hand. Fitz Lee had sent John Hood word: "Come and see the review, and bring any of your people." And just as the troopers took the field, Hood arrived with his 10,000 behind him, winding up from the Rapidan.

"You invited me and my people," Hood said, shaking hands with Fitz, "and you see I've brought them."

There was a revival of the old jibes of infantry-cavalry rivalry.

"Well, don't let them holler, 'Here's your mule!' " Fitz said.

"If they do we'll charge you," Wade Hampton told Hood.

The scoffing infantry watched as the horsemen walked before Robert Lee—he had excused the gunners, and asked the cavalry not to tire their horses in mock charges.

One Texas foot soldier growled, "Wouldn't we clean *them* out, if old Hood would only let us!"[1] And there were catcalls reminiscent of D. H. Hill's old joke: "Standing reward of five dollars for anyone who finds a dead man with spurs on!"

Robert Lee had teased the resplendent Stuart as they rode to the field, Jeb's horse with a wreath of flowers around his neck, the gift of women friends: "Take care, General, that is the way General Pope's horse was adorned when he went to the battle of Manassas."

When caps and hats blew off the heads of parading cavalry-men, Hood's men scuttled on the field and carried them off in triumph.

Gunner Neese ended the day sadly, for he rode a long-eared mule in a gun battery, and when Stuart's sharp eye caught the incongruous sight, Jeb sent an aide to remove Neese and the mule from the handsome column.

Robert Lee wrote his wife:

> I reviewed the cavalry in this section. . . . It was a splendid sight. The men and horses looked well. They have recuperated since last fall. Stuart was in all his glory.

The enemy might have been a world away.[2]

Luther Hopkins, a boy trooper from Maryland, was relieved of picket duty on the river at three A.M., June ninth, and curled in his blanket a few yards from the ford. He had hardly closed his eyes when the watchman shouted, "Yankees! Great God, millions of 'em!"

Horses splashed the ford as the camp scrambled to life. Pistol shots spurted up and down the river as pickets fell back, giving the alarm. The enemy was crossing in a dozen places, chiefly at Kelly's and Beverly's Fords.

Bluecoats came in sight, and the little picket company at Kelly's fired in an attempt to alert the main camp, a mile behind. A few men fell and the company ran.

As the pickets left the riverside woods, the first of the 6th Virginia came at a gallop among the trees; the 7th Virginia followed. The enemy slowed. "The roar of the guns in the woods at that early hour in the morning was terrific," Hopkins said. Fighting spread for three miles along the river.

George Neese was near the center of Stuart's camp, in the edge of a woods: "Just as we were rounding up the last sweet snooze for the night bullets from Yankee sharpshooters zipped across our blanket beds, and then such a getting up of horse artillerymen I never saw before. Blankets were fluttering and being rolled up in double quick time in every direction, and in less than twenty minutes we were ready to man our guns."

A half-dressed South Carolina gun crew pulled a cannon by hand to fire on the hidden sharpshooters. This halted the enemy for a few minutes and Neese thought: "If it had not been for that precious little check some of us would be on the weary road to some of Uncle Sam's elegant hotels specially devised for the royal entertainment of Southern rebels."

But Stuart was saved by his old antagonist, Grumble Jones, who mounted barefoot, hatless and coatless and got his brigade first into action. Colonel Elijah White of the 35th Battalion, with whom Jeb had squabbled in Maryland, was early in the thick of it.

Neese's gun battery joined Major Beckham's emplacement on a grassy swell in the open, but at first could not fire, since the field "was covered with a mingled mass, fighting and struggling with pistol and saber like maddened savages."

General Jones passed the cannoneers, and yelled to Captain Chew, "I'm not in command today, but do you see that gap in the woods yonder? I think the Yankees are bringing a battery in there. If they do, give 'em hell."

Canister cut down hundreds of Federals at point-blank range, but the blue tide was not to be stemmed so quickly. It lapped into the artillery camp and sent teams flying to the rear. A wagon of headquarters papers tipped over, and Federals picked up Major Beckham's official files. The battle spread.

Stuart had slept with everything packed except two tent flies, for General Lee had ordered him to cross the Rappahannock today to cover a northward movement of the infantry. He was very near the house called Fleetwood, on a hill with a long view to the river. When he woke to the sound of fighting, Stuart put his staff to work and waited impatiently for word from the front. Jones reported that the enemy, though in great force, seemed to be beaten off for the time at Beverly's Ford, and that he had taken position at Saint James Church. Stuart sent most of Wade Hampton's men to the scene.

The new Federal cavalry commander, Alfred Pleasanton, had thrown most of four divisions over the river in two columns, each supported by infantry. The quiet in Jones's front seemed to threaten danger from the other column, perhaps an attack in flank and rear. Jeb sent one of Hampton's regiments rearward and hurried the headquarters wagons away; there remained on Fleetwood Hill only couriers and his new adjutant, Major H. B. McClellan. Stuart went to the front at Saint James Church. Two subordinates had arguments with Jeb this morning. Von Borcke urged waiting for the enemy on Fleetwood Heights with both guns and horsemen. Stuart wanted to attack immediately and have done with it.

And General Jones, who saw bluecoats flanking the position from Culpeper, sent a courier to Jeb with a warning.

"Tell General Jones to tend to the Yankees in his front and I'll watch the flanks," Stuart said.

When Jones got this reply he snapped, "So he thinks they ain't coming, does he? Well, let him alone. He'll damned soon see for himself."

Captain Frank Myers, riding with Jones, said, "And he *did* see, for about 1 o'clock the flanking force appeared exactly in rear of Stuart's headquarters."[3]

Major McClellan also discovered the Federal flank attack boring in from Kelly's Ford. He scoffed at a scout's first report, thinking that General Beverly Robertson would have stopped any advance in that quarter. He sent the courier for a closer look, and the man returned at a gallop. "In five minutes, Major, you can see for yourself!"

McClellan saw a blue column already near the railroad station at Brandy. Within a few minutes the enemy would occupy Fleetwood Heights, the key to the landscape. McClellan called up a gun which had only a few defective shells and some round shot in its chests; it fired a few rounds at the enemy. McClellan also sent couriers for Stuart—all the couriers. The Federals hesitated, puzzled at sight of the lone officer and a single gun on the heights, then pulled up guns and began shelling the hill.

A North Carolina officer found Stuart incredulous. Jeb turned to James Hart of the artillery: "Ride back there, Captain, and see what all this foolishness is about."

Jeb heard the cannon in his rear before Hart was out of sight and sent the nearest regiment racing for the heights. The leading riders got there as the gun was firing its last shell, and blue troopers were coming in fifty yards below.

Jeb sent William Blackford down the front: "Order every regimental officer to get to Fleetwood at the gallop." The engineer passed the order and went rearward as thousands of riders wheeled: "It was a thrilling sight to see these dashing horsemen draw their sabers and start for the hill a mile and a half in rear at a gallop. The lines met on the hill. It was like what we read of in the days of chivalry, acres and acres of horsemen sparkling with sabers . . . flags above them, hurled against each other at full speed and meeting with a shock that made the earth tremble."

Colonel Calbraith Butler, leading the Carolinians, was knocked from his horse by a shell; his leg was gone. The same shell struck young Captain Farley. Both went to the rear in an ambulance.

Stuart watched anxiously as the enemy were driven back. "Blackford, watch with your glasses and tell me if you see infantry coming." The captain soon saw marching Federals in the distance, and Stuart sent him the six dusty miles to Longstreet. Within an hour gray infantry was in sight. General Lee was with them, but this was the cavalry's day, and both blue and gray foot soldiers waited, watching.

Luther Hopkins, who had seen the start of this inferno, looked in surprise: "I did not suppose that General Lee was within thirty miles of us. Toward sunset I saw him come riding across the fields on Traveller, accompanied by his staff. He seemed as calm and unconcerned as if he were inspecting the land with the view of a purchase."

But Lee had been shaken. He met soldiers carrying back his son Rooney, who had a serious wound. There were casualties everywhere in the cauldron on Fleetwood Hill.

Batteries and cavalry regiments fought for life in clouds of dust.

The decisive charge was made by some of Hampton's men, chiefly the 1st North Carolina. Major Hart of the artillery watched:

"The whole plateau east of the hill and beyond the railroad was covered with Federal cavalry. Hampton, diverging toward his left, passed the eastern terminus of the ridge, and, crossing the railroad, struck the enemy in column just beyond it. This charge was as gallantly made and gallantly met as any . . . ever witnessed. Taking into consideration the number of men (being nearly a brigade on each side) it was by far the most important hand-to-hand contest between the cavalry of the two armies. As the blue and gray riders mixed in the smoke and dust of that eventful charge, minutes seemed to elapse. . . . At last the mixed and disorganized mass began to recede, and we saw that the field was won to the Confederates."[4]

At almost the same moment the Cobb Georgia Legion and the 1st South Carolina had struck the enemy, Colonel P. M. B. Young leading the men over Fleetwood Heights. Young's men used only sabers: "I swept the hill clear of the enemy, he being scattered and entirely routed. I do claim that this was the turning point of the day in this portion of the field."

Even in darkness the defiant Federal guns did not cease until they were ridden down and crews had been killed with pistols. Sponge staffs knocked many riders from their saddles. The enemy at last left the field.

Stuart's scout, Farley, left memories with the staff. Soldiers sent by Colonel Butler to help the young man carried him off in "an old flat trough." Farley was in great pain, but kept smiling.

As he was loaded into the crude stretcher he pointed to his leg, lying on the ground where it had been flung by the shell.

"Bring it to me, please," he said.

Farley hugged the bleeding stump in his arms. "It's an old friend, gentlemen, and I do not wish to part with it."

He had a last word as he entered the ambulance: "Goodbye, and forever. I know my condition. I won't meet you again. Let me thank you for your kindness. It is a pleasure to me that I fell into the hands of Carolinians at my last moment."

Farley was soon dead. Esten Cooke saw his body in Culpeper

at night, dressed in a new uniform coat that he had left with a girl
in the town, telling her: "If anything happens to me, wrap me in
this and send me to my mother."

Stuart had lost over 500 men, including two colonels dead;
and Rooney Lee and Calbraith Butler would be lost for a long time.
But there were 500 prisoners, three guns, and a number of captured
battle flags. The enemy loss, it turned out, was over 900.

Stuart called the staff to set up headquarters on the spot of the
night before, as if by this gesture he would claim victory beyond
challenge. But it could not be done. Bluebottle flies swarmed over
the bloody ground so thickly, and the hill was so littered with bodies
of men and horses that tents could not be pitched. Stuart turned
reluctantly to another place; Blackford thought Jeb's pride was hurt
at having been forced from his ground by the surprise attack.

Stuart had fought the war's greatest cavalry engagement against
fine young Union commanders who would be heard from: Alfred
Duffié, Judson Kilpatrick, David Gregg, John Buford. He had used
only fifteen of the twenty-one regiments, perhaps 7,000 against the
10,000 of Pleasanton, and after savage fighting had beaten two
assault columns in turn. Every unit that had seen action was hurt,
however; it was the first great shock the corps had borne.

The army's critics were not idle. As far away as Richmond, the
chief of the Bureau of War, Robert H. G. Kean, wrote in his diary:
"Stuart is so conceited that he got careless—his officers were having
a frolic at Col. Rosser's wedding party." [Kean was in error. There
had been a frolic the night before, but Rosser had been married a
year earlier.]

Charles Blackford, now on Longstreet's staff, had a similar idea:
"The fight at Brandy Station can hardly be called a victory. Stuart
was certainly surprised, and but for the supreme gallantry of his
subordinate officers and the men . . . it would have been a day of
disaster and disgrace. . . . Stuart is blamed very much, but whether
or not fairly I am not sufficiently well informed to say."

Colonel William Oates of the Alabama infantry advanced
a new theory: The firing of Stuart's cannon in the review attracted
the attention of the Yankees, who believed that some Confederates

had mutinied. "Their anxiety to know, in part, caused them to cross the river . . . while General Stuart and his principal officers were at a ball in the village of Culpeper Court House dancing with the pretty women and having a good time. The Yankees ruthlessly disturbed the Confederates and caused them to rush to the front as the officers of Wellington's army did from the grand ball in Brussels in 1815, at the sound of Napoleon's cannon, the night before the battle of Waterloo."[5]

One Culpeper woman sent a bitter note to President Davis, anonymously:

> . . . If General Stuart is allowed to remain our commanding general of cavalry we are lost people. I have been eye witness to the maneuvering of General Stuart since he has been in Culpeper. . . . Gen. S. loves the admiration of his class of lady friends too much to be a commanding general. He loves to have his repeated reviews immediately under the Yankees' eyes too much for the benefit and pleasure of his lady friends for the interest of the Confederacy.
>
> "Southern Lady."[6]

The President's staff sent this note on to Stuart with a playful admonition to "cease your attentions to the ladies or make them more general."

It was perhaps the implied charge of immorality leveled by this critic that moved Jeb to say to Esten Cooke: "That person does not live who can say that I ever did anything improper of that description."

The Richmond *Examiner* scolded Stuart in stinging words:

> The more the circumstances of the late affair at Brandy Station are considered, the less pleasant do they appear. If this was an isolated case, it might be excused under the convenient head of accident or chance. But this puffed up cavalry of the Army of Northern Virginia has been twice, if not three times, surprised since the battles of December, and such repeated accidents can be regarded as nothing but the necessary consequences of negligence and bad management. If the war was a

tournament, invented and supported for the pleasure of a few vain and weak-headed officers, these disasters might be dismissed with compassion. But the country pays dearly for the blunders which encourage the enemy to overrun and devastate the land, with a cavalry which is daily learning to despise the mounted troops of the Confederacy. The surprise on this occasion was the most complete that has occurred. The Confederate cavalry was carelessly strewn over the country. . . .

Events of this description . . . require the earnest attention both of the chiefs of the Government and the heads of the Army. The enemy is evidently determined to employ his cavalry extensively, and has spared no pains or cost to perfect that arm. The only effective means of preventing the mischief it may do is to reorganize our own forces, enforce a stricter discipline among the men and insist on more earnestness among the officers in the discharge of their very important duty.

That volley was echoed by the more sedate Richmond *Sentinel:*

Vigilance, vigilance, more vigilance, is the lesson taught us by the Brandy surprise, and which must not be forgotten by the victory which was wrested from defeat. Let all learn it, from the Major General down to the picket.[7]

Stuart possibly felt obliged to defend himself against other criticism because of such reports. He had written General Lee in recent days, indicating that he was sensitive on the subject of Chancellorsville. That letter was to be lost, but Lee's reply made the matter fairly clear:

As regards the closing remarks of your note, I am at a loss to understand their reference or to know what has given rise to them. In the management of the difficult operations at Chancellorsville, which you so promptly understood and creditably performed, I saw no errors to correct, nor has there been a fit opportunity to commend your conduct. I prefer your acts to speak for themselves, nor does your character or reputation require bolstering up by out-of-place expressions of my opinion.

If Stuart had written a petulant note to Lee, perhaps in resentment that he had not been raised to lieutenant general with infantry command, it was his first such expression, for it appeared from another of Lee's letters that neither of them had considered Jeb's transfer from cavalry command:

> I am obliged to you for your views as to the successor of the great and good Jackson. Unless God in his mercy will raise us up one, I do not know what we shall do. I agree with you on the subject, and have so expressed myself.

There was no note of apology, at any rate, in Stuart's order to his troops after Brandy Station:

> . . . Comrades, two divisions of the enemy's cavalry and artillery, escorted by a strong force of infantry, "tested your metal" and found it "proof steel. . . ."
>
> Your saber blows, inflicted on that glorious day, have taught them again the weight of Southern vengeance. . . .
>
> Nothing but the enemy's infantry strongly posted in the woods saved his cavalry from capture or annihilation. An act of rashness on his part was severely punished by rout and the loss of his artillery.
>
> With an abiding faith in the God of battles and a firm reliance on the saber, your success will continue.

The army was immediately under way. In the early morning of June tenth, while Stuart was out with Captain Blackford and others of the staff, frightening vultures from the bodies, his troopers watched the foot soldiers moving. Young Luther Hopkins was at his picket post by the river:

"We were quietly resting in the woods, watching the infantry as they tramped by all day long, moving in a northwesterly direction. The question was asked ten thousand times perhaps that day: 'What is Marse Robert up to now? Where is he taking us?'

"In the afternoon we noticed a long string of wagons of peculiar construction, each drawn by six horses, and loaded with something covered with white canvas. Of course, we are all curious to know what these wagons contained. The secret soon leaked out. They were pontoon bridges. And then we began to speculate as to what rivers we were to cross. Some said we were destined for the Ohio, others for the Potomac."

Just before sunset bugles called in cavalry camp, and Stuart's men moved. The column rode most of the night, crossing the Rappahannock some miles above the Brandy Station field.

The troops Hopkins saw were Dick Ewell's, moving toward Winchester, hoping to drive the Federals from that town, cross the Potomac and strike into the North once more. Robert Lee had made his decision and obtained Richmond's blessing. The Army of Northern Virginia would transfer the fighting from the ravaged home counties to new fields, rich with forage. It would also ruin any Federal plans for a new drive on Richmond, this summer.

Longstreet was involved in two minor matters at Culpeper, scarcely noted, which would become important to the army.

Old Pete had come back from independent command in Eastern Virginia with more positive opinions, and he now urged upon Lee a strategy of defense to be used even on this invasion. He wrote:

> I suggested that, after piercing Pennsylvania and menacing Washington, we should choose a strong position, and force the Federals to attack us, observing that the popular clamor throughout the North would speedily force the Federal general to attempt to drive us out. I recalled the battle of Fredericksburg as an instance of a defensive battle, when, with a few thousand men, we hurled the whole Federal army back, crippling and demoralizing it, with trifling loss to our own troops.

Longstreet beset Lee with his theory for several days, and began the march resolved to see the army apply it in battle. Shortly before he left, too, he sent out a scout, a man known simply as Harrison, a veteran spy who was to sneak into Washington and discover enemy plans.

"Where will I report to you?" Harrison asked.

Old Pete would not divulge the army's goal: "I'm sure the First Corps is big enough for a man of your intelligence to find."

Harrison was off on his errand.

Two slow columns wound north, Ewell to the west, with Long-street following along the Blue Ridge. A. P. Hill's corps was last to leave the Rappahannock. By June fifteenth, Ewell's advance was already over the Potomac, and Winchester fell the next day. Long-street's men were around the Blue Ridge passes, Ashby's Gap and Snicker's Gap. The enemy began a desperate effort to break through Stuart's screen and discover the route of the infantry.

Stuart's corps was divided when the blows fell: The brigades of Robertson, Fitz Lee and Rooney Lee, the latter under Colonel J. R. Chambliss, were to the east of Longstreet's column. Grumble Jones and Wade Hampton, with their troopers, were in the rear southward, shielding A. P. Hill.

June seventeenth was clear and hot. Colonel T. T. Munford, commanding some of Fitz Lee's men, led the 2nd and 3rd Virginia along Bull Run Mountain from Upperville through Middleburg, to the pass at Aldie, setting out pickets. He stopped to gather corn on a farm a mile out of Aldie. Behind him Williams Wickham had brought the three other regiments of the brigade near the village.

Colonel Rosser and the 5th Virginia met the enemy here, as blue riders came in and gobbled up Munford's pickets, a full Federal division under General Gregg. Young Judson Kilpatrick's brigade carried the fight for the enemy—five regiments from New York, Massachusetts, Ohio and Maine. They fought like demons.

Rosser pushed back their advance for a moment with a saber charge and put sharpshooters among haystacks in an adjoining field, with a small mounted reserve behind them. Colonel Munford sent a party of fifteen dismounted men behind a stone wall to hold on until he could call up his two regiments from their corn foraging.

The Confederates were driven slowly back until the 2nd and 3rd Virginia arrived, and firing became heavy. The Federals came on an uphill road, squeezed into column of fours by deep gullies. They were met in this defile, hand-to-hand. The head of the Federal column was almost wiped out. At about this moment the graycoats in the haystacks were captured, and the enemy pulled back into Aldie, holding off Munford's final charge. The sharpshooters in the

hayfield and along the stone fence had taken terrible toll. Colonel
Munford noted:

> I do not hesitate to say that I have never seen as many
> Yankees killed in the same space of ground in any fight I have
> ever seen. . . . We held our ground until ordered by the Major
> General commanding to retire and the Yankees had been so
> severely punished that they did not follow.

Munford had lost 119 men, mostly in the 5th Virginia, which
furnished the sharpshooters; he had 138 prisoners in tow. Munford
camped a mile in rear of the battlefield.

Stuart got into Middleburg in the late afternoon. An officer saw
him in the street surrounded by women: "The scene looked like a
dance around a maypole. It lasted an hour or so until they heard the
guns."[8]

Jeb was forced to flee with the staff. Colonel Alfred Duffié and
the 1st Rhode Island slashed down the street, having snatched
Stuart's pickets before they could sound an alarm. Jeb ran for the
safety of Robertson's lines, just beyond the village, and sent Robertson to clear Middleburg. Riders fought in the dark, once leaping
a barricade in the road and scattering its guard. Von Borcke wrote
of the brief stay in this town:

"The General and I remained another hour with our lady
friends, who, with their accustomed devotedness, were busy nursing
the wounded, large numbers of whom were collected in the resi-
dences."

John Mosby reported during the day. He was a changed man,
Blackford saw, no longer the carelessly dressed scout on a shambling
nag. In recent weeks he had become famous, raiding enemy headquarters and kidnaping generals.

With the splendidly uniformed partisan chief were the rough
men of his command. It was the "only time during the war" that
Stuart saw these raiders. "They remind me of the story about Captain Scott and the 'coon," he told Mosby, "when the 'coon said,
'Don't shoot, I'll come down!' They'll look like that to the Yankees."

The ranger had news for Stuart: The Army of the Potomac

was streaming northward on a line parallel to that of Lee's infantry, but on the east of the mountains. More immediately important, Mosby had captured Federal dispatches disclosing that Stuart faced a division of infantry, as well as the blue cavalry corps. Jeb had only twelve regiments to keep this force from striking Lee's infantry in the rear.

June nineteenth opened with heavy fire at dawn, and dragged on in furious fighting. Stuart's line near Upperville was pushed back half a mile by dismounted Federal riflemen and cannon fire, until Jeb found a hillside to his liking and settled to defend it. Von Borcke was sent to place some cannon and returned with an ominous report: "They are too strong, General. So many that they overlap the line on either side."

Stuart scoffed. "I can hold here all day." He ordered some of Rooney Lee's troops into Aldie to meet another threat, but von Borcke pleaded with him to keep them on the ground. The German was sent back to the front once more.

"You see if you haven't over-estimated their number," Stuart said.

Von Borcke returned to affirm his fears. "You will have to re-treat, even if you keep the whole force together."

Stuart laughed. "You're mistaken this time, Von. I'll be in Middleburg in less than an hour. Write out a permit for the Major, here, to go into the village as commissary."

They came under fire while von Borcke wrote, and retreating men poured about them. Federals came in sight.

"Ride after those men, Von," Stuart said. "Rally them. I'll fol-low you with all I can gather."

As von Borcke got to the fighting line, the enemy was staggered by artillery fire from the flank and a charge by the 9th Virginia, which seemed to save the day for Stuart. Jeb and the German rode behind the lines, cheered by the men. The two were almost identical in dress, from plumes to spurs, and, as von Borcke said, ". . . bullets came humming around me like a swarm of bees."

A sharpshooter's bullet snipped gold braid from von Borcke's trousers. He complained to Stuart: "Those Yankees are giving it to me rather hotly on your account."

The German's military career was over in that moment:

"I suddenly felt a severe dull blow, as though somebody had struck me with his fist on my neck, fiery sparks glittered before my eyes, and a tremendous weight seemed to be dragging me from my horse."

Blackford was at his side: "I heard a thump very much like some one had struck a barrel a violent blow with a stick. I knew very well what it meant. . . . I looked around to see which one would fall."[9]

He looked first at Stuart, and saw him firm in the saddle, then saw von Borcke drop his bridle and slide. Blackford saw that the German's spur would catch in the stirrup, and rode beside him, throwing his foot clear; von Borcke went down slowly on his back. He was shot in the back of the neck. His left arm was stiff, and blood streamed from his mouth. There was a whistling from his throat. He could not speak, and motioned to the others to leave him.

Blackford could think of no way to keep the body of the 250-pound major on a restive, bucking horse until he remembered a trick taught him by von Borcke early in the war. He had a courier twist the horse's ear, holding down the head, until they were out of firing range. Von Borcke surprised them by coming to life, helping them to get him seated in the saddle, and thence to an ambulance.

He went back with shells bursting about the speeding, plunging ambulance. When he could bear it no longer, von Borcke forced himself erect and put his pistol at the frightened driver's head. "You will slow down, shells or no, or I will kill you. Stop!" They moved at a more comfortable pace until they reached Dr. Talcott Eliason of the staff.

A bullet had cut part of the windpipe and lodged in a lung. Eliason's face was grave.

"I can't expect you to live till morning. I will attend to your last wishes."

Von Borcke did not flinch; he wrote some orders for ordnance wagons to move up to the front, and went then to Eliason's house, where he was put to bed in the parlor and given opium. Members of the staff who came in after the fight disturbed him only slightly; he could hear them:

"Is he alive yet?"

"Yes, but he won't live over night."

When Stuart bent over him, von Borcke felt two tears drop on his face. "Poor Von," Stuart said, "you took this wound for me."

The German slept all night and awoke refreshed. Eliason was amazed.

There was heavy cannon fire all day, for Stuart was being pushed nearer Upperville and the fight roared on after dark.

Stuart came to the Eliason home to see von Borcke: "I may be forced back past Upperville tomorrow. I'll send an ambulance for you if it comes to that."

The German could hardly be kept in bed the next day, for stragglers ran through town, firing increased, wounded men passed, and no word came from Stuart. Von Borcke kept a courier running to and from the street. Scheibert came the long distance from Longstreet's headquarters with an ambulance, offering to take him off, but von Borcke would not leave without word from Jeb, and they waited until a cavalryman ran in with a message: Stuart had waited until the last moment, hoping to save von Borcke a move, but he must now leave at once.

The ambulance got away under fire once more, with enemy riders in the street, and von Borcke was taken two miles to a plantation house and hidden in an upper room. Yankees searched the house, but did not find him, though he waited with a cocked pistol and saber on his bed. They stayed for half an hour, and he heard them:

"We've searched every house in Upperville. There's some big Rebel officer wounded. We think it may be Stuart. They saw him fall. He must have been buried before they ran."

Stuart, Wade Hampton and Robertson visited von Borcke the next day, June twenty-first; he had recovered his voice a bit, and could croak to them. He told them goodbye with a long face. He ate a little food that day, and sat on the porch.

Jeb had fought against odds and bold, confident, well-led columns. He had fallen back some six miles, but still screened the valley behind him, halting Pleasanton at the gaps. Blackford noted that the improvement of enemy cavalry was enormous, mainly in the heavy fire from long-range carbines, and horse artillery that was a match for Stuart's own. These cavalrymen fought as if they had been taken from infantry regiments, for they knew how to fight with horses left behind.

June twenty-first found the vast theater of Northern Virginia ready for a new act: Lee's infantry thronged in the Shenandoah Valley from Winchester to the Potomac. East of the Blue Ridge and the little Bull Run Mountains, Hooker moved slowly, waiting to see where Lee led. Stuart still held the mountain ridges between the two armies.

On this day, with one of his units camped on the old battlefield at Sharpsburg, Maryland, Dick Ewell notified General Lee he was ready to move north. He was ordered to march on, though Lee had not chosen his final goal: "Your progress and direction will, of course, depend upon the development of circumstances. If Harrisburg comes within your means, capture it."

Ewell's men hurried, and Longstreet's corps crossed the Potomac behind them, embarrassing some Maryland women as they splashed from the deep ford, carrying their trousers overhead.

On the flank, hourly farther in rear of the infantry, Stuart watched. He had an explanation for Major McClellan on the fighting at the mountain passes, where he had watched, but left actual control to regimental and brigade commanders. McClellan asked why he had done that.

"I gave them all the instructions they needed, and I wanted them to feel responsibility come down on them. Then they could have whatever honor there was on the field."

For the three days of hard fighting he had paid with 510 casualties, 65 of them dead; the Federal loss was over 800.

On the morning of June twenty-second pickets came to Jeb with news that the enemy had left Upperville. Stuart advanced and camped at Rectortown. He puzzled over the disappearance of the bluecoats, who had evidently left him free to move.

There was an order from Robert Lee to Stuart in the afternoon, enclosed in a dispatch packet from Longstreet:

I judge the efforts of the enemy yesterday were to arrest
our progress and ascertain our whereabouts. Perhaps he is satisfied. Do you know where he is and what he is doing? I fear
he will steal a march on us and get across the Potomac before
we are aware. If you find that he is moving northward and that
two brigades can guard the Blue Ridge and take care of your
rear, you can move with the other three into Maryland and
take position on General Ewell's right, place yourself in communication with him, guard his flank, keep him informed of
the enemy's movements and collect all the supplies you can. . . .

But by the time Stuart read this, Ewell's advance was marching
on Greencastle, Pennsylvania, far to the north. And Jeb did not yet
know what Hooker was doing, down the slopes eastward, in Lou-
doun and Fauquier Counties.

John Mosby returned to tell him.

☆

CHAPTER 17

Gettysburg

MOSBY had been to the very center of the Federal camps, prowling a rainy night in an oilcloth coat; he came away with two prisoners and a plan of campaign, which he put persuasively before Stuart:

"Cut between the wings of Hooker's army by crossing the Bull Run Mountains and fording the Potomac at Seneca. The enemy are not moving—Hooker is still afraid Lee will strike him on the railroad, somewhere near Bull Run. It will be easy to flank them in one day, beating up wagons on the way. They will send their cavalry after you, which is what you want."

Mosby's final word impressed Stuart: "The best way to protect Lee's communications is to assail Hooker's."

Stuart agreed. He had talked over such a plan with General Lee, arguing that he could create a panic in Washington by taking the cavalry off, and could quickly rejoin the army in case of need.

Then, on June twenty-second, having read with care Lee's letter of instructions, Jeb turned to the notes from Longstreet which accompanied it.

Longstreet had written Lee:

> Yours of 4 o'clock this afternoon is received. I have forwarded your letter to General Stuart with the suggestion that he pass by the enemy's rear if he thinks that he might get through.

There was also Longstreet's explanation to Stuart:

General Lee has enclosed to me this letter for you, to be forwarded to you provided you can be spared from my front, and provided I think you can cross the Potomac without disclosing our plans. He speaks of your leaving via Hopewell Gap in the Bull Run Mountains and passing by the rear of the enemy. If you can get through by that route I think you will be less likely to indicate what our plans are than if you should cross by passing to our rear. Please advise me of the condition of affairs before you leave. . . .

N. B. I think that your passage of the Potomac by our rear at the present moment will in a measure disclose our plans. You had better not leave us, therefore, unless you can take the proposed route in rear of the enemy.

Thus Stuart had orders to hurry northward and join Ewell, though both Lee's and Hooker's armies now lay between them, and equally positive orders to pass around the enemy rear and cross the Potomac. He had, in addition, Longstreet's approval of the rearward march. This course would place the Federal army between Lee's infantry and his cavalry, but in the evening of June twenty-second, in the camps in the mountains, this was not yet evident.

Jeb wrote Flora during the day, and inserted a rather ruthless scolding, an effort to stop her anxious queries to headquarters when Stuart's letters were delayed:

Don't be telegraphing General Lee's Staff or anybody else. If I am hurt you will hear of it very soon.

There was a day's wait for the cavalry, for scouts confirmed reports that roads on the eastern slopes were full of enemy wagons, and that this, the most direct route to the river, was blocked. Night of June twenty-third brought a severe rainstorm. Stuart's troopers were scattered about Rectortown, where there was an old house at a crossroads. At bedtime Stuart went from the building into the drenching rain, unwrapped the oilcloth from his blanket and lay under a tree. Major McClellan tried to persuade him to use the house.

"No. The men must stay out in it, and I won't fare any better than they. You stay there on the porch, where you can take any dispatches that come in. You can strike a light better there."

McClellan was soon aroused. A courier handed him a note which, he saw in candlelight, was marked "Confidential." The adjutant turned it thoughtfully, and, eying the sleeping Stuart, violated orders by opening the dispatch. He later wrote:

"It was a lengthy communication from General Lee, containing the directions upon which Stuart was to act."

He took it to Stuart at once, with his candle, and read it to him under the dripping tree.

Near the end he read:

> If General Hooker's army remains inactive, you can leave two brigades to watch him, and withdraw with the three others, but should he not appear to be moving northward, I think you had better withdraw this side of the mountains tomorrow night, cross at Shepherdstown next day, and move over to Frederickstown.
>
> You will, however, be able to judge whether you can pass around their army without hindrance, doing them all the damage you can, and cross the river east of the mountains. In either case, after crossing the river, you must move on and feel the right of Ewell's troops.[1]

Stuart gave McClellan "a mild reproof" for having opened the document, told him to keep it for the night, and fell asleep. He gave no sign that he did not fully understand and appreciate the perplexing orders which were to become the most controversial of his career.

The morning was busy. Stuart left Grumble Jones and Robertson behind, because, he said, Jones was "the best outpost officer" in his command; these two brigades had more than 3,000 troopers. They were ordered to guard the passes and to follow Lee's army and join it when it had moved North.

Jeb would take Colonel Chambliss with Rooney Lee's men, Wade Hampton and Fitz Lee—who was just now back after a month of painful rheumatic attacks.

The day was spent in moving the three brigades to a rendezvous at the village of Salem, a little southwest. It was after midnight, June twenty-fifth, when they rode eastward toward the Army of

The Potomac, about 2,000 strong. They were over the Bull Run Mountains by daylight. But at Haymarket, not far from the old Manassas battlefield, Stuart found a corps of blue infantry and went into a detour, camping for the night at Buckland.

Stuart sent a note to Lee, advising him that Hancock's corps was moving north. But he sought no advice on the all-important detour of June twenty-sixth, which changed his direction. He did not so much as consult his brigadiers as he swung the column southward to pass around the enemy. He crossed the Occoquan at Wolf Run Shoals, and was now east of Hooker, with the whole enemy army between him and Lee.

He turned north to Fairfax Court House, sweeping up a few prisoners as Hampton clashed with a small enemy party. The pace was slow.[2]

The country had been stripped bare, and they had to halt three or four times daily to forage and graze horses. It had taken forty-eight hours to march thirty-five miles. In the evening of June twenty-seventh the hungry men halted several hours more, robbing the stores at Fairfax, and it was late when Stuart got them through Dranesville toward the Potomac.

Campfires of the enemy were still warm here, so that the better fords near Leesburg were probably guarded. Stuart sent Wade Hampton's vanguard toward a little-known crossing, Rowser's Ford. The men started over early on June twenty-eighth. Stuart now knew nothing of General Lee's position.

He had learned that Hooker was marching on Frederick, Maryland, but had no way to know that Ewell was seventy miles or more north of the river, at Carlisle, Pennsylvania, and that Early was camped at Gettysburg. Jeb sent a courier westward to find General Lee and report on the Federal position; the message was not destined to be delivered.

Stuart now had his hands full at the river. Not long after midnight Hampton's men were across, but the river was so wide and deep that Jeb doubted his guns and ambulances could pass over it. He called for volunteers for special duty, and the first man before him was Captain R. B. Kennon, a special courier. Stuart sent him across the river nearby to see if there were an easier way for the rest

of the column. Kennon rode his thoroughbred, Big Indian. He never
forgot the night:

"The Potomac was about a mile wide, the water deep and the
current strong. The horse swam magnificently. When he tired I
would get off on a boulder, holding the bridle to let him rest. I
reached the Maryland side. The night was calm, but no moon. Some
rest for the horse was indispensable. However, as soon as the breathing of Big Indian came back to normal I sprang to the saddle and we
took the plunge to return."

When he reached the Virginia shore a man stepped from the
bushes. Kennon recognized Stuart only when Jeb took the bridle.

"Thank God," Stuart said. "I never expected to see you again."

"Where did you come from, General?"

"I've been here all the time. Can we make it?"

"No." Kennon described the treacherous bottom, the depths
and boulders. "It's no better than Rowser's Ford."

Stuart felt the neck of the heaving horse. "What will you do?
You've ruined your fine horse."

Kennon said he would ride his servant's mount.

Stuart spoke quickly: "Kennon, I'll take Rowser's Ford. You
get what rest you can, and follow when you wake up, if you're able.
You can catch us, even if we're over. I'll promote you major for this."

He was gone. Kennon fell asleep, watched over by his slave,
who waked him at daybreak and gave him coffee brewed from
charred corn meal. The last troopers were just emerging from the
river on the far shore.[8]

The end of the crossing had been almost frantic. Gun carriages,
caissons and limbers went under the current and damaged powder
and shells. Men carried powder bags over in their hands on horses
scarcely able to negotiate the crossing. By three thirty A.M. the bulk
of the force was in Maryland.

"No more difficult achievement was accomplished by the cavalry during the war," McClellan thought.

The weary command rested on the northern bank. The vanguard caught a few sleepy Federal canal guards and broke the banks
of the canal, draining it into the river. But the horses needed rest,
especially those of the artillery, and the sun was high before the

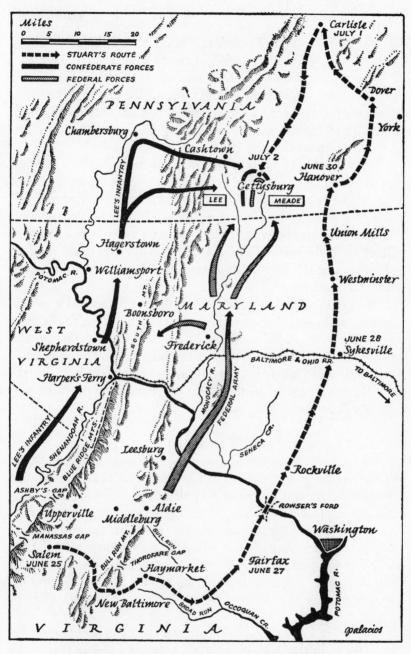

Miles
0   5   10   15   20

- - -➤ STUART'S ROUTE
▬▬▬ CONFEDERATE FORCES
▓▓▓ FEDERAL FORCES

PENNSYLVANIA

Carlisle
JULY 1

Dover

York

Chambersburg

Cashtown

JULY 2

Gettysburg

LEE   MEADE

JUNE 30
Hanover

LEE'S INFANTRY

Hagerstown

Union Mills

Williamsport

Westminster

POTOMAC R.

Boonsboro

MARYLAND

SOUTH MT.

Shepherdstown

WEST

Frederick

JUNE 28
Sykesville

VIRGINIA

BALTIMORE & OHIO R.R.

TO BALTIMORE

Harper's Ferry

MONOCACY R.

FEDERAL ARMY

SHENANDOAH R.

LEE'S INFANTRY

BLUE RIDGE MTS.

Leesburg

SENECA CR.

Rockville

ASHBY'S GAP

Upperville

Aldie

ROWSER'S FORD

MANASSAS GAP

Middleburg

Washington

BULL RUN MT.

BULL RUN

THOROFARE GAP

Salem
JUNE 25

Haymarket

Fairfax
JUNE 27

POTOMAC R.

New Baltimore

BROAD RUN

OCCOQUAN CR.

VIRGINIA

palacios

FATEFUL LINES OF MARCH TO GETTYSBURG
June 25–July 2, 1863

column moved toward Rockville. They reached this town about
noon; it was only fifteen or so miles from Washington.

There were delays, but they seemed unavoidable. Hampton's
troopers took a wagon train coming from Washington. Union soldiers in the rear fled until a wagon overturned, and others piled on it
in a melee of frantic mules kicking long legs amid bags of grain.
There was a chase of several miles.

Stuart took 125 wagons without a thought that they might
burden him, and his famished horses fed for hours from the oats of
the captured train. Troopers loaded bags of grain across their saddles.
There was another precious commodity aboard—bottled whisky.

The men were beset by scores of pretty girls from the seminary
in Rockville, who waved Confederate music and flags from windows
and gathered in the streets, taking souvenirs from every soldier they
could reach, snipping off many uniform buttons.

Most of the day was spent in Rockville, for Stuart had some 400
prisoners, and paroled them with meticulous regard for the code of
war. Officers were still working on parole papers as the column
moved, and spent ten or twelve hours on them in the villages of
Brookeville and Cooksville. It was time wasted in the end, for the
Federal government refused to honor the paroles and the freed men
went back into the fighting ranks.

As Stuart waited near Rockville on the twenty-eighth, Harrison, the scout, returned to the main army and reported to Longstreet
at Chambersburg, Pennsylvania: The Army of The Potomac had
crossed the river and was around Frederick, with Meade now commanding in place of Hooker. With the enemy almost upon him,
Robert Lee learned for the first time that the Federals were north of
the border. Not only had he heard nothing from Stuart; he did not
know where the cavalry corps was even now. He called Ewell back
from the North, just as he was moving toward Harrisburg, and began to concentrate his infantry in the hills west of Gettysburg.

After daylight of June twenty-ninth Fitz Lee's men began tearing up tracks of the Baltimore & Ohio Railroad, after a night march
of twenty miles. They added a few more prisoners, burned a bridge,

and tried to capture a train, but those which puffed along the tracks were wary, saw the raiders far ahead, and backed to safety.

After a few hours on the railroad Stuart led them to Westminster, a country town in central Maryland where they drove out two companies of Delaware cavalry as stubborn as any bluecoats they had met; the enemy fell back only after losing 67 of his 95 troopers. Two of the 4th Virginia's most promising young lieutenants were killed in the Westminster streets, Pierre Gibson and John Murray, and when women of the town begged to be allowed to bury the bodies, Jeb agreed.

There was more forage at Westminster, and Stuart spent the night there, with the column strung out as far as Union Mills on the road to Gettysburg. Here he got first word of the Federal pursuit: Kilpatrick's cavalry was at Littlestown, seven miles away. The staff talked over the problem: The enemy was probably moving toward Hanover, over the Pennsylvania line to the north. The Federals were seven miles from Hanover, and Stuart was ten. Yet he held on to the shining new Federal wagons and their teams as if they were the only evidence of his success, and as if the need for haste did not occur to him. Gettysburg was fifteen miles away, but if anyone in the column thought of that fact, it seemed of no consequence; it was not yet a prospective battleground.

On June thirtieth the leading riders entered Hanover and struck the rear of a Federal cavalry brigade on the main street.

The 2nd North Carolina charged, scattered a bluecoat regiment, the 18th Pennsylvania, and with help might have put to flight all of Kilpatrick's column.

But Stuart's line of march was split. Fitz Lee was out to the west, shielding the approach from Littlestown, and Wade Hampton was behind the slow wagon train. There was only the little brigade of Chambliss to come to the aid of the North Carolinians when Kilpatrick countercharged, and there was a chase through Hanover. Citizens in houses along the street threw up windows and fired muskets and shotguns at the graycoats.

Stuart was jogging toward Hanover when the flight approached him. He led Blackford toward town at a gallop and tried to rally the men. There was not a pause in the headlong retreat, and Blackford and Stuart soon found themselves riding almost neck and neck with the head of the Federal pursuit.

They were riding at full speed on a road lined with hedges when Stuart laughed, drew his saber, and shouted, "Rally them, Blackford!" He spurred his big mare, Virginia, jumping the hedge. Blackford followed him. They were not yet safe. A Federal flanking party ordered them to surrender, but Jeb and Blackford galloped on. Pistol shots sang around them. They rode in a field deep in grass, and neither rider saw a deep fifteen-foot ditch until they were upon it. The horses rose magnificently, Blackford a bit in advance. He turned: "I shall never forget the glimpse I then saw of this beautiful animal away up in mid-air over the chasm and Stuart's fine figure sitting erect and firm in the saddle." Blackford's own horse, Magic, cleared the ditch by a wide margin, a leap of some twenty-seven feet. The pursuing Federals halted and fired after them.

Major McClellan watched other Confederate officers gallop in the field, discover the ditch too late, and land sprawling in the shallow water at the bottom. Stuart and his staff howled with laughter "notwithstanding the peril."

The 2nd North Carolina rallied on a hill nearby and Stuart brought up a gun to halt pursuit. Wade Hampton's men went into line on the right; Fitz Lee joined on the left. The enemy approached, and there was firing, but Kilpatrick did not press the hill position. The wagons had been placed together, with details ready to burn them, but now Stuart ordered the prizes back into the road and had them rolled eastward toward the town of Jefferson, hoping to send them to York, where he expected to get information of the main army.

Stuart faced the enemy until dark, fearing an attack if he moved in daylight. A punishing night march began. Wagons hindered the regiments and broke up the columns with frequent halts. About four hundred new prisoners had been taken, and these rode in the wagon train, many of them as drivers. The mules were wild with hunger and thirst, and often bolted or bucked. More than once the procession ground to a halt, and the trouble was not discovered until officers rode the line and found a driver asleep with his weary mules standing in the traces. Stuart drove the staff to keep the column on the move. He turned north at Jefferson, and on the morning of July first reached the hamlet of Dover.

It was the day Robert Lee's advance began fighting at Gettysburg.

Fitz Lee, probing eastward toward York, discovered that General Early had left that town and gone to the West. Stuart's best guess today was that the army was concentrating to the north of Chambersburg, at Shippensburg. He groped for more information.

Major A. R. Venable of his staff was sent out from Dover, trailing Early's troops, and Fitz Lee soon afterward sent Captain Henry Lee toward Gettysburg for the same purpose. Stuart pushed the column toward Carlisle.

The tail of the column had left Dover at sunrise, and here the last of the batch of prisoners was paroled. Stuart's men plodded through the village of Dillsburg, taking horses as they went. They gathered more than a hundred in this region from people who had joined a protective league, guaranteeing defense against Confederate raiders, and had left their horses conveniently at hand. Men took all the food they could find in houses, and many robbed beehives. Women were put to work cooking for the troops.

Stuart wrote: ". . . after as little rest as was compatible with the exhausted condition of the command I pushed on for Carlisle where I hoped to find a portion of the army."

But when his commissary officers reached Carlisle in late afternoon, they found Ewell's men had long since departed; the enemy occupied the town. Stuart came up and was told that a brigade of volunteer infantry was in ambush in the town, under command of General William F. ("Baldy") Smith. Jeb sent in a demand for surrender. Smith declined, and Stuart threatened bombardment. Smith's message was plain: "Shell away." The guns were firing almost before the messenger was out of town. Stuart burned the U.S. Cavalry barracks. A civilian witness wrote:

"And now began a general flight of the inhabitants into the country and cellars and behind anything strong enough to afford hope of protection, a stream of women and children and infirm people on foot, with outcries and terrified countenances. To add terror to the scene the sky was lighted up by the flames of a woodyard in the vicinity of the rebel encampment, and about 10 o'clock the barracks and the garrison were burnt. . . . In the middle of the night there was another pause in the firing, and another call for a surrender made, to which a rather uncourteous reply was made by General Smith, and the shelling proceeded, but with diminishing power and frequency. It is supposed that ammunition had become precious in the hostile camp."[4]

The truth was that Stuart, after eight days on the move, had only now learned where Lee was: "The whereabouts of our army," he wrote, "was still a mystery, but during the night I received a dispatch from General Lee that the army was at Gettysburg and had been engaged this day."

The news was brought back by Venable and Henry Lee, with orders to hurry the column to Gettysburg. They also had glowing reports of victory over Meade's infantry during the day. Stuart left Carlisle at one A.M., with about thirty miles to go by the nearest route.[5]

The column left the wagon train behind, entrusted to Colonel R. L. T. Beale of the 9th Virginia. Beale got the wagons six miles south of Carlisle before he called a halt and watched as his weary drivers "suffering in agony for sleep, lay on the road with bridles in hand, some on rocks, and others on the wet earth, slumbering soundly." There was soon an order from Stuart, far in front, to see that Beale's command remained in the saddle all night. Beale replied that this would rob him of fresh troops in tomorrow's fighting, and Stuart, as if the factor of fatigue had not occurred to him, replied that the riders should have some sleep. Jeb himself had seen men falling asleep while their horses were trying to jump fences.

Stuart got brief rest in the night. Esten Cooke saw him halt for an hour, "wrapped in his cape and resting against the trunk of a tree, and then mount again, as fresh, apparently, as if he had slumbered from sunset to dawn."

On the morning of July second Captain Blackford rode far ahead of Stuart to the field at Gettysburg. He came onto a landscape already made terrible by long hours of the most savage fighting the army had known, but found Lee's headquarters strangely quiet after the roar of the armies meeting head-on. Across rolling fields masses of bluecoats lay on slopes stretching from tumbled rock piles called Big Round Top and Little Round Top, past a peach orchard, along the Emmitsburg Road into Gettysburg—and then, more heights, Culp's Hill and Cemetery Ridge.

But Blackford was most impressed by the homely spectacle of Lee in the grip of an uncomfortable illness. Staff officers told him he could not see the commander, though Blackford had often visited Lee's tent with messages from Stuart, and had always been admitted. But today Lee's aide took his report into the tent himself. For half an hour Blackford talked with Colonels Charles Venable and Walter Taylor of Lee's staff of Stuart's adventures in the wide circle of the enemy. Blackford was surprised to see Lee make several exits from the tent and go to the rear. "He walked as if he was weak and in pain," Blackford said, and one of the officers explained that Lee had suffered an attack of diarrhea.

Blackford also saw strange warfare in the town of Gettysburg, where infantrymen of General Rodes occupied houses; men had cut holes in walls to pass easily from room to room and house to house. The troops were naked to the waist and black with powder, firing from rear windows where they had stuffed mattresses and piled furniture as shields. Men not on duty at the windows lounged on elegant chairs and sofas and lay on thick rugs. From the windows Blackford saw the enemy dug in along the natural fortress he assumed General Lee would have occupied, if he had been "in his usually vigorous condition of health."

In these hours Stuart's column moved as rapidly as its worn men and horses would allow. Wade Hampton, with much the shorter road, was first to approach the field. He was ordered to the left of Lee's infantry, but Federal riders appeared when he neared Huntersville, a village five miles north of Gettysburg. Stuart halted Hampton to meet this threat to the army's rear and there was a brief skirmish, ended by a charge of South Carolina and Georgia troopers. Hampton held the ground until the next morning, when he found the enemy gone. General Custer, who was with the Federals, claimed victory in this action.

In the afternoon of July second, perhaps at the hour when the army was launching costly attacks in the open, the peach orchard, and facing slaughter on the rocky hillsides, Stuart rode up to face Robert Lee.

Major McClellan and Colonel Munford, among others, witnessed their meeting. "It was painful beyond description," McClellan thought.

Lee reddened at sight of Stuart and raised his arm as if he would strike him. "General Stuart, where have you been?"

Stuart seemed to "wilt," and explained his movements to Lee.

"I have not heard a word from you for days," Lee said, "and you the eyes and ears of my army."

"I have brought you 125 wagons and their teams, General," Stuart said.

"Yes, General, but they are an impediment to me now." His manner abruptly became one "of great tenderness," and he said to Stuart, "Let me ask your help now. We will not discuss this matter longer. Help me fight these people."[6]

Stuart went to his command and rested on the Confederate left. He took a long look at the field, heard officers talk of the bloody hammering of the day, and concluded that tomorrow would bring a Confederate victory. After nine days, he was in position with the army. The brigades of Jones and Robertson, which he had ordered to guard the rear and follow closely the main army, were far away, no one knew where.

The day's fighting had strewn 8,000 casualties between the armies, with the lines otherwise little changed. Lee's attacks had been delayed and delivered piecemeal: Longstreet had belatedly sent his men in on the right, around the Round Tops and Devil's Den and the Emmitsburg Road, in bloody hours that cost him 80 per cent of some regiments. John Hood was badly wounded. A. P. Hill in the center had seen a few men reach the crest of Cemetery Ridge, but they were driven back and slaughtered in the open; on the left, Ewell was later still, but got a toehold on the rugged slopes of Culp's Hill.

By nightfall, too, Lee had lost his superiority in numbers, for the whole Army of the Potomac was now up and in position. General Meade was by no means confident, however, and in a night council proposed pulling rearward to Big Pipe Creek to await attack. His commanders persuaded him to hold his forbidding line.

The Union cavalry was scattered: John Buford's division, badly hurt by collision with Lee's infantry as Gettysburg opened, was in the rear guarding the railhead at Westminster; Kilpatrick was on Meade's left, and Gregg on the right.

Confederate regiments moved in the night, closing the line. George Pickett's division came in from the rear, fresh and strong, not yet having fired a shot on this field. There was some confusion of command at headquarters, and orders for the next day's action went out verbally. Longstreet and Lee were still engaged in their strange, subtle conflict of wills; Old Pete feared a Fredericksburg in reverse on this terrain.

July third opened with a dawn artillery barrage on Ewell's front near Culp's Hill. Ewell attacked the hill, but the position was too strong, and there were no guns for support. This corps withdrew, to fight no more for the day.

Lee ordered Longstreet to strike the Union center.

"I have been examining the ground over to the right," Longstreet said. "I am much inclined to think the best thing is to move to the Federal left."

"No," Lee said. "I am going to take them where they are. I want you to take Pickett's Division and make the attack. I will reinforce you with two divisions of the Third Corps."

"That will give me 15,000," Longstreet said. "I have been a soldier all my life, in pretty much all kinds of skirmishes. I think I can safely say there never were fifteen thousand men who could make that attack successfully."

Lee continued to explain his plan; Longstreet went to his front. Hours dragged. Longstreet was once found asleep in the woods, as the gray regiments were brought up for the assault.

George Pickett wrote his bride:

> . . . Oh, the responsibility for the lives of such men as these! Well, my darling, their fate and that of our beloved Southland will be settled ere your glorious brown eyes rest on these scraps of penciled paper. . . .

The men are lying in the rear, and the hot July sun pours its scorching rays almost vertically down on them. The suffering is almost unbearable.

I have never seen Old Peter so grave and troubled. For several minutes after I saluted him he looked at me without speaking. Then in an agonized voice, the reserve all gone, he said, "Pickett, I am being crucified. I have instructed Alexander to give you your orders, for I can't."

... I saw tears glistening on his cheeks and beard. The stern old war horse, God bless him, was weeping for his men, and, I know, praying too that this cup might pass from them. It is almost three o'clock.

Alexander's 159 guns had rolled for more than an hour, blasting the line on Cemetery Ridge, a mile away across the open. Pickett's ranks were assembling in front, under the blazing sun. Their front was more than a mile wide, in three solid columns.

There was a desperate message to Pickett from General Alexander, at artillery headquarters:

For God's sake come quick. ... Come quick or my ammunition will not let me support you properly.

Pickett saw a cavalryman on his way out—Fitz Lee: "Come on, Fitz, and go with us; we shall have lots of fun there presently."

Men behind heard Pickett shout as he rode through the infantry ranks: "Up, men, and to your posts! Don't forget today that you are from Old Virginia!"

The 15,000 stepped forward.

Stuart was up early, and if he had been stung by Lee's reception after his exhausting march, he gave no sign of it. He sent the troopers back to the ordnance wagons for ammunition; they were two hours or more at the task. Newcomers were in the ranks today, one brigade of them the half-disciplined Western Virginia riders of General A. G. Jenkins. These were now commanded by Colonel M. J. Ferguson, since Jenkins had been wounded at Hunterstown the day before. This brigade, through some error, drew only ten rounds of ammunition per man.

The Horse Artillery had ammunition troubles as well, and Stuart was forced to march about noon, leaving Major Breathed with orders to follow when he could fill his caissons. Jeb took the brigades of Jenkins and Chambliss eastward on the York road; Fitz Lee and Wade Hampton were ordered to follow.

Almost as soon as Jeb moved the procession was seen by Federal scouts on Cemetery Ridge, and the warning went rearward to General David Gregg, commanding cavalry on that wing. The bluecoats were concentrated along the Low Dutch Road, where the roads to York, Hanover and Baltimore intersected.

Stuart marched two and a half miles out the York turnpike without sighting a Federal soldier. The route led through rich farmlands, thickly settled, dotted with clumps of woodland and big barns. Heat shimmered over the fields, many of which were enclosed by stone fences. Stuart turned off the highway to his right, on a country road leading to "a commanding ridge which completely controlled a wide plain of cultivated fields stretching toward Hanover on the left, and reaching to the base of the mountain spurs among which the enemy held position."

He was on Cress Ridge, whose northern slopes were clothed in woods which masked his approach from enemy scouts. In the open below, some three hundred yards away, was a big frame barn known as the Rummel Barn. Stuart took in the position at a glance, and with his instinct for terrain, made it his. His object was to shield General Ewell's left, observe the enemy's rear, and strike on the flank if the opportunity arose. Cress Ridge seemed to him ideal, for he could see almost every road leading from the rear of the Federal army, and the open fields gave him room to maneuver.

Jeb hid the two brigades in the trees until they could not have been seen from the nearby barn. The landscape gave not a hint of war, and there was no sound from the main armies, which faced each other a scant three miles away. Stuart's next move mystified his staff.

Jeb ordered one of the guns of a new Maryland battery to the edge of the woods and fired it in several directions, giving the orders himself. The shells burst far away over the empty landscape.

He did not explain to his officers. Major McClellan assumed that it was a signal to General Lee that the cavalry was in place—or that he perhaps wanted to know whether Federal cavalry was within range before leaving his wooded hill. Whatever the reason, he had announced to the enemy his exact position. There was a wait before the bluecoats appeared, however. Stuart sent a courier back to Gettysburg to bring up Fitz Lee and Hampton; he planned an attack on the rear of the enemy infantry.

After a few minutes Jeb dismounted a battalion of riders from Ferguson's command and sent them to hold the Rummel Barn and a line of adjacent fence. They were hardly in place when Federal shells fell on Stuart's position; the fire was uncannily accurate, forcing Stuart's disabled guns to pull back. Bluecoats on foot ran in the open toward the Rummel Barn and overlapped the Confederate line. Stuart poured in more men.

Fighting grew hot on the right, around the contingent from Ferguson's command; these had advanced a little when their ten rounds of cartridges gave out. Only a charge by other troopers kept the bluecoats off them. Part of the pushing enemy force was from George Custer's command; it was driven back two hundred yards.

The first mounted men appeared on the field—a swift file of bluecoats which swept forward with as much dash as the Virginia horsemen had managed in their heyday. This charge cut the gray line behind the fence, but at the Rummel Barn one of Chambliss's squadrons struck in a pile-up of men and horses and flashing swords.

Stuart saw that General Gregg did not intend to allow an assault on Meade's rear. The enemy was as stoutly determined as they had been at Brandy Station or in the mountain passes in Northern Virginia.

Just as the Federals slowed, Wade Hampton arrived with the 1st North Carolina and the Mississippi Legion, and there was charge and countercharge until all but two of Stuart's regiments were engaged. For once, Jeb outnumbered the enemy, but seemed unable to drive them. Then came the climactic Federal charge. Colonel William Brooke-Rawle, who rode with the bluecoats, left a vivid sketch of the action, which came almost at the moment Pickett's infantrymen were charging Cemetery Ridge, some three miles to the west:

"Gregg rode over to the 1st Michigan . . . formed close column of squadrons, and ordered it to charge. . . . Custer dashed up and placed himself at its head. The two columns drew nearer and nearer, the Confederates outnumbering their opponents three or four to one. The gait increased—first the trot, then the gallop. Hampton's battle flag floated in the van of the brigade.

"The orders of the Confederate officers could be heard by those in the woods on their left: 'Keep to your sabers, men, keep to your sabers.' For the lessons they had learned at Brandy Station and at Aldie had been severe. There the cry had been: 'Put up your sabers! Draw your pistols and fight like gentlemen!' But the saber was never a favorite weapon with the Confederate cavalry, and now, in spite of the lessons of the past, the warnings were not heeded by all.

". . . The speed increased, every horse on the jump, every man yelling like a demon. The column of the Confederates blended, but the perfect alignment was maintained. [The gunner] Chester put charge after charge of canister into their midst, his men bringing it up to the guns by the armful. The execution was fearful, but the long rent closed up at once. As the opposing columns drew nearer every man gathered his horse well under him, and gripped his weapon the tighter. . . . Staggered by the fearful execution from the two batteries, the men in the front line of the Confederate column drew in their horses and wavered . . . but those behind came pressing on. Custer, seeing the front men hesitate, waved his saber and shouted, 'Come on, you Wolverines!' and with a fearful yell the 1st Michigan rushed on, Custer four lengths ahead."

Now, from woods on the flank, two small Federal parties struck the flying gray column. Almost every man in the first party was cut down, but the second broke through the gray column and rode back and forth, cutting off Confederates in the rear.

Brooke-Rawle wrote: "In the meantime, the two columns had come together with a crash—the one led by Hampton and Fitz Lee, and the other by Custer—and were fighting hand to hand. For minutes which seemed like hours, amid the clashing of the sabers, the rattle of the small arms, the frenzied imprecations, the demands for surrender, the undaunted replies, and the appeals for mercy, the Confederate column stood its ground."

A squadron of the 1st New Jersey drove in, lured by sight of a

Confederate officer near a color guard: It was Wade Hampton, and he went down in this attack with a gushing head wound.

Brooke-Rawle saw with relief: "The edge of the Confederate column had begun to fray away, and the outside men to draw back . . . the enemy turned. Then followed a pell-mell rush, our men in close pursuit. Many prisoners were captured, and many of our men, through their impetuosity, were carried away by the overpowering current of the retreat.

"The pursuit was kept up past Rummel's, and the enemy were driven back into the woods beyond. The line of fences and the farm buildings . . . which in the beginning of the fight had been in the possession of the enemy, remained in ours until the end."

But Major McClellan, at Stuart's side, saw it differently: "The impetuous attack of the Federal cavalry was finally broken, and both parties withdrew to the lines held at the opening of the fight."[7]

Artillerymen on both sides had fired when they dared, trying to avoid a slaughter of their own riders. But though Major Breathed had reached the field in time, and found good positions, the Federal artillery bested him at every turn. The guns banged at each other when the cavalry retired, and Breathed was forced to watch his own defective shells explode harmlessly over the field, halfway to their target—while the Federal bursts fell relentlessly on his batteries and destroyed several guns.

The affair was over. Stuart could see across the field a bluecoat brigade drawn up in reserve, not yet fought. There seemed no way to pass the lines of Gregg. Jeb withdrew to the hill and the 1st Virginia went into a skirmish line on the field.

Stuart and McClellan rode near the barn. The premature bursting of Confederate shells was so frequent that McClellan urged Stuart to get back under cover; Stuart rode the front until he was satisfied that the enemy was through for the day.

Dr. Eliason worked at the Rummel Barn with wounded, most of them Federals, until almost eight o'clock in the evening.

The Federal loss on the field was 252; Stuart reported 181, with no return from the artillery or Ferguson's command. Losses were thus about equal, and Stuart had been unable to damage the enemy decisively.

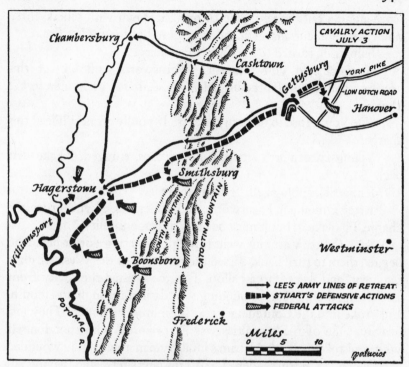

CHAMBERSBURG · CASHTOWN · GETTYSBURG · YORK PIKE · LOW DUTCH ROAD · HANOVER · CAVALRY ACTION JULY 3 · SMITHSBURG · HAGERSTOWN · WILLIAMSPORT · SOUTH MOUNTAIN · CATOCTIN MOUNTAIN · WESTMINSTER · BOONSBORO · FREDERICK · POTOMAC R.

→ LEE'S ARMY LINES OF RETREAT
▰▰▰► STUART'S DEFENSIVE ACTIONS
▱▱► FEDERAL ATTACKS

Miles
0   5   10

palacios

STUART SHIELDS LEE AFTER GETTYSBURG

After dark he led the men to the York turnpike and camped. At this hour Lee's main army was withdrawing to ridges west of Gettysburg, leaving the wreckage of Pickett's attack on the slopes before Cemetery Ridge. Stuart did not learn of this until late at night when he rode to headquarters and was told, in an atmosphere of gloom, that the army would lie the next day, and then retreat. His command was already exposed and isolated; he withdrew in the early morning of July fourth and joined the main army.

While Stuart fought, Union cavalry had struck gallantly at the far end of Lee's line, where Hood's Texans lay behind rock walls near the Round Tops, in difficult, broken terrain. The assault leader was General E. J. Farnsworth, lately promoted from captain; he was directed by Kilpatrick. There were many vain attacks.

The 1st West Virginia charged the Texans and died by the

score along a rail fence, trying to break it down with sabers; three times this regiment charged, and was cut to bits by musket fire.

Kilpatrick turned to Farnsworth: "Charge!"

"General, do you mean it?" Farnsworth said. "Over this ground, against an infantry brigade? These are too good men to kill like this."

"Do you refuse to obey my orders? If you're afraid I'll lead this charge."

Young Farnsworth stood in his stirrups, enraged. "Take that back!"

Kilpatrick apologized. "I didn't mean it."

After a moment Farnsworth said, "General, if you order the charge, I'll make it, but it must be on your responsibility."

Soon the 1st Vermont went through retreating skirmishers who begged them to turn back, passed the remnants of the West Virginia regiment, and went into a gallop. The 300 crossed the rocky front and emerged on a road in blinding sun, dashed through an ambush, and broke into the Confederate rear for more than a mile. They lost heavily. One of the casualties was Farnsworth, who shot himself with a pistol when an Alabama infantryman found him wounded and demanded his surrender. The Vermonters retreated, having accomplished their mission by drawing fire, piercing the Rebel flank and softening it for a possible infantry attack. It was in vain. The fighting was over.[8]

The cavalry brigades Stuart had left to guard the army's rear in Virginia had not closely followed the infantry, as they were ordered to do. In the welter of confusion and failure, Robertson had not crossed the Potomac until July first, and reached Cashtown, just west of Gettysburg, on July third. While Pickett's men charged and Stuart slashed vainly at the Federal flank, Robertson and Jones beat off a raid on the army's supply trains in the rear.

General Lee now ordered the rear-guard cavalry to nearby Fairfield, where the hundreds of wagons were parked. Jones, with three brigades, met the 6th U.S. Cavalry in a bloody fight in fields surrounded by stout rail fences that could not be broken. Riders charged over the open, but were halted at the rails, and fell under rifles of dismounted bluecoats. The 7th Virginia fled. Jones wrote: "A failure to rally promptly and renew the fight is a blemish in the bright history of this regiment."

The 6th Virginia came in, routed the enemy, and captured about 200 bluecoats. The wagons were safe.

Morning of July fourth brought a watery sun and lowering sky. In the infantry front men who had not eaten for more than a day crawled among the dead, rifling Federal knapsacks. Many retched at the sight and stench of the swollen corpses of men and horses which had lain there for three days. There was not a shot during the morning. General Longstreet expected a salute from the blue line at noon, greeting Independence Day, but the hour passed in silence. Old Pete said, "Their artillery was too much crippled yesterday to think of salutes. Meade is not in good spirits this morning."

Strangely, there was not a spirit of defeat in the army this morning; men waited hopefully for Federal attack on their hill. And though they could see the many casualties of Pickett's fateful charge on the far slopes, they were not in despair. That charge had cost almost 12,000 casualties, it was estimated, and of the fifteen field officers and four generals who had gone out with it, only Pickett and a lieutenant colonel returned unhurt.

The army gossiped quietly of what General Lee had said when it was over: "It's all my fault. . . . The blame rests on me. Form your line here, and be ready."

The cavalryman, John Imboden, had seen the commander late in the night, when all the staff and couriers had gone, when Lee said, "It has been a sad, sad day to us. . . . Too bad! Oh, too bad!"

It was clear, at any rate, that the campaign was ended, and that there would be no triumphal march through Washington, Philadelphia or New York. The casualties were staggering: at least 20,000 Confederate, and more than 23,000 Federal.

At one P.M. a deluge of rain fell and Imboden, trying to get off with his miles of wagons bearing wounded, struggled with mules and great wheels in mud. The wounded lay in the driving rain, and their plight only worsened when they were moved under canvas, in the jarring wagons.

The train started early and the infantry followed at dark, A. P. Hill, then Longstreet, then Ewell. The Potomac was forty miles away, and fording might be difficult. Meade's army could be expected to follow. The cavalry was divided to cover the separate lines of march, with a body left behind on the Gettysburg ridges to keep up campfires and shield the rear. The movement southward began slowly; there was not a sign of rout.

There was no rest for the cavalry.

General Imboden's role as escort to the wounded was as trying as that of the squadrons who beat off raids on the infantry. He rode in the rain on the night of July fourth, trying to reach the head of the train of misery, seventeen miles long:

"From every wagon issued wails of agony. For four hours I galloped. I was never out of the hearing of the groans and cries of the wounded and dying. Many of them had been without food for thirty-six hours. Their torn and bloody clothing, matted and hardened, was rasping the tender inflamed wounds. The road was rough and rocky. The jolting was enough to have killed sound, strong men. From nearly every wagon came cries:

" 'Oh, God! Why can't I die?'

" 'Will no one have mercy? Kill me and end my misery!'

" 'I am dying! My poor wife and children!'

"Some were praying; others were uttering the most fearful oaths and execrations. . . . There was no time even to fill a canteen of water for a dying man."

Imboden passed Greencastle, where citizens chopped down the wheels of the wagons of wounded, and were beaten off only by a cavalry squadron. There were minor attacks by the enemy, but at last he rolled into Williamsport, on the Potomac. There he had to lie in wait, with his few able-bodied men, clerks, cooks and cripples in a line of defense at the rear; the river was too high to ford, and must be bridged.

Far in the rear, in the passes of the Catoctin Mountains, Stuart's troopers fought in the rainstorm at night.

Captain G. M. Emack of the 1st Maryland cavalry defended his pass as if it were Thermopylae:

"I came across a lieutenant of a North Carolina battery, who had but one gun and only two rounds of ammunition. . . . I directed him to put both charges in his gun and await orders. Sergeant Sam Spencer was placed in rear with five men, while I advanced down the road, accompanied by Private Edward Thomas, until I met the head of the enemy's column. It was then dusk and raining; and as we wore our gum coats the Federal cavalry failed to recognize us. Without making any demonstration we turned and retreated before them at a walk, shielding the guns as much as possible."

The gun fired through the bluecoats, and in the turmoil Emack and his handful charged on horseback, and drove them back "more than a mile." As he turned back he heard: "From the shouting and firing among the retreating enemy we concluded that they had become panic-stricken and were fighting among themselves."

Emack called up the rest of his company and waited until a final enemy advance drove the rear guard from its position. Emack could smile even now as the Federals staged "a general advance with mounted and dismounted men and with artillery, firing at every step, which to us was rather amusing, as we were about a mile distant and lying snugly on the ground."

The rest of the night was fearful for Emack. A silent Federal attack came so near that a skirmisher stepped on a prone Confederate, who killed his man and opened a new skirmish. Emack's men tried to hold their position with stones when ammunition failed. Behind them, they heard the profane effort of General Jones and his staff officers to drive men of the 4th North Carolina cavalry to aid Emack's party; these riders would not budge, except for ten reluctant volunteers who came into line.

The bluecoats soon overran the position, wounding Emack and capturing more than half of his men. Federal riders dashed along the wagon train, breaking the column and taking hundreds of the vehicles and their weary teams.[9]

Even in the Federal ranks it was a formidable night. Captain Willard Glazier rode with Kilpatrick's horsemen against Emack's gun: "The darkness was so intense that the guns could be of little use, except to make the night terribly hideous with their bellowings, the echoes of which reverberated in the mountain gorges in a most frightful manner. To add to the horrors the rain fell in floods, accompanied with groaning thunders, while lightning flashed from cloud to cloud, only to leave friend and foe enveloped in greater darkness."

The Federals saw the Confederates flee "in wild dismay," and rushed along the crowded road, seizing hundreds of prisoners and wagons "mostly laden with the ripened and gathered crops of Pennsylvania and Maryland, and with the plunder of public and private stores. None who saw it will ever forget the appearance of that mountain road the day following."

Kilpatrick's men spread havoc among the wagons from three A.M. until daylight. The young general claimed to have destroyed nine miles of Ewell's wagon train, which seemed an exaggeration; Confederates were astounded at his claim of 1,860 prisoners. But there was no doubt that the blue tide had spilled through the pass into the valley beyond South Mountain, and Stuart's cavalrymen fell back.

At five P.M. of July fifth Stuart's column had a brush with the enemy near the hamlet of Smithburg, but though it seemed to the trooper Glazier that Kilpatrick had been "watching for him as a cat does a mouse," Jeb fought off the attack with ease, and followed the Federals toward Boonsboro, where they left their prisoners.

A Federal who had a glimpse of Stuart's men on this night wrote of them resting in Leitersburg: "A large number of his men were mounted on shoeless horses, whose leanness showed that they had made many a long march through and from Virginia. Or . . . they had fat horses stolen from the fields and stalls of the invaded states, but, being entirely unused to such hard and cruel treatment, were well nigh unserviceable."[10]

Stuart fought the next day near Hagerstown, just six miles from Williamsport, where the main army was concentrating for a crossing. The country was open, though much cut by fences; the two towns were connected by a straight macadamized road. The Federals were cleared from Hagerstown early, then driven from field to field, harried until they gave up a thrust at Williamsport. Jeb could not see all the fighting; a bluecoat sweep captured troopers from Robert-son's and Chambliss's brigades at Hagerstown; gray infantry turned aside to aid the riders half a dozen times during the day. It was a scramble without hope of victory; Stuart's only aim was to keep the enemy cavalry out of the army's camps. General Buford confessed Jeb's success: "Just before dark Kilpatrick's troops gave way, pass-ing to my rear, and were closely followed by the enemy. . . . The expedition had for its object the destruction of the enemy's trains, supposed to be at Williamsport. This, I regret to say, was not ac-complished. The enemy was too strong for me, but he was severely punished for his obstinacy."

The fighting north of the Potomac raged without respite until July twelfth. There was little food and almost no sleep; running fights flared on all roads of the region. The enemy did not break through, but as Lee's engineers struggled with their pontoon bridges and the river continued to rage at flood tide behind them, the troop-ers neared the limits of endurance. Toward the end they fought almost entirely on foot. On July twelfth Stuart removed his screen from the infantry position at the river side, but the enemy cavalry found the entrenchments too strong, and waited for Meade's in-fantry to come to their aid.

Major McClellan went with Stuart to the home of a Confeder-ate sympathizer in Hagerstown. At nine P.M. their young hostess invited the officers to dine. Stuart stirred briefly and shook his head. He would not eat.

McClellan knew he had eaten nothing in twenty-four hours, raised Stuart by his arm, and led him to the table: "His eyes were open, but he ate sparingly and without relish."

The young woman was anxious, thinking that the food was not to his taste. "General, perhaps you would like a hard-boiled egg."

"Yes," Stuart said. "I'll take four or five."

Silence followed, but the young woman soon had the eggs be-fore him. Stuart ate one, then rose from the table. The party returned to the parlor.

McClellan went to the piano and played, and began singing "Jine the Cavalry." Stuart joined in, becoming more animated, evi-dently for the first time fully aware of his surroundings. When Mc-

Clellan explained that he had been rude to their hostess, Stuart began an elaborate apology that lasted until they left the house.

McClellan saw him again when the toll of his long expedition seemed too much for Stuart. At night, on a turnpike near Hagerstown, McClellan and Stuart rode with one courier, as Jeb dictated dispatches to McClellan—orders for the next morning's movements of the brigades and artillery. The major needed light for writing and stopped at a tollhouse, calling for a lantern. The three riders went inside, where Stuart fell asleep as McClellan wrote. When he had finished he shook Stuart, who read the orders. The cavalry dispatches were approved as they were written, but Jeb scratched out the Maryland place names on the artillery orders and penciled in "Aldie" and "Shepherdstown."

McClellan saw that he was still more than half asleep, lost in the memories of the Virginia passes where the campaign had begun. "I aroused him with some difficulty, when my dispatch was rewritten, approved, and sent off."[11]

On the night of July thirteenth, as the Federal army began digging trenches in his front, Robert Lee started over the river. The infantry and wagons poured across in a night swept by rain, while behind them Stuart's dismounted cavalry manned their vacated entrenchments. There was a thrust by Kilpatrick's cavalry the next day, in which the enemy was allowed to come close to a crossing by the infantry, which mistook the riders for some of Stuart's. There was an hour of fighting, in which General Johnston Pettigrew was killed; the Federal cavalrymen lost heavily.

Stuart wrote of the final moments of the Gettysburg campaign: "The cavalry crossed at the fords without serious molestation, bringing up the rear on that route by 8 A.M. on the 14th."

It was almost exactly a month before that the first riders of Lee's advance had forded the Potomac, bound for invasion of the Yankee cities. It was twenty days since Stuart's brigades had made their rendezvous for the march. The greatest of the army's adventures was over.

If Stuart or the army had a sense of the cavalry's failure, there was no hint of it now, not even in Lee's orders to Jeb in the last phase: "I rely upon your good judgment, energy, and boldness . . . and trust you may be as successful as you have been on former occasions."

Jeb had written Flora on July tenth, amid rear-guard skirmishing:

> . . . I write to say God has mercifully spared me through many dangers and bloody fields. My cavalry has nobly sustained its reputation, and done better and harder fighting than it ever has since the war. Pray, without ceasing, that God will grant us the victory.

And on July thirteenth, from the riverside, he wrote her again:

> I had a grand time in Penna. and we return without defeat to recuperate and reinforce when no doubt the role will be reinacted. I shelled Carlisle and burned the barracks. I . . . went close to Georgetown and Washt. cutting four important railroads and joining our army in time for the battle of Gettysburg with 900 prisoners and 200 wagons and splendid teams. . . .
>
> We must invade again. It is the only path to peace. . . . Genl. Lee maneuvering the Yankees out of Virginia is the grandest piece of strategy ever heard of. If they had sent 10,000 reinforcements and plenty of ammunition to join him here our recrossing would be with banners of peace. . . .

☆

CHAPTER 18

The Receding Tide

THE army streaming southward in the heat of July provided at least one spectacle, for all the suffering of the Gettysburg campaign. Captain Charles Blackford recorded a glimpse of a Jeb unchanged:

"I was much amused to see Stuart pass through Martinsburg with a large cavalcade of staff and couriers and two bugles blowing furiously. Lee, Hill, Ewell and Longstreet passed, each with one or two persons with them and not even a battleflag to mark their rank. . . . I scarcely like to write this of so gallant an officer, but all of us have some weaknesses, and should be very liberal to each other."

Stuart approached The Bower in the same fashion, in such splendor that he might have been the conqueror of Gettysburg, rather than the subject of whispered criticism. His mood in camp was as gay as ever.

One day when it occurred to him that Esten Cooke's courage and nonchalance under fire entitled him to promotion, Jeb beckoned the young novelist.

"You're about my size, Cooke. But I suppose you're not so broad in the chest."

"Yes, I am," Cooke said.

"Let's see if you are," Stuart said. He stripped off his coat. "Try that on."

Cooke pulled on the coat with three stars on the collar and found it a snug fit.

Stuart laughed.

"Cut off two of the stars and wear it to Richmond," he said. "Tell the people in the War Department to make you a major and send you back to me in a hurry. I'll need you tomorrow."

Cooke was delighted, but the knighting ceremony was in vain, for Richmond officials sent him back with the assertion that "Stuart has too many majors." His friends thought Cooke's published criticism of the conduct of the war had offended the Davis administration and made his promotion impossible.

It may have been this that led Cooke to say bitterly: "I wasn't born to be a soldier. Of course, I can stand bullets and shells and all that, without flinching, as any man must if he has any manhood in him. . . . But I never liked the business of war. Gold lace on my coat always made me feel as if I were a child tricked out in red and yellow calico with turkey feathers in my headgear to add to the gorgeousness. There is nothing intellectual about fighting. It is the fit work of brutes and brutish men."[1]

Despite his failure in Richmond, Cooke became a major so far as the cavalry was concerned and Stuart afterward called him "Major"—a habit taken up by Robert Lee.

There were more important changes in the cavalry command. Beverly Robertson, who had disappointed Stuart by slow movements and failure to hold mountain passes in the Gettysburg campaign, recrossed into Virginia with only 300 men in his ranks. Robertson asked Lee to return him to the three regiments he had left in North Carolina, or give him a force commensurate with his rank. Stuart forwarded the request with a hearty recommendation that Robertson be once more removed from his command. The troublesome officer was sent to set up cavalry recruiting camps in the rear.

Richmond soon approved two divisions of cavalry, with Wade Hampton and Fitz Lee promoted major general to command them. Into the vacated posts Stuart put Calbraith Butler and Williams Wickham, and into Robertson's place, Lawrence Baker. The brigades were made smaller.

Two able men had been passed over: Tom Rosser, who was making a manful effort to overcome his excessive drinking, and writing pathetic letters about his struggle to his bride; and Grumble Jones, who was so resentful of Stuart that he had asked to be relieved before Gettysburg. Jones was incensed at Jeb's failure to urge his promotion, and an explosion followed.

Witnesses were secretive about what happened, but it was clear that Jones confronted Stuart and probably cursed him venomously. Jeb put him under arrest, charging him with using disrespectful language to his superior. General Lee sent a sketchy report of the affair to Jefferson Davis:

> I consider General Jones a brave and intelligent officer, but his feelings have become so opposed to General Stuart that I have lost all hope of his being useful in the cavalry here. . . . He has been tried by court-martial for disrespect and the proceedings are now in Richmond. I understand he says he will no longer serve under Stuart and I do not think it would be advantageous for him to do so.

Jones was sent to command cavalry in southwest Virginia, replaced by Rosser, whom Lee thought "an excellent officer in the field . . . prompt, cool and fearless, and has been wounded twice in this war."[2]

One more change was forced upon the corps, for Lawrence Baker was wounded in a skirmish, and the gifted James B. Gordon, a country merchant and political leader from Wilkes County, North Carolina, was put in his place.

The cavalry was preparing for action, but its troopers were still in distress. The enemy got word of it in an intercepted signal August seventeenth:

> Col. Corley: My command is suffering from want of clothing. What is the difficulty about getting it?
>
> Stuart.

It was two weeks later when the Federal signal corps learned that Jeb's riders were at last fully clothed.

The army fell back to the country near Orange Court House, a little to the south. There was a mood of depression around headquarters, for news from the western front was ominous: Vicksburg had fallen, laying open the Mississippi to complete conquest.

There were controversies in Robert Lee's command. George Pickett complained that his men had been sacrificed at Gettysburg, and only Lee's diplomacy silenced him. Lee himself felt the sting of failure, for he offered his resignation to Jefferson Davis:

> ... I have been prompted more than once since my return from Pennsylvania to propose to Your Excellency the propriety of selecting another commander for this army. I have seen and heard of expressions of discontent in the public journals. . . . No one is more aware than myself of my inability for the duties of my position. . . . I . . . anxiously urge the matter upon Your Excellency from my belief that a young and abler man than myself can readily be obtained.

Davis rejected the offer, saying: "Our country could not bear to lose you."

Other criticism centered about Stuart's role at Gettysburg. One source of it was Colonel Charles Marshall of Lee's staff, who was thought by Stuart's officers to be hostile to their chief. For weeks Lee urged Marshall to complete his official papers for the report on Gettysburg. Marshall collected reports from all commanders except Stuart. He wrote: "General Stuart was applied to more than once. He said he was busy preparing it, and promised me several times to send it in."

When Marshall told Lee the cause of delay, the commander urged Jeb to hurry the document. At last Stuart took his campaign report to Marshall, asked him to read it with care, and give him his opinion of the handling of the cavalry.

Marshall pored over the pages as if aware of the classic controversy which would ensue. Jeb outlined reasons for his every movement. He had crossed the Potomac east of the Union army, he wrote, because he had thought of making a raid on Washington—but was prevented by orders to rejoin the infantry as soon as possible. He also wrote that he could not obey Lee's order to join the right of the infantry, since he would have drawn the stronger Federal cavalry to that point. This move, he claimed, would have permitted the bluecoats to cross the mountains and fall upon Lee, since the cavalry could not have held all passes against them.

When Marshall had read the document Stuart asked: "Colonel, don't you think I had fair reason for not coming in on the infantry's right? I drew all the enemy cavalry away from the Catoctins, and made General Lee's wagon trains safe."

"I think it would have been far better for you to have obeyed orders, General Stuart," Marshall said. "General Lee did not order you to protect our trains. He had placed his infantry so as to do that himself. The object of keeping you on our right was to inform the army of the enemy's movements. General Lee knew nothing, since you were gone. He did not know that Hooker had crossed the river until days later."

Stuart flushed. "When I crossed the Potomac I found that Hooker had crossed the day before, and sent General Lee a message by way of Ashby's Gap."

"We never got that dispatch," Marshall said coolly. "And if we had got it, we still had no cavalry to get information for us."

"I admit I moved at my own discretion," Stuart said. "I got General Lee's last letter that you wrote for him. It seemed to allow me to take my own course. I was sure I could ride around Hooker and rejoin the army before the enemy came in."

Stuart left Marshall with obvious hard feelings between them. This was only the beginning of the controversy over Stuart's part in the Gettysburg campaign; there were to be interminable discussions of Lee's rather vague orders, and Stuart's bold interpretation of them.

Lee did not hesitate to discuss the matter with his officers. General Hoke approached headquarters one day and found Lee writing at a table. Hoke turned away.

"Be seated, General," Lee said. "I am just preparing my report on the battle of Gettysburg. I have taken all the blame. But had General Stuart kept me informed as he should have done, all would have been different. He stopped to capture a wagon train, and what was a wagon train compared with the tremendous issues we had at stake?"

Not long afterward Lee was discussing the campaign with General Henry Heth, and said to him, "After it is all over, as stupid a fellow as I am can see the mistakes that were made. I notice, however, my mistakes are never told me until it is too late."

Most important of all, perhaps, Lee told General Eppa Hunton: "It took a dozen blunders to lose Gettysburg, and I committed a good many of them."[3]

But in the field, and especially around the signal post on Clark's Mountain, Stuart seemed unaware of criticism. Charles Taylor, a Confederate signalman, recorded a scene at the semaphore station. (The scoffing infantrymen called signalmen "flag flappers"; they often halted a busy semaphorist with his snapping flags: "Say, mister, are the flies bothering you?")

Officers came to Clark's Mountain one day with a number of women. One pretty girl from Charleston, South Carolina, asked if she might send a greeting over the system. She wanted to pay her respects to "a gallant general known as a ladies' man."

The signalmen sent off her message and there was soon a reply. "Do you want me to deliver it?" the grinning signalman asked the girl.

"Why, yes, of course."

"Well, the message is: 'General Stuart sends a kiss to Miss A. B.' "

The girl blushed and left with her laughing escort.

Another witness from the same post saw more:

"General Lee would come up and spend hours studying the situation with his splendid glasses; and the glorious Stuart would dash up, always with a lady, and a pretty one, too. I wonder if the girl is yet alive who rode the general's fine horse and raced with him to charge our station.

"When they had reached the level platform, and Stuart left her in care of one of us and took the other off to one side and questioned the very sweat out of him about the enemy's position, he was General Stuart then, but when he got back and lifted the beauty into the saddle and rode off humming a breezy air . . . he was Stuart the beau."[4]

There were several weeks of peace in the country around Culpeper, with the cavalry almost in idleness; the center of Jeb's line was near Brandy Station. The enemy had at last crossed the Potomac in an effort to follow up the victory at Gettysburg, but General Meade appeared cautious and uncertain and remained on the line of the Rappahannock. Private Luther Hopkins, the observant trooper in Stuart's ranks, kept his journal as usual:

"General Stuart threw out his pickets across the fields, and just in front of us the enemy did likewise. The pickets were in full view of each other, and a long range musket might have sent a bullet across the line at any time, but we did not molest each other. At night the lines came still closer together, and we could distinctly hear them relieving their pickets every two hours. . . .

"For several weeks not a shot was fired, and so well acquainted did the pickets of each army become that it was not an uncommon thing to see them marching across the fields to meet each other and exchange greetings, and often the Confederates traded tobacco for coffee and sugar. . . . This got to be so common that General Stuart had to issue an order forbidding it."

Stuart spent the days in keeping watch over the enemy and in an almost frantic effort to recondition the cavalry. In late July he ordered "Company Q" abolished, saying that it shamed crippled men, degraded the cavalry in general, and hampered operations. There was no more banding together of unfit men and horses when the corps was moving.

He asked General Lee for better firearms, and tested the commander's patience on this score. Lee replied that he had sent an ordnance expert to Richmond to see what could be done, but added:

> There are many difficulties in the way of arming the cavalry thoroughly, and keeping it in that condition. Few cavalry arms are imported, and those manufactured in the Confederacy are generally rejected. I fear there is great carelessness, too, in the preservation of arms. . . . Where infantry arms have been issued to the cavalry, it is stated that they have either been turned in or thrown away in nine cases out of ten. . . . Recently 600 Enfield rifles and Mississippi rifles were sent to Culpeper for the cavalry division. The brigade ordnance officer declined to receive them, saying the men would not take them.
>
> From the nature of the cavalry service, it is almost impos-

sible for the ordnance officers to enforce the rules of the Department. Regimental and company commanders should be held to rigid account.

In short, Lee despaired of exercising proper discipline over the cavalry, and did not expect it to be properly armed. He added a final admonition bearing on the effectiveness of the cavalry under Stuart:

> I think your dismounted men should be speedily organized, and thoroughly drilled as infantry, and armed to be used as infantry, until they can be mounted.

Stuart tried to account for guns used by his men, and sent stern orders to his generals. The experience of Thomas Rosser, attempting to trace the discarded rifles of Elijah White's wild Virginia riders, was typical. White's men simply refused to carry guns, for their kind of war was headlong charging with sabers, and spirited night rides to surprise the enemy. Rosser sent an officer to White's headquarters with orders to make out a detailed report.

"Go ahead," White said. "Let's find out."

The officer shuffled papers of the command and said at last, "Colonel, I see that 340 guns have been issued to your command. What report do you make of them?"

White turned to his adjutant: "How many guns we got?"

"Eighty, sir."

"How do you account for the 260 missing?" the investigator asked.

White was nonplussed. There was a silence, broken by a young Comanche lolling on the tent floor: "Cunnel, ain't them the guns that busted in Western Virginny?"

"By golly, yes," White said. "They did bust. You sent us them drotted Richmond carbines, and they like to have killed all the men."

The officer solemnly recorded: "260 guns bursted in Western Virginia."[5]

And, as Lee wrote to President Davis, the whole state of the cavalry worried him, and prevented his putting the army into action against the waiting Meade:

The cavalry also suffer, and I fear to set them at work. Some days we get a pound of corn per horse and some days more; some none. Our limit is 5 pounds per day per horse. You can judge of our prospects.... Everything is being done by me that can be to recruit the horses. I have been obliged to diminish the number of guns in the artillery, and fear I shall have to lose more.

On September thirteenth, in this state of unpreparedness, the cavalry was called to action. General Meade moved at last, probably led on by news that Longstreet and his corps had been detached from Lee's army and sent into the West, where it was to join bitter fighting in Tennessee. The Union advance did not fall without warning from cavalry headquarters.

Late in the night of September twelfth, a cavalry surgeon slipped through Union lines and gave Jeb a brief report: The Yankees will cross at daylight, in force.

Stuart put the wagons and the sick and injured on the road southward and got his command into position.

Private Hopkins was on the front line as the bluecoats swarmed across. He had a surprise in store: "They began a movement toward our front, but so considerate were they that they did not open fire on us until we had gotten beyond range of their guns. This fraternal condition perhaps never existed before between two contending armies."

It was short-lived this morning. Stuart's middle division, commanded by Lunsford Lomax, fell back before a superior force under Judson Kilpatrick. Hopkins wrote:

"When we had retreated about a mile, they began firing on us. The friendly sentiment was soon dissipated, we returned the fire, and began to dispute their passage. My part of the line carried me directly through the streets of Culpeper, and the fighting in and around the town was the heaviest that we encountered. Several of our men had their horses killed, and I saw the enemy's cavalry pick up the men as they ran."

The retreat carried back to the Rapidan, and the Union army poured over the plains into its new position.

For a few more days the armies watched each other across a stream. There was little action even at cavalry headquarters. Stuart devoted some time to writing a humorous report. He had gone after the Federal General Joseph Bartlett and looted his headquarters in a night raid. He had missed the general, Stuart wrote, because that officer "fled precipitately in his nether garments."

He also added a colorful but migratory character to headquarters in St. Leger Grenfell, a Britisher who had been in the Crimean War, fought Riff pirates from his own yacht, and seen action in the Sepoy Mutiny and South American wars. He had run the Federal blockade to fight with the Confederacy. Stuart was cool toward the elderly eccentric, who affected side whiskers and stalked about with an air of icy reserve.

There was brief action on September twenty-second from which Jeb was lucky to emerge with his skin. General Buford's troopers advanced from Madison Court House and Stuart clashed with them at Jack's Shop, a tiny settlement. Confederate charges did not bend the blue lines. Jeb ordered the men to charge dismounted, and just as they were flung back, learned that a big Federal force had taken the road in his rear. Stuart was surrounded, and evidently could not handle even the force in his front.

When he tried to extricate his men in front, Buford threw in heavy attacks. There was a ford to the rear by which the Rebels might have escaped, but the flanking party, under Judson Kilpatrick, already held the crossing. Stuart moved backward, and the battle flowed into an open field. Stuart sent his artillery to a knoll and began to fight for life. Major McCellan wrote:

"Stuart's artillery was firing in both directions from the hill, and in sight of each other his regiments were charging in opposite directions. If Kilpatrick could have maintained his position Stuart must at least have lost his guns."

But Jeb was not done. He charged Kilpatrick with a regiment and when the front ranks reached the rail fence shielding the enemy, the men dismounted and pulled it down. The whole command had soon galloped through, brushing past Kilpatrick's band. They recrossed the Rapidan at Liberty Mills and when an infantry division came up, were safe. Stuart considered the action so minor he did not report on it.

Grenfell had an embarrassing day: In the midst of action, when affairs seemed hopeless, the Englishman fled, swam the river under fire, and went back to headquarters, reporting Stuart and his command captured. He could not again show his face in camp.

October opened with a new move by Robert Lee. He planned an offensive like that of the year before, when he had turned John Pope's flank. This time he intended a quick march to Culpeper to take Meade's army in a vulnerable position. By October seventh the enemy was aware that something was up. Federal signalmen intercepted Stuart's message:

> General R. E. Lee:
> Send me some good guides for country between Madison Courthouse and Woodville.
>
> Stuart

On October ninth, Stuart's third child was born, a girl, whom he advised his wife to adorn with a patriotic name, Virginia Pelham. And on that very day he led off Lee's new maneuver. The cavalry went to Madison Court House and the infantry moved after it the next day. Stuart led his regiments in a series of minor engagements, and fought without Fitz Lee, who held the position vacated by Lee's army, and was busy beating off cavalry attacks himself.

Stuart camped at Madison Court House on October ninth, and for two days skirmished toward Culpeper, where he found that Meade's infantry had crossed the Rappahannock to the north. But in this neighborhood Kilpatrick had massed bluecoat cavalry for a head-on clash.

Stuart had only five regiments, some 1,500 men, to pit against the Federal 4,000. He encountered Kilpatrick's main force on October tenth and waited several hours, fending off major action until he heard Fitz Lee's guns approaching from the Rapidan. Stuart immediately swung away from the enemy, going by farm roads for the enemy rear, planning to take Fleetwood Hill, where he had come so near disaster in the spring.

Kilpatrick saw Stuart's column moving across the open country and outraced him to the heights, placing guns there and striking in column at the Confederates.

Fitz Lee was slow in coming up, but when his regiments approached, Colonel Rosser turned the moment to his advantage by charging Kilpatrick's main body as it galloped against Stuart. Rosser wrote: "Never in my life did I reap such a rich harvest in horses and prisoners."

There was a fierce cavalry fight around Brandy Station for the rest of the afternoon. Private Hopkins saw it from the front ranks:

"After a good deal of maneuvering and waiting we saw the long lines of Union cavalry coming over the ridge and moving toward us in line of battle . . . when they got within 200 yards of us, their leader ordered a charge, and it looked as if the whole column was coming right into our ranks. . . .

"I noticed that quite a number of them, perhaps every third man, was reining in his horse, which meant, 'I have gone as far as I mean to go.' Of course . . . we knew by this action they were whipped, but the others came on, dashing right into our ranks, firing as they came. The dust and smoke from the guns made it almost impossible to distinguish friend from foe."

After this there was a lull, when Hopkins and his commanders wondered what lay behind the ridge in front. Their curiosity was soon satisfied, for they saw the first onslaught of Fitz Lee's men:

"Presently we saw a magnificent sight. The Colonel of the 5th Virginia regiment, mounted on a beautiful black horse, moved forward, calling upon his regiment to follow him. It was Colonel Rosser.

"As the regiment moved toward the enemy's lines at a gallop, the cry went up and down the ranks, 'Look at Rosser! Look at Rosser!' Everybody expected to see him tumble from his horse, shot to death, but he went forward, leading his men, and when the enemy discovered that we were coming in earnest, they turned on their heels and fled. . . . When we reached the top of the ridge we found that the enemy were disappearing in the distance as fast as their flying horses would carry them."

These affairs had a very different look from the saddle of Willard Glazier, the brave diarist in Kilpatrick's New York Light

Regiment, who described the heavy fighting at Brandy Station on October eleventh, where Kilpatrick was all but surrounded:

"Nothing daunted, Kilpatrick proved himself worthy of the brave men. . . . Forming his division into three lines of battle . . . he advanced. . . . He ordered his band to strike up a national air. . . .

"Custer, the daring, terrible demon that he is in battle, pulled off his cap and handed it to his orderly, then dashed madly forward in the charge, while his yellow locks floated like pennants on the breeze. . . .

"Fired to an almost divine potency, and with a majestic madness, this band of heroic troopers shook the air with their battle cry, and dashed forward to meet the hitherto exultant foe. Ambulances, forges, and cannon, with pack horses and mules, all joined to swell the mighty tide. . . . The Rebel lines broke in wild dismay. . . . No one who ever looked upon that wonderful panorama can ever forget it. On the great field were riderless horses and dying men; clouds of dust from solid shot and bursting shell occasionally obscured the sky; broken caissons and upturned ambulances obstructed the way, while long lines of cavalry were pressing forward in the charge, with their drawn sabers glistening. . . .

"The Rebel cavalry, undoubtedly ashamed . . . reorganized their broken ranks, and again advanced. . . . For at least two long hours of slaughter these opposing squadrons dashed upon one another over these historic fields . . . and at times the blue and gray were so confusedly commingled together that it was difficult to conjecture how they could regain their appropriate places. . . . It was a scene of wild commotion and blood. This carnival continued until late at night, when the exhausted and beaten foe sank back upon safer grounds to rest, while our victorious braves . . . gathered up their wounded and dead companions, and, unmolested, recrossed the Rappahannock."[6]

In any event, it had been a bloody day for cavalry, and it ended with the last of the Federals north of the Rappahannock. General Lee pressed on, still trying to flank Meade; Stuart led the way upstream on October twelfth, and fought General Gregg's cavalry near Warrenton Springs. Rosser and his men, who had been left behind, spent a hectic day trying to stem the onrush of the Federal infantry, as Meade pushed southward, trying to puzzle out Lee's intentions. After nightfall, some of the cavalry bands were moved about in the woods near Brandy Station, playing loudly to deceive the enemy as to the size of the Confederate force. The musicians need not have troubled, for during the night Meade learned that Stuart was on his flank and retreated to the open country around Manassas. Stuart led the chase, and on October thirteenth took his men into a trap which provided laughter for the army for months.

Lee's infantry lay around the town of Warrenton, with Meade's advance some nine miles east, at Warrenton Junction. Between the two was the village of Auburn, no more than a post office, a blacksmith's shop, and a house. The country was rough, forested and hilly, and near the village was Cedar Run, a steep-banked creek.

Stuart went through Auburn, where he dropped off Lomax and his brigade, and with two brigades and seven guns advanced toward the Orange and Alexandria Railroad. He sent William Blackford ahead to scout.

Some three miles outside Auburn the road dropped into the open plain, across which ran the railroad. Blackford went no farther. Below him was Meade's wagon train, thousands of wagons parked together under heavy guard. Blackford lay in a clump of brush and sent a courier back for Stuart, who soon arrived.

Blue divisions marched along the tracks as the horsemen watched, a major movement, Stuart thought. He called Major Reid Venable:

"Go through Auburn, where Lomax will be holding the road open. Tell General Lee the enemy is going north along the railroad, and in a big hurry. The army could hit him in the flank."

Venable left them. Stuart continued to study the tempting park of wagons, but concluded that the main Federal army was much too near to risk an attack. A courier galloped up.

"Enemy back of you!" he said. "A whole damned army!"

When Stuart, Blackford and their little party reached the brigades, they saw two Federal corps marching through Auburn. Lomax and his command had already been driven off. Venable had been forced far around the village, through the hills.

Stuart and his two brigades were cut off from Lee's infantry by an entire wing of Meade's force—with the rest of the enemy just to the east. Jeb looked about for means of escape.

North of them broken and wooded ground tumbled to the horizon. To the south, beside the road he held, was a deep millrace, too wide to cross. Stuart instantly found a simple means of saving himself.

Virtually within sight of the Federals in Auburn a small wooded valley opened on the road. He herded the command into this hidden pocket, and with the enemy marching all about, had the men lie quietly the rest of the day. He placed pickets in two bodies twenty yards apart, with orders to remain in hiding when large troop formations came by—but to allow single horsemen to pass and trap them between posts. This stratagem caught several Federal couriers in the night, and told Stuart some of Meade's plans.

It was an anxious night. Most of the men lay in a grassy field atop their ridge, looking down on the Federal army, which marched past no more than 150 yards below. Stuart and his staff heard talk of Union soldiers. Blackford recorded the night watch:

"General Stuart threw himself down by my side and laid his head on me and in an instant was fast asleep. Hour after hour passed and the General's head on my middle became rather heavy for comfort, but I was reluctant to disturb him. It got so bad at last that I was compelled to move it gently to another part of my body, but this awoke him and I then snatched a few hours' sleep."

Most of them did not sleep. Since they were so near the enemy, Jeb had each ambulance mule guarded by a soldier; when the animals brayed they were beaten into silence with saber scabbards.

Late in the night Jeb sent five men off with word of his plight, told them to try and break through the enemy lines, reach General Lee, and ask for a diversion of artillery fire on the village of Auburn. All of them got through by the ruse of falling into the Federal column, marching for a time, and dropping out on the far side. Stuart's command waited for rescue in the midst of the enemy infantry.

Officers proposed plans of escape. One said:

"We can leave the guns and wagons, mass the squadrons, and ride over the Yanks. We'd be gone before they knew what hit 'em."

Jeb shook his head. "I won't leave 'em a gun or a wagon," he said.

He proposed a scheme of his own: "We could stop one of their wagon trains, and turn it off to the west, as if some superior officer had ordered it—and then fall in behind it with the whole command, and march off to safety."

The staff laughed over the plan, but it was abandoned. Daylight came.

The Federals in their front turned to the opposite side of the road to cook breakfast. Stuart was forced to wait.

Anticipating the attack by General Lee, he had his gunners load all the artillery pieces, ready to be pulled to the roadside by hand. The sun was almost an hour high before the cavalrymen heard from the Army of Northern Virginia, a rattling of musketry sweeping up the road.

Stuart turned his seven guns on the breakfasting Federals at point-blank range, and the camp was soon a shambles of flying coffee pots, pails and flaming brands. The brave Federals put out a skirmish line, but General Gordon led a mounted charge of North Carolina troopers and swept them back.

The fight broke off after a few moments and the cavalry was safe. Stuart complained that Lee's infantry had come up too slowly; the foot soldiers protested that Stuart's artillery shells had fallen in their front, holding them back. The army followed the enemy.

Stuart's report of the affair grumbled over the failure of the infantry: "A vigorous attack with our main body at the time that I expected it would have assured the annihilation of that army corps."[7]

Meade was now concentrated around Bristoe Station, on the Orange and Alexandria Railroad slightly to the east. The Confederate infantry followed him there, and with A. P. Hill in the van, recklessly charged. Within fifteen minutes Hill's corps had 1,000 casualties and the enemy took five of his guns.

General Lee did not hide his disappointment at this end of the campaign. Frank Peak, one of Jeb's troopers, overheard him scolding Hill on a roadway: "General Hill, your line was too short and thin."

Another heard Lee say as he looked over the bleak scene of

Bristoe, "Very well, General, bury these poor men and let us say no more about it."

The infantry pulled back to the south, but there was a final bit of action for Stuart, who followed Meade to the neighborhood of the old Manassas battlefields. Jeb called the clash The Buckland Races.

On the night of October eighteenth, Stuart went into camp at Buckland, a bit southwest of Manassas. He was alone, for Fitz Lee was below him at Auburn. At dawn on October nineteenth the enemy advanced by the road from Fairfax Court House. The Federal Willard Glazier wrote:

"Dripping wet and somewhat stiffened with cold, we were ordered in battle array early in the morning, and the command, about 2,000 strong, advanced toward Buckland Mills. The Rebel pickets were quickly withdrawn, and their whole force slowly and without resistance retired before us."

But Stuart had a reception planned. As he began to fight Kilpatrick, Jeb had word from Fitz Lee that he was on his way to Buckland; Fitz added a shrewd plan of battle: "Let Kilpatrick come on, and withdraw in front of him down the Warrenton Road. When he has passed Buckland I will come in with my command and cut him off in the rear." Stuart adopted the plan, and through the morning retreated, leading on the Federals. The trap worked to perfection.

Glazier described the situation:

"With some degree of hesitation, yet unconscious of immediate danger . . . Our advance brigade had just passed New Baltimore, when Fitz Lee . . . fell upon our rearguard and opened upon our unsuspecting column with a battery of flying artillery. . . . Stuart, who had hitherto retired before us quietly, now turned about and advanced upon us with terrible determination. . . . Scarcely had we time to recover our sense from the first shock of attack upon our rear and front, when General Gordon, with a third division of cavalry, until now concealed behind a low range of hills and woods on our left, appeared with a furious attack, which threatened to sever our two small brigades."

Only a determined attack on Fitz Lee got Kilpatrick past the barrier in his rear, and the flight was on. The Federals lost over 300 men in the action, many of them drowned in the creek near Fitz Lee's force. The affair ended with Stuart charging the New York Harris Light in a roadway, as Glazier said: "Amid deafening yells. Our men stood firmly, almost like rocks before the surging sea. We were soon engaged in a fierce hand-to-hand conflict." Glazier was captured here.

Stuart had taken almost 1,400 prisoners in the ten days of skirmishing. His loss was 400. It was Stuart's last victory over the Federal cavalry corps.

His troopers were far from comfortable, for they fought under miserable conditions in this weather. Private Hopkins complained:

"In this section the farmers had no chance to plant crops. The trees had already been stripped of fruit. We could not even find a persimmon and we suffered terribly with hunger.

"We were looking forward to Manassas with vivid recollections of the rich haul that we had made there just prior to the second battle of Manassas, and everybody was saying, 'We'll get plenty when we get to Manassas'. We were there before we knew it. Everything was changed. There was not a building anywhere. The soil, enriched by debris from former camps, had grown a rich crop of weeds that came halfway up the sides of our horses, and the only way we recognized the place was by our horses, tumbling over the railroad tracks.

"While fighting just below Manassas, the enemy threw a shell in among the led horses, which burst and killed several of them. A short time after that, while lying in camp, our stomachs crying bitterly for food, someone suggested that we try the horseflesh. I remember pulling out my knife and sharpening it on a stone preparatory to cutting a steak from one of the dead horses, but just at this point a caravan on horseback arrived with a supply of food. We had a rich feast, and were happy again."

About this time, when the cavalry were fording a stream beside a bridge, General Lee scolded General Lomax. The cavalrymen were wet to the knees.

"My, General!" Lee said, "you should have used the bridge below."

Private Hopkins commented: "I suppose General Lomax thought that as we were soldiers we ought not to mind a little wetting even if the cold November winds were blowing."

Lee put the army into camp around Culpeper, and defended the line of the Rappahannock once more. But on November sixth Meade came forward, after repairing the railroad, and the next day stormed over the river at Kelly's Ford and a neighboring railroad bridge. Confederate infantry losses were heavy. The army dropped back below the Rapidan once more. There was a brief rest.

Meade pushed over the Rapidan at Germanna and Ely's Fords on November twenty-sixth. Hampton's troopers aided the infantry in checking him, but the Federals remained in threatening position south of the Rapidan, and General Lee had his infantry dig trenches along Mine Run, hopeful that he was to be attacked.

Hampton, who was only now recovering from his head wound suffered at Gettysburg, offered Lee the key to possible victory at Mine Run—but it was in vain.

On November thirtieth the enterprising South Carolinian rode on reconnaissance to the right flank overlooking Federal lines. If infantry could strike here, he reasoned, Meade could be rolled up. Stuart inspected the flank, agreed with Hampton's diagnosis, and passed the information to Lee.

The following movements were too slow, for when Lee pulled two divisions out of the trenches to throw them around the flank, he found the enemy had recrossed the river. Lee could not hide his disappointment.

"I am too old to command this army!" an aide heard him growl. "We should never have permitted those people to get away."

Stuart had sent William Blackford to General Lee with the report of a scout that Meade was ready to move, and the captain saw Lee in a rare mood. The commander walked about his headquarters angrily: "Captain, if they don't attack us today, we must attack them! . . . We must attack them, sir! And you young men must exert yourselves. You must exert yourselves, sir!"

The Federals were gone, in any event, and the cavalry could

not be blamed for the lost opportunity. Blackford reported a final scene as the armies lay near together in the frost:

A farmhouse between the lines, almost picked clean, was the refuge of a lone turkey, which sometimes strutted in the roadway in no man's land. One day a Federal soldier shot the bird, after many attempts, and amid the triumphant shouts of his companions, ran into the open to retrieve his game. A shot from the Confederate lines killed him. A Rebel then dashed into the road, reaching for the turkey. A Union bullet killed him, and the two bodies lay, freezing, across that of the turkey.

Lee's headquarters were glum. Richmond was trying to persuade the commander to go to the West, in an effort to save Tennessee, and he once left for Richmond, saying to Stuart, "My heart and thoughts will always be with this army," as if he feared he could not return. In the end President Davis sent Joseph Johnston to the border command.

Lee's health was poor, and he had word of the death of Rooney's wife and children. The suffering of the men moved him, and he was forever writing Richmond in an effort to get shoes, blankets and food. Fevers became common in the city of huts in which the army lived.

One of winter's victims brought great sadness to Stuart: Sam Sweeney succumbed to smallpox, and the band was never the same, though there was still music almost nightly.

There was a cavalry review in the cold weather, of which Captain Frank Myers of the 35th Virginia Battalion wrote: "The brigade was ordered to join the division on the historic plains of Brandy Station, where General Stuart purposed holding another of his 'spread-eagle' grand reviews, which did no good except to give Yankee spies an opportunity to count the exact number of cavalry attached to the Army of Northern Virginia, and to display the foppishness of Stuart, who rode along his war-torn lines with a multitude of bouquets, which fair hands had presented to him, fastened in his hat and coat."[8]

Stuart had comfortable quarters, which he styled "The Wigwam," and wrote to Flora in Lynchburg, asking her to visit him, saying that he enjoyed the luxury of a private entrance, and that he had her favorite camp horse, "Lily of The Valley," in fine condition for her. He advised her to bring a riding habit.

There was at least one gay pause in the routine of camp life, a ball held in Montpelier, the old home of President Madison, an occasion remembered by many cavalry veterans who saw Stuart, Fitz Lee, Williams Wickham and the rest of their officer corps dancing with women of the region.

Stuart also made occasional trips to Richmond, and for the first time capital society was able to lionize him. General Gorgas, chief of Confederate ordnance, saw him in January, 1864, at the home of Mrs. George Randolph, when a party was enjoying charades. Also in the group were other major generals, Hood, Buckner and Elzey, and a number of brigadiers. Gorgas noted: "Stuart is fond of society, but entirely abstemious as to drinks."

And Mrs. Semmes, wife of the Senator from Louisiana, landed Stuart for a party in her home opposite the Confederate White House. Many leading figures were on hand for the charity affair, among them President and Mrs. Davis, Secretary Judah Benjamin, Secretary of Navy Mallory and his wife, and Burton Harrison, the President's secretary. Several diarists were there, including lovely Constance Cary, soon to become Mrs. Burton Harrison; Mrs. James Chesnut, wife of a leading Presidential advisor; and T. C. deLeon, who seemed to be everywhere in the city.

The crowd had gathered to dance and watch a series of charades and tableaux, now the rage in the city.

The stage was soon set for the spectacle for which the crowd had come. The audience was seated and actors appeared as a band of pilgrims on a stage dominated by a cross and an altar. An orchestra struck up a tune: *Hail, The Conquering Hero Comes!*

DeLeon was impressed: "Forth strode grand Jeb Stuart in full uniform, his stainless sword unsheathed, his noble face luminous with inward fire. Ignoring the audience and its welcome, he advanced, his eyes fixed upon the shrine until he had laid the blade, so famous, upon it. Then he moved to a group, and never raised his eyes from the floor as he stood with folded arms."

The evening was an immense success. DeLeon recorded more

than one such visit by Stuart, some of them made with Esten Cooke, when Jeb's "manly voice would troll out—merrily, if none too correctly—the camp ditty linked with his name: 'If you want to catch the devil, just jine the cavalry.'"

Constance Cary saw Jeb and Fitz Lee in another night of charades in a Richmond home—when they went on a strike which was quelled by her pretty cousin, Hetty Cary. Stuart and Lee were detailed to help hold aloft the scenery, and were packed into a closet behind a butler's pantry to steady a ladder for the performers.

"I won't stay here," Stuart said, "unless Miss Hetty will come and talk to me." He won that concession, but when the show began and Constance took the stage, Jeb's attentions to Hetty caused pandemonium. Constance wrote:

"Just as I had seated myself upon the stile, held up by General Stuart in the rear, and Vizetelly was prepared to make his swaggering entrance from the side . . . my perch gave way and I slid to the ground."

She darted behind the scenery to scold Stuart, who "protested abject penitence for having forgotten for the moment and let go, and promised better behavior." Miss Cary was firm, however, and the laughing Stuart was banished into the audience and the show went on with Fitz Lee holding the ladder. Fitz declared virtuously: "No young lady can make me forget my responsibility as a step ladder."

But Constance Cary was not entirely lost in the careless laughter. "In all our parties and pleasurings, there seemed to lurk a foreshadowing of tragedy, as in the Greek plays where the gloomy end is ever kept in sight."

One officer sorely missed by the city's young women was von Borcke, who had been nursed back to health in the Price home, Dundee, since his wounding before Gettysburg. Connie Cary had found the Prussian giant fascinating the year before: "To dance with him the swift-circling, never-reversing German fashion was a breathless experience, and his method of avoiding obstacles in the ballroom was simply to lift his partner off her feet, without altering his step, and deposit her in safety farther on."

But now, though he was sometimes seen in Richmond, he was

"painfully thin and emaciated," Connie Cary thought. His throat wound was still dangerous, for the bullet was lodged against his windpipe, and any unusual exertion upset him. He wheezed horribly through his wound at every breath. He once startled Miss Cary:

"Once, when sitting in our drawing room he insisted upon leaning over the back of a sofa to pick up a wandering thimble from the floor, the effort bringing on a frightful fit of coughing and struggling for breath, which my mother dealt with skilfully, while we girls assisted with tears streaming from our eyes."

Von Borcke got some satisfaction from a joint resolution of thanks from Congress in January, and he noted that the last foreigner to win such an honor was Lafayette. The resolution said in part:

Having ... by his personal gallantry on the field ... won the admiration of his comrades, as well as of his Commanding General, all of whom deeply sympathise with him in his present sufferings from wounds received in battle, therefore—Resolved by the Congress of the Confederate States of America, that the thanks of Congress are due, and ... tendered to Major Heros von Borcke for his self-sacrificing devotion to our Confederacy.

The Prussian occasionally saw Stuart in Richmond, and once or twice visited the cavalry camp near Culpeper.

He wrote: "I was received on all hands, from the General down to the last courier, with so much tender attention that I was deeply touched, and felt it hard to tear myself from the gallant fellows."

He tried to take the field, but a short time on horseback brought on a relapse, and he again went to a sickbed.

Jeb soon suffered another loss from the staff: William Blackford left him to help organize an engineer corps for General Lee. Stuart was out of camp on the January day when Blackford left, but he sent him a letter:

To say that I part with you with regret is a poor expression of what I feel. To no member of my staff have I felt the same bond of attachment, dating to the ever memorable First

Manassas. . . . We do not part as those who part to meet no
more. . . . I trust we shall meet again, with no tears to shed,
but glad in the sunshine of victory, till peace shall encircle with
her rainbow the Independent Confederate States.

They had met for the last time. With Blackford's departure,
all but Esten Cooke of the old-time staff had gone. Jeb had intimate
ties with his surgeon, Dr. John Fontaine, and with young Theo
Garnett, but the veterans with whom he had lived through so much
were all gone: Burke and Farley and Pelham, Hardeman Stuart and
Channing Price, dead, and von Borcke wounded.

There was a final challenge from the enemy before the winter's
end. On February twenty-eighth two Federal corps lurched forward
through the snows from Culpeper toward Madison Court House,
and General Custer, with about 1,500 horsemen, took Charlottesville. Stuart went toward the town with Wickham's brigade through
a sleet storm, but found the enemy had retired. Stuart turned north
in the hope of catching Custer; when he reached his road of retreat
one regiment had already passed the spot. Jeb settled down to wait
for the main column.

It was an unpleasant night, for freezing rain pelted men and
horses and when morning came the command was in a pitiable state.
Custer's column, in superb condition, charged down the road,
knocking aside the few pickets in its path, and passed Stuart toward
its base.

While Stuart was occupied in this region, the enemy launched
its major attack, a raid on Richmond by almost 4,000 of Judson Kilpatrick's cavalrymen. The raiders crossed the Rapidan at Ely's Ford,
and with Stuart out of the way and Lee's infantry snug in its camps
to the west, struck for the capital. They rode through The Wilderness in the sleet storm and spent the night at Beaver Dam Station,
huddling around huge fires to keep warm.

Kilpatrick split his force during the day, sending southward
about 500 men under young Colonel Ulric Dahlgren, who rode with
a wooden leg—he had lost a limb in the Gettysburg fighting. Dahlgren's men went through Spotsylvania Court House to approach

Richmond from the south, while the Rebel chase concentrated on Kilpatrick's men to the north. Dahlgren was to fight his way to the Rebel prison at Belle Isle, free the 15,000 Union soldiers held in its pens, and dash through the city to rejoin Kilpatrick.

By morning, Kilpatrick was within five miles of Richmond on the north, on Brook Turnpike, banging away with his few guns. Nothing had been heard from Dahlgren. Kilpatrick gave up at dark, recrossing the Chickahominy to camp. Some of Dahlgren's men came in with an ominous report.

The 500 had reached the James without incident, but when Dahlgren tried to cross the river with the aid of a freed Negro, he ran into trouble. The spot to which the Negro took him was high and unfordable, and there were no boats. Dahlgren, in a nasty temper, hanged his guide and tried to approach Richmond on the north bank of the James.

Dahlgren ran into the outskirts of Richmond as the light began to fail, and was stung by infantrymen at every turn. He went northward, crossing a network of roads, but there was no escaping the Rebels. The column had broken in two, and 200 of them, at Dahlgren's heels, were off somewhere in the darkness.

By now, as Kilpatrick must have suspected, the cavalry regulars of the Army of Northern Virginia were on his trail. Stuart was too far away to reach him, but Wade Hampton, leading 306 men of the 1st North Carolina, crept upon Kilpatrick's camp at Atlee's Station in the night while a snowstorm raged, ran up his artillery to close range, and blew the camp apart. Kilpatrick went into retreat, losing 87 men as prisoners, 133 horses, and much equipment. Hampton's men hung on Kilpatrick's rear the next day, until he retreated to Williamsburg. Nor was that all.

The Rebel advance drove Dahlgren and his little band off the main highways, as he made his way toward Gloucester Point. He crossed the Pamunkey and Mattaponi Rivers, and was seen by cavalrymen who were recruiting in the area. They laid a trap for him.

On the bitter night of March third Dahlgren ran into an ambush near King and Queen Court house, laid for him by Lieutenant James Pollard of the 9th Virginia with a few regulars and some of the Home Guard—about 150 men in all.

Dahlgren's half-frozen troops were almost in the midst of the Rebels before they were aware of danger. Dahlgren was one of the first to fall, shouting, "Disperse, you damned Rebels!" The Confederates stripped his body, taking the wooden leg as a souvenir and robbing his hand of a ring. The command surrendered, finding its escape impossible. Pollard took 135 troopers and 40 Negroes prisoner.

Soldiers found orders on Dahlgren's body, and reported them to Richmond. As Pollard's messenger made his way toward the capital he met some officers of the 9th Virginia, who listened eagerly to his news of the ambush and examined the papers found on Dahlgren's body. Colonel R. L. T. Beale remembered inspecting them:

"Nearly every paper had been copied in a memorandum book; they consisted of an address to the command, the order of attack . . . upon the city of Richmond, enjoining the release of the prisoners, the killing of the executive officers of the Confederate Government, the burning and gutting of the city, directions where to apply for the materials necessary to setting fire to the city, and an accurate copy of the last field return of our cavalry made to General Stuart, with the location of every regiment."

Beale forwarded all papers to Richmond except the memorandum book, and when publication of the papers brought a furor of Confederate protest, Beale was interrogated by officers and asked to produce the book. General Lee wrote General Meade, asking if this type of warfare had his approval, and a denial was issued from Washington.

The raid ended in failure, but it had thoroughly aroused the capital and given it a new sense of insecurity. As Captain Myers of the cavalry wrote:

"The Yankee nation is indelibly disgraced by the objects of the expedition, and Stuart's laurels wilted by his failure to annihilate the whole party."[9]

Spring came on imperceptibly. Longstreet returned to the army from the west. The Yankees got a new commander in March, a stranger: U. S. Grant, who had been winning victories in the Western theater. He installed a new cavalry commander, Philip Sheridan.

Stuart wrote frequently to Flora, urging cheerfulness upon her, for her own letters were full of her fears. He once wrote that she must be gay at all costs. For one thing, she must never wear black, no matter whose death came next. He added:

> There is an old lady here, who danced a jig with my great uncle at my mother's wedding. She wears a turban and is an elegant old lady. Major Venable remarked the other day that she is never so happy as when she is miserable. It reminds me of my darling, when she will insist on looking on the dark side in preference to the bright. . . . Have you heard the words of *When This Cruel War Is Over?*

He gave her brief glimpses of his camp life:

> I think I will make Cooke write my reports when he comes back, I am so behind on them. I have brigade reviews every day . . . every General and Colonel in the infantry appears to have his wife along.

There were now about 8,000 cavalrymen on the rolls, a miracle in itself. But Stuart was not satisfied. He sent a remarkable dispatch of instruction to General J. R. Chambliss:

> April 4th, 1864
> (Confidential)
> General: I wish you to bear in mind a few considerations . . . as the commander of the outposts on the lower Rappahannock.
> Keep out scouts who will be competent. . . . Endeavor to secure accurate information and telegraph it clearly, avoiding the possibility of ambiguity for which telegrams are noted. It is very important to state time and place of enemy's movement. . . . Bear in mind that your telegrams may make the whole army strike tents, and night or day, rain or shine, take up the line of march; endeavor, therefore, to secure *accurate* information. . . .
> Do not let a feigned movement deceive you . . .
> Above all, *Vigilance*, VIGILANCE! VIGILANCE![10]

CHAPTER 19

In The Wilderness

B. L. WYNN, a Mississippi sergeant, was in command of the Clark's Mountain signal post on the night of May third. He was asleep when one of his men shook him awake near midnight.

"Look. Yanks moving."

It was true. Through his telescope Wynn saw dark forms slipping by against the distant campfires of the enemy, thousands of them, in regular order. Wynn flashed a message rearward toward the headquarters of General Lee. There was a quick reply:

> See if they are going toward Germanna Ford or Liberty Mills.

Wynn could not make out the direction of the Federal advance in the darkness. The signal flares flashed through the night. At daybreak Wynn saw that the blue columns had turned downriver, and that the attack would be launched through The Wilderness. General Grant would be pushing across at Germanna Ford. It was quite a sight Wynn beheld: Miles of men and vehicles, an army of almost 103,000, with 50,000 horses and 4,000 wagons. General Lee waited south of the river with little more than half that force.[1]

Lee sent the infantry of Ewell and A. P. Hill into The Wilderness to meet the threat, down parallel roads through the overgrown hilly and gullied terrain. Stuart went at once to his picket line on the river, carrying only one courier with him. His staff had orders to break up the comfortable camp at Orange Court House.

The gunner George Neese, in the Horse Artillery, wrote in his diary:

May 4—I heard today that the Yankee army is crossing the
Rapidan in great force, and that General Lee is on the march
to meet it. If that is true, we will soon be in the middle of some
bloody work. This evening at sunset we broke camp and are
now marching to the front. Farewell, my peaceful cabin.

Stuart and his staff slept that night behind the pickets. The
troopers were moving behind them, going to the right wing of the
army.

Early on May fifth General Lee sent for Stuart to guide the
infantry, and Jeb trotted along the Plank Road with A. P. Hill's
corps until they met the enemy. General Lee came up about noon,
when heavy firing broke out, and with Stuart, Ewell and Hill studied
the situation. The Confederate infantry lay on either side of the
Plank Road and confused fighting raged everywhere in the scrub.
Ewell's men broke and streamed in panic down the road; John Gordon's men restored the line. The bloody fighting went on through
the day.

The cavalry saw less of it than their commander. Private Hopkins wrote:

"It was mostly in heavy timber and thick undergrowth. The
first day we did not see the enemy, but we knew he was there, for
the woods were ringing with the sound of his guns, and bullets were
hissing about our ears. We knew somewhere in front of us was the
enemy, and it was our mission to find him. Suddenly we heard two
shots: pop-pop. We all knew what that meant. The armies of Lee
and Grant had met, and as far as I know, these were the first two
shots fired in the battle of The Wilderness. . . . We took the hint and
halted. The regiment was dismounted and the led horses were taken
back."

Gunner Neese had marched all night and was so sleepy that he
dozed, almost falling from his horse. He was evidently near Stuart in
the late morning, for he said:

"Today about 11 o'clock we sighted the first new goods of the
season in the way of live bluecoats. . . . They opened fire with their
artillery and fired on our cavalry at first sight and right away . . . and
were trying to do some ugly work from the start. We put two of our

rifled guns in position and replied. . . . Undoubtedly the Yankee batteries did the best and most accurate firing today that I have seen or been exposed to . . . their shrapnel shot exploded all around and over us, and the everlasting ping and thud of shells, balls and fragments filled the air with horrid screams for an hour. . . ."

Neese's battery fought in a field of dry broom sedge about two feet high, and the gunner was incensed as the "cowardly Yanks" set the field on fire.

Thomas Rosser's men had a sharp cavalry engagement with General Wilson far on the right, at Todd's Tavern.

The second day's onslaught by Grant was almost too much, for bluecoat charges drove the veteran Rebel infantry so hard that the men fled unashamed past General Lee, and the front was restored only by the timely arrival of Longstreet—and by Lee dashing toward the enemy himself, to be halted only by the frantic appeals of his troops. The armies grappled all day, and suffered fearful casualties. General Longstreet was badly wounded. The cavalry's share of it was a serious brush on the flank. Stuart still had found no opportunity to test the strength of the new Federal cavalry corps.

No one reported the day's passage more graphically than Stuart's gunner Neese, who fought on the flank with the Horse Artillery:

"The fierce, sharp roar of deadly musketry filled our ears from morning to night, and a thick white cloud of battle smoke hung pall-like over the fields. . . . The smoke was so thick and dense sometimes during the day that it was impossible to discern anything 50 paces away, and at midday the smoke was so thick overhead that I could just make out to see the sun, and it looked like a vast ball of red fire. . . . The country all along the lines, which is mostly timber land, was set on fire early by the explosion of shell and heavy musketry; a thousand fires blazed and crackled. . . . The hissing flames, the sharp roar of musketry, the bellowing of the artillery mingled with the yelling . . . the wailing moans of the wounded . . . all loudly acclaimed the savagery of our boasted civilization and the enlightened barbarism of the nineteenth century. Even the midday sun refused to look with anything but a faint red glimmer on the tragical scene being enacted in the tangled underbrush where the lords of creation were struggling and slaughtering each other like wild beasts in a jungle."

Late in the night, when the battle had died out, Neese watched the fires in the forest:

"The night is dark, and the woods around us are all on fire; all the dead trees scattered through the woods are ablaze from bottom to top, and the fire has crept out on every branch, glowingly painting a fiery weird scene on the curtain of night."

Daylight of May seventh brought calm; General Lee suspected Grant of a new maneuver, and he began to swing southward to Spotsylvania Court House, where he assumed Grant must strike next. By nightfall it was plain that Grant was moving; Lee's infantry was already on its way to intercept him.

In the meantime, Fitz Lee, with his division dismounted, was thrown in the Federal path. The troopers took terrible punishment, but were driven off only after daylight of May 8.

This morning found Stuart hastening toward Spotsylvania. Gunner Neese had a close look at him.

"Our orders to leave bivouac and hasten to the front this morning at daylight were urgent and pressing, and we had no time to prepare or eat any breakfast, which greatly ruffled some of our drivers. When we neared the enemy's line we awaited orders, and one of our drivers was still going through the baby act about something to eat and having no breakfast.

"Just then General Stuart and staff came along, rather on the reconnaissance order, and halted a moment in the road right where we were, and heard the gallant grumbling and childish murmuring of our hungry man."

But Jeb did not react as Neese expected. Stuart fished into his own haversack, pulled out two biscuits, handed them to the complaining driver, and trotted off under the stares of his astonished artillerymen.

Private Hopkins, going rearward with the Horse Artillery, was one of the first to see the working of Lee's strategy in withdrawing to Spotsylvania:

"When we fell slowly back, we looked behind us and saw a gorgeous sight. It was Grant's line of battle moving forward as if

on dress parade, their brass buttons and steel guns with fixed bayonets glistening in the sun, their banners floating in the breeze. The
first thought among the soldiers was, 'Has Grant stolen a march on
Lee? Is Richmond doomed?' It certainly looked so, but we kept on
falling back.

"As we entered the woods we suddenly came upon Lee's infantry lying down in line of battle, waiting the enemy's advance. As
we approached them, word was passed up and down the line not to
cheer the infantry. This was the custom in the face of a battle, when
the cavalry, retiring from the front, gave way to the infantry.

"They opened their ranks and let us pass through, and we
formed in line some distance behind them. The infantry was entirely
concealed from the enemy's view, and up to this time I am quite sure
Grant did not know that he was facing Lee's army at Spotsylvania
Courthouse. He was soon to be undeceived in a manner most tragic."

U. S. Grant rode through The Wilderness in the night of May
seventh with yellow storms of fire in the thickets around him. He
left 18,000 casualties uncounted behind him, determined to hammer
past Lee to Richmond. He knew only: "Our losses in The Wilderness were very severe."

He was accompanied only by a small cavalry escort. Federal
infantry cheered madly at sight of him. Grant supposed that this was
because the path led south, at last, and there was hope that the worst
of the rebellion was over. He remembered the yells above all else:

"The cheering was so lusty that the enemy must have taken it
for a night attack. At all events it drew from him a furious fusillade
of artillery and musketry."

Grant rode the strange roadways, until he reached a fork and
took the right, where scouts imagined they saw the tracks of Sheridan's cavalry. A picket came back with the tale that he had heard
Rebels marching. Grant retraced his steps, and shortly after midnight was at Todd's Tavern.

His vanguard was pushing down the Po River, a slight but deep
stream with high, overgrown banks which snaked down out of The
Wilderness. Beyond it lay the village of Spotsylvania, the prize for
which the armies raced.

It was not an imposing place: Three houses, a small church and a scattering of outbuildings sat on a level plain, surrounded by low hills. The land was barren and wild, chiefly covered in scrub oak, not more than fifteen feet high, but thickly tangled so that men could hardly push through it. There were rare clearings, occupied by mean houses.[2]

Confederates had begun to arrive in large numbers soon after Luther Hopkins and the artillery rode through the hidden infantry. Another gunner, Willie Dame, who went in with the crack Richmond Howitzers, recorded a hard night march, undertaken without sleep. The next day brought worse:

"The morning of May 8 broke, foggy and lowering, and found us still moving swiftly along . . . our battery seemed all alone on a quiet country road. The birds were singing around us, and it seemed to us, so sweet! Everybody was impressed by the music of those birds. The note of a bird was a sound we rarely heard.

"By and by the sun came out and began to make it hot for us. At last, just about 12 o'clock, our road wound down to a stream . . . and then we went up a very long hill, a bank, surmounted by a rail fence on the left side of the road, and the woods on the other.

"Just as we got to the top (our battery happened just then to be ahead of all the troops). . . . a farm gate opened into a field, and there, covering that field, was the whole of Fitz Lee's division of Stuart's cavalry. These heroic fellows had for two days been fighting Warren's corps of Federal infantry, which General Grant had sent down to seize this very line on which we had now arrived. They had fought dismounted, from hill to hill, fence to fence, from tree to tree, and so obstinate was their resistance and so skillful the dispositions of the matchless Stuart, that some 30,000 men had been forced to take about twenty-six hours to get seven or eight miles, by about 4,500 cavalry. . . . This was a 'white day' for the cavalry."[3]

Stuart had spent most of the day as an infantry officer, herding Anderson's men toward Spotsylvania while Fitz Lee's weary troopers went back stubbornly, in lines so tight that only the full pressure of the oncoming Yankee columns pushed them across a road junction near Spotsylvania. Casualties were heavy, but when the dismounted troopers came within sight of the courthouse they saw the reassuring lines of Anderson's graybacks behind them, already digging in. Lee's objective was safe.

Pelham's old battery checked the first Federal rush at the courthouse. The four guns were under command of Captain P. P. Johnston, and though James Breathed had been promoted major of the battalion, he fought at Johnston's side. They tore up charges of Union cavalrymen and made a spectacular defiance of the enemy.

The guns barked steadily until the blue skirmish line, seeing the battery without apparent support, charged it with a yell.

Breathed and Johnston kept the guns hot until the last moment, and only when Federals were shouting for them to surrender from three sides did Breathed order the guns to the rear. The driver of a team fell under the fire, and Breathed jumped into the saddle and took the piece from the field. He soon outdistanced the enemy.

As the bluecoats swept over the crest of a ridge they met an unexpected volley from Anderson's prone infantry. The blue wave fell back; the battle of Spotsylvania had fairly begun.

Stuart sat near the courthouse where Federal columns were concentrating. General Anderson asked his help once more, and Stuart put dismounted troopers into line, stretching the infantry ranks to the left. He remained for several hours, but as troops from other corps came down from The Wilderness and the infantry fighting assumed major proportions, the command passed from his hands.

Major McClellan was worried about Jeb during these hours: "He exposed himself to fire with more than his usual disregard of danger, in spite of the repeated and earnest remonstrances of several of the infantry officers."

Only McClellan of his staff was with him now, and Stuart kept him galloping with messages.

McClellan at last realized, after he had been sent on several unimportant missions, that Stuart was simply protecting him from danger. He protested:

"General, my horse is weary. You are exposing yourself, and you're alone. Please let me remain with you."

Stuart smiled, but he sent McClellan off to Anderson once more.

More and more bluecoats appeared in front. Night brought
sporadic fire, and then quiet. May eighth drew to a close.

Stuart left the scene which General John B. Gordon would one
day describe to audiences, holding his long arms horizontally from
the shoulders: "My dead were piled that high, and three days after
the battle I saw wounded men trying to pull themselves from under
the mass of the dead above them, and the slopes were so slippery with
blood that my soldiers could not stand until the ground had been
carpeted with the bodies of their fallen comrades."[4]

U. S. Grant's unassailable calm had ended a squabble at Federal
headquarters during the day. Little Phil Sheridan, scarcely taller
than a musket, had been spilling over with fury, and let his temper
flow into official dispatches: If he was to fight cavalry, let him fight
it. George Meade would hobble them forever, with his everlasting
nibbling away at the command, taking troopers to guard wagon
trains, prisoners, picket lines. If this war was to be won on horseback,
the cavalry corps must be concentrated to fall on the enemy flank
and rear. He could take it to Richmond, now or any day. Meade
made evasive replies. Grant overruled him, and sent his favorite
horseman off on the first proper raid of Federal cavalry Virginia had
seen.

"I directed Sheridan verbally to cut loose," Grant said, "pass
around . . . Lee's army and attack his cavalry; to cut the two roads—
one running west through Gordonsville, Charlottesville and Lynchburg, the other to Richmond. . . ."

Phil Sheridan understood. He began at once to improve on
Grant's intentions. There was dangerous country below, but Stuart's
brigades were growing thin; he would cut around the Confederate
fringes and go for Richmond. If Stuart came into his path, all the
better.[5]

☆

CHAPTER 20

Yellow Tavern

THE bluecoat riders were ready before dawn of May ninth. Sheridan found them with one day's rations in their knapsacks, and half rations, at that. But no matter; it was a trifling detail when stakes were so high. Merritt's division was put in the lead. It moved from camp at Silver's Plantation near Fredericksburg at four thirty A.M. Sheridan had the rest moving by five o'clock.

They wound southeast past Tabernacle Church and into the Telegraph Road, the main north-south artery from Fredericksburg to Richmond. The column went by Massaponax Church as it struck this road, and there was seen by Confederate pickets. The report that these riders took to Williams Wickham, at the nearest headquarters, almost defied belief:

The column seemed endless, from 12,000 to 15,000 troopers, with artillery and wagons. They stretched out over thirteen miles of road. And this time they were not galloping desperately. They walked, as if they meant to take their time, and feared nothing.

Coming down the Telegraph Road, the blue troopers crossed the Ny, the Po and the Ta, any of which would have made a good line of defense for Stuart. The Federal vanguard moved slowly at the streams until, near the village of Jarrald's Mill, the last of these three watercourses was crossed without a sign of the enemy. Then Sheridan thought: "Our ability to cross the North Anna was unquestionable." Once he crossed this river to the south, Richmond would be within his grasp. The pace quickened.

Within two hours after Sheridan had cleared Massaponax Church, Wickham's pursuit was well under way. Stuart soon had the news himself. He advised headquarters at eight A.M.:

General R. E. Lee:

General—There is a demonstration of the enemy's cavalry on the Fredericksburg road about one mile and a half from
Spotsylvania Courthouse. If it amounts to anything serious I
will be sure to inform you in time to change your dispositions.
I have sent a regiment down to engage them and see what it
means.

Stuart was then off across country eastward to strike the Telegraph Road. He could take only Fitz Lee and the brigades of Lomax
and James B. Gordon, for Rosser must be left to guard Lee's infantry. Even when Stuart joined Wickham and combined forces, he
would have no more than 4,000 riders, but he pressed on as if he gave
no thought to the odds. The force approached the Telegraph Road
as darkness came.

Stuart by now had news that Sheridan's vanguard had left this
main road and turned southwest through the villages of Mitchell's
Shop and Chilesburg toward Beaver Dam Station. The word must
have spurred the chase, for not only was the greatest remaining store
of food and medicine for Lee's army at Beaver Dam; Flora and the
children were there, too, in Sheridan's path. She was visiting with
Colonel Edmund Fontaine at his plantation house, in what had
seemed yesterday a place of safety.

Sheridan's men kept to a methodical pace as Stuart pounded
after them. At four P.M. Wickham fell upon the Federal rear.

The little skirmish at Mitchell's Shop was gallant enough, but
Wickham's men were pawing at a massive force. The big blue regiments, the 6th Ohio and the 1st New Jersey, stood firm on a hill
near Mitchell's Shop as Wickham dashed his squadrons against them
one after another—he had only 1,000 men.

Major McClellan recorded that, when one or two attacks had
recoiled, Wickham called Captain George H. Matthews of the 3rd
Virginia, a veteran up from the ranks, saying, "I know Matthews
will go through."

Matthews formed a column of fours and led the handful of
troopers into the Federal line, bowled over riders until he forced the
head of his column through—and was lost to sight. The blue ranks

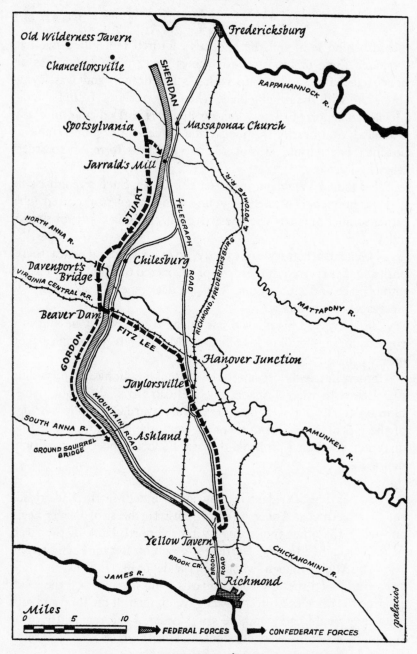

Old Wilderness Tavern

Chancellorsville

Fredericksburg

RAPPAHANNOCK R.

SHERIDAN

Spotsylvania

Massaponax Church

R.F.&P. R.R.

Jarrald's Mill

STUART

TELEGRAPH ROAD

NORTH ANNA R.

Davenport's Bridge

VIRGINIA CENTRAL R.R.

Chilesburg

RICHMOND, FREDERICKSBURG & POTOMAC R.R.

MATTAPONY R.

Beaver Dam

FITZ LEE

GORDON

Hanover Junction

MOUNTAIN ROAD

Taylorsville

SOUTH ANNA R.

Ashland

PAMUNKEY R.

GROUND SQUIRREL BRIDGE

Yellow Tavern

CHICKAHOMINY R.

JAMES R.

BROOK CR.

BROOK ROAD

Richmond

Miles

0   5   10

→ FEDERAL FORCES   → CONFEDERATE FORCES

palacios

STUART BLOCKS SHERIDAN'S RICHMOND RAID
May 9–11, 1864

closed behind him, and the Federals captured ten, killed five and
wounded three of his band. Matthews went to the ground as his
horse fell, but scrambled up with a saber drawn, and was laying
about him with the ringing blade when he was shot, "from behind,"
McClellan reported. The admiring Federals carried him, mortally
wounded, to a nearby farmhouse and made him as comfortable as
possible. The skirmish was over; there was little to report to Stuart
when he arrived.

Jeb joined Wickham just after this brush. Such strength as he
had was now concentrated. A young staff lieutenant reported Jeb's
rather somber manner when he arrived after his hard ride of sixteen
miles:

"General Stuart rode up quietly, no one suspecting he was there,
until a soldier crossed the road, stopped, peered through the darkness
into his face and shouted out, 'Old Jeb has come!' In an instant the
air was rent with huzzas."

Stuart waved his plumed hat to the troopers, but he said in a
voice sounding "sad" to his officers: "My friends, we won't halloo
until we get out of the woods."[1]

Stuart hurriedly organized the chase. He split his force, sending
Fitz Lee with three brigades on Sheridan's trail. He took James
Gordon's command with him westward, toward Davenport's Bridge
of the North Anna. From there he would be able to move in any
direction. It seemed probable that the Federal objective was Richmond itself.

By this time Sheridan's leading corps, under Merritt, had crossed
the North Anna at Anderson's Ford, just northeast of Beaver Dam,
and while the other two corps lay on the north bank of the river,
Merritt detached George Custer for a raid on Beaver Dam Station.

The Michigan men swept in on the depot like Indians, and their
yells frightened the few Rebel guards, who began firing the sheds
housing the priceless stores. Custer gave his men all the food and supplies they could carry and, he said, "ordered the remainder to be
burnt." The bonfire was enormous, and the fragrant odor of burning
bacon drifted over the landscape for days.

Custer's men destroyed about 1,000,000 rations of bacon and

more than 500,000 of bread. He listed the staples on hand in railroad cars and depots: bacon, flour, sugar, meal, molasses, liquor, medical stores, small arms, hospital tents. All went up in the night. Yellow light glowed from the clouds.

Flora Stuart watched the glare, and with her friends and children waited fearfully for the Federal troopers to descend upon the Fontaine house.

Custer's wreckers spread along the tracks of the Virginia Central Railroad and tore them up for ten miles. They burned three trains of cars—100 cars in all—and two locomotives. The telegraph wires were pulled down for miles, and culverts and bridges along the railroad were ruined. One of the most heartening coups to the Federals was the liberation of 400 of their men lost to the Rebels in The Wilderness; in the liberated throng were two colonels, a major and other officers. There was a hilarious reunion.

General Merritt had only one regret, that through "a misconception of orders or some other cause," the fires were lighted, betraying their position to the enemy and destroying needed supplies.

Stuart, however, had no need of the pillar of fire to guide him. He galloped south to Davenport's Bridge, where his vanguard sighted the enemy. General Merritt had sent his 5th Michigan Cavalry there to guard the flank of his Reserve Brigade as it crossed the river farther to the east.

Stuart's troopers made the 5th the victims of their intimate knowledge of the country. The memory of the affair remained only in Merritt's formal report of the day's work: "In withdrawing, this gallant regiment, with its accomplished commander, Captain Arnold, at its head, charged and made its way through a very superior force of the enemy which, by crossing blind fords on the river, had interposed between him and the main command. Of necessity some few officers and men were lost as prisoners."[2]

Stuart had nothing else to detain him, and early on May tenth, through increasingly humid heat, he trotted into Beaver Dam, at a moment when the enemy rear guard was pulling out of the ruined village.

With only Major Reid Venable of the staff at his side Jeb rode to the Fontaine house, up a drive which wound for a mile and a half from the station, bordering the railroad of which Colonel Fontaine was president.

Flora greeted them at the house. Venable recorded the scene in sparse words:

"Mrs. Stuart came out, and after a few words of private conversation, the General (not dismounting) bade her a most affectionate farewell."

Then, having done no more than lean from his saddle to kiss Flora for the last time, Stuart wheeled his horse—he was riding the stout gray General today—and with Venable behind him went swiftly down the drive.[3] In her final glimpse Jeb's wife undoubtedly saw him as Esten Cooke had pictured him, magnificent on horseback, with none of the awkward long-leggedness of his walk, wearing tall black boots now mud-spattered from hard riding, and, though dressed to the nines, "looking like work," as usual.

At some point nearby, Stuart wrote his first dispatch of the day to General Lee:

May 10, 1864—8:45 A.M.

One of the 4th Virginia Cavalry reports the enemy at 7:30 o'clock this morning had reached a point on the road to Trinity Church [in Richmond], about one mile below Beaver Dam, going toward Richmond. . . . Fitz Lee is now crossing [at Anderson's Ford]. The other brigades, Gordon's and Lomax's, will . . . sweep down on the south side.

Stuart began a conversation in a tone his companion thought strange. Venable wrote:

"After riding some distance in silence, he told me he never expected to live through the war, and that if we were to be conquered, he did not want to live."

Stuart gave no hint of this frame of mind when he met Fitz Lee near Beaver Dam; instead he gave orders for the continuing chase. Stuart found that the main body of the enemy had gone south into the Old Mountain Road, running a general east-west course parallel to the South Anna River. Jeb once more divided his command: Fitz Lee would go with him, with the brigades of Lomax and Wickham. Gordon's North Carolinians would follow Sheridan's rear. Stuart would move to Hanover Junction in an effort to get between the enemy and Richmond.

He sent a dispatch to General Braxton Bragg in Richmond, the chief of staff to President Davis. There was little of the ornamental rhetoric here:

> General: A large body of the enemy's cavalry reached Beaver Dam yesterday at 5 P.M. and is now advancing in the direction of Richmond. . . . My cavalry have been fighting them all day yesterday and are still in his rear pushing on. Their rear left Anderson's Bridge at 8 A.M., where they camped last night.

Later in the day he sent another message into Richmond: The road to Richmond was barricaded with trees felled by Yankee raiders, and he was forced into a parallel route. He intended to spend the night at Taylorsville, just below Hanover Junction. He expressed only optimism to Bragg, as if this were only one of the ineffectual hit-and-run Yankee cavalry raids of the old days:

> Should he attack Richmond I will certainly move in his rear and do what I can; at the same time I hope to be able to strike him if he endeavors to escape. His force is large, and if attack is made on Richmond it will be principally as dismounted cavalry, which fight better than the enemy's infantry.

Stuart reached Hanover Junction long after dark. Here he learned that Sheridan's advance was on the South Anna by mid-afternoon, no more than twenty miles from Richmond.

Fitz Lee insisted that the troopers could no longer bear the punishment, but the weary column plodded a bit longer before Stuart gave in and allowed a halt.

He had wired Bragg at nine P.M. from Hanover of the Yankee position around Ground Squirrel Bridge on the South Anna, adding:

> There is none of our cavalry from this direction between the enemy and Richmond. Has the enemy made any demon-

stration upon Richmond? Please answer tonight, if practicable, as I am very anxious to give my command a night's rest, if compatible with duty.

His men already fell asleep in their saddles and at the roadside.

He got Bragg's reply to his query about the enemy and sent a message in return: He had just learned that Sheridan had gone into camp and would not menace Richmond further tonight. His scouts reported that the Federals were to have moved at midnight, however, and Jeb added in the message to Bragg:

> I am moving to Ashland. If I reach that point before the enemy, I will move down the Telegraph Road.[4]

The Richmond in which the anxious General Bragg dealt with Stuart's dispatches was in something of a state. Colonel Josiah Gorgas, the ordnance chief, wrote in his diary of the disaster at Beaver Dam, and of a fight to the east at Drewry's Bluff, where the infantry of Generals Butler and Beauregard had clashed. Gorgas could see from his window:

"The affair was done to attract the enemy from Petersburg. . . . The woods are on fire where the fight took place today and the horizon is lined with fires tonight in that direction. . . ."

Even if Stuart's cavalry saved the city from Sheridan, there was always the menace of Butler on the James, below the city. And Gorgas, in position to know the Confederate weaknesses, confided to his diary almost in the same moment:

"Hoke has, it is said, relieved Pickett at Petersburg. Pickett is very dissipated, it is said."

He was unable to give undivided attention to the journal, however, for as he wrote:

"I slept but a few hours . . . having been called up by messages, and kept awake by the ringing of alarm bells and the blowing of alarm whistles the most of the night. At five this morning I went to Mr. Seddon's office and found him laboring under the impression that the last hours of Richmond were at length numbered."

The city's militia, Gorgas recorded, had been shifted in the trenches, to the side now threatened by Sheridan; they were reinforced by a brigade of old men in uniform. The high Confederate official complained:

"As all my officers and clerks are in the field I am obliged to attend to details myself and have trudged about the streets until I am thoroughly tired."

There was another diarist in the city, Mrs. Alexander Lawton, wife of the Confederate Quartermaster General:

"There was a great alarm in the city. Many ladies sat up all night, dressed in all their best clothes with their jewelry on. Congressmen besieged the War Department all night—so that General Bragg was called out of bed to go down to them after midnight."

In the darkness, some twenty miles north of the troubled capital, Stuart and his command slept at last. Jeb took precautions. He called Major McClellan:

"Go with Fitz Lee's men. I've told them we must move at 1 o'clock. Go to Lee's bivouac, and don't close your eyes until you have seen them mounted and on the march, and on the dot of 1 o'clock."

Stuart went to sleep near Taylorsville. He crawled under a blanket with Reid Venable and was soon snoring, evidently as worn as his men.

Colonel Bradley Johnson, detailed to guard bridges, was nearby with a small band of Maryland cavalry. Stuart had sent a courier to him with a request for some guns, since he had so few himself, and probably must face Sheridan tomorrow. Stuart promised to return the battery promptly, if Johnson would part with it.

In reply Johnson rode through the night in search of Stuart, wandering among the sleeping squadrons. Johnson recalled:

"I rode at once to Taylorsville to see General Stuart. He was lying flat on his back, his head on a saddle, and so fast asleep that McClellan and I turned him over without being able to waken him."

Johnson dealt with McClellan. He was obliged to protect the bridges, he said, under orders from General Lee, and could not join the chase of Sheridan. Further, he wanted to be positive that Stuart would take the best care of his guns.

"I have brought the pick of the command's batteries," he told McClellan. "I want it returned as soon as possible—and intact."

McClellan assured him the guns would be safe, and Johnson rode off to his post.

At one A.M. McClellan roused Fitz Lee and watched sleepily until the riders were moving. Stuart was also awake by now. McClellan was overcome as the move got under way:

"I lay down to catch, if possible, a few minutes' rest. The party rode off as I lay in a half-conscious condition, and I heard some one say: 'General, here's McClellan, fast asleep. Shall I wake him?'

" 'No,' he replied, 'he has been watching while we were asleep. Leave a courier with him, and tell him to come on when his nap is out.' "

McClellan slept and later caught up with the column, which was trotting toward Ashland, in the direction of Richmond.[5]

Now Jeb led the main column to the intersection of the Telegraph Road and the Mountain Road, which came in from the west, where Sheridan was. Not far below the intersection—perhaps half a mile—was an abandoned inn, Yellow Tavern, a paintless ghost of another era.

The spot was just six miles from Richmond, at the northern end of the Brook Turnpike. The gunner George Neese described the landscape: "A beautiful, rich and productive country of fertile land. The Brook Turnpike is an excellent macadamized road leading out of Richmond . . . through a gently rolling country of green fields and cultivated farms and gardens."

At six thirty A.M. Stuart reported to Bragg:

> General, the enemy reached this point [Ashland] just before us, but was promptly whipped out after a sharp fight by Fitz Lee's advance, killing and capturing quite a number. General Gordon is in the rear of the enemy. I intersect the road the enemy is marching on at Yellow Tavern, the head of the turnpike. . . . My men and horses are all tired, hungry and jaded, but all right.

Two and a half hours later, at nine A.M., Jeb sent off two messages by couriers. One, to Bradley Johnson:

As the enemy may double back . . . you will oblige me very much by arranging it so that I may get the information in time to turn upon them before they get away. Be sure to barricade the roads with felled trees, in case they start in that direction. . . . Communicate with me by way of the Telegraph Road.

The other to General Bragg:

The head of my column reached Yellow Tavern at 8 A.M. No enemy had passed. Citizens and furloughed soldiers report them in heavy column gone toward Dover Mills. I will sweep across after them. I heard some firing toward their place of encampment about 7 A.M. Probably Gordon engaging them. The Central road is safe to Hanover Junction.

In short, Stuart was uncertain of Sheridan's next move, and could not yet determine his proper position. But in every line of his dispatches was the determination to strike, whatever the odds. His chief concern was the possibility of the enemy's escape.

McClellan rode beside Jeb as they came near Yellow Tavern. The Major found his commander pensive:

"We conversed on many matters of personal interest. He was more quiet than usual, softer, and more communicative . . . the shadow of the near future was already upon him."

Major Theo Garnett overheard Stuart chide one of his brigade commanders who said, "We'll never catch Sheridan. He's too fast and too big for us."

Stuart snapped: "No! I would rather die than let him go!"

Stuart was at Yellow Tavern itself by ten o'clock, with no enemy in sight. To the north the country was wooded and rough, becoming more level and open nearer the Tavern. There was a stream nearby; fenced fields almost surrounded the spot.

If he could depend upon General Bragg and the home guard to hold Richmond, Stuart would prefer to remain at Yellow Tavern, where he could hang on Sheridan's flank and worry him as he moved across the country. He must make sure of Richmond's safety, however. He sent McClellan galloping down the Brook Turnpike to see Bragg and get help, if possible. The day grew warmer as the

column waited. In the distance, from time to time, were sounds of
Gordon's hammering at the Federal rear.

In the Union column May tenth had passed almost peacefully.
Sheridan noted that, since he at last had food for men and horses,
"our next object was to husband their strength and prepare to fight."

There was a "futile" and light barrage of artillery fire from the
Confederate pursuit as his bluecoats left the North Anna, but the
column was too big for a full-scale assault by Gordon's party, and
the advance went on. Sheridan recalled it as a tranquil passage
through the rolling country: "The march was without much incident, and we quietly encamped on the south bank of the South Anna
(at Ground Squirrel Bridge) where we quietly procured all the
necessary forage, marching from fifteen to eighteen miles."

Sheridan also began to suspect that he had Stuart at last:

"It now became apparent that the enemy in following up our
rear, had made a great mistake, and he began to see it, for when we
leisurely took the Negro Foot road to Richmond, a doubt arose in
his mind as to whether his tactics were good, and urged his horses
to the death so as to get in between Richmond and our column. This
he effected, concentrating at Yellow Tavern."

The forces moved toward a collision in the late hours of May
tenth. Sheridan recorded his moves:

He ordered a brigade under General Davies to destroy a train
and tracks at Ashland; this force "rejoined the main column at Allen's
Station, on the Fredericksburg Railroad. From Allen's, the entire
command moved on Yellow Tavern, Merritt in advance, Wilson
next, and Gregg in rear. The enemy here again made an error in
tactics by sending a large force to attack my rear, thus weakening
his force in front, enabling me to throw all my strength on that
which opposed my front, and fight this force with a small rear
guard."

Sheridan was right, but the affair in his rear early on May
eleventh, though it was faint in his ears and posed no problems of
command, was fierce enough to men on the ground. The scene was
Goodall's Tavern, an old country hotel eighteen miles north of

Richmond, where part of Sheridan's command had spent the night. General Gordon and the North Carolina troopers galloped into the midst of the Federals at dawn. The 1st North Carolina, one of the finest of Stuart's regiments, was in front.

Colonel W. H. Cheek of the 1st recalled part of it: "The enemy filled the old hotel and all its outhouses, stables, barns with sharpshooters. Without artillery, we could not dislodge them. The fight between the dismounted sharpshooters lasted several hours."

General Gordon at last came up, took command, and sent Cheek to a flank with a squadron of the 5th North Carolina; this drove the enemy skirmishers in "great disorder" to their main body, and then Gordon's men clashed with Sheridan's rear strength, head-on. Cheek never forgot it:

"We had the most desperate hand-to-hand conflict I ever witnessed. The regiment we met was the 1st Maine, and it had the reputation of being the best cavalry in the Army of the Potomac. Saber cuts were given thick and fast on both sides. The staff of my colors received two deep cuts while the sergeant was using it to protect himself from the furious blows of a Yankee trooper. We drove them from the field, but our pursuit was stopped by a battery of artillery and a second mounted line which they had established a short distance in the woods at Ground Squirrel Church. . . . Here we had another hand-to-hand fight, which resulted in our breaking and hurling them back in confusion into the road. Here again was the saber freely used, and here it was that while I was pursuing a fleeing foe with the point of a saber in his back, his companion sent a bullet crashing through my shoulder."[6]

Colonel Cheek became a prisoner, the rear-guard skirmish was over, and the head of the Federal column, now almost a dozen miles to the south, came down on Yellow Tavern. The rear action, in brief, was gallant and spectacular, but Sheridan was only toying with Gordon.

In the blue ranks, with Company E of the 5th Michigan, Colonel Russell Alger commanding, was a trooper destined to play a vital role in the day's action. His name was John A. Huff. He had enlisted in October, 1861, at the age of forty-two, joining the 2nd U.S. Sharpshooters, which was to become famous as Berdan's Sharpshooters. He had won a prize as the regiment's best shot, an expert among hundreds of crack marksmen. But in 1863, after being wounded, he had been discharged on a surgeon's certificate: Disabled and unfit for duty.

Huff had returned to Michigan, but a year later, in January, 1864, had re-enlisted, this time in the 5th Michigan Cavalry. He had joined his regiment in Virginia not long before the coming of U. S. Grant and the spring offensive.

The army knew little enough about Huff, and until now had no occasion to know more. He was born in Hamburg, N.Y., the son of a journeyman Canadian carpenter who had migrated into Michigan by way of New York State and Ohio.

Trooper Huff was married, and had been a carpenter before the war. He had blue eyes, brown hair, and a light complexion; he was five feet eight and a half inches tall.

In the late morning of this May 11, 1864, as he rode down the last miles of the Mountain Road to the junction with the Telegraph Road, Private Huff, now forty-five, had only his age to set him apart from others of Company E, Fifth Michigan, Alger's regiment, Custer's brigade, Merritt's division.[7]

Stuart waited in the spring sunshine with perhaps 1,100 tired troopers, all that he had left to him today of the Cavalry Corps. Rosser was far away with the main army at Spotsylvania, and Gordon was in the rear of Sheridan. Two brigades, and no more. They filed around the tavern, seeking the best of the scanty cover.

About this time he wrote his last two dispatches—one dated nine forty A.M., the other evidently sent at about ten thirty. Both were addressed to Bragg. The first said in part:

> . . . The enemy is moving down the same route of march already indicated—that is by a road leading into the head of the Brook Turnpike. . . . I desire to keep in their rear and flank . . . if they can be kept in check we hope to punish them severely.

The second was written from very near Yellow Tavern itself:

> The enemy seems to be making demonstrations here only—but we cannot exactly tell yet—I think his attack more likely to be made somewhere between Brook Turnpike and James River—Please caution our troops not to let anybody of cavalry advance on any road without being halted—a sufficient distance and its real character, whether friends or foes, investigated.

Jeb turned to the disposition of his oncoming troops.

Lomax's brigade came in first and took position along the road with its left flank near Yellow Tavern. Lomax left Colonel Henry Clay Pate in charge and went to the rear to observe things from a hilltop with his staff. Pate scouted the ground and moved his skirmish line in a gully at the edge of a woodland, with pickets hidden in a growth of trees. The line was three quarters of a mile long, trailing from the junction of the roads southward to the Tavern.

Wickham's brigade came in on the right of Lomax, pushing the line north of the road junction some two and a half miles, to a place known as Half Sink. Most of the artillery was placed along the line of Lomax, since it was most exposed. There were now ten guns, including those of the Baltimore Light Artillery which Jeb had borrowed from Bradley Johnson. Sheridan's approaching column carried an estimated thirty-six guns.

The Confederates were dismounted, waiting; behind the lines Negroes and orderlies held the horses, which snatched at scant grass and switched their tails at the first flies of the season. Two cannon were exposed in the road, not far from the Tavern. Others were screened by undergrowth, on the sector where Pate commanded.

Colonel Pate, whom Stuart had first met in the days of John Brown in Kansas, had often clashed with his chief during the war; there were bitter feelings between the two. Pate got first attention of the enemy today.

The bluecoats came near noon. The first wave was commanded by Colonel Thomas Devin, 6th New York, who had orders to clear Brook Turnpike.

Devin found other Federals in the woods ahead of him who had not yet attacked—troopers of the Reserve Brigade. He studied Stuart's line about the Tavern and changed his tactics:

"Advancing the 17th Pennsylvania through the woods on the right, I swung around on the Turnpike, driving the enemy from and seizing the cross roads leading to Ashland and Hanover Court House. . . . I was then ordered to make a reconnaissance toward Richmond."

Devin's squadrons had no trouble circling Stuart's rear. They cut between the gray troopers and the capital and held Brook Turnpike, and went boldly to Richmond's outskirts, where the home guard was in trenches ahead of them. The advance of Devin stopped there, where its men could literally hear the heartbeat of the Confederacy: "The bells could be heard ringing, locomotives whistling, and general alarm and bustling seemed to prevail in Richmond," Devin remembered.

Back at Yellow Tavern, facing Stuart, Custer pushed his Michigan regiments into line, and General James Wilson strung another brigade on Custer's left. For two or three hours, just after noon, Sheridan's commanders perfected their line of attack.

Stuart watched. His frame of mind even now was probably about that of young W. W. Burgess, who lay with the Marylanders of Company K, 1st Virginia:

"Our only fear was that Sheridan would get away, as usual. That we would not whip him if we caught up with him did not enter our minds. . . . The enemy's cavalrymen were an insignificant looking set of men, but their horses and equipment were excellent."

Cyrus McCormick, a boy private of the 6th Virginia, watched the attack from near the Confederate center, where he and an elderly man stood picket under one of the aspen trees lining the road. When bullets began whizzing McCormick urged his little horse between the Tavern wall and a tree. The old man, whose horse was fat, could not make it, and after frantic spurring was stuck fast between tree and building.

McCormick wrote:

"We had been there half an hour when there appeared a great

cloud of dust enveloping quite a troop of horsemen. As soon as this
poor old man saw them he said, 'You do what you choose. I'm going
to surrender.' I said, 'Oh, don't talk such nonsense. Those must be
our own men. I don't understand how the Yankees can have gotten
on our right so suddenly.' Just then the cloud of dust raised, and the
awful apparition turned out to be General Stuart and his staff. . . . I
took position immediately behind them."

Stuart studied the enemy with field glasses. McCormick looked
behind and was humiliated to see the old man still stuck against the
Tavern. He spoke in an undertone, "not dreaming that anyone could
hear me except the old man."

"You're a coward and ought to be ashamed of yourself! Come
out of there!"

Stuart and his officers roared with laughter. McCormick flushed
red. He remembered:

"General Stuart . . . had thrown his leg over the saddle and was
in the act of writing a dispatch. Captain Walter Hullihen . . . was
with this party, and Stuart turned to Hullihen."

"Do you know that boy?" Stuart asked, nodding to McCormick.

"Yes," Hullihen said. "He belongs to Company D of the Sixth."

Stuart held the dispatch to McCormick. "Take this to General
Lomax as fast as you can, and tell him to send it to General Fitz Lee."

McCormick rode after Lomax but his frightened horse squatted,
and moved only when whacked on the head with a sword. The animal then ran madly, and the courier collided with Lomax as he delivered the message. McCormick asked permission to return. Lomax
shook his head.

"You certainly can't go back where you left General Stuart.
You'd better go back to your own squadron, down this road."[8]

Federal attacks were pushing forward. Colonel Pate's men
countercharged and fought hand-to-hand. Wickham sent in a
mounted charge to help.

Stuart rode to the spot. If Pate could not cling to his position,
the line must be abandoned. Jeb seemed to forget past antagonisms,
or to be pleading with Pate to forget. He held out his hand and Pate
took it, smiling.

"Colonel," Stuart said, "you have done all any man could do. How long can you hold?"

"Until I die," Pate said.

"You're a brave man," Stuart said. They again shook hands, and Jeb rode back nearer the center.

The chief bugler was with him, and protested mildly under the fire: "General, I believe you love bullets."

"No, Fred, I don't love 'em any more than you do. I go where they are because it's my duty. I don't expect to survive this war."

They went by staff officers crouched under a hill, beneath a battery in action. Stuart asked Reid Venable to ride with him and they approached a gun surrounded by wounded men and horses.

Venable watched Stuart: "He stopped a while at this gun and encouraged the men to hold their position, as he expected reinforcements."

Venable scolded him for reckless exposure. "Men behind stumps and fences are being killed, and here you are out in the open."

Stuart laughed. "I don't reckon there is any danger," he said.[9]

Now the Michigan troopers came into action. Custer was a striking sight with his long yellow hair and black velvet uniform as he maneuvered his troops into position. Custer sketched the operation:

"The enemy was strongly posted on a bluff in rear of a thin skirt of woods, his battery being concealed from our view by the woods, while they had obtained perfect range of my position. The edge of the woods nearest to my front was held by the enemy's dismounted men, who poured a heavy fire into my lines."

Custer ordered the 5th and 6th Michigan, dismounted, to charge. Colonel Alger commanded this assault; they ran forward over the uneven footing, many bodies dropping, and at last gained the woods. Custer ordered these two regiments to hold on there with carbines until further orders.

He looked over the field until he was satisfied:

"From a personal examination of the ground, I discovered that a successful charge might be made upon the battery of the enemy by keeping well to the right. With this intention I formed the 1st Michigan in column of squadrons under cover of the wood."

But the Rebel artillerymen were ready. Custer saw:

"As soon as the 1st Michigan moved from the cover of the woods the enemy divined our intention and opened a brisk fire from his artillery with shell and canister.

"Before the battery . . . could be reached there were five fences to be opened and a bridge to cross, over which it was impossible to pass more than three at one time, the intervening ground being within close range of the enemy's battery."

While the 1st Michigan hammered over the narrow bridge and up the slope, losing heavily, Custer's buglers were crowing the charge.

The blue riders came off the bridge bravely, fell into line and galloped, overwhelming the Confederate battery by sheer force of numbers.

"When within two hundred yards of the battery," Custer wrote, "they charged it with a yell which spread terror before them."

The Federals took two cannon and a handful of prisoners; this was the prized battery Colonel Johnson had brought to Stuart.

The Confederate line sagged back for about a quarter of a mile and re-formed.

Custer sent in the 7th Michigan, and its riders drove almost into the muzzles of Stuart's guns before their commander fell and they were hurled back. There was a lull.

From every segment of the Confederate line men saw bluecoats swarming thickly in the woods; there was no way to compute the odds against them. At two o'clock, during this brief quiet, Major McClellan returned from Richmond, reporting that the enemy held Brook Turnpike in their rear and had forced him into a wide detour. Stuart did not seem to be alarmed.

McClellan's news was encouraging on the whole. Bragg had about 4,000 irregular troops in the city's trenches, and expected three brigades of infantry from Petersburg at any moment. Bragg was confident he could hold the city.

Stuart told McClellan that "heavy fighting" had raged in his absence. Fitz Lee's men had lost most heavily. One of the dead was

Colonel Pate, shot as his line was overwhelmed and he shouted, "One more round, boys, and then we'll get to the hill."

Stuart told McClellan he would hold his present position, since he could stay on Sheridan's flank if Bragg marched out to catch the raiders; perhaps they could take Sheridan between the two forces.

He sat talking with McClellan for more than an hour.

Behind them in Richmond, Heros von Borcke was aroused from his convalescence by reports of the cavalry's troubles and by the sound of "light guns, which I recognized so well." He felt "electric fire" in his veins, and tried everywhere to borrow a horse. At last, finding every available animal already in service, he buckled on his sword and pistol and went through the streets.

He came upon a wagon, and before the astounded driver could protest had commandeered one of his bony Government horses, thrown his saddle upon him and ridden away. He trotted through the entrenchments and past the last Confederate pickets, asking directions as he entered open country.

Pickets told him Federals were between Stuart and the city, but pointed out a road which would take him to Jeb without danger. Von Borcke galloped on. He had just crossed a bridge when a band of Union cavalry dashed upon him, firing and yelling for his surrender. The German wrote:

"I turned my pony's head around, and galloped off to the rear and an exciting chase ensued for several miles, till it was put a stop to by our pickets, whom I reached completely exhausted."

Von Borcke went to Bragg, who was watching from the fortifications, and begged him to send infantry to Stuart's aid:

"The cautiousness characteristic of that General, however, induced him to resist my appeals, and finding further effort useless, I slowly retraced my steps to Richmond."

Von Borcke barely made it, for the exercise was too much for his wound. Blood streamed from his mouth, and he stopped, "half fainting," in a nearby house, and was put to bed.[10]

About four in the afternoon the massing Federal columns charged again at Yellow Tavern. A wave of skirmishers spilled out of the woods and a mounted brigade rode down guns on Stuart's line. Jeb outdistanced McClellan on his jaded horse, and the major was forced to watch his chief disappear on the left flank, where the trouble seemed to be most serious.

Several men saw Stuart as he approached the besieged line. Private N. W. Harris of Company G was one:

"We were ordered to dismount, and the last words I ever heard from old Jeb were, 'Boys, don't stop to count fours. Shoot them! Shoot them!' And we did shoot them. There was a deep cut in the road with a good fence to the left and in front of us. The Yankees were charging with sabers and slashed at us over the fences, but we soon piled them up so as to completely blockade the road with dead horses and men. As soon as General Stuart saw we had blocked the road and stopped their advance, he rode off in the direction of Troop K, and that was the last I ever saw of him."

This was Company K, Maryland riders of the 1st Virginia, from whose ranks Private J. R. Oliver noted Jeb's calm:

"General Stuart came riding slowly through the woods, whistling and entirely alone. He took a position directly between Fred Pitts, a young man from the Eastern Shore of Maryland, and myself, with his horse's head extending over the fence.

"My left elbow was touching the boot on General Stuart's right foot, while Pitts was equally as close to the General on his left."

Pitts did not remember the details quite so clearly, but said:

"I am certain that when General Stuart joined us he was entirely alone. I saw him speak to Captain Dorsey and then lost sight of him for a few minutes, on account of a little trouble we were having with the people in front of us. It was a pretty hot place."

Another witness was Captain Connally Litchfield of Company D, 1st Virginia, who saw Stuart behind the firing line, "in rear about ten feet of the sharpshooters, seemingly in a gay mood, and was whistling. His horse was in a canter."

Private Oliver observed Jeb as he sat with Company K:

"He had been with us for a few minutes when some of General Lomax's mounted men made a charge up the road and were driven back by a regiment of Federal cavalry which, when they got to our line of battle, filed to the left along the fence in front of our command, passing within ten or fifteen feet of General Stuart."

Captain Gus Dorsey, commanding this company, was near Stuart, in the center of the seventy-odd men of K Company. Stuart shouted, "Bully for Old K! Give it to 'em, boys!"

McClellan watched him empty his big silver-chased pistol at the retreating Federals, who were being pushed by a charge of the 1st Virginia.

Stuart continued to call to the troopers, "Steady, men, steady!"

A bluecoat horseman who had been dismounted in the charge trotted back with his companions, pistol in hand, just across the fence from Stuart.

The Federal was Private John Huff.

Huff fired on the run at the big man on the gray horse, with almost casual aim.

Oliver saw the general press a hand to his side. Stuart's head dropped. His hat fell off.

"General, are you hit?" Oliver asked.

"Yes."

"You wounded bad?"

"I'm afraid I am," Stuart said, "but don't worry, boys. Fitz will do as well for you as I have."

To the courier at his side Stuart said, "Go ask General Lee and Doctor Fontaine to come here."

The courier found Lomax and told him the news, then found Fitz Lee on the left of the line.

Dorsey recorded his own impressions of the moment:

"Stuart reeled on his horse and said, 'I am shot.' And then, 'Dorsey, save your men!' "

Dorsey caught the general to hold him in his saddle and troopers took Jeb toward the rear. Oliver wrote:

"As we were taking him back Tom Waters, of Baltimore, led his horse while Fred Pitts and myself, one on either side of him, went back about one hundred yards."

Stuart protested, and Captain Dorsey gently remonstrated, "We're taking you back a little, General, so as not to leave you to the enemy."

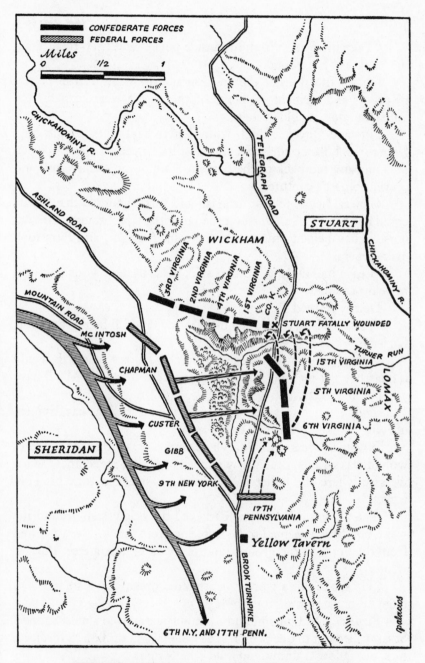

THE KILL: SHERIDAN VS. STUART, YELLOW TAVERN
May 11, 1864

"Take the papers from my inside pocket and keep them from the Yankees," Stuart said.

Dorsey fished inside the uniform and drew out a small packet of papers and mementoes. Some of the papers were torn by the bullet, but bore no blood stains.

Pitts and Oliver left Jeb with Waters while they sought help from the ambulance corps. Stuart was still slumped on General when the company ran back to the fence to hold off an enemy rush and prevent Stuart's capture.

General began to toss his head and turn about, so that Stuart could not handle him. Dorsey called to Pitts, who brought his own horse. They helped Stuart onto the calmer mount, and Pitts took over General.

"Leave me, Dorsey," Stuart said. "Get back to your men and drive the enemy."

Dorsey refused.

"I'm afraid they've killed me, Dorsey, and I'll be no more use. Go back."

"I can't obey that order, General," Dorsey said. "I would rather they get me, too, than leave you here for them. We'll have you out in a shake."

They took Jeb farther to the rear, and most of the cavalrymen, obeying his order, returned to the front.

Private Burgess of the Maryland company saw that the general's wound was serious: "He was wounded mortally, as we knew when we saw where the bullet had entered his side and torn his gray jacket."

The wound had by now darkened the bright sash around the waist, and Stuart seemed to be suffering from shock. He was lifted from the horse to the ground, and propped against a tree. Burgess wrote:

"He spoke not a word nor uttered a groan as we assisted him from his horse to the ground."

Fitz Lee, Dr. Fontaine and an ambulance arrived almost at once. Stuart called out to Lee as soon as he caught sight of him: "Go ahead, Fitz, old fellow. I know you'll do what's right."

Reid Venable was by now at the General's side to record

Stuart's cry of defiance. As men lifted the big body into the ambulance, a few troopers from the disorganized line ran rearward. Stuart raised himself to a painful sitting position and shouted: "Go back! Go back! Do your duty as I've done mine. I would rather die than be whipped!"

Venable thought the tone of his voice was "imperious."

Some of the men who had retreated turned about and went into the skirmish line once more. Others did not. Private Hopkins, who was nearby at this moment, reported:

"Some of our men mounted the fence in the rear and fled across the fields. Others stood their ground and were captured, I among them. . . . There was a little culvert across a ditch in the road. . . . Some of our men crept under this culvert and escaped. Probably two hundred of us were captured."

The ambulance bearing Stuart began to roll. A courier who followed it briefly watched:

"I followed it close behind. He lay without speaking as it went along, but kept shaking his head with an expression of the deepest disappointment."

Another witness was the eighteen-year-old Private McCormick. He wrote of the ambulance in more vivid detail:

"The mules became unmanageable in the close fighting. They had a cool driver, but they dashed down over the steep bank with Stuart inside. The right hind wheel flew up in the air, and I thought, oh, God, he is going to be dragged to death.

"But the ambulance righted itself when it struck the road, and down the road toward the Chickahominy it went."

McCormick followed for a time with the head of his horse inside the rear of the ambulance, but as the vehicle began to pick up speed, thought he should go back to the firing line. He wrote:

"The last thing I saw of him he was lying flat on his back in the ambulance, the mules running at a terrific pace, and he was being jolted most unmercifully. He opened his eyes and looked at me, shook his head from side to side as much as to say, 'It's all over with me.' He had folded arms and a look of resignation."

As Stuart left the Tavern fighting raged in rear of the speeding wagon.[11]

CHAPTER 21

"God's Will Be Done"

MAJOR VENABLE took command of the ambulance, and when it had rolled into the lowlands near a bridge, he had it halted so that Dr. Fontaine could make an examination.

Lieutenant Hullihen was there by now, and helped Fontaine to turn Stuart on his side. The physician unhooked the double-breasted jacket, unwound the stained silk band, and inspected the wound.

Stuart turned to Hullihen: "Honey-bun, how do I look in the face?"

"You are looking all right, General," Hullihen told him. "You will be all right."

"Well," Jeb said slowly, "I don't know how this will turn out, but if it is God's will that I shall die I am ready."

Doctor Fontaine was not cheered by what he saw. He was afraid that the shock of the bullet, penetrating near the liver, might kill Stuart immediately.

Fontaine urged him to take some whisky as a stimulant.

"No," Stuart said. "I've never tasted it in my life. I promised my mother that when I was a baby."

Venable joined Fontaine in urging him to take a drink. The general held up his hands.

"Lift me," he said. "Old fellow, I know you will tell me the truth. Is the death pallor on my face?"

"I hope not," Venable said. "There is some flush on your forehead."

Stuart seemed to take heart, and agreed to take a drink of the whisky.

He looked at the soldiers who had gathered around the wagon.

"Go back to the front," he said. "I will be taken care of. I want you to do your duty to your country."

The ambulance went off once more. There were only the driver, the two staff members, Hullihen and Venable, Dr. Fontaine, a couple of couriers, and three riders of the general's escort: Ellis, Thompson and Carpenter.

It was nearing dark. Out on the front Stuart's men were being pushed from their position at Yellow Tavern.

Richmond was only six miles away, but the jolting wagon was forced into a detour around back-country roads to avoid Federals along Brook Turnpike. Stuart rode for hours, tortured by the jarring of his wound.

They trailed through Mechanicsville in the night, and from there Garnett rode ahead to have a bed made ready at the home of Dr. Charles Brewer, Stuart's brother-in-law. Garnett was also to report to General Bragg.

The wagon crossed the Chickahominy at least twice, and it was late before the wheels stopped at last. In the merciful quiet, Stuart made out that he was at the Brewer home. He heard the voice of Flora's sister, Maria, Mrs. Brewer. The house stood on Grace Street, between Jefferson and Madison.

Stuart was carried into the house at eleven o'clock. A low brick wall enclosing the garden was covered with yellow roses, and the scent of them was strong. The air was heavy.

It soon began to rain, and a thunderstorm broke over the city.

Fontaine called other doctors, and they did the little that was possible to make Stuart more comfortable. He seemed to rest more easily after a few hours, when the shock was apparently wearing off.

News spread through the city and a crowd gathered even before daylight. Women wept in the throng and several children stared curiously at the house and the solemn adults. Men passed in and out of the house. Dr. Brewer left the place on an errand before dawn.

Von Borcke had spent a "long, refreshing" night after his hemorrhage of the day before, and hurried out of bed when he heard the voice of Dr. Brewer from the darkness.

"Von Borcke! It's Stuart. He's wounded."

The German dressed as Brewer explained that Jeb had been taken to his home. "He wants to see you," the doctor said.

Von Borcke found several men in the sickroom. Stuart managed a smile.

"I'm glad you've come, my dear Von. You see they've got me at last. But don't feel uneasy. I don't think I'm as badly wounded as you were, and I hope I'll get over it as you did."

The general did not seem exhausted, for he told the detailed story of his wounding, and though his voice was slow, it was strong and steady, and he seemed to forget nothing. After a time von Borcke stepped back from the bed and went out to send a telegram to Flora.

The message was late leaving the city. There was no direct line to Beaver Dam, since the wires along both the Virginia Central and the Fredericksburg Railroad had been cut, and there were many relays as the message slowly approached Flora by way of distant Lynchburg and Gordonsville.[1]

Flora Stuart had a breakfast guest on May twelfth—Captain William Blackford. Jeb's old staff officer had gone to Beaver Dam with engineers and all other troops he could collect in an effort to help beat off Sheridan's raid. His men camped near the Fontaine house, and Blackford paid Mrs. Stuart an immediate visit.

The captain noticed no unusual strain about Flora. There was little news of the cavalry, beyond the fact that Stuart was on Sheridan's trail. And that, Blackford said, made all "feel quite content."

Breakfast over, Blackford returned to his camp.

He had hardly left the house when a messenger rode up the drive with a telegram for Mrs. Stuart. Colonel Fontaine first read it privately:

General Stuart has been seriously wounded. Come at once.

Fontaine put it into his pocket and did not tell Flora immediately. He summoned a locomotive to carry her to Richmond and asked his wife to give her the news.

Blackford saw Flora leave on the strange conveyance, watching from the camp as the engine puffed into the station without cars. A carriage went swiftly down the Fontaine drive. After questioning men around the depot, Blackford learned that Flora and her children had gone to her wounded husband.[2]

They left Beaver Dam at one P.M. in the rocking engine, off to Ashland over the last undamaged stretch of rails. At the last moment Flora got an escort, Rev. George Woodbridge, who had been visiting his son, a cavalryman. Another friend, Charles Carter, of Hanover County, also accompanied her.

The engine puffed along the track for two hours before they reached Ashland, for the engineer was an amateur, a volunteer haled into service by Fontaine. There were new troubles at Ashland. The rails into Richmond had been torn up.

An ambulance stood near the station, and though several wounded cavalry officers were in it, ready to go into the city, they hobbled out and insisted that Mrs. Stuart take it, instead. Woodbridge accepted it for her and they lurched off over rutted and miry roads. A storm broke over them as they left Ashland, and the dark sky, lit by lightning and loud with thunder, added to the fright of the children. The wagon did not halt.

There were frequent calls from passing soldiers, and always Woodbridge asked for news of Stuart. They were usually told: "No news, but we heard his wound was not serious."

At eight P.M. they reached the Chickahominy, where they found the Confederate cavalry had destroyed the bridge in the face of Sheridan. After a wait in the storm a cavalry picket was found to lead the driver to a ford a mile or so away. The wagon splashed through the water in a frantic hurry.

Just before reaching the city the wagon was halted; it was ten o'clock, and the storm still rolled. Woodbridge suddenly saw dark masses of men and horses just in front of the wagon, and along the roadside. A rider was at the head of the wagon horses. The wagon stopped, and once the wheels had halted, Woodbridge heard the challenge: "Who's there? Stand!"

Woodbridge found it was a Confederate sentry, and told him Mrs. Stuart was in the wagon, on her way to the general's side.

"Thank God!" the sentry said. "My pistol cap snapped twice when you didn't answer my challenge, and wouldn't fire."

These were men of Lomax, driven back on the city, defending the approaches against Sheridan. The wagon rolled into Richmond at the height of the storm, which was so severe that the steeple of St. John's Church was blown away.[3]

In the bedroom where four doctors now worked, Stuart's condition changed rapidly during the day of May twelfth. There was occasional delirium, followed by periods of ease and quiet. In the morning he seemed to get relief from his pain, and the doctors became hopeful; perhaps he might survive the wound, after all.

Someone who left the room told a newspaper reporter that Stuart's mind wandered as Jackson's had, almost a year ago to the day, when Stonewall was on his deathbed. Jeb had given snatches of orders to his commanders, this man said, urging them against the enemy. Once he had shouted, "Make haste!"

McClellan, who had reported to General Bragg, at last arrived at the Brewer house. He found Stuart "calm and composed, in the full possession of his mind," but said their conversation was interrupted by "paroxysms of suffering."

Stuart told McClellan to dispose of his official papers and to send his personal belongings to Flora. That was not all.

"I want you to take one of my horses and Venable the other. Which is the heavier rider?"

"I think Venable is."

"Then," Stuart said, "let Venable have the gray and you take the bay."

Stuart stirred again.

"You will find in my hat a little Confederate flag, sent to me by a lady from Columbia, South Carolina. She wanted me to wear it on my horse in battle and send it to her. Send it."

McClellan searched the big plumed hat for some time before he found the flag; it was tucked beneath the stained sweat band. The staff had known nothing of this request from the distant woman patriot, but later, in the papers, McClellan found the letter from this admirer.

Stuart had another request: "My spurs. I want them sent to Lily Lee in Shepherdstown. The gold ones, I mean. My sword I want to go to my son."

There was a roll of cannon fire in the distance. Stuart turned eagerly to McClellan: "What's that?"

"Bragg sent Gracie's brigade out to take Sheridan in the rear on Brook Turnpike. Fitz is going after the vanguard at the Meadow Bridges. It may be them, hitting him now."

That seemed to remind Stuart of the action at Yellow Tavern, and he told him feelingly of the death of Henry Pate, and of their reconciliation. McClellan then recorded Jeb in a melodramatic moment as he spoke of the men still fighting Sheridan:

"He turned his eyes upward and exclaimed earnestly, 'God grant that they may be successful.' Then turning his head aside, he said with a sigh, 'But I must be prepared for another world.' "

They listened to the guns for a time, and Stuart said, "Major, Fitz Lee may need you."

McClellan stood, and took Stuart's hand to say good-bye.

As he left, President Davis entered the room, and McClellan halted to overhear the conversation.

"General," Davis said, "how do you feel?"

"Easy, but willing to die, if God and my country think I have fulfilled my destiny and done my duty."

McClellan went out of the room.

The Reverend Joshua Peterkin, of St. James Episcopal Church, visited the bedside, and prayed with Stuart. Jeb had a request:

"Sing," the general said. "Let's sing 'Rock of Ages.' " The room resounded to the slow tune of the old hymn, and Stuart joined in a low voice. He seemed weaker when he finished.

During the afternoon, on one of Dr. Brewer's visits, Stuart asked, "How long can I live, Charles? Can I last through the night?"

"I'm afraid the end is near," Brewer said.

Stuart nodded.

"I am resigned, if it be God's will. I would like to see my wife. But God's will be done."

He asked for Flora several times during the afternoon. When

the pain became intense, ice was placed on the wound, and Stuart held it there himself.

After a time Stuart talked again of disposing of his property among friends and relatives; there was precious little to be left to Flora or anyone else.

The specific bequests in his will were rather pathetic. He left Flora his class ring, diplomas, commissions and wardrobe, and added:

> I give & bequeath to my son the saber used by me in the war of my country's independence with the injunction to draw it whenever his country's rights are violated or her territory invaded.

And the document repeated an injunction Flora had read before:

> I desire my children to be educated South of the Mason and Dixon Line, and always to retain the right of domicile in the Confederate states.

During May twelfth, just north of the city, Sheridan had moved against Fitz Lee at the Chickahominy, where he found the Meadow Bridges burned. But though there was fierce fighting, Sheridan did not seriously attempt to storm Richmond—probably because it did not attract him as a temporary objective, and could not long be held by his cavalry.

The Federal riders went away eastward, toward the blue infantry of General Butler. The lead corps, in fact, camped near the great house Shirley, on the James, with others strung out behind as far as the Meadow Bridges. In the rear James Gordon, "The Murat of the Army of Northern Virginia," struck hard at the enemy. At Brook Church he tied up an entire brigade of the Federal rear with the 1st and 2nd North Carolina.

Bragg sent fresh artillery from Richmond, but when Gordon put it into action and enemy canister showered them, the green crews ran for a ditch and could not be driven out.

Gordon raged at the "bandbox artillery" and its cowardly men, and his veterans laughed at the gunners from Richmond. "We asked them to go back to their guns," one soldier wrote, "but they looked at us as if we were surely crazy. Gordon became utterly disgusted."

In this frame of mind Gordon galloped into the shell-swept road as if he would charge the Yankees alone. He pitched from his horse, mortally wounded.

Men carried Gordon rearward and put him into an ambulance, which took him into Richmond after dark. A throng gathered about it.

Theo Garnett was in Stuart's room by now, holding the general's pulse, which throbbed faster and faster. Garnett wrote:

"Suddenly a loud shout arose from a crowd of men and boys passing along Broad Street. Awakening with a startled look, Stuart said, 'Go and see what it means.'"

Garnett hurried into the street and saw an ambulance pushing through the rain toward the capitol. Someone said it carried a wounded general to the hospital. After a few moments Garnett returned to Stuart.

He found Jeb almost asleep, and did not repeat to him either the rumors or the fact: Stuart's able lieutenant, James Gordon, had passed the house on his slow way to his deathbed.

Von Borcke sat on Stuart's bed, holding his hand. The German fed him ice, and Jeb crunched it rapidly. Jeb drew von Borcke closer to him.

"My dear Von, I am sinking fast now. But before I die I want you to know that I never loved a man as much as you. I pray you may live a long and happy life. Look after my family when I'm gone, and be the same true friend to my wife and children you have been to me."

Von Borcke, at any rate, had that recollection when he came to write his memoirs.

The memories of others were less heroic.

Soon Stuart said to Dr. Brewer:

"I am going fast now. God's will be done. . . ."

He was gone. The pulse was still. It was twenty-two minutes before eight, in the evening of May twelfth.[4]

More than three hours later Flora arrived in the wagon. One who rode with her wrote: "A certain quiet resting on all about the house instantly impressed them, and words were not necessary to convey to the . . . wife the sad intelligence."

Flora's children were taken by quick hands, and she was soon alone with him in candlelight, the pale image she had so long held in her mind's eye. Despite stunning grief, perhaps it did not seem so strange to her. She had feared it from the start, and had read it in almost every line of his letters, in the war and in the long-gone days of Indian raids on the frontier.

Others tried to help. Her sister Maria snipped off a lock of the red-golden hair from Jeb's head, tied it with a ribbon and thrust it into an envelope. And she, or one of the staff, assembled the few items found in his pockets:

A pincushion, thin and round, on one side a blue background with the legend worked in gold embroidery: "Gen. J. E. B. Stuart"; on the reverse side in red and blue a Confederate flag, with the legend: "Glory to Our Immortal Cavalry!"

There was a copy of one of Stuart's orders to his troops, ringing with familiar phrases:

> We now, as in all battles, mourn the loss of many brave and valued comrades. Let us avenge our fallen heroes; and at the word, move upon the enemy with the determined assurance that in victory alone is honor and safety.

There was a letter to his wife, telling of plans to bring her to his headquarters within a few days.

An original General Order of congratulation to the victorious infantry he had led at Chancellorsville.

A letter from his brother W. A. Stuart in Saltville, Virginia, the owner of White Sulphur Springs.

A letter asking Jeb to find a government job for a friend.

There was a poem on the death of a child, taken from a newspaper.

A New Testament.

A handkerchief.

A lock of his young daughter's hair.[5]

The Richmond Whig of May twelfth, on the streets as Stuart died, reported on the state of the populace:

> The greatest excitement felt in this city yesterday was caused by a dog fight in Tobacco Alley, which occurred about 6 o'clock P.M.
>
> Two fice, one yellow and white with a long tail, the other black and lobbed, after the manner of a terrier . . . were the combatants. . . . Several hundred soldiers watched. . . . The long-tailed fice's owner withdrew him . . . no match.

And on the following day, unaware that the cavalry chief was dead, this newspaper said:

> General Stuart was reported improving last evening. The rumor of his death at noon, which caused so deep a sensation among the resident and transient population of Richmond, was speedily dissipated by an announcement from his surgeon that he was getting on well. . . . We trust that he may live to meet and repel many a Yankee raid.

The Army of Northern Virginia, off at Spotsylvania, was resting after one of its most terrible blood baths, in firing that had felled large trees; Lee's ranks had been broken, and the line held only by hand-to-hand battle. Casualties had been ghastly, enough to make men forget The Wilderness.

Several officers were near General Lee when he got a dispatch telling him of Stuart's wound.

"Gentlemen," Lee said, with obvious emotion, "we have very bad news. General Stuart has been mortally wounded."

After a time Lee said, "He never brought me a piece of false information."

And when Lee heard of the end, not long afterward, he said, "I can scarcely think of him without weeping."

The funeral was held May thirteenth at St. James Church, with the Rev. Mr. Peterkin officiating. It was late, about five in the afternoon, before the procession reached the church, and in the air were sounds of fighting at Drewry's Bluff, rolling strongly up the James.

There was no music on the streets, and no military escort, since the Public Guard was in the field. The city was so nearly under siege that customary honors could not be thought of today. The metal coffin was carried into the church by the pallbearers, among them Generals John Winder, George Randolph, Joseph Anderson, and A. R. Lawton, and Commodore Forrest. The men bore their burden up the center aisle as the organ played and the choir sang. Flora wept in the front of the crowd, her sobs drowned by the cannon fire.

President Davis was there, and Generals Bragg and Ransom and other Confederate and city officials—but none of the dusty troopers. A part of the Episcopal service was read by The Rev. Mr. Peterkin, followed by a hymn and a prayer.

The coffin went out to the waiting hearse, which was topped with black plumes suggestive of Jeb's own. Four white horses drew him to Hollywood Cemetery. There were few carriages in the procession through the streets, and the short concluding portion of the funeral service was read by The Reverend Charles Minnegerode of St. Paul's Church in his heavy German accent. Stuart's coffin was placed in a vault, and the carriages moved off.

Just as the funeral party left the cemetery the rain began once more.[6]

The next day there was a general order from Fitz Lee at cavalry headquarters:

> A terrible duty has to be performed in announcing to this division the death of Major General J. E. B. Stuart. . . . His name and fame, bright as the keen blade of his trusty saber, is at this moment encompassed by no boundaries. Great, glorious and good, his loss to his country, to our army, especially to his troopers, is inconsolable.
>
> Whilst his bright glancing eye can no longer see, his clear ringing voice no longer be heard . . . may the principles he has taught us, the example he has shown us, be not lost. Stuart had no superior as a soldier. . . . Let the remembrance of his mighty

deeds, his hopeful devotion, his buoyant courage, inspire us to emulate him, however feebly, and whilst weeping for our beloved chieftain, our sabers must be thrust to the hilt, and our motto be, Independence or Death.

And the *Richmond Examiner* of May seventeenth, as if Stuart had become the symbol of Confederate defiance, cried:

We have it from the lips of prisoners, that the Yankee honor and glory of having fired the chance shot that laid the gallant Stuart low is claimed by a Yankee dog, one Major Hogan, of the Pennsylvania reserves, who made a boast of it, and was complimented by such kindred mastiffs as Generals Merritt, Wilson and Davis. . . .

Hogan claims to be the slayer of the Confederate lion, the shaking of whose mane and angry roar kept the Jackal North in a perpetual terror. True to their cowardly instinct they feared him living, but insult him dead, by honoring his assassin. . . . Stuart's troopers still live, and as true as they live Hogan will die if ever found on the soil of the "Old Dominion." They swear it. Stuart has not fallen to sleep unavenged.

The apoplectic editorial voice, relentlessly critical of Stuart in life, was lost in gunfire which came ever nearer the city and the otherwise unidentified Hogan and his claim to fame were forgotten. Richmond fought for its life.

For a long time there appeared on Stuart's grave each day a mound of spring flowers.

☆

Notes

CHAPTER ONE

OLD JOHN BROWN

[1] From the Shepherdstown, Va., *Register*, Oct. 29, 1859; cited by Oswald Garrison Villard in *John Brown, A Biography Fifty Years After* (hereafter Villard), whose account of the Harpers Ferry raid is the finest.

[2] Harry Hunter described the Thompson murder in the New York *Tribune*, Oct. 29, 1859. Other details of killings and atrocities are from a rare little book, *The Strange Story of Harpers Ferry*, by Joseph Barry, a witness (hereafter Barry).

[3] A. R. Boteler left this story, in *Century* magazine, July, 1883, p. 399. This is one of the most detailed narratives of these moments. Lawson Botts was soon to be Brown's defense attorney.

[4] Stuart's role is described in a letter to his mother from Fort Riley, Kan., Jan., 1860. It is now in possession of a descendant of hers, Stuart B. Campbell of Wytheville, Va. The saber attachment developed by Stuart is Patent #25,684, of Oct. 24, 1859.

[5] The narrative of Lieut. Green, cited here and later in this chapter, is the only eyewitness story of Brown's capture in the enginehouse. From *The North American Review*, Dec., 1885, p. 564.

[6] This striking glimpse of cowardice and bravery in the face of danger comes from an affidavit of G. A. Schoppert, a witness, cited in Villard, p. 452.

[7] These details are from Stuart's letter, "The Mason Report" (Senate Committee Report #278, 1st Session, 36th Congress, Washington, 1860), and from Boteler's account.

[8] From Boteler's story. Though this does not seem of a piece with other accounts, there is no ground for rejecting it. Boteler, though an intense partisan, was a Princeton graduate, and a man of broad political and worldly experience.

422

[9] This dialogue is from the New York *Herald*, Oct. 21, 1859.

[10] C. W. Tayleure to John Brown, Jr., June 15, 1879, a copy of which is in the Maryland Historical Society Library, as cited by Villard. Vivid glimpses of atrocities, again, are from Barry.

CHAPTER TWO

THE YOUNG WARRIOR

[1] Letter of Sept. 4, 1849, now in Confederate Museum, Richmond, Va.

[2] Stuart sketched his visits to Monticello and Washington in a letter of June 3, 1850, now in Virginia State Library, Richmond; West Point records provided from files by Sidney Forman, Archivist, U.S. Military Academy.

[3] Fitz Lee's account is in Southern Historical Society Papers (hereafter SHSP), Vol. 1, p. 99.

[4] From Register of Delinquencies, #7, 1849–54, U.S. Military Academy.

[5] This and following quotations in this chapter from a series of letters from Stuart to his cousin, Bettie Hairston, many undated, but from his West Point years. The collection, unpublished and not previously consulted by Stuart biographers, is in the Southern Historical Collection, University of North Carolina Library.

[6] Cited by John Thomason in *Jeb Stuart* (hereafter Thomason), p. 21, and confirmed by members of the Stuart family.

[7] This daguerreotype, reproduced in the illustrated section following page 210, is among the treasures of the Confederate Museum. The letter, June 19, 1854, now in the same collection, is from Stuart to an unidentified friend.

CHAPTER THREE

ON THE FRONTIER

[1] Details of this journey are from Stuart's letters to Bettie Hairston, Univ. N.C. Library, dated Jan. 4–10, 1855.

[2] Sketches of animal life from Stuart to Jack Hairston, Mar. 31, 1855, Univ. of N.C. Library.

[3] Stuart's letter to an unidentified girl, evidently at West Point, Apr.

21, 1855, fixing the beginning of his beard, is in Va. State Library; his letter to John Stuart appeared in the Staunton *Jeffersonian*.

⁴ Venable's relations with Stuart in St. Louis are sketched in SHSP, Vol. 37, p. 61.

⁵ The original of this note is owned (1957) by Stuart's granddaughter, Mrs. Virginia Waller Davis, of Alexandria, Va.

⁶ Stuart to "Cousin Brown," Aug. 10, 1855, original in Va. State Library.

⁷ Stuart's letter to an unknown girl, dated Nov. 25, 1855, is in Confederate Museum; P. St. Geo. Cooke to John Esten Cooke from *John Esten Cooke, Virginian*, by J. O. Beaty (hereafter Beaty), p. 75.

⁸ The story of the battle of Black Jack and subsequent events in Kansas, including documents cited, are from Villard, p. 200.

⁹ A full description of this trying expedition is in Stuart's letters to Flora, July–August, 1857, cited in Major H. B. McClellan, *The Life and Campaigns of Maj.-Gen. J. E. B. Stuart* (hereafter McClellan), pp. 20–27.

¹⁰ Authority is Benjamin Blake Minor, to whom Stuart showed his invention, in SHSP, Vol. 36, p. 269.

¹¹ This revealing letter is in Va. State Library, dated Nov. 11, 1859.

¹² Elizabeth Stuart's fiery—and somewhat insulting—letter to R. E. Lee is in Va. State Library, dated Apr. 23, 1861. It seems to have escaped the attention of all students and biographers of Stuart and Lee.

CHAPTER FOUR

First Blood

¹ This letter from Stuart to Flora, like many in this and the following chapter, is in the Keith M. Read Collection of the Emory University Library, Atlanta, Ga.; they were published in 1943, in a booklet edited by Bingham Duncan.

² Stuart's quoted letter on P. St. Geo. Cooke, May 19, 1861, is in Confederate Museum; the rivalry between Stuart and Ashby is cited by General John Imboden in *Battles and Leaders* (hereafter B&L) Vol. 1, p. 123.

³ Stuart to Col. James W. Allen, June 10, 1861; original in Duke University Library.

⁴ George C. Eggleston, *A Rebel's Recollections*, p. 110.

⁵ W. W. Blackford, *War Years With Jeb Stuart*, p. 15.

⁶ Geo. C. Eggleston, *Recollections of A Varied Life*, p. 78.

[7] The description of Falling Waters is from Official Records, Vol. 2, p. 160 ff.; Stuart's capture of an enemy company is from John Esten Cooke, *Stonewall Jackson*, p. 51; also from Jackson's report and Stuart's letter to his wife.

[8] Eggleston, *Rebel's Recollections*, p. 114 ff.

[9] Blackford, *War Years*, p. 18.

[10] The Federal misfortunes are taken from *Official Records, War of the Rebellion* (hereafter OR) Vol. 2, pp. 167–8, 178.

[11] Jubal A. Early, as cited in McClellan, p. 35 ff.

CHAPTER FIVE

GATHERING THE CLAN

[1] These vivid glimpses of Stuart, from drumming on horseback to his gay espionage, are from *Wearing Of the Gray*, by John Esten Cooke, pp. 195, 214; Cooke's best-known novel, *The Virginia Comedians*, had appeared in 1854, and he was an army celebrity. At war's end he buried silver spurs at Appomattox to keep them from the enemy.

[2] Munford is cited in Beaty, p. 81; the story of the Sweeneys, their banjo and minstrelsy, is from the *Spring Quarterly*, 1949, of Los Angeles County Museum, California, the institution owning what is said to be the "original" banjo, made by Joe Sweeney. The museum also provided a copy of the only known photograph of Sam Sweeney, a daguerreotype.

[3] Cooke's comments from his *War Diary*, the original of which is in Duke University Library; the incident of the captured letters is from Beaty, p. 81.

[4] Eggleston, *Rebel's Recollections*, p. 123; stories of Hagan and Stuart's weary pickets from the same source, pp. 121, 128.

[5] Flora Cooke at the front is drawn by C. M. Blackford, *Letters from Lee's Army*, pp. 42, 57; Major H. B. McClellan, in SHSP, Vol. 8, p. 191, reported the exchange between Poe and Stuart; Robert Hooke's comment is in a letter to his father, Colonel William W. Hooke, Aug. 28, 1861, the original of which is in Duke University Library.

[6] Statement of Mrs. Virginia Stuart Waller Davis, Stuart's granddaughter, to the writer, Alexandria, Va., Nov., 1956. Mrs. Davis was reared by Flora Stuart.

[7] Blackford, *Letters from Lee's Army*, p. 57.

[8] This series of letters from Stuart to Flora is in the Emory University Library, Keith M. Read Collection.

[9] Details of the chaplain's life from *The Rebel Scout*, by Thomas Nelson Conrad, pp. 45, 47, 102.

[10] *Confederate Scout: Virginia's Frank Stringfellow*, by James D. Peavey, p. 48.

[11] Stuart to John Cooke in the P. St. Geo. Cooke Papers, Virginia Historical Society, Richmond.

[12] Davis's stern note is in *OR*, Vol. 5, p. 1063.

CHAPTER SIX

THE PENINSULA

[1] This picture of the inauguration and Richmond of the period is drawn largely from T. C. DeLeon, *Four Years in Rebel Capitals*, pp. 88, 163 ff.

[2] This retreat is depicted by Blackford in *War Years*, in various scenes, pp. 59–62.

[3] The singular election is described in *War Years*, pp. 62–3.

[4] Stuart describes Pelham's role in *Photographic History of The Civil War*, Vol. 9, pp. 84–5.

[5] Cooke's sketch of Farley is in *Wearing of the Gray*, pp. 146, 411, 437, etc. The latter references are to "Darrell," a thinly disguised Farley.

[6] Williamsburg action from McClellan, pp. 47–50. The best general account of the battle is in D. S. Freeman's *Lee's Lieutenants*, Vol. 1, p. 174 ff., but the cavalry is scarcely mentioned.

[7] The Charleston *Mercury*, May 20, 1862, reported Johnston's song.

[8] Sketch of von Borcke from Constance Harrison, *Recollections Grave & Gay*, p. 130; *von Borcke*, Vol. 1, p. 130; Blackford, pp. 69–70.

CHAPTER SEVEN

FAME AT A GALLOP

[1] Mosby's version of the origin of the raid, though not corroborated by other sources, rings true, and there is no reason to suspect its accuracy; his accounts are numerous, use having been made here of that in SHSP, Vol. 26, p. 246 ff., and *Memoirs*, p. 110.

[2] Stuart's battle plan is in the Confederate Memorial Institute, Richmond; a digest is in *Wearing of the Gray*, p. 175.

[3] *OR*, Vol. 11, Pt. 3, p. 590. Stuart's elaboration is in his own report of the raid, *OR* Vol. 11, Pt. 1, p. 1038, a prophetic guide to his career: "These circumstances led me to look with more favor to my favorite scheme, disclosed to you before starting, of passing around." Somehow this intention of Stuart's escaped his previous biographers—but not Dr. Douglas Southall Freeman.

[4] The narrative of the raid is based, as is much of Stuart's story, on von Borcke, John Esten Cooke, and H. B. McClellan; minor details come from other witnesses: John Mosby, Richard Frayser, George A. Townsend.

[5] Moves of the Federal pickets from *OR*, Vol. 11, Pt. 1, p. 1004, etc.; reports of all officers involved will be found here.

[6] Even the stilted prose of official records (*OR*, Vol. 11, Pt. 1, pp. 1006–13) does not conceal the strange drama of Gen. P. St. Geo. Cooke, as he gropes after the raiders led by his son-in-law. The clash of opinion and proffered fact from the Federal side, however, may cause students to share the confusion of the Union command. Suspicion of General Cooke probably led to his prompt transfer from this army.

[7] From Townsend's vivid, charming book, *Rustics in Rebellion*, p. 118.

[8] Burial of Latané is drawn from T. C. DeLeon, *Belles, Beaux and Brains of the Sixties*, p. 286, and from a more detailed account by Mrs. Kate B. Newton Christian, granddaughter of an eyewitness.

[9] Mosby's *Reminiscences*, p. 229.

[10] The Federal impression that the army dealt with no more than a casual raid may be found in *OR*, Vol. 11, Pt. 1, p. 1017.

[11] From Cooke's *War Diary*, Duke University Library.

CHAPTER EIGHT

A WEEK OF MIRACLES

[1] Opening moves of the cavalry in the Seven Days, and headquarters scenes, are from von Borcke, pp. 47–52; Cooke's *War Diary*, and Blackford, p. 71.

[2] Jackson's halt above Mechanicsville has not been fully explained; Stuart's behavior is described in *Thomason*, p. 180.

[3] This incident from H. K. Douglas, *I Rode With Stonewall*, p. 104; the brief sketch of Cold Harbor here is drawn from von Borcke, Cooke,

Douglas, Blackford, and Richard Taylor, the latter in *Destruction and Reconstruction*, p. 107. There are minor conflicts in the accounts of these witnesses.

⁴ Stuart's own account, in his official report, is the most important document on cavalry moves of this week, though staff officers illuminate them with graphic detail. A startling minority view of Stuart's behavior, which could not otherwise be substantiated by the writer, is J. Churchill Cooke's, in *Confederate Veteran*, July, 1931, p. 248, which says: "The morning after the battle of Mechanicsville Jackson sent for me and ordered me to find General Stuart and tell him to report immediately. . . . I had not the least idea where to find him. . . . A cavalryman told me he had gone to the White House. . . . I reported to General Jackson. He became very angry and said he would dismount every cavalryman and put them in the ranks."

⁵ Blame for burning of the White House cannot be fixed; Gen. Silas Casey, the Federal commander, ordered Government stores fired, but says the house was burned against his orders.

⁶ Von Borcke, Vol. 1, p. 70, perhaps inaccurate as to timing, for Stuart already had an urgent call to aid the army at Malvern Hill.

⁷ One of the most controversial incidents in Stuart's career—Evelington Heights—had its origin in a book by Col. Walter Taylor of Lee's staff, who thought Stuart's action in firing from the hill was "maladroit," and that it cost Lee total victory; H. B. McClellan of Stuart's staff treats this at length in his life of Stuart, p. 83 ff., summoning up much detail. In this narrative, the writer has put chief reliance on the official records.

⁸ In conflict between von Borcke and Stuart's report it is not clear whether Stuart or Stephen D. Lee led this expedition; since von Borcke said specifically that it was Stuart, and *OR* is silent, he is placed there in this narrative.

⁹ From Cooke's *War Diary*.

¹⁰ This incident, observed by Longstreet's men, is cited in Thomason, p. 209.

CHAPTER NINE

EASY VICTORIES

¹ The original of this letter, described by Mosby as "the best I could get" from Stuart, is in Confederate Museum; chief reliance for this tale of adventure, capture and espionage is Mosby's *Memoirs*, p. 125 ff.

[2] Blackford's *War Years*, p. 94.

[3] Mosby's *Memoirs*, p. 130 ff.

[4] G. A. Townsend, *Rustics in Rebellion*, p. 241.

[5] C. M. Blackford, *Letters from Lee's Army*, p. 110; and *War Years*, p. 98, note.

[6] This tale from von Borcke, Vol. 1, p. 103.

[7] The Verdiersville escapade, in which lie concealed symptoms of Confederate weaknesses in command, is reconstructed here from the accounts of Mosby, von Borcke, J. E. Cooke in *Wearing*, p. 204 ff. and Stuart in *OR*, Vol. 12, Pt. 2, p. 275.

[8] Details from Willard Glazier, *Three Years in the Federal Cavalry*, p. 25.

[9] Stuart's report, in *OR*, Vol. 12, Pt. 2, p. 726.

[10] There are minor discrepancies in the versions of this story in the accounts of Blackford, von Borcke and Stuart; the more likely one seems to be Stuart's, followed here.

[11] Von Borcke and Blackford again disagree as to details in the story of Miss Lucas, the captured Federal, and the bottle of wine, but between them they fully authenticate the incident.

[12] George M. Neese, *Three Years in the Confederate Horse Artillery*, p. 102.

[13] Major Roy Mason, in *B&L*, Vol. 2, p. 528.

[14] The note, Stuart to Pope, is cited by H. K. Douglas, *I Rode With Stonewall*, p. 134; Jackson's quip is in *Confederate Veteran*, June, 1926, p. 221; the song appears in Richard B. Harwell's *Confederate Music*.

[15] These comments of Lee from *OR*, Vol. 28, p. 54; and J. William Jones, *Life & Letters of R. E. Lee*, p. 391.

CHAPTER TEN

Exit John Pope

[1] These details are from Blackford's *War Years*, p. 108; and von Borcke, Vol. 1, p. 133.

[2] Stuart's moves are taken from his report in *OR*, Vol. 12, Pt. 2, p. 733 ff.

[3] *B&L*, Vol. 2, p. 534.

[4] From *War Years*, pp. 112–15, and *OR*, *loc. cit.*

[5] Von Borcke, Vol. 1, p. 137.

[6] *B&L*, Vol. 2, p. 529.

[7] Stuart's report in *OR*, Vol. 12, Pt. 2, previously cited, gives details of his movements and those of cavalry units throughout the Second Manassas campaign, including comments on his subordinates.

[8] Longstreet in *B&L*, Vol. 2, p. 525.

[9] This sketch from J. E. Cooke in *Wearing of the Gray*, p. 152.

[10] *Confederate Veteran*, Sept., 1922, p. 329.

[11] Von Borcke, Vol. 1, p. 162 ff.

[12] This sequence, with the ambush and skirmish leading to the battle of Chantilly, is von Borcke's.

[13] Blackford's *War Years*, p. 137.

[14] Laura Herbert McAlpine, in *Confederate Veteran*, Dec., 1913, p. 579.

CHAPTER ELEVEN

BLOODY MARYLAND

[1] Neese, *Three Years in the Confederate Horse Artillery*, p. 111 ff.

[2] Dudley to Flora Stuart, cited in Thomason, p. 265.

[3] Frank Myers in *The Comanches*, p. 107 ff. Officers of this command bore an active dislike for Stuart, thus this incident, like others in the work, is perhaps given in a biased version. It is, however, the only account of the clash.

[4] Von Borcke and Blackford again join to give this picturesque account of life at Stuart's headquarters.

[5] General Walker, in *B&L*, Vol. 2, p. 605.

[6] Von Borcke, evidently sated with night life, gave the dance with the "Irish girls" brief mention; the letter, Stuart to Flora, is cited in Thomason, p. 289.

[7] General Cox, in *B&L*, Vol. 2, p. 584.

[8] SHSP, Vol. 25, p. 148.

[9] Stuart details his movements in *OR* 19, Pt. 1, p. 817, etc.; his handling of the Lost Order problem is sketched by D. S. Freeman in *Lee's Lieutenants*, Vol. 2, p. 173.

[10] Blackford, *War Years*, p. 144.

[11] *War Years*, p. 148, gives the only detailed account of this interesting probe of Federal tactics.

[12] Jackson's planned attack in face of the fearful odds of Sharpsburg emerges in Walker's account in *B&L*, Vol. 2, p. 679, and in Stuart's report in *OR*, as cited above.

[13] Channing Price to his mother, Oct. 1, 1862; original in collection of McDonald Wellford, Richmond.

[14] This dispatch used by courtesy of Ralph Newman, Chicago.

CHAPTER TWELVE

ENEMY COUNTRY

[1] The account of Stuart's visit is in von Borcke, Vol. 1, p. 276. The poem is from *Confederate Veteran*, July, 1928, p. 255. A variant is in H. K. Douglas, *I Rode With Stonewall*, p. 193.

[2] The dance and charades are described by Blackford and von Borcke, with the latter, as usual, reserving a heroic role for himself. One interesting mystery of the materials cited here is a missing program of music sung at a farewell concert at The Bower before the Chambersburg Raid, in Stuart's hand. This is described by D. S. Freeman, *Lee's Lieutenants*, Vol. 2, p. 286, and said to be in the H. B. McClellan papers, in Confederate Memorial Institute. A search of this depository by the writer and officials of the Virginia Historical Society, curators, failed to disclose the document.

[3] The orders of Lee and Stuart are in *OR*, Vol. 19, Pt. 2, p. 55 ff.

[4] From this point the narrative of the raid rests chiefly on one of the most remarkable of Civil War letters, a description of the raid by Lieut. Channing Price for his mother, giving many details. The original is in the Univ. of N.C. Library, Southern Historical Collection.

[5] Blackford, *War Years*, p. 165; Blackford is also the authority for most of the details on looting in Pennsylvania on this raid.

[6] McClure's narrative, the most substantial Northern account of the operation, is in his book, *Lincoln and Men of War Times*, p. 372.

[7] From *Border Raids into Pennsylvania During the Civil War*, by J. Melchior Sheads, an unpublished history thesis at Gettysburg College, 1933. Sheads cites the *Gettysburg Compiler*.

[8] Federal moves may be reconstructed in detail from *OR*, Vol. 19, Pt. 2, p. 38 ff.

[9] From *The Grayjackets*, by "A Confederate," p. 308.

¹⁰ J. Melchior Sheads, *op. cit.*, citing the *Washington Star*.

¹¹ Sheads, citing an account by William Storrick in "a Chambersburg newspaper."

¹² Stuart to Lily Lee, Dec. 5, 1862; original in Duke University Library.

CHAPTER THIRTEEN

WAR IN WINTER

¹ *Letters From Lee's Army*, p. 132.

² Douglas, *I Rode With Stonewall*, p. 196.

³ These quotations are from Cooke's *Wearing of the Gray*, pp. 29, 30, 39.

⁴ This revealing letter is cited in SHSP, Vol. 8, p. 454.

⁵ Stuart's letter to Flora, cited here, appears in SHSP, Vol. 8, p. 454; his letter to Lily Lee is in the Duke University Library.

⁶ This incident is related with obvious relish in von Borcke, Vol. 2, p. 61.

⁷ The preceding order by Stuart on Burke's death is in the Duke University Library, as is his letter to Lily Lee; the snowball battle is sketched in von Borcke, Vol. 2, p. 83.

⁸ From the manuscript collection of Van Dyk MacBride, of Newark, N.J.

⁹ John Esten Cooke in *Stonewall Jackson*, p. 375.

¹⁰ The story of Pelham's most famous hour is drawn from von Borcke, Vol. 2, p. 117; *Wearing of the Gray*, p. 133; and from *OR*, Vol. 21, p. 553.

¹¹ This scene is reported in *Mine Eyes Have Seen the Glory*, by L. Minor Blackford, p. 209. It was taken from a "printed, but not published" work of the Blackford family, Susan Leigh Blackford's *Memoir*, Vol. 1, p. 272.

¹² This incident is offered by Douglas in *I Rode With Stonewall*, 205; the story of the planned night attack is reconstructed from von Borcke, Vol. 2, p. 128; for Dr. Hunter McGuire on Jackson's part, see Davis, *They Called Him Stonewall*, p. 361.

¹³ Stuart-Custis Lee, Dec. 18, 1862, Duke University Manuscript Collection.

CHAPTER FOURTEEN

Pelham's Last Fight

[1] SHSP, Vol. 5, p. 40.

[2] The "Christmas," or "Dumfries" raid is drawn from McClellan, p. 196. The text of Stuart's famed telegraph message of contempt is not exact; the writer could not find its original, and numerous versions exist in secondary sources.

[3] For other bitter comments by McLaws on his brother officers see Davis, *They Called Him Stonewall*, p. 387.

[4] Stuart to John R. Cooke, Feb. 28, 1863; microfilm copy in Univ. of N.C. Library.

[5] The narrative of Kelly's Ford, the movements of Stuart and Pelham's death rest chiefly on Gilmor, *Four Years in the Saddle*, pp. 64–74; and H. H. Matthewe in SHSP, Vol. 38, p. 379. H. B. McClellan left varying accounts and in his life of Stuart gave meager and unconvincing details. The story that Pelham died while shouting, "Forward!" to his men seems unlikely, and Gilmor's less dramatic account is followed here.

[6] Cited by D. S. Freeman in *Lee's Lieutenants*, Vol. 2, p. 466, from a letter of Peter Pelham to Edwin P. Cox.

[7] This poetic fragment has been often reprinted. Pelham's posthumous commission as Lieutenant Colonel is in the Confederate Museum.

CHAPTER FIFTEEN

Chancellorsville

[1] Stuart to —— Price is in the collection of McDonald Wellford of Richmond, Va.

[2] The chronicle of the Price brothers is from *War Years*, p. 204 ff.; efforts to locate the published diary have been in vain; the Price family heirs know nothing of the journal's whereabouts.

[3] Stuart to an unidentified colonel is in the Duke University Library.

[4] Stuart's role in the opening phases of Chancellorsville may be traced in von Borcke, Vol. 2, p. 209; McClellan, p. 226 ff., and in Stuart's official reports.

[5] Morrison's little-known account is in *Confederate Veteran*, May, 1905, p. 231.

[6] This important and previously unpublished letter of Evalina Wellford is in the McDonald Wellford collection.

[7] The Lee-Jackson plan of their most celebrated maneuver is detailed in SHSP, Vol. 34, p. 12 ff. and B&L, Vol. 3, p. 204.

[8] Jackson's greeting of Beckham is reported in McClellan, p. 234; the sketch of Stonewall in this action is derived from the account of Capt. R. E. Wilbourn; for a full account, see Davis, *They Called Him Stonewall*, p. 402 ff.

[9] From Cooke's *Stonewall Jackson*, p. 430.

[10] Col. W. L. Goldsmith in *Under Both Flags*, as cited in *The American Iliad*, Eisenschiml & Newman, p. 402.

[11] Gordon McCabe in SHSP, Vol. 37, p. 61, tells the story of Venable's joining Stuart.

[12] This letter is in the Duke University Library.

[13] From von Borcke, Vol. 2, p. 258.

CHAPTER SIXTEEN

PRELUDE TO INVASION

[1] *Wearing of the Gray*, p. 317.

[2] This most famous of Stuart's reviews is sketched from von Borcke, Vol. 2, p. 263 ff. and *War Years*, p. 206 ff., with George Neese and Luther Hopkins as minor contributors.

[3] *Comanches*, p. 183.

[4] Hart, as cited in McClellan, p. 277.

[5] *Letters from Lee's Army*, p. 175; and Wm. C. Oates, *The War Between the Union & The Confederacy*, p. 189, reflect contemporary opinion that Stuart was caught napping at Brandy Station.

[6] This amusing document is in the Virginia Historical Society collection.

[7] These admonitions are from the Richmond newspapers cited, both of the date of June 12, 1863.

[8] John Mosby in *Stuart's Cavalry in the Gettysburg Campaign*, p. 62.

[9] The narrative of the fighting for these mountain passes is drawn from *War Years*, p. 218 ff., from Mosby, *op. cit.*, p. 62 ff.; McClellan, p. 296 ff., provides a reliable guide, including reports from both sides.

CHAPTER SEVENTEEN

GETTYSBURG

[1] This synopsis of events in the crucial formative stage of the Gettysburg campaign depends heavily on Mosby, *Stuart's Cavalry*. Though this book is in general partisan special pleading, Mosby undoubtedly described his own role accurately in this phase. The documents cited here are well known, but present no real basis for condemnation of Stuart's role, since he was given such wide latitude by Lee, and the situation was further confused by Longstreet. Though the controversy over Stuart's part in Gettysburg is the most important one involving his career, its argument today is bootless. The telling document seems to be Lee's order to Stuart of June 23. Major McClellan thought this lost, but D. S. Freeman found it in *OR*, Vol. 27, Pt. 3, p. 923.

[2] McClellan, p. 321, is the authority for Stuart's having sent a report to Lee on this day. Not unnaturally, he is alone, since he handled the dispatch as adjutant, and says that Lee obviously did not receive it.

[3] Captain R. B. Kennon to his daughter, Clara V. Kennon; the original is in the Virginia State Library.

[4] Conway P. Wing, *History of Cumberland County, Pennsylvania*, as cited in J. Melchior Sheads's unpublished thesis, Gettysburg College, 1933: *Border Raids into Pennsylvania During the Civil War*. This manuscript was made available through the courtesy of Dr. Frederick Tilberg, historian at the Gettysburg National Military Park.

[5] There are at least two other accounts of the calling of Stuart to Gettysburg. John W. DuBose, in *Confederate Veteran*, Oct., 1917, p. 242, says Lee sent twenty scouts after Jeb; Edwin Selvage, in *Confederate Veteran*, Dec., 1922, p. 445, says he and eight cavalrymen led Stuart to the field. In the narrative here, Stuart's own report is followed.

[6] This striking, and perhaps astonishing, scene, is created almost verbatim from an account in the Anne Bachman Hyde Papers, Univ. of N.C. Library. It is based on diary entries of Mrs. Hyde in 1915, after conversation with T. T. Munford; she was also a pupil of Major McClellan in his later years, and was thoroughly familiar with the circumstances. This is the most detailed known account of the famed confrontation of Lee and Stuart.

[7] The story of Stuart's cavalry action at Gettysburg is from McClellan, p. 337 ff.; and Brook-Rawle in *Annals of the War*, p. 467 ff.

[8] This glimpse of the bloody Federal cavalry attack is drawn from a witness, Capt. H. C. Parsons, in *B&L*, Vol. 3, p. 393.

[9] Emack's account, as given to Major McClellan, is cited in McClellan, p. 353 ff.

[10] Captain Glazier in *Three Years in the Federal Cavalry*, p. 270.

[11] Stuart's weariness is detailed in McClellan, p. 365.

CHAPTER EIGHTEEN

The Receding Tide

[1] G. C. Eggleston, *Recollections of a Varied Life*, p. 70.

[2] *OR*, 29, Pt. 2, p. 771, has Lee's comment on Rosser and his passing mention of the court-martial of Jones.

[3] Marshall's detailed account of Gettysburg strategy, highly critical of Stuart, is in *Aide-de-Camp of Lee*, Sir Frederick Maurice, editor, p. 195 ff.; the Hoke-Lee exchange is in *Confederate Veteran*, Sept. 1912, p. 562; Heth-Lee, SHSP, Vol. 4, p. 160; Lee-Hunton, in Hunton's *Autobiography*, p. 98.

[4] The signal post incidents are drawn from Taylor in *Confederate Veteran*, Aug., 1932, p. 304; and the same magazine, Vol. 2, p. 12, by H. W. Manson.

[5] *Comanches*, p. 158.

[6] Cavalry movements as the Bristoe Campaign opened stem from *OR*, 29, Pt. 2, p. 263 ff.; McClellan, p. 372; Hopkins, p. 119; and Glazier, p. 333.

[7] Stuart's amusing entrapment is reconstructed from accounts in Blackford, p. 238; SHSP, Vol. 37, p. 66; McClellan, p. 386.

[8] *Comanches*, p. 234.

[9] Beale's sidelight on the well-known Dahlgren Raid story is in SHSP, Vol. 3, p. 219; Frank Myers adds his biting comment in *Comanches*, p. 251.

[10] SHSP, Vol. 3, p. 192.

CHAPTER NINETEEN

In The Wilderness

[1] This glimpse of the opening of the battle of The Wilderness is given by Wynn in *Confederate Veteran*, Vol. 21, p. 68; see also *B&L*,

Vol. 4, p. 118; accounts of action following are in Neese, p. 258; and Hopkins, p. 145.

[2] Grant described these moves in his *Memoirs*, p. 411.

[3] William M. Dame, *From the Rapidan to Richmond*, p. 96.

[4] Hopkins, p. 156.

[5] Grant sketches the conflict in Federal Command in his *Memoirs*, p. 412; his order to Sheridan to make his raid is recalled on p. 420.

CHAPTER TWENTY

YELLOW TAVERN

[1] Judith B. McGuire, *Diary of a Southern Refugee*, pp. 269–70.

[2] The Federal reports, basic to this account, are in *OR*, Vol. 36, Pt. 1; Sheridan's on p. 776; Merritt's on p. 812; Custer's on p. 817.

[3] The only account found by the writer of the last meeting of Flora and Stuart is in a letter from A. R. Venable to Fitz Lee of 1885, which is in the Virginia Historical Society, Richmond. The letter contains minor errors of fact, but is invaluable in reconstructing the scene of Stuart's wounding and death.

[4] Dispatches from Stuart and Fitz Lee from Yellow Tavern and vicinity are in *OR*, Vol. 51, Pt. 1, p. 905. Fitz Lee made famous as the "last dispatch" the six thirty A.M. message of May 11, but two later ones are owned by Rev. David H. Coblentz of Clover, S.C., and are described in the Fall, 1956, issue of *Manuscripts*, the publication of the Manuscript Society.

[5] Incidents in this portion of the narrative are from McClellan, p. 411, and an account by the same author in SHSP, Vol. 24, p. 227.

[6] Colonel Cheek, in Clark's *N.C. Regts.*, Vol. 1, p. 465.

[7] Though positive proof is lacking, the writer accepts the Federal version that John Huff killed Stuart; in the absence of evidence to the contrary, and bolstered by reports of Col. Alger and Custer in *OR*, Vol. 36, Pt. 1, p. 828, the Huff story seems substantial enough.

Facts used in this account are from: National Archives, Huff's service folder; *Record of Service of Michigan Volunteers in the Civil War* (Michigan Adjutant General's Office), Vol. 35, pp. 3, 75; Records of the G.A.R., Lansing, Mich.

Huff was mortally wounded at Hawes' Shop a few days after Yellow Tavern, thus his career is difficult to trace. He is buried in Armada, Mich.

⁸ Stuart's early movements at Yellow Tavern are detailed by: Devin, *OR*, Vol. 36, Pt. 1, p. 834; Burgess, SHSP, Vol. 36, p. 121; McCormick, *Confederate Veteran*, March, 1931, p. 98. (McCormick is probably also the author of the "anonymous" account in *B&L*, Vol. 4, p. 194.)

⁹ These incidents are from R. S. Morgan on Pate in *The University Memorial*, p. 589; T. S. Garnett, in *Confederate Veteran*, Dec., 1911, p. 575; and Venable to Fitz Lee, as cited above.

¹⁰ Von Borcke, Vol. 2, p. 308.

¹¹ Accounts of eyewitnesses, in sequence, from these sources: Harris, *Confederate Veteran*, Feb., 1909, p. 76; Oliver, *Confederate Veteran*, 1911, p. 531; Litchfield, statement to Flora C. Stuart, 1907, ms. owned by Mrs. Virginia Stuart Waller Davis, Alexandria, Va.; Dorsey, SHSP, Vol. 30, p. 236; McCormick, *Confederate Veteran*, Mar., 1931, p. 98; Hopkins, *From Bull Run to Appomattox*, p. 158; Burgess, SHSP, Vol. 5, p. 121; Pitts, *Confederate Veteran*, Feb., 1909, p. 76.

There is doubt as to the horse Stuart rode at the time of his wounding, but in Hopkins, p. 269, he is placed on his gray, General. Other witnesses introduce complications, mentioning a bay and a sorrel mare.

CHAPTER TWENTY-ONE

"GOD'S WILL BE DONE"

¹ Details of the sketchy story of Stuart's trip into Richmond are from McClellan, p. 415; Venable's letter to Fitz Lee, cited in Chapter 20; and in von Borcke, Vol. 2, p. 310.

² Blackford's *War Years*, p. 252.

³ The narrative of Flora's ride to Stuart's deathbed seems to have been written by one of her companions. In SHSP, Vol. 7, p. 140, it is credited to an anonymous "source entitled to the very highest consideration." The writer may have been the Rev. Mr. Woodbridge. Several other accounts involving Mrs. Stuart exist, most of them vague, romantic and erroneous.

⁴ The writer's search yielded few reliable witnesses at Stuart's deathbed: McClellan, Venable, von Borcke and T. S. Garnett are used here. Von Borcke's picture of Stuart's dying moments is suspect, but is the only one found.

⁵These items, and perhaps others which have since disappeared, were

given to Mrs. Stuart soon after her husband's death by relatives in attendance. They are now owned by Mrs. Virginia Stuart Waller Davis, of Alexandria, Va.

[6] The funeral scene, as sketched by the *Richmond Examiner*, is cited in SHSP, Vol. 7, p. 109.

☆

Acknowledgments

I am indebted to scores of people for aid with this book, in particular to:

Mrs. Virginia Stuart Waller Davis of Alexandria, Va., granddaughter of Stuart, for letters, photographs, advice, permission to inspect mementoes, especially those found on Stuart at death, and for general advice.

Richard B. Harwell of Chicago, for discovery of letters, especially one of Stuart's mother to R. E. Lee, for wise counsel, instruction in Confederate music, and his guide to the "fiction" in John Esten Cooke's war novels.

Ray D. Smith of Chicago, owner of a great Civil War collection and creator of the first index to *Confederate Veteran* magazine, especially for the use of Stuart references among his five hundred thousand index cards.

Major General John R. Peacock of High Point, N.C., an infallible source of aid, guide to rare sources, including the only known photograph of Sam Sweeney.

McDonald Wellford of Richmond, Va., whose valuable family letters shed new light on Stuart at Chancellorsville, and who provided other papers and photographs through the kindness of Miss Louise Price of Richmond.

Van Dyk MacBride of Newark, N.J., for use of a Stuart note to Miss Belle Hart and other assistance.

Mrs. Charles R. Hyde of Chattanooga, Tenn., a former student of Major H. B. McClellan, who furnished valuable material on Stuart at Gettysburg through a carefully recorded interview with Gen. T. T. Munford in 1917.

Sidney Forman, Archivist and Historian, U.S. Military Academy,

West Point, N.Y., and his assistant, Joseph M. O'Donnell, for academic and delinquency records of Stuart.

Manly Wade Wellman of Chapel Hill, N.C., for material and advice.

Harvey Young of the Department of History, Emory University, Atlanta, Ga., for counsel on the authenticity of certain Stuart letters.

Ralph G. Newman of Chicago, for advice, aid in location of source material, and permitting use of a dispatch from Stuart to George B. McClellan.

Virgil Carrington Jones of Washington, D.C., for aid on sources, especially on the Dahlgren Raid against Richmond.

Thelma Joseph, of the Michigan Historical Commission, Lansing; F. Clever Bald, University of Michigan Historical Collections; and J. R. Winters of Washington, D.C., for aid in research on John A. Huff, the probable slayer of Stuart.

Ruth I. Mahood, Curator of History, Los Angeles County Museum, for a copy of a rare photograph of Sam Sweeney.

Roy Bird Cook of Charleston, W. Va., for material, especially on Harpers Ferry.

O. H. Felton of Lyons, Ill., for pointing out rare Harpers Ferry sources.

John M. Jennings and his staff, especially Mrs. J. M. Slaughter, of the Virginia Historical Society, Richmond.

Miss India Thomas and Miss Eleanor S. Brockenbrough of the Confederate Museum, Richmond, for guidance and material.

Carroll G. Bowen of the University of Chicago Press for encouragement and advice.

Colonel John Virden of Army Times Publishing Co., Washington, D.C., for support and a valuable lecture on Gettysburg delivered at the Army War College.

Rev. David Herr Coblentz of Clover, S.C., for pointing out the two final dispatches of Stuart's career, in his collection.

Miss Mattie Russell and Mrs. Elizabeth Harrison of the manuscript division, and Jay Luvaas, of the G. W. Flowers Collection, Duke University Library, for much aid throughout.

James W. Patton and the staff of the Southern Historical Collection, Louis R. Wilson Library, Chapel Hill, N.C., who provided material indispensable to this book.

J. Ambler Johnston, William H. Stauffer and Samuel J. Moore of

Richmond's Civil War Round Table, for considerable aid, especially on Stuart's Ride Around McClellan, June, 1862.

Ezra J. Warner of La Jolla, Calif., for information on Confederate general officers.

Mrs. Ruth Burdick of St. Petersburg, Fla., for use of a body of letters of her grandfather, Clarke Dodge of the Army of The Potomac.

Gerard O'Brien of Hyattsville, Md., for location of materials, especially the field books of Stuart.

Jacquelyn Jurkins, manuscript division, Wisconsin Historical Society, for aid in obtaining microfilm copy of Stuart's field books.

Mrs. Louise F. Catterall of the Valentine Museum, Richmond, for aid on photographs and general sources.

Thomas E. Snook of New York City, for information on casualties of the war, of which he has made an exhaustive study.

Dr. Frederick Tilberg, historian of Gettysburg National Military Park, for loan of the typescript of Border Raids into Pennsylvania During the Civil War, a 1933 Gettysburg College thesis by J. Melchior Sheads.

Mrs. Charles Murray of Washington, D.C., for use of letters of Richard Gilliam Gary, 4th Virginia Cavalry.

Brunnhilde McIntyre, my tireless companion and assistant.

Carl O. Jeffress and Miles H. Wolff of the Greensboro, N.C. *Daily News*, whose generous co-operation provided time for this work.

Col. Margaret B. Price of the North Carolina State Library, Raleigh, for major assistance on source materials.

Olivia Burwell and the staff of the Greensboro Public Library, and Charles Adams and the staff of the Library of the Women's College, University of North Carolina.

My wife and children, for patient understanding and active, able assistance.

BURKE DAVIS

Guilford College, N.C.

☆

Bibliography

General Reference

The American Iliad, Eisenschiml and Newman, Indianapolis, 1947.

The Alexander Letters, 1787–1900, Savannah, Ga., 1910.

Annals of The War, Written by Leading Participants, North and South, Philadelphia, 1879.

Battles and Leaders of The Civil War, R. U. Johnson and C. C. Buel, Editors, 4 vols., 1887–88.

Biographical Register of the Officers and Graduates of the U.S. Military Academy, Geo. W. Cullum, 4 vols., Boston, 1891.

A Calendar of Confederate Papers, D. S. Freeman, Richmond, 1908.

The Civil War Diary of Gen. Josiah Gorgas, Univ. of Ala., 1947.

Confederate Music, Richard B. Harwell, Chapel Hill, N.C., 1950.

Confederate Portraits, Gamaliel Bradford, Boston, 1917.

Confederate Veteran, 40 vols., 1893–1932, Nashville, Tenn. (Indexed, 1956, by Ray D. Smith, Chicago.)

Histories of the Several Regiments & Battalions from North Carolina in The Great War, 1861–65, 5 vols., Walter Clark, ed., Raleigh, N.C., 1901.

Journal of Southern History.

The Land We Love, Charlotte, N.C., 1866–69.

R. E. Lee, D. S. Freeman, 4 vols., New York, 1934.

Lee's Confidential Dispatches to Davis, D. S. Freeman, New York, 1915.

Lee's Lieutenants, D. S. Freeman, 3 vols., New York, 1942.

Letters of General J. E. B. Stuart to his Wife, 1861, Bingham Duncan, ed., Emory University Library, 1943.

The Life of Johnny Reb, Bell I. Wiley, New York, 1943.

The Life of Stonewall Jackson, J. E. Cooke, Richmond, 1863.

Military History of Carlisle and Carlisle Barracks, by T. G. Tousey, Richmond, 1939.

Our Living and Our Dead, Raleigh, N.C., 1874–76, 3 vols. plus an odd number.

The Rebellion Record, Frank Moore, ed., 12 vols., New York, 1862–71.
The South to Posterity, D. S. Freeman, New York, 1939.
Southern Historical Society Papers, Richmond, 49 vols., 1876–1944.
The Story of The Confederacy, Robert S. Henry, Indianapolis, 1931.
The War of The Rebellion: A Compilation of the Official Records of the Union and Confederate Armies, 70 vols., Washington, 1880–1901.

Newspapers

Charleston, S.C., *Mercury*
New York *Herald*
New York *Tribune*
Richmond *Examiner*
Richmond *Sentinel*
Richmond *Whig*
Shepherdstown, Va., *Register*
Staunton, Va., *Jeffersonian*
Washington *Star*

General Magazines

Century, Harper's Monthly, North American Review, South Atlantic Quarterly.

Manuscript and Documentary Sources

Chicago Historical Society.
    Charles E. Gunther Collection.

David Herr Coblentz, Clover, S.C.
    Stuart dispatches, 11 May, 1864.

Confederate Museum, Richmond, Va.
    Stuart papers, scrapbook, arms, effects.
    John Esten Cooke papers.

Mrs. A. J. Davis, Alexandria, Va.
    Papers, chiefly letters, of Stuart, John E. Cooke, numerous other Confederate leaders. Relics, photographs.

Duke University Library.
    J. E. B. Stuart papers.

Robert W. Hooke papers.
John Esten Cooke papers.

Gettysburg National Military Park Library.
Border Raids into Pennsylvania During the Civil War, an unpublished thesis by J. Melchior Sheads, Gettysburg College, 1933.

Van Dyk MacBride, Newark, N.J.
Stuart letters.

National Archives.
Service Record, John A. Huff.

Ralph G. Newman, Chicago.
Stuart letters.

Miss Louise F. Price, Richmona.
Papers of R. Channing Price, Stuart, Fitz Lee.

U.S. Census, 1860.
Macomb Co., Mich.

U.S. Military Academy.
Register of Delinquencies.
Academic Records.

University of North Carolina Library.
Hairston-Wilson papers.
R. Channing Price papers.
Philip St. Geo. Cooke papers.
Anne Bachman Hyde papers.

Virginia Historical Society, Richmond.
John E. Cooke papers.
Stuart papers.
H. B. McClellan papers.
A. Reid Venable papers.

Virginia State Library, Richmond.
Stuart papers.

John Letcher papers.
R. B. Kennon papers.

McDonald Wellford, Richmond.
Papers of Stuart, Channing Price, Evalina Wellford.

Biography, Memoirs, etc.

Alexander, E. P., *Military Memoirs of a Confederate*, New York, 1907.
Barry, Joseph, *The Strange Story of Harpers Ferry*, Martinsburg, W.Va., 1903.
Beale, G. W., *A Lieutenant of Cavalry in Lee's Army*, Boston, 1918.
Beale, R. L. T., *History of the 9th Virginia Cavalry*, Richmond, 1897.
Beaty, J. O., *John Esten Cooke, Virginian*, New York, 1922.
Bill, Alfred H., *The Beleaguered City: Richmond, 1861–65*, New York, 1946.
Blackford, Chas. M., *Letters from Lee's Army*, New York, 1947.
Blackford, L. M., *Mine Eyes Have Seen The Glory*, Cambridge, Mass., 1954.
Blackford, W. W., *War Years With Jeb Stuart*, New York, 1945.
von Borcke, Heros, *Memoirs of the Confederate War*, London, 1866, 2 vols.
Chamberlayne, C. G., *Ham Chamberlayne, Virginian*, Richmond, 1933.
Chesnut, Mary B., *A Diary From Dixie*, Ben A. Williams, ed., Boston, 1949.
A Confederate [Pseudonym], *The Grayjackets*, Philadelphia, 1867.
Conrad, Thomas N., *The Rebel Scout*, Washington, 1904.
Cooke, John Esten, *Wearing of the Gray*, New York, 1867.
———, Mohun, N.Y., 1893.
Cowles, Wm. H. H., *The Life and Services of Gen. James B. Gordon*, Raleigh, N.C., 1887.
Dame, Wm. M., *From the Rapidan to Richmond*, Baltimore, 1920.
Davis, Burke, *Gray Fox*, New York, 1956.
———, *They Called Him Stonewall*, New York, 1954.
Davis, Jefferson, *The Rise and Fall of The Confederate Government*, New York, 1881, 2 vols.
De Fontaine, F. G., *Marginalia*, Columbia, S.C., 1864.
De Leon, T. C., *Four Years in Rebel Capitals*, Mobile, Ala., 1890.
———, *Belles and Beaux and Brains of the '60's*, New York, 1909.
Douglas, H. K., *I Rode With Stonewall*, Chapel Hill, N.C., 1940.
Eggleston, Geo. C., *A Rebel's Recollections*, New York, 1875.

———, *Recollections of a Varied Life*, New York, 1910.

Garnett, T. S., *General Stuart*, Washington, 1907.

Gilmor, Harry, *Four Years in The Saddle*, New York, 1866.

Glazier, Willard, *Three Years in The Federal Cavalry*, New York, 1874.

Gordon, John B., *Reminiscences of the Civil War*, New York, 1903.

Grant, U. S., *Personal Memoirs*, 2 vols., New York, 1885.

Harrison, Constance C., *Recollections Grave and Gay*, Richmond, 1911.

Henderson, G. F. R., *Stonewall Jackson and the American Civil War*, New York, London, 1898, 2 vols.

Hopkins, Luther W., *From Bull Run to Appomattox, A Boy's View*, Baltimore, 1908.

Hunton, Eppa, *Autobiography*, Richmond, 1933.

Johnston, Jos. E., *Narrative of Military Operations*, New York, 1872.

Jones, J. B., *A Rebel War Clerk's Diary*, Philadelphia, 1866, 2 vols.

Jones, J. Wm., *Life and Letters of Robert Edward Lee*, Washington, 1906.

Lee, R. E., Jr., *Recollections and Letters of General Robert E. Lee*, New York, 1904.

Longstreet, James, *From Manassas to Appomattox*, Philadelphia, 1895.

Marshall, Charles, *An Aide-de-Camp of Lee*, Sir Frederick Maurice, ed., Boston, 1927.

McCarthy, Carlton, *Detailed Minutiae of Soldier Life*, Richmond, 1882.

McClellan, Henry Brainerd, *The Life and Campaigns of Maj. Gen. J. E. B. Stuart*, Richmond, 1885.

McClure, A. K., *Lincoln and Men of War Times*, Philadelphia, 1892.

McGuire, Judith W., *Diary of a Southern Refugee*, Richmond, 1889.

McKim, Randolph H., *A Soldier's Recollections*, New York, 1910.

Mercer, Philip, *The Life of the Gallant Pelham*, Macon, Ga., 1929.

Morgan, R. S., *The University Memorial*, Baltimore, 1871.

Mosby, John S., *Stuart's Cavalry in The Gettysburg Campaign*, New York, 1908.

———, *Memoirs*, Boston, 1917.

———, *War Reminiscences*, Boston, 1887.

Myers, Frank M., *The Comanches*, Baltimore, 1871.

Neese, George M., *Three Years In The Confederate Horse Artillery*, Washington, 1911.

Oates, Wm. C., *The War Between the Union and the Confederacy*, Washington, 1905.

Owen, Wm. M., *In Camp and Battle With The Washington Artillery of New Orleans*, Boston, 1885.

Peavey, James D., *Confederate Scout: Virginia's Frank Stringfellow*, Onancock, Va., 1956.

Pickett, Geo. E., *Heart of a Soldier*, New York, 1913.

Taylor, Richard, *Destruction and Reconstruction*, New York, 1879.

Taylor, Walter H., *Four Years with General Lee*, New York, 1877.

Thomason, John W., Jr., *Jeb Stuart*, New York, 1930.

Townsend, Geo. A., *Rustics in Rebellion*, Chapel Hill, N.C., 1950.

Villard, Oswald G., *John Brown: A Biography After Fifty Years*, Boston, 1910.

Wing, Conway P., *History of Cumberland County, Pa.*, Philadelphia, 1879.

Index

449

WGRL-HQ BIOGRAPHY
31057000443955
STUART DAV
Davis, Burke,
Jeb Stuart, the last
cavalier /